EMBODYING DIFFERENCE

Embodying Difference

The Making of Burakumin in Modern Japan

Timothy D. Amos

University of Hawai'i Press
HONOLULU

Embodying Difference: The Making of Burakumin in Modern Japan

Hardback ISBN 9780824835781
Paperback ISBN 9780824835798

First published in South Asia by Navayana Publishing
155, Second Floor, Shahpur Jat, New Delhi 110049. Phone 91-11-26494795
www.navayana.org

Simultaneously published outside South Asia by
University of Hawai'i Press, 2840 Kolowalu Street, Honolulu, HI 96822 USA
www.uhpress.hawaii.edu
Library of Congress Cataloging-in-Publication Data

Amos, Timothy D., 1973–

Embodying difference: the making of burakumin in modern Japan / Timothy D. Amos.
p. cm.
First published in New Delhi by Navayana Publishing
Includes bibliographical references and index.
ISBN 978-0-8248-3578-1 (hardcover: alk. paper) — ISBN 978-0-8248-3579-8 (pbk.: alk. paper)
1. Buraku people. 2. Caste—Japan—History. 3. Caste-based discrimination—Japan. 4. Marginality, Social—Japan. I. Title.
HT725.J3A47 2011
305.5'68092—dc22

2010041902

Printed and bound in India

Contents

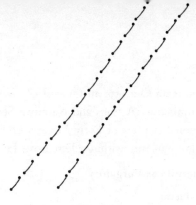

Acknowledgements vii
Explanatory Note on Style xi

1 **Introduction to the Buraku Problem** 1
Introduction
Reinstating the Ambiguity of Burakumin
Ideational Aspects of the Buraku Problem
Discourses of Difference
Book Outline
Burakumin and Dalits

2 **The Problem of Buraku History** 33
Introduction
The Master Narrative: Ancient Period (Before 1185)
Medieval Period (1185–1600)
Early Modern Period (1600–1868)
Modern Period (1868–)
Empirical Problems
Conceptual Problems
The Master Narrative at Work: Touring Imado and Naniwa
Towards a Discursive History of Difference

3 **The Problem of Buraku Discrimination** 74
Introduction
Buraku Discrimination
Formation of Early Modern 'Outcastes'
Lives of Early Modern Outcastes

When is an Outcaste an Outcast/e?
Discriminatory Actions and Narrative Sequences
Ideational Aspects of Early Modern Outcaste History
Cordon Sanitaire within a Discursive History of Difference

4 **Modernity as Purgatory** 111

Introduction
Civilizing Social Frontiers
Early Meiji Transformations in 'Former Outcaste' Communities
Towards a Specialization of Difference
Formation of 'Buraku Culture'
Conclusion

5 **Walking to Liberty in Osaka** 149

Introduction
Background
Special Measures and Internal Struggles
Towards 'Human Rights Culture'
State Human Rights Cultural Discourse
Local Human Rights Cultural Discourse
Liberty Osaka and Human Rights Culture
Conclusion

6 **Narrating Buraku Experience in Contemporary Japan** 189

Introduction
Background
Anti-Buraku Structuralist Narratives
Burakumin Creating Buraku History
Re-reading Uramoto's History
History and Liberation

7 **Epilogue: Return from Discursive Exile** 211

Notes 227

Bibliography 273

Index 295

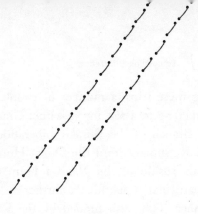

Acknowledgements

I began collecting documents and records related to burakumin from various locations in Japan as a Masters student in the History Department at Tohoku University in Sendai (1997–2000). With the gracious help of Yoshida Masao, Shigeta Masao, and several others, I copied a number of documents from the Saitama Prefectural Archives, the Higashi Matsuyama City Library Document Centre, and the home of Suzuki Mikio.

Large numbers of historical documents were also gathered during a three-month fieldwork expedition undertaken in 2003 as part of my PhD tenure in the Division of Pacific and Asian History at the Australian National University (ANU). At that time, Gerald Groemer (Yamanashi University) helped me locate additional material. Arai Hirofumi and Shirai Tetsuya at the Saitama Prefectural Archives offered generous assistance in helping me gain access to restricted documents in their holdings. Professor Ōtō Osamu also kindly permitted me to use the facilities in the History Department at Tohoku University, and to attend his highly instructive *komonjo* (old documents) class and weekly seminar.

More material was collected in 2007 during two separate fieldwork trips to Japan in May/June and September. The first trip was generously funded by the Faculty of Arts and Social Sciences Staff Research Support Scheme at the National University of Singapore.

During these trips, a number of people freely offered their time and expertise to assist my research: Uramoto Yoshifumi from the Tokyo Branch of the Buraku Liberation League, Ota Kyōji and Maeda Katsumasa from the Osaka Human Rights Museum, and Arimoto Toshio of the Naniwa Human Rights Culture Centre were particularly helpful. A further field trip was conducted in December 2008 (also funded by the Faculty of Arts and Social Sciences at the National University of Singapore), and a number of people including Tomotsune Tsutomu, Mizuno Matsuo, and Satō Takayuki freely offered their time to answer my queries about the nature of modern buraku discrimination.

Many teachers, colleagues, and friends have offered generous advice and assistance to me over the years. Tessa Morris-Suzuki has been an exceptional academic guide. During my PhD candidature, and thereafter, she has constantly challenged my ideas, thinking, and expression both personally and through her work. Watanabe Hideo, Kumada Ryōsuke, and Okuyama Toshimi (now retired) at Akita University; Ōtō Osamu at Tohoku University; Ann Curthoys and Debjani Ganguly at the Australian National University; and Noel Weeks (now retired) from the University of Sydney, have all been excellent advisors. Vanessa 'Buffy' Ward, Curtis Anderson Gayle, Steven Jarvis, Motoe Sasaki-Gayle, Robin Fletcher, Julian Kusa, Noah McCormack, Kōhei Kawabata, Michael Leininger-Ogawa, Brett Baker, Gavan McCormack, Yoshikazu Shiobara, Hiroko Matsuda, and Yasuko Kobayashi have all offered thoughtful comments and suggestions relating to this research during my PhD candidature.

More recently, my colleagues in the Department of Japanese Studies at the National University of Singapore have offered tireless support. Scot Hislop has sounded out many of the ideas contained in this volume. Timothy Tsu went through some of the early material and liberally provided me with his characteristic knowledgeable comments and advice. Simon Avenell has also enthusiastically engaged with important issues in this book, particularly offering invaluable comments about the overall structure in the first three chapters. Romit Dasgupta (now back at the University of Western

Australia) accompanied me on one of my excursions to Osaka and I benefited greatly from his critical eye and his company. Leng Leng Thang, Beng Choo Lim, Hendrik Meyer-Ohle and other Departmental members have also liberally offered me feedback and support in my research endeavours, for which I am exceedingly grateful to them.

An earlier version of a section in Chapter 1 was originally published as "Outcaste or Internal Exile? Ambiguous Bodies in the Making of Modern Japan" in the Special Issue, "Exile and Social Transformation", edited by Paul Allatson and Jo McCormack, in *Portal Journal of Multidisciplinary International Studies* vol. 2, no. 1 (2005).[1] I wish to thank the UTSe Press for kindly granting me permission to use this material.

An earlier version of sections in Chapters 2 and 4 appeared as "Binding Burakumin: Marxist Historiography and the Narration of Difference in Japan," *Japanese Studies*, vol. 27, no. 2, 2007.[2] These sections are reproduced with permission from Judith Snodgrass, editor of *Japanese Studies*.

My families—the Honda and Amos families—have provided inexhaustible generosity, patience, advice, and understanding to me throughout all my research endeavours. My partner, Aki Honda, has been persistent, fearless, prudent, loving, consistent, and endlessly positive throughout this effort.

Finally, I offer my thanks to S. Anand, who provided me with the opportunity to work with Navayana on this monograph. My hope is that this research will make some contribution, however modest, to his greater work. The reviewer chosen by Anand to scrutinize this manuscript, Elyssa Faison, also gave detailed comments and suggestions of an insurmountable quality on numerous occasions.

My heartfelt thanks go to everyone, though words alone cannot express my feeling of debt. Rest assured, however, while written with the immeasurable help and support of all those mentioned above, this monograph is my own work and its faults or inadequacies are only attributable to me.

Explanatory Note on Style

Japanese words, apart from a handful of exceptions, are placed in italics throughout the book using the Hepburn system for Romanization. Macrons have been applied wherever appropriate. Exceptions to this rule and the application of a modified Hepburn system are determined by the following criteria:

— If the words cited are in commonplace use in English (like Tokyo or Kyoto)

— If the words are deemed to be in commonplace usage in English language accounts of Japanese history (like shogun or Edo)

— If the words contained in passages are taken in direct quotation from other authors and macrons and italics have not been applied in the original instance

— Where alternative systems of Romanization have been used by scholars and this has become a matter of public record (like Naitoh)

Japanese place names are generally Romanized in full with designations of places such as *kuni*, *gun*, *machi*, and *mura* translated into their respective English equivalents: province, county, town, and village. An exception is that pertaining to official titles of primary and secondary research works. In the case where the meaning of a place name would be lost with a direct transliteration, however, an English equivalent has been used (for example, the *shimo* in Shimowana Village has been translated as 'Lower' as opposed to Upper).

Japanese names are written with the family name preceding the given name as per custom. The exceptions are when the author's name appears in the opposite order in the source cited or the author is more commonly known by names (or has published work) in the conventional English language order.

Pre-Meiji dates have not been converted into the Gregorian calendar equivalents unless otherwise stated, so that the Japanese date *Kansei ninen nigatsu hatsuka*, which would normally be read as 20 February 1790, is, in fact, 4 April 1790.

All Japanese words, apart from the words *eta* and *hinin*, are placed in italics only in the first instance of usage. Capitals, moreover, are only applied to the first word of a proper Japanese language phrase.

1

Introduction to the Buraku Problem

'Burakumin, Die!'
'Human Garbage!'
Endless discriminatory graffiti and phone calls.
One person confronts another; tells them to die.
Such terrible things.

Discrimination is a heavy burden.
Youth still worry about marriage;
People fuss over ancestry, pedigree, birthplace, and the like.
Discrimination's roots are deep.
Who spreads the fertilizer;
Pours waters on this tree of discrimination?
Sad people who judge others
With preconceptions and prejudice.

One line of the Suiheisha Declaration says:
'Our ancestors yearned for Liberty and Equality;
They were their enforcers.'
They fought for Freedom.
Equality is everyone's birthright.

There is not a single person,
Who leaves their mother's womb,
Planning to be discriminated against.

I pity those who discriminate.
Problems shouldn't arise just by being born.

Give to children the fragrance of the earth,
Light from the sun,
The love of humanity.
Give to people with no knowledge of war
Peace, Freedom, and Equality.

Life is beautiful.
Don't dismember it by discriminating.

Degrading and shaming people should never happen.
From our mother's womb –
Beautiful people.
People are precious.
People are wondrous.

— Maeda Katsumasa (1989)

If Buraku are a problem of the past, then why do you discriminate against them? If they are a thing of the past, then who am I that is hurt by your remarks? Am I a ghost?

— Uramoto Yoshifumi (2003)

Introduction

The first epigraph is a poem authored by an elderly burakumin activist and friend, Maeda Katsumasa, who lives in Osaka Prefecture, Japan. Originally written in November 1989, the epigraph was given to me by Maeda as part of a privately bound collection of his writings entitled *The Sun Will Rise Again: People are Precious* (*Taiyō ga mata noboru: ningen wa tōtoi*). The poem, which shares its heading with the collection's subtitle, speaks about a troubling social issue in Japan, usually referred to as 'buraku discrimination' (*buraku sabetsu*), or more generically, the 'buraku problem' (*buraku mondai*). The poem reveals an issue which in its rawest form involves some members of mainstream Japanese society who bully, threaten, or perpetrate violence against the people called 'burakumin'.

But who are the burakumin? Why do people discriminate against them? When did this discrimination begin? And why does the problem still persist in Japanese society today? For answers to these questions, one must turn to the work of scholars who have tried to explain this problem.

The word 'burakumin' comprises two parts: 'buraku', meaning hamlet, and 'min', meaning a person or people.[1] It literally refers to people who live in a distinguishable subsection of a village presumed to have substantial communal ties.[2] These distinct communities were historically ostracized by surrounding villages and townships due to a dominant social perception that they were polluted because they engaged in occupations linked with death, such as tanning and burial. While estimates differ, the origins of many of these communities are thought to date back to at least the medieval period (twelfth to sixteenth centuries). Despite the absence of external marks or racial or genetic dissimilarities which might set them apart from other Japanese, these 'outcast people' (*senmin*/*hisabetsumin*), over time, came to be referred to pejoratively by names like *eta* and *hinin* (discussed in more detail below), usually written with Chinese ideographs meaning 'much pollution' and 'non-human'.

Early unifiers of Japan, such as general and statesman Toyotomi Hideyoshi (1536–1598) of the Sengoku period, adopted policies such as the 'Sword Hunt Edict' (*katanagari-rei*), which hastened the establishment of a fixed social and legal status system.[3] Later, in the eighteenth century, outcaste groups were forced through strict state legislation to live separately from the rest of mainstream society and were forbidden to engage in other occupations.[4] They were also officially assigned low-level policing and execution duties, further reducing their social standing within their communities. Intermarriage became criminalized, social mobility was restricted, and hereditary systems of succession were institutionalized. These factors, combined with an authoritarian period of *Pax Tokugawa*[5] (1603–1868) rule, built on Confucian ideology stressing rigid hierarchical relations, led to the development of a highly stratified social structure reminiscent of a caste system. And though outcaste status was abolished through a so-called Emancipation Edict issued in 1871, concrete measures guaranteeing their successful merger back into mainstream society were not pursued. Outcaste groups, particularly the descendants of former *eta* groups, remained a modern leftover of a backward feudal past, experiencing further victimization as a result of economic inequalities inherent in modern capitalist society. In more recent times, their upward mobility has also been hampered by restricted access to important life opportunities such as tertiary education and white-collar employment. Many burakumin today continue to reside in areas officially recognized as former outcaste settlements and claim ancestral links to these earlier groups.

This story about burakumin, while seldom found in precisely identical versions, does tend to retain the vast majority of points outlined above when recounted by both Japanese and Western scholars.[6] The common threads of the narrative are that: (a) burakumin are a bounded community with a point of historical origin; (b) buraku discrimination, whether state-sponsored or based on popular social sanction, has existed in an external, structural form (legislation, practice) over a long period of time; and (c) buraku history has remained relatively intact as a single entity from the premodern period through to the present. These three key building blocks of the mainstream narrative are found in countless Japanese language academic and pedagogical texts, albeit in different combinations and with different points of emphasis.

This master narrative, however, when subjected to close scrutiny, seems to raise more questions than it answers, particularly for the historian. To what extent can continuity between premodern and modern burakumin communities actually be empirically verified?[7] What proportion of contemporary burakumin directly descend from premodern *eta* and *hinin* groups and prewar 'special buraku' (*tokushu buraku*) communities?[8] To what extent do the majority of geographical places in which modern-day buraku are located neatly correlate (or meaningfully overlap) with the historical sites of outcaste communities? To what degree is the discrimination that contemporary buraku communities face the same as that experienced by historic outcaste communities? On what basis do burakumin today distinguish 'buraku discrimination' from other forms of prejudice (such as a blanket hatred of all minority groups)? And to what extent can this narrative be considered as a story told by burakumin in order to frame their plight in a particular way for the purposes of engaging in contemporary identity politics?

This book, after a decade-and-a-half-long search for answers to these kinds of questions, argues that there needs to be a fundamental reconceptualization of the buraku problem for two main reasons. Firstly, the master narrative outlined above is built on empirically and conceptually questionable foundations; and secondly, mainstream accounts tend to overlook the very important role burakumin and other interested parties play in the construction and maintenance of the narrative. By continually drawing a straight line between premodern *eta* and *hinin* groups and today's burakumin, and equating the types of discrimination suffered by members of this community today with that faced by premodern outcaste groups, the Japanese government, the general population, scholars, and burakumin activists tend to overlook some of the real changes that have often taken place both in *who* is identified (or self-identifies) as members of socially marginalized groups in Japan and *how* they experience that identification. Clinging to this master narrative, moreover, serves to restrict the ways in which burakumin can productively and more inclusively identify in the present to imagine a liberated future for themselves.

Reinstating the Ambiguity of Burakumin

The master narrative of buraku history as outlined above makes certain assumptions about the history of burakumin, which tends to lack empirical support and conceptual rigour, thereby making it difficult to retain as an explanatory model. Within the mainstream interpretation, burakumin are usually presented unambiguously as people who objectively exist in the world: a minority outcaste group bound by a common experience of discrimination, which stretches from the distant past to the present. The actual ambiguity of burakumin, however, becomes patently obvious upon close empirical and conceptual scrutiny.

First, on an empirical level, the linkages in buraku history, when carefully examined, are often found to be suspect: they lack sufficient evidence. Available evidence suggests that buraku communities have disparate points of historical origin, particularly in eastern and western Japan.[9] In addition, only about half of the current buraku residents actually claim ancestral connections to premodern outcaste groups.[10] The Japanese government and burakumin organizations also strongly disagree on the best method for counting the locations of all buraku areas and buraku-related populations.[11] The usual tools that researchers use to test the empirical foundations of truth claims, moreover, are often not available to the buraku historian. In short, the empirical ground upon which the mainstream view of buraku history is built is unstable.

A handful of examples gleaned from the work of Western scholars are sufficient to demonstrate the difficulty of envisaging uniform and continuous physical buraku history. Ian Neary, for example, argues that about half of the buraku communities in Tottori Prefecture were 'formed during or after the *Bakumatsu* period' (mid-nineteenth century), revealing that in some cases, buraku communities can have modern origins in the orthodox sense of being newly created around the time of the emergence of political institutions closely related to modern government and the emerging Meiji regime.[12] Noah McCormack also indicates many examples of discontinuity in buraku history in his research, including: the elevation of *eta* to commoner status during the early 1870s; the modern reconstruction of old outcaste areas; the movement of new poor into outcaste neighbourhoods during the 1870s; and the emigration of elites out of buraku in the 1900–1910s.[13] John B. Cornell also recorded the following observation about Okayama Prefecture, his area of fieldwork, in the late 1960s: 'To a much higher degree than in comparable ippan [literally 'general', that is, non-buraku] communities, residence in the Buraku is impermanent.'[14] Although awaiting further investigation, extant research reinforces the preliminary conclusion that individual 'buraku communities' are probably better understood as having unique, fluid, and often quite divergent histories.

There is, moreover, marked disparity in the statistics surrounding the total numbers of burakumin. The figures vary depending on who is doing the counting. The Buraku Liberation League (*Buraku kaihō dōmei*; hereafter BLL) has almost universally opted for a figure of about three million people.[15] This figure relies on extremely old and unreliable documentation, problematic counting methods, and a basic assumption about a universal historical continuity between premodern outcaste and modern buraku communities. The Japanese government, however, has consistently maintained a figure of between one and two million while devising policy and funding.[16] The government, though, appears to have derived this figure on the basis of the unilateral setting of geographical boundaries, which, in turn, were not based on thorough research and proper consultation. As a consequence, organizations like the BLL have consistently maintained that the government has only partially addressed the buraku problem because all buraku areas were not targeted by government policies. As William Wetherall has pointed out, though, at least some of the 'buraku areas' claimed by the BLL are not counted because residents do not wish to be recognized as such. This means that BLL counting methods are also somewhat ethically problematic: they incorporate groups of people as 'burakumin' who do not wish to be identified in that way.[17]

Another significant problem relates to the issue of verification. Claims by burakumin that they have descended from premodern outcaste communities often have to be taken at face value because they cannot be subjected to adequate processes of empirical substantiation. Legal restrictions are placed on access to certain official government records like early Meiji period censuses that may help in confirming alleged linkages between contemporary buraku families and premodern outcaste groups.[18] While in one sense, being a positive measure that has helped prevent the abuse of these records for discriminatory purposes, it has also meant that historical continuities and linkages are, more often than not, matters of statements of belief rather than empirically demonstrable facts. Furthermore, some families and community representatives have destroyed records or put them out of reach of the public for fear that later generations would be able to reconstruct undesirable linkages.[19] It is difficult, for example, to find any substantial documentation about premodern outcaste communities in northeastern Japan despite considerable evidence showing that they once existed in quite significant numbers.[20] The result of lack of proper resources for verification means that researchers are well-advised to interpret claims of burakumin status based on outcaste heritage as probably true but also in some cases possibly imagined.[21]

Secondly, quite apart from the empirical tenuousness of the mainstream account of outcaste history, the ideas upon which buraku history is based are also conceptually fragile. In order to better articulate this point, however, a more detailed discussion of key terms is first in order.

The two main terms repeatedly used to refer to burakumin and their antecedents in the Japanese language literature are hisabetsumin (literally 'people who are discriminated against') and senmin (literally 'base people'). Hisabetsumin is commonly used in contemporary Japanese academic writing as a politically correct term to predominantly refer to burakumin and their antecedents. It has, in recent times, often come to replace the previously popular senmin which is actually the more exact equivalent of the English word 'outcast'. Despite the slightly different nuances contained in the two terms, their relatively high degree of discursive fungibility suggests that they may be both adequately translated into English as 'outcast'. As mentioned earlier in the chapter, however, Gerald Groemer has argued that Japanese historians have tended to make important distinctions between medieval and early modern marginalized groups in Japan in terms of their potential social mobility which are not necessarily reflected in nomenclature. Groemer suggests that this distinction should be preserved in English by referring to medieval marginalized groups as 'outcast' and their early modern counterparts as 'outcaste'. Groemer's distinction is important and finds support in the work of David Howell. Howell, while mindful of the possible shortcomings of the term 'outcaste', uses it exclusively in his examination of the *eta* within the early modern Japanese status system, even intimating at one point that this group may well have been 'constrained by an ideology of essential identity such as...caste'.[22]

Employment of the term outcaste, however, also poses problems.

First, there is no direct translation of the word outcaste that is commonly used in Japanese to generically refer to burakumin or their antecedents. Second, classification of Japanese premodern scholarship on marginalized groups through an outcast/outcaste distinction attributes a conceptual clarity to this body of work which (with some notable exceptions) has rarely been there; little explicit or sustained comparative debate emerged among Japanese scholars in the postwar period about the meanings of terms such as senmin and hisabetsumin, the possible 'caste-like' features of early modern Japanese society, and/or the relevance of the concept of caste in the Japanese context. Third, there is a seemingly innocent, yet undoubtedly deeply significant distinction between the terms outcast and outcaste. The latter term, purely by the inclusion of the last vowel, semantically mutates, creating a sense of permanent exclusion, a nuance that is not necessarily fully contained in the word outcast.

In this volume, following Groemer's usage, I employ the term outcast when translating the terms senmin/hisabetsumin in relation to medieval groups of marginalized status, and outcaste when these same terms are used to refer to early modern low status groups. The term outcaste, however, is also mobilized in two additional ways in the following pages: as a translation of the Edo period expression *eta-hinin-nado* (eta, hinin, etc); and as an analytical category to discuss the changing character, significance, and potential of *eta*, *hinin*, burakumin and other conceptually similar marginalized figures in discourse (called below a discursive history of difference). Outcaste is chosen over outcast for this last important role not only because I believe it most accurately captures the reality effects of this particular form of social marginalization (*cordon sanitaire*), but because it reflects the difficulty that those who experience this 'temporal displacement' have in either achieving liberation from it or attaining a degree of social restoration.[23]

As the central aim of this volume is to highlight the contingent nature of buraku identity in Japan, and to demonstrate widespread empirical, conceptual, and ideational problems concealed within the common framework of buraku history that deals with political action in the context of identities assumed to be knowable, it is important here to also distinguish between my uses of the term outcaste (particularly in its third application as analytical category) and the translation of the terms senmin/hisabetsumin in Japanese writings on low social status when they are used to incorporate medieval outcast, early modern outcaste, and burakumin in the sense of a generic outcaste. In order to preserve the ambiguity of this broader usage of these terms, and to better distinguish them from my employment of the term outcaste, they will hereafter be translated as 'outcast/e' in discussions of the master narrative of buraku history. Following Groemer, the expression outcast/e is intended to embody the sense in which the marginalized Japanese subject is usually considered 'outcast' (in the orthodox sense of someone who is 'cast out'), and increasingly subjected to intense discrimination over time, but where ultimately the question of what kind of marginalization they experience (caste discrimination or otherwise) is basically left unanswered.

Returning then to the question of the conceptual fragility of the ideas upon which buraku history is based, it is clear that the above two terms repeatedly used to refer to burakumin and their antecedents in the Japanese language literature—hisabetsumin and senmin (outcast/es)—insufficiently describe people who lived in either eighteenth century *eta* villages or early twenty-first century buraku communities. The current head of the Suzuki household, Suzuki Mikio, a traceable descendant of a Tokugawa outcaste community leader in Saitama (just west of Tokyo), whom I met in 1999 and whose ancestors I have written about in detail elsewhere, certainly did not appear to qualify for the label outcast/e.[24] The label is, therefore, plainly deficient in the first place because it only illuminates one possible aspect (albeit an important one) of the lives of people like Suzuki. Outcast/e here is also a problematic label because its application actually works to reinforce an ambiguous historical distinction and normatively ensures the Suzuki family's position as contemporary subjects of social exclusion.

There is, moreover, little that is self-evident about the idea of the outcast/e. Few people would disagree that the historical antecedents of the burakumin (*eta*, *hinin*), as well as modern buraku communities, have been targets of social exclusion in Japan and that a rubric of similarity between them can be drawn up on the basis of a perceived common experience. But as Hatanaka Toshiyuki notes, difference, along with close resemblance, is also a defining characteristic of buraku history. 'The "buraku problem",' he writes, 'is not a problem caused by something in the people who are "discriminated against". People who are "discriminated against" are products of the social and political structure of each particular historical period. Conceptually, therefore, "burakumin" do not exist objectively beyond historical periods.'[25] What Hatanaka is arguing is that there is nothing inherent in the current head of the Suzuki family that makes him a burakumin; and neither is there a 'buraku-ness' that can be intergenerationally transmitted. Burakumin, he argues, are people who are 'discriminated against' in distinctive ways during a given historical period. It is not immediately obvious, therefore, what the definition of 'burakumin' (in the sense of a socially marginalized person) has been during each historical period and whether people like Suzuki actually qualify for the label.

Kurokawa Midori reveals in her groundbreaking research how the labels used to refer to Japan's outcastes changed rapidly over time in the modern era. Between the eighteenth and the twentieth centuries, terms like *eta*, *hinin*, tokushu buraku, and burakumin were used in relation to outcaste groups and each period-specific signifier reveals a conceptually quite different perception of social difference.[26] The former terms (*eta* and *hinin*) referred to people who were labelled according to the quality or quantity of their humanity (that is, they were often written with the characters 'much pollution' 穢多 or 'non-human' 非人, respectively). The latter term burakumin 部落民, however, refers specifically to people defined by a physical location (that is, 'hamlet'). Logics that defined pre- and post-Meiji outcaste communities clearly differed in important ways, suggesting a critical divergence in the nature of these 'outcaste problems'.

In a similar vein, the idea that burakumin are, in some way, a 'minority' akin to an ethnic group is contestable. While there may appear to be some superficial similarities between, say, burakumin and Zainichi Koreans,[27] a close analysis tends to reveal numerous crucial differences between them. Burakumin do appear on the surface to have a collective identity founded on reasonably objective factors like occupation and religion just as ethnic minority groups claim a distinctive collective identity based on relatively tangible factors like language or religious affiliation. Common history and geography also appear to be just as important for burakumin as they are for many ethnic groups. Yet, while the conditions for belonging to a particular ethnic minority group are often empirically veritable (poor language ability, distinct religious practices, and widely recognized phenotypical differences are relatively obvious and common [though not unproblematic] reasons for discrimination), the foundational sources for buraku identity are far less tangible.[28]

Arguably, the most important sources of buraku identity (and concurrently the most important external markers of buraku status) relate to occupation, ancestral lineage, and geographical location. As regards occupation, many buraku communities have long histories of engagement with certain occupations like leatherwork and tanning, and there is clearly an important link between traditional popular perceptions about these industries and discrimination against burakumin. As regards ancestral lineage and geographical location, too, many burakumin have personal histories which link them physically to premodern outcaste groups (*zokujinshugi*) and/or particular residential areas associated with groups of people who performed certain occupations (*zokuchishugi*). It is for this reason that the buraku problem is often characterized as a problem of 'work and descent'.[29]

During the Tokugawa era, when the three main islands of the Japanese archipelago primarily comprised a patriarchal society made up of large numbers of agricultural producers, legally bound to particular plots of land and communities, it was doubtless relatively straightforward to develop reasonably accurate mental associations about the kind of families living in particular areas. Far more residential continuity existed as compared to the modern era, and stereotypes or caricatures had a stronger degree of potency than they do today. Non-agricultural producers or persons who engaged in non-agricultural pursuits were ostracized for being different. Popular stereotypes, moreover, were reinforced by the Tokugawa state through legislation, which further demonized these communities. The literati also tended to exacerbate this stereotype by further speculating that *eta* and *hinin* groups were subhuman or of foreign origin. Members of such communities, bound by a legal framework and social expectations of the transmission of occupation and land to descendants, became marginalized in both a literal and figurative sense. Birth in a very real way became a major determinant of one's status and identity in premodern (and to some extent early modern) Japanese society.

Yet, it is also true that there never existed the degree of uniformity in occupations that people generally assume in former outcaste communities.[30] Premodern outcaste communities were considerably more fluid entities than the above kind of explanation usually permits us to see.[31] The records of Lower Wana Village, for example, where Suzuki Mikio's ancestors were village heads, are replete with instances of people from all backgrounds moving in and out of the community.[32] Recent research on the leather industry also indicates that numerous people from non-outcaste community backgrounds successfully entered the leather industry after the Meiji Restoration.[33] It is, therefore, difficult to speak meaningfully about the burakumin existing historically as a relatively uniform minority group, continuously bound together over time through blood line and geography. People flowed in and out of socially marginalized villages from sometimes quite distant regions at a significant rate. Certainly, continuity was the norm for a good many residents in premodern outcaste communities (as can be evidenced in the case of the Suzuki family). While considerable similarities may have existed between many buraku areas in the past (they were usually poorer, less fertile areas than the non-buraku ones, and were often not included in land surveys during the Tokugawa period), these communities were also scattered throughout the Japanese archipelago and the consistency, uniformity, or relational linkage among them is questionable. Many of these areas, moreover, received extreme makeovers during the postwar period through a massive injection of public funds so that it is now virtually impossible to use the downcast nature of these areas as a unifying source of buraku identity.

Other sources of buraku identity such as religion do exist, and great importance has been attached to them by some burakumin. Many early modern outcaste communities, for example, were adherents to either Pure Land Sect Buddhism (*Jōdō shinshū*) or White Mountain Shinto (*Hakusan shinkō*), and some burakumin (like Maeda Katsumasa who was introduced in the beginning) still attach great importance to these beliefs. But it is also true that neither of these faiths (or associated practices) was solely the property of outcaste communities nor were they used as strict litmus tests for distinguishing former outcaste communities throughout Japan from other members of the population. Christian missionaries, moreover, quickly moved into many former outcaste areas in the Meiji era. Increased freedom of religion after the Meiji Restoration meant that a real diversification of religious beliefs emerged in many of these areas.

On a conceptual level, therefore, burakumin and their historical antecedents, rather than being treated as an ethnic group, are, in many respects, best regarded as 'social minorities' wherein groups of people are temporally bound together through shared experiences of discrimination and for various political reasons.

Ideational Aspects of the Buraku Problem

A further problem with the master narrative of buraku history lies in the fact that it does not sufficiently address the ideational aspects of buraku existence. Burakumin, like all social groups, create and recreate themselves on a cognitive level. The buraku problem, therefore, needs to be seen as much more than just a historical form of discrimination against particular people linked by familial lineage or geographical location and grounded in ancient stereotypes about occupations. It is intimately linked to the ways in which the burakumin (and 'non-burakumin') narrate their experiences in the present and the kinds of identities they assume for the purpose of achieving future liberation from discrimination. Burakumin like Maeda Katsumasa and Uramoto Yoshifumi (a Tokyo-based historian and buraku activist, and author of the second epigraph discussed at length below) are not simply products of a history of discrimination. They are also active members of political organizations like the BLL, dedicated to fighting buraku discrimination and educating others about the plight of a minority group which they belong to and strongly identify with. Explanatory models of the buraku problem must, therefore, account for the ideational aspects of this social movement if they are to retain descriptive value.

Certainly, many burakumin may legitimately be defined as members of old outcaste communities cut off from mainstream society long ago by both a figurative (conceptual, discursive) as well as a physical (geographical, endogamous) isolation. Yet, at another level, burakumin must also be said to have a long history of discrimination because they imagine and construct their existence in that way. Maeda's poem communicates this aspect of the buraku problem well: 'Discrimination's roots are deep,' he writes. Maeda remonstrates that young people residing in buraku communities today still worry about whether their marriages would be opposed by interfering parents or disrupted by inherited ideas of 'correct blood lines' and 'family lineage'. The buraku problem, he informs us, is an old one—a historical problem—which persists in contemporary life. Other parts of Maeda's poem also reinforce this kind of perspective. Referring to the 'Suiheisha Declaration',[34] a document from 1922, which first called upon members of 'former outcaste' communities to unite in a historical struggle for recognition of basic human rights, Maeda describes how burakumin in the early twentieth century spoke of their ancestors as 'enforcers' who 'fought for freedom and equality which is everyone's birthright'. The poem insists that the kinds of experiences that burakumin are forced to endure in the present are rooted in a troubled past and should find no place in modern life.

Other buraku authors, however, go even further and tell us that the buraku problem is actually a more complex phenomenon than even Maeda's poem permits us to see. Buraku discrimination does not simply stem from hatred based on myths driven by superstitions about what is considered pure and impure in Japanese culture. Such an interpretation conflates what is evidenced as buraku discrimination in everyday life with the real causes of discrimination. Generations of buraku activists and scholars have insisted that discrimination against them is not merely something that lurks in the hearts and minds of Japanese people. It is, rather, a problem that resides in the very social structures that Japanese people have collectively constructed and now occupy. Contemporary writers like Miyazaki Manabu (a buraku activist and social commentator) argue that in contemporary Japanese society, buraku discrimination continues to exist as it has always done but has merely changed its mode of existence. Growing up in the city of Kyoto and surrounded by discrimination, Miyazaki writes that 'life experiences' (*taiken*) have to be understood in order to fully comprehend the historical continuity of buraku discrimination.[35] In other words, the outward evidences of discrimination found in everyday life described in Maeda's literary offering, while giving us a sense of the kinds of experiences he endures, are merely symptomatic of a problem which runs much deeper. To understand this level of the buraku problem, burakumin need to personally narrate their individual experiences of discrimination to facilitate a correct knowledge of the problem.

Citing instances from his own life, in early 2008, Maeda revealed in a guest lecture to my students that he was illiterate for a considerable part of his early life. Writing his name in bold strokes on the white board, he related to us his experiences of learning how to read and write in his late teens. Students of Japanese history generally learn in textbooks that by the turn of the twentieth century, Japanese 'primary school education was almost universal, and those moving in from the rural areas as well as those growing up in the cities were for the most part literate.'[36] 'Almost universal', however, is a phrase that Maeda believes obliterates the history and experiences of many burakumin like himself who, along with other family members, endured the burden of illiteracy because of poverty and institutional discrimination evidenced in areas like schooling.[37] His working life, which was spent in activism, fighting discrimination, and working on projects beneficial to buraku communities in western Japan, moreover, provides the very proof of the existence of a long and continuous buraku problem. Becoming secretary of a local branch of the BLL in the early 1970s, Maeda went on to work as the Director of the Toyonaka (Osaka Prefecture) Municipal Committee for the Promotion of Buraku Industry from 1974 to 2002, organizing buraku-related projects in the Osaka area. As of 2009, despite having officially retired, Maeda continues to work as the Director of the Committee for Human Rights Culture and Town Development in Toyonaka City, as a Child Welfare Commissioner, and as a volunteer staff member at the Osaka Human Rights Museum. Unsurprisingly, Maeda's fight against buraku discrimination sometimes brought him into conflict with the local community. On one occasion, for example, he was involved in a clash with local residents because they objected to the word 'liberation' being included in the name for a community hall. They apparently did not want outsiders to mistakenly think that the area in which they lived and where the hall was being erected was a 'buraku area'.[38] The fact that Maeda's entire life, and the lives of many others like him, have been spent combating a historical form of prejudice known as buraku discrimination is to them a clear indication that the buraku problem is not just a product of bad education or warped thinking. It is rather a phenomenon embedded in the very fabric of Japanese society.

Perhaps the incident that inspired the words of the second epigraph at the beginning of this chapter provides the clearest example of the ideational aspects of the contemporary buraku problem. The epigraph is taken from the Epilogue to a book entitled *Edo/Tokyo no hisabetsu buraku no rekishi: Danzaemon to hisabetsu minshū* (The History of the Buraku in Edo/Tokyo: Danzaemon and Outcastes) authored by Uramoto Yoshifumi and published in 2003. The epigraph reveals the words that Uramoto felt compelled to utter to his friends earlier in life when they attempted to console him after another of his acquaintances denied his identity as a burakumin. His friends argued that there was no reason to be upset because the buraku problem was actually a thing of the past. At this, Uramoto became severely distressed. He reportedly replied: 'If buraku are a problem of the past, then why do you discriminate against them? If they are a thing of past, then who am I that is hurt by your remarks? Am I a ghost?'

In order to better understand Uramoto's plea to his friends for recognition as a burakumin, it is important to first briefly examine the incident that triggered these words. The 'Mass Discriminatory Postcard Affair' (*tairyō sabetsu hagaki jiken*), as the incident is sometimes called in Japanese, began when Uramoto received a package in the mail in May 2003 as he was preparing a manuscript for publication in his series on the history of Edo/Tokyo burakumin for the Tokyo edition of the *Kaihō shinbun* (Liberation Newspaper). The package contained items that Uramoto could not recall ordering. This first package was followed soon after by another parcel, and then another. Expensive books and luxury items that Uramoto had no recollection of purchasing continued to arrive on his doorstep, which, as per the anonymous sender's arrangement, had to be purchased by Uramoto upon delivery. Then, in due course, a handwritten postcard arrived, this time at Uramoto's office at the Tokyo headquarters of the Buraku Liberation League (BLL). On it was written in Japanese, 'For an eta, Uramoto Yoshifumi is pretty up himself. I'll kill him.'[39]

Additional postcards and memos arrived at other residences and workplaces too. The handwriting on many of these postcards seemed strikingly similar to the one on the postcard sent to Uramoto. This kind of harassment continued sporadically for several years. Unbeknown to me at this stage, Uramoto was also responding to the perpetrator on the BLL Tokyo website. His decision to fight back against this discrimination at one stage even produced a written pledge by the perpetrator to stop discriminating (*shūketsu sengen*). The barrage of hate mail eventually recommenced, however, when Uramoto stated on his web page that he would never forgive the responsible party unless they came forward and sincerely apologized.[40]

Uramoto responded to the attacks on him by reluctantly

suggesting in the Epilogue to his book that they were, in fact, reflections of wider reaching structural realities of discrimination targeting burakumin. Uramoto informed his readers that he was prepared, at one time, to consider the present act of discrimination an isolated incident. However, since he had encountered such harassment numerous times throughout his life, he was forced to conclude that it was part of a larger pattern of hate.[41] In Uramoto's view, this disturbing case of discrimination against himself and other buraku community members was proof of the continued existence of a buraku problem in Japan, and symptomatic of a society that had not properly come to terms with buraku identity. This incident caused Uramoto to remember the earlier incident when a friend quite close to him questioned his continued insistence that he was a burakumin when there was, he alleged, 'no such thing as burakumin in Tokyo'.

These comments had clearly stung Uramoto but it was the remarks made by other friends attempting to console him that eventually drew his strong response. Presumably concerned that Uramoto's maintenance of a buraku identity during a period when there were no truly visible buraku communities in Tokyo was akin to him keeping a 'dead issue' alive and inflicting a kind of 'self-harm', his friends had tried to reassure him of the good intentions behind their statements. Memories of this painful incident—wherein those closest to him refused to acknowledge his identity—flooded back to Uramoto, spilling over onto the pages of his book, as he struggled to deal with the wilful actions of an unknown person in the present who degraded him and threatened his life for asserting the very same kind of distinctiveness.

Uramoto's words, and the context in which they were uttered, illustrate well the ideational aspects of the buraku problem. More than just a historical form of discrimination against a particular group of people, the buraku problem is also intimately related to contemporary questions of narration and identity. Uramoto, Maeda, and other burakumin like them, are not simply products of a history of discrimination. They are also active members of political organizations like the BLL, dedicated to fighting buraku discrimination and educating others about the plight of a minority group which they strongly identify with and belong to. Burakumin construct narratives that link the premodern past to contemporary discrimination and instruct people about the proper ways to think about that history in the present. Buraku studies like the one that Uramoto authored necessarily engage in discussion of the sorts of identity that burakumin claim for themselves in the present as well as outline strategies for a liberated future. These appeals, however, are certainly not universally subscribed to by all 'burakumin'. Some people in Japanese society, moreover, clearly find them highly objectionable. Efforts to construct meaningful narratives for buraku liberation and strategies for identity politics based on a long and continuous history are, however, confounded by the immutable fact that times change and along with them the ways in which people identify themselves.

The buraku problems of Uramoto and Maeda's youth, as well as those found in their various literary offerings, despite suggesting certain strong continuities with the past, do not describe exactly the same problems. As noted above, government statistics from the mid-1990s onwards reveal that only about half of the people who resided in areas designated as former outcaste districts in Japan at that time claimed 'ancestral connections' to premodern outcaste groups. These numbers are undoubtedly much lower today and recent research also indicates a flux of immigrant populations into various buraku areas in western Japan.[42] These kinds of statistics are usually taken as evidence (often by conservative political elites but also by some activists) that the buraku problem was basically resolved by the turn of the twenty-first century. Indeed, even the most militant sections of the buraku liberation movement have conceded that the living conditions of many burakumin are now far superior to those who lived even one generation ago.

With an apparent decline in the social acceptability of buraku discrimination and enhanced economic status, the attention of buraku activists has turned, in recent times, to different pressing social concerns like civil and human rights abuses against other minority groups. One result of these advances has been a sharp decline in buraku youth activism and government funding. A number of commentators in recent times have even publicly suggested that the funding of development projects in buraku areas has gone well beyond the point that was necessary and even led to a culture of corruption and excess within buraku liberation circles.[43]

The core organization of the buraku liberation movement, BLL, however, despite the virtual drying up of government funding and subsidies in recent years, remains relatively strong and committed.[44] Increased prosperity in officially recognized buraku areas and improved social conditions have not automatically led to the organization's dissolution. Committed activists claim, with ample justification, that discriminatory incidents involving burakumin, still occur with considerable frequency. Buraku communities may also be more drastically affected by the growing socio-economic divide between the rich and poor (*kakusa mondai*) visible in Japan in recent years (though the evidence is still mostly anecdotal). Addressing issues related to living conditions, economic disparity, and access to education and employment opportunities for burakumin has clearly not led to the disappearance of discrimination as many once thought it would. Some cynical observers like those mentioned above try to link recent allegations about the continuity of buraku discrimination to organizational discontent over a massive drop in funding. Yet, a more feasible response is that the buraku problem is far more complex than politicians and government bureaucrats, and perhaps even many scholars and activists, initially envisaged.

Not simply a problem of a uniquely bonded people who share a common history shaped by a distinctive experience of discrimination, the buraku problem is clearly a perplexing and recalcitrant social issue closely related to how people identify themselves (in the case of burakumin, how they identify with a history of discrimination and how they articulate a desire for future liberation). The identities that considerable numbers of burakumin like Uramoto forge are firmly rooted in a personal and collective history of discrimination. While significant numbers of people appear happy to leave a buraku identity behind them as opportunities to disappear into the anonymity of mainstream Japanese society arise, others continue to insist that their history should never be glossed over or forgotten. Burakumin, this latter group argues, should be able to claim any identity they choose in contemporary Japanese society, free from attack or ridicule. Until the time comes when that kind of society is realized, the buraku problem can never be considered as 'resolved'. And even if it is, some like Uramoto insist that burakumin need to feel free to claim whatever identity they choose in Japan: even a buraku identity long after all discernible forms of discrimination against them might disappear.

Discourses of Difference

Highlighting the empirical and conceptual problems evident in mainstream research and addressing the ideational processes at work within buraku identity formation leads one to conclude that 'burakumin' need to be understood as considerably more ambiguous bodies. This book argues that, contrary to the master narrative outlined at the beginning of this chapter, 'burakumin' do not simply represent a fixed, clearly delineable outcaste minority group, which has existed in a relatively constant form throughout Japanese history. 'Burakumin', rather, perhaps to some extent like discourses such as 'black' or 'Asian', is best understood as originally a modern depreciative term that came to be applied retroactively to refer to subjects who in all historical epochs are perceived to have encountered similar experiences of social marginalization. 'Burakumin' is essentially a twentieth century Japanese term which has come to categorize a number of diverse *socially* distinct populations (as opposed to *biologically* distinct populations) into one common group.[45]

'Burakumin' is a discourse of difference directly rooted in the prewar term 'tokushu buraku' ('special buraku'), which emerged during a period marked by an increased prevalence in ideas of nation, race, and capital.[46] These ideas, combined together with the unique set of circumstances that Japan and its citizenry faced during the latter half of the nineteenth century, led to an increased state and public concern with domestic sociocultural differences at the turn of the twentieth century. These domestic sociocultural differences were constantly reconfigured through changing commonsense notions about the nature of human associations, the historical development of societies, the existence of homogeneity within populations, and the importance of progress. While borrowing the idioms and practices surrounding historical practices of social marginalization, and rooted in an assumption of the absolute continuity of an old 'outcaste problem', the idea of 'buraku' emerged through a complex process that saw virtually all sociocultural differences being framed as part of a special historical problem linked to the social backwardness of a distinctive group of people.

'Tokushu buraku', however, was also quickly mobilized into a discourse of political resistance by a radical group of activists and intellectuals during the first quarter of the twentieth century. By the early twentieth century, it had become a radical oppositional discourse in the hands of activists, intellectuals, and other groups who were beginning to openly identify with the label. On the basis of a thorough theorization of their 'historical struggle', concerned activists transformed the particularization of their difference at the hands of the state and society into a confrontational struggle advocating collective mobilization and emancipatory resistance. Inspired by radical philosophy and operating under oppressive conditions for much of the second quarter of the century (including a period of brief hiatus during the Asia-Pacific War), many of these same activists and intellectuals came together again during the early postwar period to revive the movement under the new banner of 'burakumin'. The idea of 'burakumin', therefore, as a reasonably well-defined group of marginalized subjects rooted in a premodern past with a body of shared memories and a sense of collective destiny, is of a very recent vintage. Elite Marxist historians involved with a small group of former Suiheisha activists succeeded in establishing a unified discourse on the physical and conceptual continuity of 'burakumin' only during the early postwar period.[47]

Most histories of 'burakumin' to date have usually identified and discussed a specific group of people linked by blood and discriminated against over time by mainstream Japanese society. This volume posits that this understanding, while certainly capable of representing the experiences of a large number of people who are identified as (or self-identify as) burakumin, on the whole tends to obscure the real changes that have occurred over time in relation to who have been socially marginalized in Japanese history and how they experienced those exclusionary practices. Building upon the logic that 'typicality and marginality are matters of discursive construction rather than numbers,'[48] the focus in this book is placed on the way particular labels and associated discourses have been applied to (and are adopted by) certain groups under different socioeconomic and political institutional regimes. By doing so, the many historical discontinuities evident in the historical records become increasingly visible and the particular political struggles that socially marginalized people have engaged in over time are better contextualized and comprehended.

People physically, conceptually, or discursively connected to 'buraku' communities unquestionably feel the effects of real discriminatory actions against them: that fact is not in dispute. But it is first their existence as discourse that permits people to be constructed as 'outcastes' or 'burakumin'.[49] 'Buraku history', therefore, is not merely an accurate sequencing of empirical records that relate to outcaste groups with similar discriminatory experiences that occur over time. It is also the product of a chosen structural historical methodology and the outcome of the practice of narration itself.[50] 'Buraku discrimination', moreover, does not simply exist latently in society or in the collective minds of human subjects. It is first and foremost a form of power expression found within manifestations of distinct human behaviours (such as speech acts).[51]

Eta, *hinin*, and burakumin are not inexorably connected in an empirical sense and the concepts commonly used to bind them are troubled. There are, therefore, compelling grounds for arguing that *eta*, *hinin*, and burakumin should, in fact, be treated as discursive labels embedded in historical narratives which are concurrently functions of power relations within contemporary institutional settings. 'Burakumin' emerges as a discourse of difference within a larger politics of nomenclature determined by a particular ordering of the Japanese social world. It is a label used to refer to a state of 'outcasteness' in contemporary Japan that must be understood alongside a myriad of other terminologies (both contemporaneous and historical), defined by larger processes of social ordering rooted in period-specific notions of normality and difference. 'Burakumin', as a discourse of difference, is merely one among many discourses used to define and bind together socially marginalized persons on the Japanese archipelago. It specifically refers to Japanese people in postwar society who can loosely be termed as members of an imagined community that is believed to have emerged as a result of the common experiences of social marginalization originating in inherited circumstances.[52] 'Burakumin', therefore, is a discourse that portrays the defining characteristics of the community it refers to as being marked by strong historical continuity and permanence despite strong evidences in the historical records indicating a considerable degree of fluidity and temporality amongst many of its members.

'Burakumin' is also a spatial rather than a temporal signifier, used to signify the abnormality of a particular place that needs to be marked off by a 'sanitary cordon' (*cordon sanitaire*). It is markedly different to the older term '*eta*', which is commonly considered to be its early modern precursor. '*Eta*' was not a spatial referent but a temporal one. It referred to the state or condition of one's humanity—a condition that sought to banish affected subjects into a kind of 'solitary confinement' (*reclusion solitaire*) for the duration of their lives. *Eta* (and *hinin*) were particular marginalizing discourses that experienced a narrowing in definition in the early eighteenth century as part of a process of the bipolarization of Tokugawa subjects into 'commoners' (*heinin/heimin*) and 'outcastes' (*eta-hinin-nado*). This bipolarization emerged due to a shift in the practices of warrior governance and ideas of sovereignty, as well as a growing conceptualization of a firm geopolitical body called 'Japan' and a 'commoner' who could legitimately reside within its borders.

Terms like '*eta*' and 'burakumin', when aligned chronologically, also reveal an intriguing pattern of historical significance. While both spatial and temporal referents were liberally used during earlier historical periods to refer to marginalized states, referents that have dominated public and official discourse on outcast/es (senmin/hisabetsumin) in modernity have tended to be spatially orientated expressions. People signified by these discourses of difference, however, have consistently tended to choose others or adapt existing ones to imbue their plight with a more temporal association. 'Burakumin' have insisted, sometimes through quite violent protests, that state and society in Japan fasten prefixes such as *mikaihō* (yet-to-be-liberated) or *hisabetsu* (who-are-discriminated-against) to their designation: an act that superficially suggests an appeal for respect. Yet these acts also bespeak a deeper significance. They reveal the central importance that the struggle over language plays in combating social marginalization in Japan and the necessity of inscribing temporal meaning into labels of self-identification when envisaging a radical liberation movement.

Book Outline

This book presents and supports its arguments in the following way. Chapter 2 begins by offering a detailed account of the mainstream narrative of buraku history in which burakumin are defined as members of old outcaste communities who were cut off from mainstream society long ago by both social and institutional discrimination. The chapter goes on to highlight specific empirical and conceptual problems with this narrative that came to light during archival work on the 1871 Emancipation Edict and readings of critical Japanese literature on the buraku problem. The chapter then demonstrates how the master narrative of buraku history is actually mobilized on the ground in two 'former outcaste' areas in eastern and western Japan. It concludes by demonstrating that 'burakumin' is actually best conceived as a label of marginality that falls within a larger discursive history of difference.

Chapter 3 addresses the problem of buraku discrimination, demonstrating the empirical and conceptual problems inherent in mainstream accounts of this phenomenon that see it as a historically continuous 'idea' with certain 'structural effects'. Through an examination of early modern outcaste groups, the chapter establishes that an assumption of uniform and continuous discrimination against them is untenable, as is the idea that members of these groups were universally of low social status. Numerous problems are then also pointed out on a conceptual level. Ideas that an outcast/e (senmin/hisabetsumin) can be an all-encompassing subjectivity, that discrimination is expugnable from daily life, and that discrimination is an action that can be objectively narrated, are all critically discussed. The chapter next addresses some ideational aspects of early modern outcaste history by depicting the ways in which outcaste communities negotiated status in early modern Japan. It then concludes by reinterpreting early modern outcaste discrimination against the *eta* and *hinin* communities as part of larger period-specific processes of social ordering involving the bureaucratization of the warrior class and the expansion of proto-nationalist thinking.

Chapter 4 presents a history of the modern transformations of former outcaste communities in Japan and traces the development of the 'buraku problem' from the beginning of the Meiji period through to the early 1930s. It analyses the discursive history of social difference that emerged in the writings of elites from the late Tokugawa through to the early Meiji period and juxtaposes these images of an increasingly uniform minority-like community against the real changes that were actually occurring in 'former outcaste' communities. Contrasting the discursive and material formation of 'former outcaste' communities makes it clear that while some historical continuities are clearly evident, sweeping change also occurred in many areas. Far from the discourse of 'burakumin' following any clearly determined linear path of development, competing ideas about what constituted Japan's social margins actually proliferated during the period in question. The idea of social outcastes was constantly reconfigured through changing 'commonsense' notions about the nature of human associations, the historical development of societies, the existence of homogeneity within populations, and the importance of progress (which this chapter argues usually conformed to the principles of probabilistic association, homogenization of difference, time-lag effects, speciation, and perpetual recalibration). The end product of this complex discursive history of difference, the chapter concludes, was the emergence of the idea of a reasonably well-defined group of marginalized subjects rooted in a premodern past with a body of shared memories and a sense of collective destiny.

Chapter 5 discusses the postwar development of buraku liberation activism in Japan and recent moves by the BLL to engage in an activism based in 'human rights culture' (*jinken bunka*). It argues that the most striking example of this kind of activism in Japan today is the Human Rights Museum, Liberty Osaka, located on the site inhabited by members of a historic outcaste community in western Japan. This kind of activism, it shows, is not merely a buraku concern. National and local governments also engage in 'human rights enlightenment activities' (*jinken keihatsu katsudō*) and 'human rights culture town development' (*jinken bunka machizukuri*) through the creation of posters, promotional videos, brochures, festivals, and monuments. Human rights promotional materials produced on national government, local community, and BLL levels, though, portray and articulate human rights culture in markedly different ways. This chapter, through a comparative analysis of state, local community, and BLL cultural material related to the promotion of human rights, reveals the distinctive and yet also somewhat restrictive ways in which burakumin are attempting to create and recreate a struggle for liberation in contemporary Japan.

Chapter 6, using the history and comments provided by Uramoto Yoshifumi that are discussed briefly in this chapter, as well as other resource material, points to problems related to the narration and ownership of mainstream 'outcast/e (senmin/hisabetsumin) history' in contemporary Japan and explores the question of why 'buraku history' seems weightier than other forms of history. The chapter expands upon the arguments introduced in earlier chapters and contends that by changing the way we view history—by seeing 'burakumin' as an imagined community and by accepting the idea that narratives surrounding that community are ones of convenience and that discrimination itself is a natural act necessary for human survival—we make possible a potential liberation from the binary of 'buraku' and 'Japanese', and, therefore, the need to identify ourselves within the language of the perpetrator of the discriminatory act.

Burakumin and Dalits

One final word should be mentioned here on the comparative aspects of the buraku problem. Readers will no doubt be drawn into a mental comparison between burakumin and dalits, people formerly known as 'untouchables' and commonly considered to be of the lowest rank or even outside the Indian caste system. Perhaps unsurprisingly, Western observers stumbling across the existence of burakumin in Japan have drawn heavily upon stereotypical imagery of Indian 'untouchables' to describe their plight. The familiarity in the West with the Indian 'untouchable', through colonial experience and the role that Westerners sometimes played in the definition of caste in that context, readily draw students of the buraku problem into comparisons with India. Burakumin are commonly framed as the historical remnant of outcaste groups located at the bottom of a premodern Japanese caste-like system.[53]

This linkage, however, has frequently been made quite recklessly and independently of the research findings of Japanese historians, who caution against arriving at such a simplistic association.[54] Indigenous terms in the Indian context that are used to refer to caste, such as *varna* (order, class, kind) and *jati* (birth groups), find no real equivalents in Japanese history. The key Japanese term *mibun* or 'status', particularly prevalent in early modern Japan (seventeenth–nineteenth centuries), functioned to some extent in a similar way to varna in India by idealizing a handful of human callings to the exclusion of others. These idealized callings, however, were delimited not in ancient religious texts in Japan but rather in early Confucian ones. Their historical importance, moreover, was somewhat negligible. It was really only through their re-introduction by neo-Confucian scholars during the early Tokugawa period that they found any ideological traction, proving useful as a justification in a political economy predicated upon the exploitation of peasant labour by warriors. The idea of 'birth' (*sujō*), moreover, while indeed being important in premodern Japan, particularly medieval and early modern Japanese society, must be understood in relation to other indigenous concepts used to express familial groupings like *uji* (clan) and *ie* (household), whose statuses could historically improve by rendering faithful service to rulers.[55] The roles of indigenous beliefs like Shinto and the central role of the imperial institution in defining and ordering Japanese cosmology, moreover, as well as the syncretic features of Japanese religion in incorporating Buddhist and other belief systems, reveal a distinctive set of historical conditions for the construction of status in Japan.

The considerable differences that exist between the Indian caste and Japanese status, however, should not obscure the similarities that also exist between them.[56] Visions of burakumin as 'untouchables', despite the colonial undertones that such a linkage might seem to imply, are not unfounded. The link is not simply the product of a Western imagination. The second line of Maeda's poem quoted above reveals an issue at the heart of buraku discrimination, which also preoccupied Louis Dumont in his classic work on Indian caste.[57] The reference to 'human garbage' hints at the central place that concepts of 'pollution' (*kegare*) and 'purity' (*kiyome*) play in the mechanics of buraku discrimination. Within buraku discrimination, the quality of a particular humanity is treated as being vastly inferior to others. This is usually not considered to be a temporary condition within individuals either, but rather an unalterable state that requires the discriminator to immediately and perpetually sever equilibrious social contact. Maeda's poem reveals that one of the most common forms that this kind of discrimination takes is marital discrimination. Some people in contemporary Japan, he writes, are still unable to wed partners of their own choosing because prejudiced ideas about the importance of family lineage persist in present-day Japan. Dalit and buraku experience, therefore, should also be acknowledged as undeniably similar in some very important respects.[58]

People on the Japanese archipelago in premodern times, moreover, were historically aware of subcontinental forms of social categorization and the existence of an Indian outcaste. The word candala (*sendara*), for example, is used in a considerable number of old Japanese texts. The early twelfth-century text *Konjaku monogatari* (The Tales of Times Now and Past) recorded, for example, that 'the word caṇḍāla is still feared'.[59] The late thirteenth-century dictionary *Chiribukuro* (The Dust Bag) also defined the word sendara as people 'in India who kill living things' and in the same section explained that people called *kiyome*[60] (literally 'purifiers') are sometimes called eta.[61] The Muromachi dictionary *Jinten ainoshō* (Rubbish Sack Extracts with Dust), written in the late fifteenth or early sixteenth century and containing extracts from the *Chiribukuro*, mentions that a group of people known as *kawaramono* (river-bed dwellers) were 'heavily polluted' and were just 'the same as the dirty scavengers (*etori*) of meat in India called sendara.'[62] The connection between Japanese and Indian outcasts, once made by scholars in the medieval period, remained a useful source of explanation for intellectuals in later periods.

Direct reference is not made to 'sendara' in the official lineages (*yuisho*) of eighteenth-century outcaste communities. In many cases, these communities trace their roots back to Japanese gods and creation myths surrounding the birth of Japan. Some outcaste communities, however, clearly linked their origins back to Indian rulers, gods, and specific subcontinental geographical regions. "Record of the History of the Butcher", for example, a 1707 text written by an outcaste community in Kyoto, placed its historical origins in India. [63] It was certainly not uncommon for members of particular Buddhist sects in early modern Japan to link their ancestry to gods in order to increase their social standing. By the beginning of the eighteenth century, however, intellectual and popular discourses increasingly treated outcaste communities as 'foreign bodies' that originated in Korea or China and some outcaste communities may have felt compelled to include foreign ancestry in their lineages. Within this context, some outcaste communities fabricated elaborate stories surrounding their origins in an attempt to legitimize both real and imagined social practices in the eyes of warrior officials in order to ensure that as communities they could retain special privileges (*tokken*) and, therefore, the continuity of social standing and economic livelihood.[64]

Clearly, these linkages made by early modern outcaste communities are important. There is meaning in linkages being sought after with India rather than with Korea or China.[65] The social realities of an eighteenth-century *eta* community plainly matched the historical depictions of their Indian counterparts that was made available in literature and kept alive through popular imagination and discourse. These conceptual and discursive linkages demonstrate the reality of historical practices of discrimination between certain Tokugawa communities. Mental and physical protective barriers were erected around 'non-outcaste' communities in order to protect them from the dangerous influence of outcastes. This harmful power was undoubtedly conceived of as a kind of 'untouchability' or 'pollution', popularly thought of as being transferable to 'non-outcaste' communities through close contact or interaction. 'Untouchability' or 'pollution' meant that these communities were framed in the language of 'Orientalism': problematic people such as *eta* emerged from within a foreign 'Other'.

The buraku problem, then, is in certain respects similar to the problems facing dalits in India and in some respects quite different. More research needs to be carried out on the comparative aspects of caste. This study hopes to lay one foundation for such future studies by asking how we can better understand the nature of this problem in the Japanese context.

2
The Problem of Buraku History

Introduction

The buraku problem is commonly described as a historical form of discrimination directed at a specific group of people linked by blood lineage or geographical location, and grounded in ancient stereotypes about the polluting effects of certain kinds of occupational activities. This master narrative of buraku history, however, based on the assumption of a strong and uniform historical continuity between a 'core body' (*kaku*) of premodern outcast/es (senmin/hisabetsumin) and modern-day burakumin, is, in certain important respects, empirically unsubstantial and conceptually frail. The narrative is also problematic because it neglects to take into account important ideational aspects of the buraku problem.

Historical records reveal, for example, that the period from around the 1860s through to the 1870s was a tumultuous time for all people living on the Japanese archipelago. This period, which witnessed the Meiji Restoration and the so-called 'Status Emancipation Edict' (*mibun kaihōrei*), also resulted in great social upheaval for former outcaste communities. Many former *eta* and *hinin* experienced colossal and complex changes in their daily lives as a direct result of state policy. However, 'emancipation' was also conceived of and indeed experienced in markedly different ways, depending on the socioeconomic level and political affiliations of members of these communities. In short, available evidence suggests that buraku history is a story that needs to be narrated with equal concern for the obvious discontinuities found in the records.

Narratives of buraku history rooted in this mainstream interpretation, moreover, rarely reflect critically on the kinds of concepts being mobilized in their support. Scholarship has almost uniformly assumed that the burakumin are a minority-like group, historically marginalized within an ethnically homogenous 'Japanese society'. As a consequence, scholarly discussions have raged for much of the postwar period over where to locate the 'true historical origins' of a firmly bound 'other' called burakumin. Excessive concern with buraku origins has led to an almost blanket obliviousness to the crushing weight that scholars themselves actually ascribe to a 'buraku past' through subscription to modernist, Japan-centric narrative structures. Even if a clear line can be drawn through familial genealogy or geographical continuity from the premodern period to the present day for some burakumin, fixation with straightforward chronologies and sequential orderings has taken collective attention away from an explanation of how social marginalization actually occurred in Japan to how buraku history progressed over time. Herman Ooms, drawing on the work of Edward Said, has cautioned thus against the pursuit of historical origins: 'to talk of a beginning is to engage in a highly interpretative discourse, and a very problematic one.' Ooms reminds his readers that ultimately a fetish for origins is closely linked with the historian becoming 'the last in a long line of victims of a particular ideological project.'[1] Some of the conceptual problems that lie at the heart of the mainstream view of outcast/e history can come into clear view only through a questioning of our concepts rooted in certain notions of time and a commonsense acceptance of causality.

Ideational aspects of buraku history have also been obscured by unquestioning support for the master narrative. Buraku history is intimately linked to the ways burakumin (and 'non-burakumin') narrate their experiences in the present and the kinds of identities they assume for the purpose of achieving future liberation. Resolutely clinging to a story about burakumin, which emphasizes their uniform historical continuity, masks the real changes that have often taken place both in who is identified (or self-identifies) as burakumin in modern Japan, and how they experience that identification. At one important level, buraku history does not have an objective existence. It is, rather, a contemporary practice rooted in identity politics. Recent guided tours of two 'former outcaste' areas in eastern (Imado) and western (Naniwa) Japan reveal how the master narrative is actually employed on the ground in contemporary Japan in ways which provide a basis for important, yet ultimately still speculative, practices of personal and collective identification. Such practices suggest a need to re-imagine alternate ways of thinking about buraku history, which can foster creative and more inclusionary modes of identification within contemporary liberation politics.

This chapter thus begins by offering a detailed account of the mainstream narrative of buraku history wherein burakumin are defined as members of old outcast/e communities cut off from mainstream society long ago by both social and institutional discrimination. The chapter then goes on to highlight specific empirical and conceptual problems with the narrative that emerged during archival research on the 1871 Emancipation Edict, and through a reading of Japanese literature that critically addressed the buraku problem. The chapter then demonstrates how the master narrative of buraku history is currently being mobilized on the ground in two areas in eastern and western Japan. It finally concludes by arguing that reconfiguring 'burakumin' as a generic label of marginality within a larger discursive history of social ordering based on ideas of irreconcilable normality and difference is one productive way of re-imagining buraku history.

The Master Narrative: Ancient Period (Before 1185)

Reference works compiled by Japan's leading outcast/e historians reveal that a number of marginalized groups existed during the ancient period (from the seventh to the twelfth centuries), but the most prominent were the senmin (literally 'base people').[2] These groups were also referred to as 'the five outcasts' (*gosen*) and 'the five kinds of outcasts' (*goshiki-no-sen*). Japanese scholars have usually interpreted the word senmin to mean 'slaves' during this early period.[3] These slaves officially existed in ancient Japan within the *ritsuryō* (legal codes) system: a structure borrowed from the Tang Dynasty in China wherein people were officially divided into 'citizens' (*ryōmin*: literally 'good people') and 'outcasts' (senmin).[4] The expression 'the five kinds of outcasts' referred to five types of privately and publicly owned slaves: state-owned imperial mausoleum guards; house slaves who belonged to people holding public office; publicly-owned non-hereditary, non-tradable house slaves; privately owned non-hereditary, non-tradable house slaves; and private slaves who belonged to wealthy 'citizens'.[5] At the beginning of the ritsuryō system, marriage between citizens and slaves was outlawed and offspring conceived between the two were enslaved. At the beginning of the Heian period (the eighth to the twelfth centuries), this law was repealed. Marriages between the two groups were permitted, and all children were deemed as citizens. This virtual turnaround in policy was probably aimed at preventing the further shrinkage of an already dwindling citizen population. But it is also argued that this action led to the end of a politically motivated system of social status.[6]

This did not necessarily mean, however, that outcast/es (senmin/hisabetsumin) suddenly vanished from society. Low status groups are usually argued to have existed even before the establishment of the ritsuryō system. Outcast/e groups can also emerge in societies without complex political systems. The *bemin*, for example, were subservient groups who served the imperial court, the imperial family, and the wealthier regional families (*uji*) in pre-ritsuryō Japan. They were later incorporated into the political and social organizational system of the ritsuryō state with some of them becoming servants of low social status.[7] Some scholars have taken this point as an indication that the outcast/e is born at an early point in Japanese society, probably during the Yayoi period (500 BCE to 300 CE), when wealth first started accumulating.[8] Other scholars, however, insist upon tracing the origins of the burakumin to the later ancient period.[9] Yamanaka Yorimasa, for example, writes that the appearance of the concept of 'impurity' (kegare) could only come about after the emergence of a belief in the 'sacred purity' (*shinsei*) of the Emperor. This concept, he claims, emerged at the very beginning of the ancient Japanese state under the reign of Emperor Tenmu.[10] The idea that the ideology of impurity has ancient origins and significantly contributed to the emergence of a buraku problem in Japan is widely supported in academic circles. Most scholars, however, tend to distinguish between what might be termed as the 'conceptual' and 'physical' origins of burakumin.[11] The birth of ideas like 'pollution' and 'purity' are not seen as being directly equated with the origins of a firmly bounded minority group, whose core membership has been preserved throughout history to the present. Rather, the end of the official system of slavery during the ancient period, the relative fluidity of the medieval period, and the absence of historical documentation demonstrating any clear historical continuity between these two periods means that researchers are more inclined to place the physical origins of the burakumin among the outcast groups that gain historical visibility during the medieval period. Many pedagogical texts and histories written by activists (or historians with strong activist ties), however, prefer to support the idea of the much later early modern (circa seventeenth to the mid-nineteenth centuries) origins of the burakumin (for reasons discussed below).[12]

Medieval Period (1185–1600)

The *chūsei* or medieval period (circa twelfth to the sixteenth centuries) followed the ancient period. Like its European counterpart, it is commonly typecast as a superstitious age. It is also seen by many academics as the period that witnessed the emergence of the people who would become known as burakumin. During the last two decades, with the wide dissemination of ideas like 'pollution' and 'purity' in texts related to buraku history, the medieval period has, for many scholars, become the period that witnessed the emergence of the Japanese outcast/e (senmin/hisabetsumin) through ideas of 'untouchability' (*fukashoku*).[13] Because there is no formal, politically motivated system of social status in medieval Japanese society, the period is generally considered to be what Harada Tomohiko once labelled as 'fluid' (*ryūdōteki*).[14] This implies that people in medieval society are ostensibly thought to have been able to alter their own social standing through physical and social mobility. The idea of medieval fluidity also tends to contribute to arguments that the buraku problem somehow arose 'naturally' (*shizen hassei*) from within medieval society and not as a result of earlier state-sanctioned discriminatory policies.[15]

The dictionary *Burakushi yōgo jiten* (Dictionary of Buraku Historical Terms) broadly categorizes the medieval outcast into three types: those related to occupation, place, and character/appearance. These three types are further divided into two distinct categories—artists/entertainers and people of low social status. The artist/entertainer group included outdoor performers, indoor performers, and those who excelled at various types of artistic accomplishments. Some of these artists did exist during the ancient period, but most appear to have emerged during the medieval period. At the beginning of the medieval period, artists lived in temples, shrines, or under the watchful eye of individual lords. They were apparently targeted for discrimination for numerous reasons: because of their itinerant nature; because they had the special privilege of receiving a tax exemption from their lords for their services; and because they often had religious functions that made them objects of fear within local communities. Historical evidence also suggests a fundamental shift in the nature of the outcast during the mid-to-late medieval period. Discrimination based on ideas of pollution and purity gave way to occupation-based discrimination.[16]

Medieval outcasts of low social status not linked to artist/entertainer groups included a range of different groups, whose names reflected their occupations, places of residence, and character/appearance. *Eta* and *hinin*, for example, had names denoting a sense of vulgarity and uncleanness. *Shuku*[17] and kawaramono, while still incorporating a sense of uncleanness, also signified particular landmarks like dwelling places and dry riverbeds. Groups like kiyome (purifier) and *kawata* (tanner)[18] had names relating to their occupations. Others, like *hōmen* (literally meaning the 'released'),[19] were outcasts because they had been convicted of crimes. Some groups had life circumstances that dictated their name and status like *kojiki* ('beggars') and *raisha* ('lepers').

Scholars who work on the medieval–early modern historical divide have ascertained some links between the historical settlements of some medieval outcast groups and early modern *eta*, *kawata,* and *hinin* communities.[20] Since geographical linkages between some outcast groups of the late medieval period and twentieth-century buraku communities can be established, the idea of burakumin having medieval origins becomes logically sustainable. Texts like the *Burakushi yōgo jiten*, however, also issue a cautionary note. Each of the terms used for medieval outcasts during the medieval period did not necessarily refer to one specific group. *Eta*, for example, did the work of kawata and kiyome. The kawaramono also basically constituted the same group. Different words were used according to the specific work that people did and regional differences were also common.[21]

Scholars have also frequently alluded to a possible linkage between the word '*etori*' that dates back to the ancient period and *eta* that emerges during the medieval period. Etori referred to a group of people employed to slaughter animals and provide carrion for the Emperor's birds of prey. *Eta*, on the other hand, were people who engaged in butchery and tanning activities. The similar names and activities of these groups have often provided a loose basis for placing the physical origins of the *eta* (and, therefore, the burakumin) in the ancient period.[22] Few scholars, however, openly support this explanation today. The vast majority of Japanese historians and burakumin writers look to the late medieval period as the point wherein a convergence between burakumin and premodern outcast/e groups (senmin/hisabetsumin) can be witnessed. This is the period wherein it can be empirically demonstrated that outcast/e communities (*qua* buraku communities) were politically constructed and confined to a marginalized status.[23] Nevertheless, texts designed for academic consumption within outcast/e historiography and pedagogical texts designed to instruct readers about the buraku problem continue to diverge on the question of origin. A majority of the pedagogical texts argue for the late sixteenth century as the point of burakumin origin. However, the historian Tsukada Takashi has highlighted a significant theoretical problem with this position. While regional warlords made clear legal demands for the formation of tanning cartels during the sixteenth century, their laws and ordinances were actually only targeting social groups that already existed.[24]

Early Modern Period (1600–1868)

The early modern period within the mainstream view of buraku history is argued to have heralded a time when elites deliberately intervened in the lives of outcaste groups. They created a social system and institutions that prevented these groups from achieving self-determination. It particularly restricted them in relation to social status, occupation, and residence.[25] When certain members of the warrior class attempted to unify the country, new institutions designed to maximize political control were put in place. Some of these systems included giving monopoly rights to occupational groups in exchange for complete compliance on certain issues particularly relating to residence and occupation.[26] Cadastral surveys (*kenchi*) established an unprecedented degree of linkages between land, occupation, and taxation, creating a relatively fixed group of agricultural producers (*onbyakusho*), who were to be placed in a special relationship with the ruling warrior elites. Along with the land surveys, warriors were moved into castle-towns (*heinō bunri*) and the peasantry was disarmed (katanagari). All non-agricultural producers were effectively excluded from membership of the peasant class and subsequent laws such as the ban on the mortgaging of farming land (*tahata eidai baibai kinshirei*) cemented outcastes into their lowly statuses.

Tokugawa society was splintered into multiple domains, averaging over 260 throughout the course of the Tokugawa period, with the Tokugawa shogun (the hereditary military dictator who ruled federally during the early modern period) located in the city of Edo. A steady yet awkward peace was maintained during the period through a variety of measures. A system of alternate attendance or residence was arranged for the warrior heads of fiefs to pay their respects to the shogun in the city of Edo (*sankin kōtai*). Laws for the conduct of warriors and nobility were promulgated. Domain lords were strategically relocated to different regions. A prohibition of foreign missionary activity and domestic travel within Japan was issued and bans were placed on the mortgaging of farming land. The establishment of population registers and the compulsory membership of households in the Buddhist religious sects were the final steps in the production of a status system (*mibunsei*) that saw Japanese society become heavily stratified. Confucian notions of society and systems of hereditary succession formed the conceptual basis for this system, which also included a moral imperative for the preservation of the status quo. Further compounding the harsh reality of strict social stratification, the Tokugawa shogunate increasingly used judicial legislation as a means of enforcing and reinforcing distinctions based on these policies.[27]

Over time, limitations were placed on movement, residence, occupational change, and marriage. Even clothing and hairstyles were subjected to harsh legislation. The creation and application of these restrictions was predicated upon a growing sense of elite desperation for social order. It was often argued, and in some cases rightfully so, that social instability was challenging the very foundation of Tokugawa rule. Widespread mercantilism, peasant bankruptcy and desertion, urban drift, increased vagrancy, and a perceived decline in public morality (evidenced in suicides resulting from love affairs, and from economic overindulgence) were interpreted as ripping apart the moral and social fabric of Tokugawa society. The response was often a neat categorization and segregation of people based on their occupational differences and prescribed duties, and the instilling of a popular fear of divergence from the status quo.[28]

Pedagogical texts frequently claim that burakumin were, therefore, 'created' (*kōchiku/hensei/zōshutsu*) by elites according to the logic of 'divided rule' (*bunretsu/bundan shihai*) based upon an ordering of society into four social statuses (*shi–nō–kō–shō* or 'warrior–farmer–artisan–merchant') borrowed from classical Confucianism. Popular control was basically maintained by encouraging segments of the population to be content with their poor social status because other groups were treated with even greater disdain. One high school textbook, edited by the well-known historian Kodama Kōta, puts it in the following way: 'Below the farmers, artisans, and merchants were placed people with low social status called *eta* and *hinin* and they had multiple restrictions placed on many different aspects of their lives including residence and clothing. The purpose of this was to let the farmers, artisans, and merchants know that there was a social status below them in order to divert discontentment away from warrior rule. The shogunate and various fiefs throughout the early modern period encouraged people to think that this kind of discrimination based on social status was permanent.'[29]

By the early eighteenth century, the attitude of many of the rulers and political advisors was to tighten the shogunate's grip on the reins of power by dealing with the aforementioned social problems in a firm and uncompromising way. This resulted in periods of social reform (*Kyōhō kaikaku*—1716–1745, *Kansei kaikaku*—1787–1793, and *Tenpō kaikaku*—1841–1843). Adopting measures that strengthened the policy separating social classes was a significant part of reforms based on a fear of social disorder.[30] '*Eta*' and '*hinin*', though originally generic labels used to refer to a variety of marginalized groups during the late medieval/early Tokugawa period, became referents for fixed outcaste groups that were made to undertake specific duties. Although there are numerous regional differences, the *eta* were generally obliged to undertake the duties of flaying, tanning, leatherwork, and sandal-making. The *hinin* engaged in begging, disposal of animal carcasses, and the burial of vagrants. But outcaste groups were also made the official punitive arm of the Tokugawa shogunate, and the bestowing of 'special powers' (*tokken*) on them such as guard and execution duties detrimentally affected their social standing in local communities. Burgeoning legislation aimed to push outcaste groups even further to the margins of Tokugawa society.

By the eighteenth century, *eta* and *hinin* groups, through the creation of an extremely rigid system of social status, had apparently become locked into their outcaste status. Institutions put into place by the unifiers of the country (particularly, Toyotomi Hideyoshi and

Tokugawa Ieyasu) were reinforced by later shogunate policies. One particularly salient outcome of these policies was the systematic organization of outcastes in eastern Japan under the *eta* leader Danzaemon.

Danzaemon was the hereditary title of a leader of the majority of *eta* and *hinin* communities in eastern Japan and his residence was located in Edo (Tokyo) during the early modern period (1600–1868). As one of eastern Japan's most powerful leather bosses, he is thought to have become the official supplier of leather to the Tokugawa shoguns and received monopoly tanning rights from the first ruler Ieyasu. Little reliable information exists about where the Danzaemon originally came from and the actual number of generational heads it produced, but scholars generally agree that Danzaemon was probably an independent leather-making family during the late medieval period that became the dominant leather cartel in eastern Japan through a process of staving off regional competitors. Scholars also suggest that there were probably thirteen generational heads of the Danzaemon family line (though it is debatable as to whether the first few bearers of the title Danzaemon were real people). From around the mid-seventeenth century onwards, Danzaemon was forcibly relocated with his sizable community to Imado and the area became known colloquially as 'New Town' (*Shinchō*).[31]

During the decades that directly preceded the Meiji Restoration of 1869, the Tokugawa status system became something akin to the Indian caste system. Laws were promulgated relating to clothing, hairstyle, residence, occupation, marriage practices, and even the value of human life. According to one often-quoted ruling, an *eta* life was only worth one-seventh of a commoner's.[32]

Modern Period (1868-)

The mid-nineteenth century saw the unwelcome arrival of a Western presence in Japan and the onset of gunboat diplomacy. Most Japanese rulers and officials did not dispute the need for independence from an encroaching West that had succeeded in dominating relations with Japan by drafting a number of humiliating treaties. But the envisaged strategy for remaining independent was often strongly contested. Eventually, the implemented approach was 'enlightenment' (*bunmei kaika*), a concept and, thereafter, policy that advocated the adoption of Western practices, including popular egalitarianism. As a result, a so-called 'Emancipation Edict' (*mibun kaihōrei*) was promulgated in 1871, abolishing the official labels and statuses of *eta* and *hinin,* and elevating them to the position of 'new commoner-citizen' (*shinheimin*).[33] The Meiji government, however, did not adopt any other policy that would back up this decree of emancipation. Modernization-driven economic policies only facilitated an increase in poverty for 'former outcastes', thereby worsening their plight. Furthermore, many people from non-outcaste backgrounds objected to the new political policy of emancipation, and former outcastes became oppressed on all sides, particularly during the decade or so immediately following its promulgation.[34]

The Meiji government, while pursuing policies of industrialization, removed the former outcaste monopoly on leather production, thereby opening the way for entrepreneurs. This forced the 'new commoner-citizens' to take up cheap wage labour. Wealthier members of former outcaste communities adopted policies of self-improvement as a way to alleviate their abject poverty and the new discriminatory challenges they were facing. Many used a large portion of their own wealth in order to address some of the problems.[35] Facing economic problems after the Russo–Japanese War (1904–05), the Japanese government set about a course of local improvements by encouraging regional communities to adopt community-based measures to improve their living standards (and, therefore, their ability to pay taxes).[36] Quite apart from this movement, however, some burakumin began to form independently self-aware associations to combat the oppressive situation that they confronted. These actions became pronounced during the early 1910s and developed into full-scale national activities by the 1920s. From around the same time, the grassroots Suiheisha movement (1922–1942) and the government-backed *Yūwa* movements began to compete for the support and backing of members of the 'special buraku' (tokushu buraku) community.[37] Rather than merely accepting the claim that 'special buraku' were responsible for the state of their communities, members of the radical Suiheisha movement declared a pride in their '*eta* heritage' and decided that they would unite together to fight all evidences of discrimination against them in society. They did this by publicly 'denouncing' (*kyūdan*) anyone who was thought to advocate or maintain discriminatory practices against former outcastes.[38] The oppressive climate of the 1930s, along with severe restrictions that were placed on social and political activism through the Peace Preservation Law, eventually led to the integration of the two movements and ultimately an abandonment of the association altogether in 1942.

The Suiheisha movement was soon resurrected during the early postwar period. Closely aligned with Marxist ideology during the early postwar years, the Buraku Liberation League (BLL), founded as the National Committee for Buraku Liberation (NCBL) (*Buraku kaihō zenkoku i'inkai*) in 1946, which changed its name to BLL in 1955, reached its heydays in the 1950s, bringing about large-scale changes in society through the distinctive practices of 'denunciation' and 'administrative struggle' (*gyōsei tōsō*).[39] The most noticeable achievement of the movement was the forcing of a political response from the Japanese government in 1965 that led to the passage of a 'Special Measures Law' (*Dōwa taisaku jigyō tokubetsu sochihō*) in 1969. As part of this policy, large sums of money were injected into efforts to improve living conditions and education in the *dōwa* districts (the Japanese government's term for buraku areas), and 'dōwa education' (*dōwa kyōiku*) was incorporated into many school curricula.[40] The creation of the Special Measures Law also led to a significant split in the movement, one that was to lead to much antagonism between the League and other buraku-related groups during subsequent decades.

While most buraku groups are in agreement that the government measures adopted to deal with the buraku problem were successful in achieving their aims, there is still intense debate surrounding the negative impact of the government's refusal to pass a law to make buraku discrimination illegal.[41] The early twenty-first century saw the end of many official government policies towards burakumin (most significantly a repeal of the Special Measures legislation), and some have used this measure to speak about the end of buraku history. The liberation movement, nevertheless, particularly the BLL, remains relatively strong, despite a noticeable decline in youth activism and government funding. The media, too, generally remained quiet about this issue for a majority of the postwar period, but has found a voice in recent times, particularly about matters that negatively reflect upon the activities of the League.[42]

Empirical Problems

Despite the popularity and prevalence of this master narrative, however, careful empirical research suggests that buraku communities are probably best understood as having unique, fluid, and often quite divergent histories. There are, for example, cases wherein 'former outcaste' communities disappeared *en masse* after the Meiji Restoration. Honda Yutaka has revealed that certain *eta* communities like the Hashimoto Township (Kanda) in Tokyo vanished during the modern era. Honda also notes that most premodern *hinin* communities are not actually included in twentieth-century buraku censuses.[43] In addition, Noah McCormack has noted the movement of 'new poor' into outcaste neighbourhoods during the 1870s in western Japan, further bringing into question the 'pure continuity' that is supposed to exist between premodern outcaste populations and modern-day buraku communities.[44] As mentioned in Chapter 1, a cursory survey of the postwar writings of Anglophone scholars on outcaste communities reveals that the status of premodern *eta* and *hinin* villages could appear and disappear during a range of historical periods (including the postwar period) for a variety of reasons. My own archival research on the 'Emancipation Edict' of 1871 outlined below also presents interesting interpretative challenges for subscribers to the master narrative of buraku history.[45]

The Tokugawa outcaste order was legally abolished in 1871 through a document commonly referred to as the Emancipation Edict intended to enable members of former outcaste communities to become 'commoner-citizens' (*heimin*). The Emancipation Edict, though, was not a piece of legislation simply plucked out of thin air. In 1868, a move towards legal emancipation was already in motion with the official 'elevation' (*hikiage*) of the *eta* leader Danzaemon as well as seventy of his closest aides to 'commoner status' (*heinin mibun*). The 1868 document gave several official reasons for Danzaemon's status promotion, such as the fact that he assisted when the fire burnt down one of the main gaols in Edo, and that he had gathered together an army of outcastes to assist the shogunate in an attack on the Chōshū fief.[46] Danzaemon's elevation in status was also accompanied by a change in name to Dan Naiki and he quickly spread this good news throughout all the surrounding towns and villages.[47]

Dan Naiki also sent an appeal to the new Meiji government soon after, which attempted to facilitate the emancipation of *eta* communities under his jurisdiction. Essentially a plea for the abolition of all outcaste statuses, Dan Naiki referred to 'several hundred years of continual abuse' during the preceding feudal era and lamented that 'even though we are no different to human beings born under heaven, the fact that humane associations are [still] not possible is a truly deplorable fact.'[48] Naiki's communication also gave some indication of what he believed was necessary for 'status emancipation' (*mibun hikiage*). He wrote about the need to eradicate the 'two despicable Chinese ideographs' (*niji no shūmei*); the 'outlawing of the label *eta*' (*eta no meimoku on-nozoki*); and the 'expurgation of their past bad name' (*jūrai no shūmei issō*).[49] Interestingly, he requested no change in 'occupation' (*shoku*), 'area of residence' (*ba*), 'official duties' (*yaku*), or 'privileges' (*tokken*): all features of *eta* status during the Tokugawa period that are considered important by scholars.[50] It appears that for Dan Naiki, status emancipation referred primarily to social acceptance facilitated through the removal of discriminatory labels.

Just as Danzaemon's elevation in status was posited in terms of what he had done for the late Tokugawa shogunate, however, so too subsequent requests by other *eta* groups for status elevation predating the Emancipation Edict were often based upon arguments of what outcaste communities could provide for the shogunate. The *eta* of Watanabe Village in Sesshū province (discussed in detail below), for example, listed as one of their main arguments for emancipation in 1870 the fact that they had been ready and prepared to fight foreigners encroaching on Japanese soil with halberds if need be (when there was initial talk of 'expelling the barbarian')—a loyalist intention that was abruptly interrupted when a peace treaty was signed with the outsiders. This new development had clearly demoralized the *eta* community, and they were greatly disconcerted that they should continue to be regarded as polluted because they were meat-eaters even though flesh-eating foreigners were living on peaceful terms with the rest of the population. The Watanabe village community requested the authorities to officially strike down the social and legal status designation of the two Chinese characters for *eta* meaning 'much pollution'. [51]

By 1870, moreover, some *eta* communities had clearly taken matters of emancipation into their own hands. Many attempted to terminate their outcaste status of their own volition, and endeavoured to seize the uneasily defined spaces of normality. An official inspector, who was employed to describe popular conditions in the countryside to the central government, reported in 1870 that there were rumours that farmers and merchants running restaurants, bath-houses, and barber shops, were being forced out of business because *eta* customers were entering their stores. The inspector further records that in Okayama, the bath-house owners were able to find ways to counter this exercising of agency. By calling themselves 'inner town baths' (*chōnai furō*), and giving out wooden passes to their customers, they could refuse entry to those customers who did not have these passes, presumably in this way being able to maintain the regimes of exclusion set in place against *eta*.[52]

In August 1871, the Emancipation Edict was formally promulgated through the remonstrations of mostly well-placed politicians of quite elite backgrounds. Danzaemon's understanding of what an elevation in status entailed was mirrored somewhat in the eventual legislation of 1871: 'From here on, the names *eta*, *hinin*, etc. are abolished; and they shall be the same as commoners with regards to status and occupation.'[53] The Edict, however, also made reference to 'status' (*mibun*) and 'occupation' (*shokugyō*) quite apart from the issue of 'names' (*shō*). Status, here, presumably referred to the extraordinary body of legal documents that proscribed different rights and responsibilities for *eta*, *hinin,* and other unnamed groups throughout the course of the eighteenth and nineteenth centuries. This section of the Emancipation Edict nullified these laws. Being made 'the same as commoners with regards to… occupation,' meanwhile, was a prescriptive order that denied the future necessity of certain tasks being performed by people of 'special status'. For the new Meiji government, then, status emancipation for *eta* meant not only the removal of discriminatory labels but the prescriptive measure of raising the position of 'former outcastes' with respect to their occupation and legal status to the level of 'commoners' (an action which also presumably involved the retraction of Tokugawa legal prohibitions and the stamping out of related discriminatory social practices).

There can be little doubt that one key motivation for the promulgation of the Emancipation Edict was the desire of oligarchs and bureaucrats to establish a more efficient national space. The *eta* and *hinin* communities were perceived to be troublesome eyesores in the process of nation-building that was being diligently inspected by Western powers (more on this in Chapter 4). Nakano Itsuki, a prominent politician at the time, argued for the emancipation of *eta* because the land of these people had traditionally been measured differently, something he believed needed to be made uniform in the 'Empire' (*kōkoku*).[54] The eventual Emancipation Edict also included an order to report to the authorities if there was a custom in local villages of waiving land taxes for 'outcastes' (*eta–hinin*–nado). Clearly, an interest in unifying taxation practices and creating a new and complete base of taxation was one motivation behind its promulgation. Kumagaya Teizō and Inazu Itsuki, who were also politicians involved in the debate on emancipation, argued that they did not perceive any foreseeable problems in getting members of the outcaste communities to assist in performing national labour services. Others too, commented on the need to include outcastes in a national household registry.[55]

When the news of the dissemination of the Edict eventually reached both 'outcaste' and 'commoner' communities, there were, predictably enough, mixed reactions. Some prefectural governments took the promulgation of the Edict as an opportunity to lecture both 'commoner-citizens' and 'new ordinary citizens' on the importance of the Edict. The Ehime Prefectural government, for example, advised those who had difficulty in accepting the Edict to understand that the *eta* were a product of Japan before it was civilized, that *eta* too were most undoubtedly the Emperor's subjects, and that they were exactly the same as 'commoners' (heinin) in terms of their nature and intelligence. At the same time though, *eta* were advised to work hard at their farming, to live cleanly, to tidy up after themselves, to wash meat thoroughly, to be careful of body odour, and to avoid all actions that 'commoner-citizens' (heimin) considered to be unclean.[56]

Several months after the promulgation of the Edict in January 1872, some disturbing reactions also began to surface. The *eta* of Nakazui village in Okayama Prefecture had used the law as a spring pad to recoil from the spaces of exile that they had been forced to occupy during the Tokugawa period. They requested permission from the prefectural government to resign from all duties related to criminal investigation, banishment of beggars, and disposal of dead animal carcasses. The local villagers reacted to this predictably by complaining that they were being inconvenienced by such a petition, and subsequently retaliated by refusing to allow the outcastes access to communal land set aside for cropping, vegetable production, and natural fuels such as firewood. Moreover, store owners from the neighbouring villages, though perhaps not even being directly related to the conflict, began to refuse to sell products to members of the *eta* community. The problem quickly reached an impasse when a 'former *eta*' (*moto eta*) villager, who was turned away from a local tavern, was joined by local *eta* villagers in a large-scale demonstration. According to the document, the angry non-*eta* villagers then banded together, summoned together three 'former *eta*' village heads, and over a period of time, brutally killed them all.[57]

At the local village level in eastern Japan, however, status emancipation was clearly being interpreted differently from region to region. In one village in the former Musashi Province (present-day Saitama Prefecture), for example, the contents of the Emancipation Edict were explained to the villagers as meaning: the abolition of legal *eta* status; the legal permissibility of bearing surnames, using the title 'farmer', wearing clothes such as *haori* and *hakama*, and entering the houses of village officials in the future; and equal participation of everyone in performing official duties (*yaku*).[58] In the same community, moreover, the village elders were informed that they would now be regional governors.[59] Other people in a neighbouring Musashi village were simply informed that everyone was now 'the same as everybody else', a declaration that understandably led to a celebration in which alcohol was consumed freely.

In another nearby village, several petitions concerning the Emancipation Edict were sent by one 'former eta, but now ordinary commoner-citizen' (*moto eta ippan heimin*) to the local authorities about a month after it was issued, in which he protested against the local village head's treatment of himself and his family. His ancestors had worked for the village for about 200 years as mountain guards in exchange for a minute allowance and permission to work a small plot of land near his residence (that was non-taxable because it was infertile). The local village official, who owned the land 'north, south, east, and west' of the 'former *eta*'s' residence, upon receiving the Edict, released him from his guard duties, forbade him from tilling his plot of land (that was formerly exempt from taxation but was presumably taxable land now) because he was now an 'ordinary commoner', and informed him that he should move off the land and leave the village along with his aged father, wife, and blind child. This former *eta* villager commented in the document that there had been 'no greater joy for them' than the Emancipation Edict and he interpreted it as something that promised the possibility of a 'stable life' (*anjū*). But it was now being transformed into a piece of legislation enabling other villagers to 'crush them under their feet' (*fumitsubushi*). To this 'former *eta*', the Edict meant the possibility of losing his job, his land, and his place in the village.[60]

Conceptions of 'status elevation' (*mibun hikiage*) clearly differed in the late 1860s and early 1870s at the central and local government levels, as well as between Danzaemon and members of regional *eta* communities. For some, 'elevation' meant outlawing an epithet with pseudo-legal status; for others, it meant the removal of discriminatory legal and social practices; and for others again, it meant the promise of a stable life. Danzaemon's conceptions of what constituted an elevation in status were markedly different from those of isolated *eta* families living in areas like rural Saitama. However, not only did people conceive of emancipation from their former statuses differently, but the realities of emancipation were also affected by legislation in very different ways. While the former outcaste in the above story was eventually permitted to remain in the village, Danzaemon's transition to modernity was different again. Officially incorporated into the Edo City Magistrate's office as a commoner of samurai status (*yoriki kaku*) in 1869, he held numerous important government posts during the years after the Restoration. Eventually, too, Danzaemon's descendants disappeared into the anonymity offered to first-class citizens within modern Japanese society.[61] In many respects, Danzaemon appears to have been an individual who, to quote Carol Gluck, 'landed on [his] feet' during the 'rapid institutional change' of the early Meiji period, which 'was like a tectonic shift in the ground of social existence.'[62]

As early as the late nineteenth century, the association between Danzaemon's former residential area of Imado (discussed more below) and early modern outcaste groups was beginning to fade. *Tokyo chiri enkakushi* (A Historical Record of the Geography of Tokyo), a book published in 1890, included the following comment about Danzaemon's former residential area: 'In older times it was called Shinchō and was an *eta* settlement. Its leader Dan Naiki lived there. Kameoka received its current name in 1871 and became a normal district broken up into three blocks.'[63] Ten years later, in 1900, the book *Ijin no genkō* (Words and Deeds of Great People) was published in Tokyo and actually listed Danzaemon as among the 'fifty greatest people' in Japanese history.[64]

As will be seen further in Chapter 4, post-Meiji urbanization in

Tokyo assisted in blurring the boundaries between 'former outcaste' areas and modern slums. In addition, momentous events like the Great Kantō Earthquake (1923) and the incendiary bombings of World War II (1944–45) also forced mass relocation and large-scale town reconstruction. The Allied Occupation and related land reforms further assisted in dissociating many areas in the greater Tokyo region with 'outcasteness'. Arai Kōjirō notes that the links between Imado and 'former outcastes' became so tenuous that the area was not even included in the Japanese government's dōwa policy in the 1960s.[65] Although this kind of urban history still awaits closer investigation, emerging research like the kind outlined above, which focuses on the Emancipation Edict, reinforces the conclusion that individual 'outcaste (*eta-hinin-nado*) communities' (as well as individual 'outcastes' themselves) are better understood as having unique, fluid, and often quite divergent histories. Any modern history of burakumin built on sound empirical analysis, therefore, must pay just as much attention to the realities of discontinuity as it does to stable connection.

Conceptual Problems

Conceptual problems are also found within the master narrative of buraku history. The historian Hatanaka Toshiyuki has insisted, for example, that the formulaic conception of 'premodern *eta* (and sometimes also *hinin*) = modern burakumin' is basically a 'theory of continuity' (*keifuron*) which mistakenly frames the problem as one of a fixed group of historical outcast/es rather than 'status' (*mibun*). According to Hatanaka, early modern outcaste and modern buraku problems are linked in the sense that both are status problems, but they are nonetheless essentially different issues, which have developed within distinct social structures. He argues that burakumin do not have any inherent characteristics that define them as burakumin but they are rather people who are subjected to discrimination at certain times for period-specific reasons. Premodern outcast/es (senmin/hisabetsumin) and modern burakumin, therefore, are not fixed categories and cannot be narrated in the way that one would speak of other, ethnically distinct minority groups.[66] The vast majority of buraku histories, however, have continually assumed a Japanese state and a Japanese race moving along a timeline with a fixed group of burakumin located at the bottom of, or external to, this social system.[67] Thus academic research, which has been conceptually bound within such an interpretative framework, has been largely preoccupied with the question of where to locate the historical origins of burakumin. Hatanaka has labelled this fixation with buraku beginnings as *rūtsu-sagashi* or 'the search for roots'.[68] Excessive concern with the uncovering of buraku origins has led to a mass of research publications, which simply describe how 'burakumin' developed over time rather than attempt to explain how processes of social marginalization actually occur in society.

Scholars do, naturally, designate different points of historical origin and derive dissimilar explanations of the root causes of the buraku problem. Most accounts, though, still maintain a high degree of consistency in explaining the key, critical chronological phenomena involved in this history, particularly those related to changes in political history. For many scholars, the key to understanding the buraku problem has been twofold: (a) to explain how this group historically came about; and (b) to understand the essence of who the burakumin are today. It is generally hoped that an understanding of burakumin achieved through a robust investigation of these two questions will eventually lead to buraku liberation in the present. Grasping how the burakumin came about is tantamount to coming to terms with the history of those who have been excluded. Comprehending the essence of who burakumin are today implies understanding how historical outcast/es tie in with the burakumin of modern Japanese history.

Discerning the emergence of burakumin is essentially related to how scholars view the problem of historical development. Closely linked to this question is the problem of the nature of historical continuity. Is history a self-propelling force or is it moved through human agency? For those who favour the idea that change is its own master, the historical origins of the burakumin tend to be pushed back further in time, and greater attention is paid to the social origins of human discriminatory behaviour. For others though, change is an entirely political act, instigated by a human hand, and, therefore, burakumin origins tend to be more closely associated with recent historical actions of particularly powerful individuals or institutions. The mainstream view of Japanese outcast/e (senmin/hisabetsumin) history is distinctive in that it tends to emphasize the role of human agency in the creation of history, and therefore highlights the 'political origins' (*seijiteki kigen*) of burakumin. The support for these two different interpretations has tended to polarize between professional academics and activists, especially in recent years. The former group tends to support theories that depend upon ideas of social origins, while the latter group supports arguments of political origins. This is not really surprising though, if one considers the different work undertaken by these two groups. Both are concerned with pedagogy, but historians in recent times are more concerned with 'objective narration' (in a modern positivist sense), while activists deal with tangible political outcomes. Different activitics and interests clearly reflect distinct narrative choices in buraku historical studies.

An understanding of the identity of burakumin today is based upon the difficult process of comprehending the contemporary realities of buraku discrimination while at the same time understanding how recent social permutations are ultimately outcomes of historical forces. This means comprehending historical forms of the burakumin and buraku discrimination and the manner in which they have metamorphosed into their present shape. In mainstream academia, it is essentially the time that the early modern Japanese state achieved a degree of unification (from the time of Toyotomi Hideyoshi, late sixteenth century, onwards), when the state played an increasing role in legislating discriminatory practices, which scholars believe is the definitive period that shaped buraku history. Researchers generally acknowledge that this does not automatically signal burakumin origins but most writers tend to concede that it was from around this time onwards that early modern Japanese society became heavily stratified, and legally backed systems of heredity and endogamy forced outcaste communities into a position from which they were unable to return. Outcaste communities were essentially locked into status, occupation, and residential arrangements from around this time: a situation that many believe remained virtually unchanged right through to the postwar era.

Scholars, however, generally pay little attention to the 'origins' (*kigen*) that are being referred to in relation to burakumin. The vast majority of historical works treat origins as being singular and absolute. It is, therefore, assumed that there is either only one essential cause for the buraku problem or multiple causes each of which may ultimately be traced back to a singular, absolutely definable point of origin. The reasons for the meticulous search for buraku origins are no doubt complex, but three factors can be said to significant contribute to this research trend. First, it is due to the prevalence of a particular historical method itself. In many of the texts written on the buraku problem, the assumption is made that burakumin, non-burakumin, and Japanese society constitute rigid structures that can be reconstructed and analysed. Twentieth-century modernist epistemological trends have also encouraged an application of these categories as objective historical realities. It is, therefore, believed that sufficient research can help to thoroughly expose the roots of a problem. Scholars, moreover, have often failed to recognize that they are actually predisposed to finding the categories they employ to analyse the buraku problem. Second, a majority of the research has assumed a modernist narrative of historical development, whereby burakumin are believed to be a product of what has historically preceded them. And third, in a majority of the texts, the 'Japanese' are considered to be a homogenous ethnic body devoid of any difference, and buraku discrimination is consequently portrayed as an evolutionary phenomenon rather than an *a priori* social condition. All Japanese outcast/e (senmin/hisabetsumin) history appears to culminate in 'buraku history', and 'burakumin' are, therefore, commonly categorized as an externalized Japanese underclass.

The Master Narrative at Work: Touring Imado and Naniwa

Buraku history, then, is not simply a story about an ancient group of outcast/es (senmin/hisabetsumin) who linger on in present-day

Japan. Historical records reveal that any straightforward linkage between premodern outcast/e groups and contemporary burakumin is only a partial story that selectively privileges certain kinds of evidence. The idea that buraku history is essentially a history of outcast/es, of which burakumin constitute a stable 'core' is also a conceptual model embedded in a particular methodology and politics. There is, however, another important ideational aspect that needs to be explored in relation to the question of buraku history, which is that many burakumin are dependent on the master narrative of current buraku history in order to explain their own experiences of discrimination and to construct meaningful identities for themselves (and others) that might better facilitate liberation. Non-burakumin, too, such as government officials employed in areas deeply implicated in buraku history, employ the master narrative in their engagement with the public and their dealings with buraku residents. The importance of these points was driven home to me during recent guided tours of two 'former outcaste' areas in both eastern and western Japan: Imado (Asakusa, Tokyo), and Naniwa (Naniwa, Osaka).

I went to Imado to visit the buraku historian and activist Uramoto Yoshifumi (introduced in Chapter 1), one hot summer Sunday afternoon in May 2007. I was deeply impressed by Uramoto's book on the history of outcastes in early modern Edo, published in 2003. In it, he had described in vivid detail groups, particularly *eta* and *hinin*, who had lived in the eastern part of Japan around present-day Tokyo during the early modern period. Uramoto's book began with the late sixteenth century and finished with the Meiji Restoration and the early 1870s, but the Epilogue included Uramoto's recent firsthand experience of buraku discrimination that he encountered as a publicly visible member of the Tokyo branch of the BLL. Aside from being deeply impressed by the quality of Uramoto's empirical research into outcaste groups in early modern Japan, I wished to learn more about this thought-provoking endnote to his book. One question in particular that intrigued me during a close reading of his book was the linking of the prejudice prevalent during the Tokugawa period (1600–1868) with contemporary buraku discrimination. There was no mention in his book of a period of 130 years or so about which I wanted to know more.

It being nearly a decade since I had last walked the area, I alighted at Asakusa Station a little earlier than necessary and headed north for a stroll along the banks of the Sumitagawa. Cutting back west around Asakusa nanachōme (just south of Imado), I came across numerous buildings related to the leather industry. There was the 'Leather Hall' (*Hikaku kaikan*), as also numerous specialist leather shoe shops of various sizes like Haruta and Sunarō, and leather specialty stores such as Hosoya. The abundant signage in the area ('For all your leather needs – Kimizuka!') clearly indicated that the area had a history of engaging in leatherwork. As I was walking along the narrow main street of Imado, my eyes were drawn to a moderately sized sign hanging vertically from the side of a narrow three-storeyed building that read 'Tokyo Liberation Hall'. Stopping outside the front of the building, I found a narrow entrance way blocked at the top by a half-drawn shutter. Ducking under the screen, I climbed the staircase to the second floor where I discovered a sizable office with partitioned desks and a middle-aged man shuffling about inside. I knocked, entered, introduced myself, and handed over a business card and a tin of Malaysian sweets hastily bought at Changhi Airport in Singapore several days earlier. Uramoto greeted me warmly and then led me to the third floor of a building where we settled on a comfortable lounge. As we took our seats, he explained that 'Liberation Hall' housed different yet closely linked buraku organizations. Uramoto's offices were located on the second and third floors of the building, and he produced two business cards that confirmed him as both a BLL Tokyo branch activist and a researcher at the Tokyo Liberation Research Institute.

Uramoto began his discussion of buraku history in Tokyo by producing a few maps of varying ages. He began to show me what the area of Asakusa and Imado had looked like several hundred years ago and what it looked like today. It was clear from Uramoto's description that much had changed over the last 150 years in this area. Outcaste groups pejoratively labelled as *eta* and *hinin* were historically involved in a wide range of activities in the area including tanning, leatherwork, guard duties, public execution, and even medicine (for example, there is ample evidence to show, as discussed below, that people of both *eta* and *hinin* statuses performed official autopsies and even made simple medical potions). These duties were quite understandably considered of great importance by the warrior officials of the time.

Being particularly interested in learning more about the modern history of burakumin in this area, I asked Uramoto if there would be a sequel to his book addressing the issue. He replied that there was still so much to know about the early modern history of the buraku that it would take a while to thoroughly research this chapter of history. He remarked, however, that he would one day turn his attention to the more recent past. Although wishing to press this point further, Uramoto kindly offered to take me on a guided tour of Imado (which he had originally designed for high school students), and assuming that I would hear more about this problem on our tour, I gratefully accepted the offer. We set out on foot to survey numerous landmarks concealing stories about where the lives of 'commoners' and 'outcastes' had intersected in older times.

For the most part, Uramoto spoke enthusiastically about the rich history located in this 'hidden side' of Tokyo's past. But his countenance also darkened several times during the course of our afternoon walk, with the jovial look on his face giving way to one reflecting deep concern. The first time this happened was in relation to a discussion on the current state of democracy in Japan. When asked about the reasons for his interest in early modern history and his thoughts about why he considered it important, Uramoto responded by revealing how excited he had been to witness proud people from outcaste communities who stood up for their local independence, during the course of his study of Tokugawa Japan. There were people who resisted the temptation to—or who, in fact, probably had little desire to—simply 'leave everything to those in charge'. Early modern Japanese history documents the existence of people who were not simply passive recipients of rule but historical agents who positively and often vigorously participated in the construction and maintenance of their own communities. According to Uramoto, the early modern history of Japan's outcaste communities needed to be taught and studied precisely because of the feeble nature of Japan's postwar democratic system. Democracy, according to Uramoto, is not just about voting politicians into power but, more importantly, it signifies a grassroots struggle of people in different localities to collectively fight for and secure their own future.

The second time Uramoto's face darkened was during a discussion of members of the buraku communities who hid their identities. He declared that there are considerable numbers of burakumin still living in Imado today, who had ancestors that worked for and lived together with Danzaemon. In spite of that, however, they are apparently reluctant to come out into the open and admit who they are and where they came from. Unless people in present-day Tokyo actually come forward and identify themselves, Uramoto stated, there is no real way for people to tell whether or not they are burakumin. He emphasized that the buraku problem is different from problems related to ethnic or racial discrimination because it was not immediately obvious who a burakumin is (this is, of course, not strictly true as there are numerous other minority groups in Japan such as the Zainichi Koreans who may also qualify for the label 'invisible').[69] Uramoto's point, though, was that burakumin are even more invisible than this community because there is no real 'buraku language' and 'buraku culture' considered completely unique to buraku communities any more. Traditional buraku industries like *taiko* drum-making[70] are today treated by most people simply as 'Japanese culture'. Uramoto stated that many people living in Imado simply wished to preserve their anonymity and blend into society. He added, though, quite strikingly: 'wakaru kedo ne' (I understand, of course).

The third time Uramoto became disconsolate during the course of our discussion that afternoon was when we arrived at the Ekōin Temple near the old Kotsugahara Execution Grounds near Minami Senju Station. In the car park of the Ekōin Temple, about 50 metres away from Minami Senju Station in Tokyo's Arakawa Ward (neighbouring Asakusa), stands a brick wall with an intriguing tablet full of carved images of snakes weaving through skulls, weight scales, semi-naked Adam- and Eve-like figures, and strange-looking fish. Next to the tablet is a plaque dated 4 March 1959, which reads:

> In memory of the autopsy that gave birth to Western Learning (Rangaku). In 1771, the 4th day of the third month of the eight year of Meiwa, Sugita Genpaku, Maeno Ryōtaku, Nakagawa Jun'an and others, came here to watch an autopsy (*fuwake*). There were people before this time who had seen one, but Genpaku and company brought with them a copy of the Dutch medical textbook *Tafel Anatomia*. They compared what they saw with the diagrams in the book and were taken aback with its accuracy. On the way home, these three men, in a state of excitement, decided to translate the book for Japanese doctors and without delay commenced the task. Therein, after much agonizing, they published the five volume series *Kaitai Shinsho* in the eighth month of the third year of An'ei in 1774. This was the beginning of the proper translation of Western technical texts. After this Western Studies (Rangaku) began to flourish, this text being the catalyst for the blossoming of Japanese modern culture.

The story of Sugita Genpaku and the translation of this Western text is a long-familiar one in Japan. However, as Uramoto pointed out to me, a very important part of Genpaku's original story is missing. One need only go as far as Genpaku's well-known early nineteenth-century text *Rantō kotohajime* (The Beginning of Western Learning) to find a vivid description of the moment when he and many other famous physicians and scholars of the time confirmed with their own eyes the internal organization of the human body.[71]

Genpaku describes how he went to the approximate area where the Ekōin monument now lies and along with Ryōtaku and others who travelled to the Kotsugahara execution grounds that day, witnessed the autopsy of a female criminal known colloquially as 'green tea lady' (about which, unfortunately, nothing is really known).

Genpaku's own passage relating to the events which transpired that day is detailed below:

> From here, we all went to the place where the autopsy was going to be performed at Kotsugahara. The autopsy was to be [performed] by an *eta* called Toramatsu, who was also highly skilled at explaining what he was doing. On this day, Toramatsu was going to perform the autopsy but because of an apparent illness, his father, an old man [ideographs for 'old butcher' used] of 90 years of age, came as his replacement. He was a healthy old man. He had performed autopsies numerous times since his youth, saying, 'I have opened up several people.' Autopsies, until that day, were left to *eta*. While cutting open the body they would point out different places informing us, 'These are lungs. This is a liver. These are kidneys.' All the while the observing doctors would simply come to watch and then return home. All they could say was, 'We actually viewed the inside of the body.' No labels were really attached to the different body parts so all they could do was watch the butcher point things out and nod.
>
> This day, too, the old butcher pointed out this and that: the heart, the kidneys, the gallbladder, the stomach. He pointed to something and said "I don't know the name, but I have performed this procedure on several people since I was a youth and I am positive that this was inside all of them."[72]

As I worked my way through these texts a few weeks after meeting Uramoto for the first time, I was able to better understand his sense of disquiet. No mention at all is made of the Edo outcaste community in the plaque that marks this epoch-making event. I sensed during our discussion at Ekōin Temple and then during our brief walk to Minami Senju Station where we bade each other farewell that dealing with blatantly revisionist history might sometimes be just as painful for some burakumin as the experience of discrimination itself. It was clear through my discussions with Uramoto, and during our journey through early modern *eta* and *hinin* history that afternoon, that the group of people claimed by many burakumin to be their ancestors had developed a distinct body of knowledge which no one could gain access to without actually travelling to this area and interacting with its residents.

It was also clear to me while walking the area and listening to Uramoto talk that though some traces of early modern outcaste history are still deeply embedded in the Asakusa cityscape, much had also transpired in the modern era to obliterate these linkages. Despite this discontinuity, however, Imado remained for Uramoto a 'buraku area' where 'many burakumin lived', where the disappearing traces of a premodern world were preserved with the hope that its rich history and a crucial identity would not be lost. Uramoto spoke with knowledge and conviction, and his love of Tokyo, Imado, and Japanese people of all historical epochs who occupied and shaped this area was highly evident in all his discussions. People who had occupied the lowest strata of Japanese society during the early modern era were referred to throughout the afternoon as 'hisabetsu burakumin' (literally 'burakumin who are discriminated against'). Uramoto linked his buraku identity with both the people who lived in this area several hundred years ago as well as the area itself; and this was despite the profound changes that the area had experienced during modern times and the fact that he had not been born in Tokyo.

Moving east to west several weeks later, I was struck by the even heavier burden that buraku history bore in this part of Japan. My destination, Naniwa, was the site of an old outcaste community in Osaka. The area is distinctive these days for a number of reasons but none more so than because Liberty Osaka (*Libati Osaka*), or, the Osaka Human Rights Museum, was established there in 1985 by the BLL. The museum, discussed in greater detail in Chapter 5 of this book, is dedicated to the memory of the historical plight of Japan's minority groups and their struggles for basic human rights protections. Naniwa is also home to the Buraku Liberation Human Rights Research Institute (*Buraku Kaihō Jinken Kenkyūjo*) established during the period when the controversial buraku activist Asada Zennosuke was at the helm of the buraku liberation movement in the late 1960s.

On my way to the Liberty Osaka one morning, I casually wandered inside the Osaka Municipal Naniwa Human Rights

Cultural Centre near Ashiharabashi Station with the hope of perhaps picking up a few brochures or booklets. To my surprise and delight, however, I caught a glimpse of a sign advertising a 'documents exhibit room' (*shiryō tenjishitsu*). With the proposition of exploring this room proving too tempting to decline, I went about securing the permission of the office secretary to see it. I was soon led to the exhibition room on the third floor by a municipal official, who introduced himself as Arimoto Toshio. The floor was dark and locked despite it being 11 am on a Tuesday morning, and Arimoto quickly opened the main exhibition room and led me inside. We began our clockwise circuit of a space that reminded me of a small classroom, perusing a series of maps lining the walls that revealed the historical development of an outcast/e (hisabetsumin) community in this district of Naniwa. The maps revealed a process whereby a historical outcast/e community was pushed further and further outside the Osaka city limits by a succession of premodern warrior governments until it settled in its current location. The maps suggested that the places occupied by members of this community were historically conceived of as 'impure spaces' because of the occupations they undertook. As a result, the community was gradually and repeatedly pushed to the outer limits of the city. Premodern officials were clearly interested in the services these people could offer (taiko drum-making, execution duties, police duties, fire-fighting duties, etc.), for they came under the official employ of the Tokugawa state, but at the same time, they were refused status as fully-fledged members of the same social world.

One map in the exhibit that was particularly striking was the reproduction of *Osaka meisho ichiran* (Compendium of Famous Views in Osaka) drawn by Gountei Sadahide in 1855. Exhibited in the main room, it provided what was essentially a view of Osaka at the end of the Tokugawa period cast from an imaginary elevated perspective somewhere near Osaka Castle. Although there was only limited space for labels on this map (only seven villages were listed for the entire Osaka area), it remarkably included 'Watanabe Village'—the name of the Naniwa outcaste community at this particular historical juncture. The inclusion of an outcaste village on any map in the Tokugawa period, particularly a reference to it with its actual name and not an epithet, is purportedly rare (though certainly not unheard of). The area that most communities occupied was often not even counted in the official measurements of distance between townships. Arimoto's explanation that the artist 'had to include the village otherwise the map would seem strange [biased or selective]' was interesting. He seemed to think that Gountei would have preferred not to include this name on the map if he had a choice but the Naniwa area had become such a hive of economic activity that it simply could not be ignored. This point was reinforced when other images and exhibit pieces were examined. The Naniwa community had grown quite famous for taiko drum-making and retained its fair share of wealthy and renowned artisans. In fact, the main park in present-day Naniwa is the site of the former mansion of an early modern taiko drum-maker, who had supplied drums to shrines in far away places like Tottori Prefecture, even producing a massive towering drum for the famous Shitennōji Temple in Osaka. Naniwa found its way on to maps by the end of the premodern era because the residents of Naniwa had literally put it there through their skill and productivity. Although they were doubtless continual targets of social discrimination because of their perceived 'outcasteness', numerous outsiders also moved to the area with the dream of etching out a new life for themselves in an economically productive and socially vibrant village.

The way in which the maps of Naniwa's outcaste community exhibited in this room were lined up next to each other was striking as they demonstrated a process of geographical marginalization, which was linked, in some sense, to a perception of the low social status of the village. A map produced during the Warring States period (sixteenth century), for example, showed a 'Watanabe no sato' (Watanabe County) located on the northern banks of Okawa (Yodokawa). A map produced in 1687, however, showed 'Watanabe Village' as part of Lower Naniwa Village near the Kizu River. A map produced 110 years later, though, simply referred to an 'Eta Village' located near the intersection of the Itachi River and the Jūsangen

River. The 'Naniwa outcaste community' had, in fact, relocated six times during its history, sometimes moving quite substantial distances before coming to rest at its current location.[73]

While these maps revealed a history of state (both shogunate and fief-based) discrimination against a particular group of people in early modern times in Osaka, the exhibit also seemed to be concealing a tale of disjuncture. To what extent, I wondered, did people actually follow the state's directives and obediently relocate? Presumably, many families moved to other villages, counties, and even provinces, disgruntled with the arbitrary nature of these state ordinances. If so, wouldn't it be difficult to claim that large numbers of identifiable families (a *kaku* or 'core' as the Japanese literature puts it) continued to be targets of discrimination over time? Hatanaka Toshiyuki has demonstrated in his research that considerable numbers of people in the Osaka region moved in and out of early modern outcaste communities in pursuit of wealth and livelihood.[74] The exhibits, moreover, did not really touch on the degree to which ancestral links between premodern and modern outcast/e (hisabetsumin) groups are empirically demonstrable. Presumably, few if any documents could actually demonstrate that the 'core' of each outcast/e community was essentially transferred to the new residential area when the Osaka authorities relocated them. The assumptions made by the organizers of the exhibit about historical continuity, therefore, appeared to necessitate much deeper examination.[75]

As Arimoto and I continued to trace the chronological history of Naniwa walking clockwise around the exhibit room, numerous other interesting details about the present-day community emerged. Naniwa's Eishō Elementary School, for example, built in 1872, was the second oldest primary school in the Osaka area, and the Osaka Human Rights Museum is currently located on the very site where this school was initially built.[76] Arimoto's discussion about the construction of Naniwa's two main railway stations—Ashiharabashi and Imamiya— was also intriguing. Prewar photographs reveal the way in which these stations were constructed so that no ordinary access was available from the buraku areas: all the station exits were located on the opposite sides of the railway tracks. This discussion, however, was followed immediately by a picture of dozens of women dressed in immaculate kimonos standing in front of impressive shopfronts waiting for soldiers who were returning from various battlefronts. The combination of all of these pictures and stories seemed to suggest that Naniwa was both very wealthy (a point that Arimoto confirmed) and yet a target of severe discrimination. This was difficult to comprehend and needed further explanation. Presumably, considerable wealth could also mean increased social mobility and, therefore, offering opportunities for people to escape social discrimination as well. This point, however, was not touched upon either in the exhibits, or in the explanations offered to me.

Arimoto concluded our tour with a discussion of the multiple facelifts that the Naniwa area had experienced in recent years, including the construction of an impressive 'human rights and *taiko* drum road' in 2002 (which the Osaka municipal and prefectural governments basically funded). Arimoto, reflecting on this new road running through the heart of the community, stated that in recent times, the Naniwa area itself had come to serve as a kind of 'field museum' (*chi'iki hakubutsukan*). When people come to visit the area, largely to see the exhibits at Liberty Osaka, they are reminded that the actual physical place where the museum is located is a 'former outcaste' or 'buraku area'. Visitors to the Naniwa Human Rights Culture Centre are reminded that this buraku area has a rich history, particularly in leather production and taiko drum-making, and that it has assumed its current impressive form through the hard work of its residents. Interestingly, however, when I told a staff member at Liberty Osaka about my discussion with Arimoto a little while later, he responded by informing me that Arimoto was 'not a burakumin' but rather a 'government official from outside the area'. The master narrative of buraku history then is clearly practised not only by burakumin who engage in identity politics but also by government officials who work with them in local communities (more on this in Chapter 5).

Towards a Discursive History of Difference

A tour through communities in places like Imado and Naniwa reveals that buraku history is indeed inextricably bound to the lives of the people who deal with the buraku problem in some capacity in their everyday lives. While historical continuities can and do exist between contemporary buraku communities and early modern outcaste settlements, it is clear that these linkages are not always as precise, stable, or all-encompassing as historians and activists often portray them to be. Linkages are, to a certain extent, imagined in the present for the purposes of personal and collective identification in order to better facilitate (or perhaps even manage) political activism. Imagined linkages, however, are portrayed as real by those who are dependent on this history for their identity. For these people, buraku history is purely an accurate and objective representation of the facts that laid the foundations for their current condition.

Yet, as Harry Harootunian has argued in another context, perspectives which insist that history is entirely 'knowable' and accessible through a universal 'commonsense' make the assumption that an ascertainable 'sequential code governs the transmutability of an event into a story-worth representation.'[77] Such an assumption, moreover, serves to efface a narrative's own status as discourse. In the case of burakumin, disparate records of acts of discrimination against premodern and modern groups of socially marginalized persons are clearly sequenced together in chronological order based on an assumption that history itself shapes the master narrative of buraku history. Such a representation obfuscates the fact that the master narrative is itself a discourse of hegemonic proportions, based on a selective mobilization of historical evidence, having achieved its status through the negation of other views.

'Burakumin', this volume contends, is therefore, usefully reinterpreted as a discourse that emerged in the twentieth century; a term applied retroactively to refer to marginalized subjects of all historical eras. Originating in the prewar term 'tokushu buraku' (special buraku), it came to categorize a number of diverse socially distinct populations into one common group, thereby achieving the status of a master narrative in the early postwar era.

In the post-Meiji period, domestic sociocultural difference was constantly reconfigured through changing 'commonsense' notions about the nature of human associations, the historical development of societies, the existence of homogeneity within populations, and the importance of progress. Borrowing the idiom of historical practices of social marginalization, 'burakumin' emerged through a complex process that saw virtually all sociocultural differences being framed as part of a special historical problem linked to the sociocultural backwardness of a distinctive kind of ancient people. This process occurred as a result of what Sakai Naoki has identified as the emergence of three dominant regimes of social ordering in modernity—race, class, and nation.[78]

National, racial, and capitalist modes of thought came to feature prominently in post-Meiji discursive formulations of social marginalization. National thinking helped propel ideas of belonging based upon notions of citizenship. Members of the *eta* and *hinin* communities came to be referred to as 'former outcastes' and 'new commoner-citizens' (*shinheimin*). The merger of 'outcaste' and 'commoner' space into a single unity—national space—basically meant, however, that 'former outcastes' were, from the beginning, presumed to be incapable of immediately achieving 'ordinary' status. Despite this fact, some 'new commoner-citizens' (and on occasion, entire communities) chose to work towards social and national integration, and a considerable number undoubtedly experienced a degree of emancipation from former practices of social discrimination. Wealthier members of former *eta* villages were not only permitted 'new commoner-citizen' status, but on occasion, were even offered leadership positions within the new state apparatus. For many others, though, the Emancipation Edict simply meant the continuation of socially oppressive practices under a new guise. Most subjects ascribed the labels 'former outcastes' and 'new commoner-citizens' (or who consciously adopted them) tended to have limited options in their struggle for emancipation.

Some chose to follow the advice of condescending elites and moved overseas; others moved to new frontiers like Hokkaidō as 'new commoner-citizens'; while still others migrated to cities, more often than not to new urban slums (which, in turn, also became targets of discriminatory political policies and social attitudes in most cases).[79] Regardless of the choices they made, however, many rapidly came to form part of the swelling ranks of Meiji Japan's emerging 'second class' citizenry.[80] Social difference from this period onwards was homogenized, stigmatized, and clearly linked to the issue of membership within the national polity.

Race was another important lens through which social difference was reconstituted in the post-Meiji period. The advent of the modern nation-state and the neat overlap that it was 'discovered' to have with a unique and supposedly homogenous body of ethnic Japanese served to propel ideas about the foreign racial origins of Japan's 'former outcaste' groups. Certainly, talk of the alleged 'foreignness' of *eta* and *hinin* had existed for some time. Western travellers to Japan during the Tokugawa period had written about a highly stratified society wherein the lowest strata were thought to have foreign origins. Early modern Japanese scholars and intellectuals also supported such ideas. The intellectual Kaiho Seiryō (1755–1817), for example, asserted that 'Eta are the descendants of barbarians who originally came from foreign lands; they are not the descendants of our Shrine of Amaterasu. Barbarians are the same as wild beasts.'[81] Hoashi Banri (1778–1852) called them 'the descendants of barbarians who lived of old in the northern provinces.'[82] Modern academics continued with this line of speculation but with a newfound respect for modern technologies of scientific classification. The pioneering Japanese anthropologist Tori'i Ryūzō (1870–1953), for example, posited that former outcastes 'do not conform to the shape of Mongoloids but closely resemble Malayan–Polynesians.'[83] Popular twentieth-century writings on the Japanese outcaste also mirrored these racial sentiments. The Yomiuri newspaper, for example, published an article in 1918 entitled 'Special Buraku People and Riots'.[84] The word 'tokushu' (special) in this document, however, was printed with the character *shu* 種 (rather than 殊), signifying a distinct category and suggesting a meaning closer to race. This variation of the word 'special' was also found in the early writings of the folk studies scholar Yanagita Kunio (1875–1962).

Capitalist modes of thought also played an increasingly important role in the reconstruction of 'outcasteness' in modern Japan. The facilities used to house vagrants during the Tokugawa period were partially built according to an economizing logic that tried to make these individuals productive and useful. At the same time, however, these institutions were primarily constructed in an attempt to stabilize a social status system perceived to be increasingly threatened by disruptive social forces. *Hinin* were permitted to operate in official begging guilds during this period, and it was widely recognized that mendicancy was a legitimate activity with strong religious connections that needed to be strictly regulated and policed rather than outlawed. In the post-Meiji period, however, new facilities designed for housing the poor were established along with other Meiji state legislation that outlawed beggary. Poor citizens began to be uniformly treated as unproductive bodies who needed to acquire trades and skills in order to be considered useful to society.

The late Meiji term 'buraku' needs to be understood within this larger discursive history of difference wherein social difference ('abnormality') came to be identified and classified in different ways during the modern era. Notions of difference and abnormality undoubtedly exist in all historical periods but changes clearly occur in the ways in which it has been conceptualized and articulated. One important way whereby these changes can be witnessed is by examining the different spatial and temporal emphases found within terms used to categorize social difference. Historical words like 'kawaramono'as well as modern terms like 'buraku', for example, reflect a state of 'outcasteness', which lays primary emphasis on a spatial dimension: outcastes are people who reside in a particular 'outcaste place' requiring the construction of a physical cordon sanitaire. Abnormality, however, can also be expressed through a lens that emphasizes temporality. Old words like *eta*, *hinin*, and senmin all reflect this other dimension of 'outcasteness'. They refer to people who are in a particular state of 'outcasteness' because of a supposed inferior quality of their humanity and who therefore need to be placed in a kind of social lock-down or 'solitary confinement' (reclusion solitaire).

Interesting observations about these kinds of discourses of difference can also be made when they are listed in chronological order. Firstly, the total number of divergent labels is striking. What appears to constitute social difference is undoubtedly highly subjective and, therefore, in constant need of revision and reiteration. Referents continually change over time, a process Kurokawa Midori has called *tsukurikaerareru shirushi* or 'constantly reconstructed signification'.[85] By this, Kurokawa means that the words used to refer to burakumin have perpetually changed throughout history and these continual shifts are evidences of the changing societal perceptions of burakumin in mainstream Japanese society. The idea that these terms *singularly* refer to a specific historical minority group known as burakumin is, however, contestable. The view adopted here is that they are better regarded as generic labels, which refer to a general state of 'outcasteness' owned by or applied to groups of people in respective historical periods that are assumed to be historically constant. Terms like *eta*, *hinin*, shinheimin, tokushu buraku, and burakumin are actually period-specific designations and, therefore, conceptually quite different. While commonly considered to refer only to distinct people who have experienced a common history of discrimination, they are, in fact, discourses used to signify a constantly changing notion of 'outcasteness' defined in relation to an imagined dominant majority community ('nation', 'people', 'society', etc.).

A second important observation that can be made when listing these labels chronologically is that they reveal colossal changes in the way 'outcasteness' has been viewed on the Japanese archipelago over time. Medieval 'outcasteness' was labelled in terms that both reflected spatial and temporal elements. Outcastes could be simultaneously referred to in terms that framed them geographically (through phrases like 'kawaramono') as well as in terms of their human condition ('kiyome'). During the early modern period, too, this state of 'outcasteness' was referred to both through the lens of spatial geography ('kawata')[86] as well as human condition (*eta*, *hinin*, etc.). With the onset of modernity, referents that have dominated public and official discourse on 'outcastes' in modernity have also alternated emphasis, but it is clear that there has been little official state or public acknowledgement of any temporally orientated expressions during the twentieth century. 'Tokushu buraku', 'burakumin', and 'dōwa chiku jūmin'[87] have all been the dominant labels used to refer to this state of social difference in the twentieth century and they are unmistakably spatial referents signifying the dominance of the nation as a regime of social ordering in modernity.

The fact that this situation arose during the twentieth century is no coincidence. Neither is it surprising that people who have commonly identified with (or have been identified with) these labels either chose alternate appellations or inserted certain prefixes or suffixes which modified the ways they were being signified in order to incorporate a temporal dimension. 'Tokushu buraku', for example, was a term often externally applied to the socially marginalized people in the early twentieth century. The term preferred in the Suiheisha Declaration, however, was the old appellation of 'eta'. Even the term 'buraku' usually became 'mikaihō buraku', 'hiappaku buraku', or 'hisabetsu buraku' in the hands of people who identified with the label.[88] These modifications are highly significant because they served to alter a spatial reference to a temporal one by reinstating the transitory dimensions of the outcaste condition. The fact that 'outcasteness' has almost consistently been referred to in the modern era in spatial terms, particularly by the state, is important because it reveals an official policy of promoting a single path to liberation—through eventual emersion into a national body. Emphasizing the temporal realm in 'outcasteness', however, has been an important empowering strategy for the socially marginalized: it contains a latent potential for reinfusing identity politics with radical action. Highlighting the temporal realm of 'outcasteness' also serves to humanize victims and personalize discrimination, thereby better facilitating a politics of action and redressal.

3
The Problem of Buraku Discrimination

Introduction

'Buraku discrimination' (buraku sabetsu) is usually portrayed as a disturbing social phenomenon perpetuated throughout history by ancient, marginalizing ideas of 'pollution' (kegare). Over a long period of time, this kind of harmful ideology, combined with other social, economic, and political factors—intentional state-sponsored discrimination in the early modern period was particularly important—to produce enduring structural impediments that prevented 'burakumin' from being able to conduct normal lives. Material inequalities in the modern era, like poor housing conditions in buraku residential areas and low matriculation rates amongst buraku youth, are, therefore, seen as both a result and evidence of buraku discrimination. The maintenance of errant ways of understanding and appraising burakumin in present-day Japan, moreover, is interpreted as a residual obstacle to the complete resolution of the problem.[1]

This common formulation of buraku discrimination, however, also entails empirical and conceptual difficulties. An empirical analysis of the way in which the putative early modern ancestors of burakumin—*eta* and perhaps to some extent *hinin*—emerged between the seventeenth and nineteenth centuries reveals a complex process of marginalization that is in conflict with this kind of understanding of buraku discrimination. Closely related to this point, moreover, lies the problem of the highly ambivalent status of some members of the early modern Japanese outcaste groups. Some leaders of the *eta* and *hinin* communities actually had considerable wealth and social standing: a point that those who advocate the universally low social status ('outcast/e status') of early modern *eta* and *hinin* groups generally fail to accommodate.

Problems also beset this explanatory model of buraku discrimination on a conceptual level. Firstly, the idea that an outcast/e (senmin/hisabetsumin)—either in burakumin, *eta*, or *hinin* form—is an all-encompassing subjectivity can be challenged. *Eta* and *hinin* in early modern Japan were not merely politically defined socio-legal statuses, but more importantly, invidious descriptors that categorized certain people who were considered abnormal by early modern standards as 'impure' and 'subhuman'. The term outcast/e (senmin/hisabetsumin) is, therefore, an inaccurate description of people made to assume these labels because it only illuminates one aspect (albeit an important one) of their lives. Secondly, the idea that 'discrimination' is action based on false ideology or its structural effects tends to misrepresent the phenomenon as something other than a fundamental discursive process of selection and ordering. Acts of differentiation, alienation, and marginalization are arguably foundational human activities evidenced in the very structures of language and modes of communication. Buraku discrimination, therefore, does not simply reside in the collective minds of human subjects or in social structures but is an expression of power found within distinct human behaviours like speech and actions, and accessed (as well as built) through narratives. Narratives of discrimination, moreover, are stories that arbitrarily sequence discriminatory acts in line with a particular politics. The whole idea of discrimination, as well as the strategies designed for liberation from it, therefore, have to be understood with an eye on the ideational concerns of the narrator.

This chapter begins with a discussion of the master narrative of buraku discrimination before going on to demonstrate some of the empirical and conceptual problems inherent in it. It then examines the ideational aspects of early modern outcaste history by revealing how a range of historical actors in early modern Japan, including members of *eta* groups, themselves actually participated in the discursive construction of 'outcasteness' that both affirmed and problematized the *eta* and *hinin* difference. The chapter concludes by outlining an alternate way of viewing a history of discrimination in early modern Japan, reframing it within the larger history of discursively constructed difference introduced in the previous chapter.

Buraku Discrimination

Buraku discrimination is often portrayed as a recalcitrant prejudice that permanently ejects people from Japanese society because of a mistaken belief in the inferior quality or contaminated nature of their humanity (thereby recreating them as outcast/es). Outcast/e discrimination leading to the formation of ostracized groups is usually considered to be different from other forms of discrimination in that it involves the assembly and rigid enforcement of a kind of *cordon sanitaire* (literally 'sanitary cordon' or 'quarantine line'), which attempts to permanently protect people from 'contamination' or the 'polluting influence' of others.[2] The specific labels applied to burakumin throughout Japanese history are, therefore, usually understood as being reflective of the reasons as to why they were discriminated against during certain periods. *Eta* (and to some extent *hinin*), considered to be the actual physical antecedents of modern-day buraku communities, had appellations that declared them as 'polluted' (*kegareta*) or 'inhuman' (*hito ni arazu*) because they handled objects like animal carcasses and dead bodies that were reckoned to be unclean. Buddhist notions of the 'polluting force of death' (*sesshō*) as well as Shintō preoccupations with 'purity' (*shinsei*) are usually considered paramount in the creation and perpetuation of the buraku problem in the Japanese context.[3] Burakumin, in this formulation, emerged as a direct result of ancient but mistaken ideologies that fostered 'fear and loathing' of them while de-emphasizing their common humanity.[4]

The 'sanitary cordon' has been described in numerous ways in relation to burakumin but literature often contains references to a 'discriminatory mechanism' or 'function' (*sabetsu no mekanizumu/kinō*) that facilitates the segregation of outcast/e communities from 'mainstream society' (*ippan shakai*).[5] The 'discriminatory mechanism' that produces and supports sanitary cordons differs according to time and place but there are generally believed to be strong historical continuities in the kinds of discrimination faced by buraku communities in Japan. Minegishi Kentarō, for example, outlines the 'customary discrimination' (*shūzokuteki sabetsu*) of *eta* and *hinin* communities during the early modern period underpinned by numerous types of exclusionary practices like the 'avoidance of social interaction' (*bekka*), 'refusal of social contact' (*bekki*), 'avoidance of intermarriage' (*bekkon*), and 'maintenance of separate dwellings' (*bekkyosho*).[6] These kinds of discriminatory practices were apparently prevalent enough in early modern times to compel some Meiji state officials to specifically instruct 'former outcaste' communities to 'purify themselves' (*mi wo kiyome*) in order to better facilitate their acceptance as 'commoners' in mainstream Japanese society after the promulgation of the Emancipation Edict.[7] Scholars who closely monitor buraku discrimination in contemporary Japan, moreover, emphasize the continued prevalence of social taboos related to marriage, employment, and residence.[8] Recent incidents such as the release of detailed lists revealing the whereabouts of buraku communities onto the internet, the public outing of famous TV personalities, politicians, and movie stars from buraku districts, and the tendency towards spreading vicious rumours about the buraku areas during periods of social unrest provide further evidence that old segregationist habits persist in contemporary Japanese society, albeit to differing degrees.[9]

The erection of a sanitary cordon is generally understood as an attempt at social sterilization: a widespread method for combating the perceived effects of ancient ideologies related to pollution. For example, Sukhadeo Thorat, a leading academic who happens to be a dalit, describes the situation for dalits in a rural Indian village:

> From the age when you learn to walk and talk, the limits are delineated: residential, physical, and social isolation combined with

> day-to-day humiliation. All rural Dalit children face one form of humiliation or the other. At school, there is hardly any interpersonal relationship between the Dalit student and the teacher, and the feeling of isolation is heightened.[10]

Writing in an earlier period, B.R. Ambedkar (1891–1956), a dalit and one of the founders of modern India, said:

> It is not a case of social separation, a mere stoppage of social intercourse for a temporary period. It is a case of territorial segregation and of a cordon sanitaire putting the impure people inside a barbed wire into a sort of a cage. Every Hindu village has a ghetto. The Hindus live in the village and the Untouchables in the ghetto.[11]

The buraku activist/writer Kawamoto Yoshikazu, while growing up in a village on the outskirts of the city of Tsuyama, Okayama, recalls an analogous state of exclusion:

> About the time I entered elementary school, I began to sense that the village in which I grew up was being looked at differently by the people around me. It is difficult to say precisely what made me feel this way, but as I lived from day to day, I noticed little things, like stares that I had never experienced before in my own village. What kind of stares? Of course it's extremely difficult to put my finger on what these stares were, even if I felt them strange myself. Virtually impossible...[12]

The sentiments expressed here, referring to a complex physical and psychological isolation, reinforce the idea that there is a real human state that might be termed as 'outcasteness'. The isolation experienced by Kawamoto is clearly reminiscent of that mentioned above by Ambedkar in relation to the Indian 'untouchables', wherein 'impure people' are put 'inside barbed wire' or 'into a sort of a cage'. Outcast/e subjects are forbidden to inhabit certain spaces, in spite of the fact that they live in the same place, and over time, there emerges a deep sense of ambiguity over whether 'their kind' of people ever truly belonged. There is often no personal memory of a safe and stable connection to the collectivity; perhaps only suggestions of the existence of a better time in the past glimpsed through fragments of historical records or recent events that hint at the possibility of a better world to come. Outcast/es, however, often have no clear memory of a historical moment of separation. As Ambedkar notes: 'The origin of Untouchability lies buried in a dead past which nobody knows. To make it alive is like an attempt to reclaim to history a city which has been dead since ages past and present it as it was in its original condition.'[13]

Sanitary cordons, therefore, involve much more than just a form of physical and conceptual quarantine. The outcast/e, while being subjected to sanitizing practices in the present, is also the subject of them through time. A consequence of the creation of a cordon sanitaire is the establishment of a forced state of reclusion solitaire (a kind of 'solitary confinement'). Outcasteness is not only a spatial state of exclusion, but also a collection of sequential moments that drive excluded individuals and communities further from their original state of belonging and the likelihood of re-occupying 'acceptable spaces' of 'normality'. History serves as a constant reminder of a long past exclusion. Through its mere existence, time cruelly hints at the impossibility of future belonging. Describing the practice of cordon sanitaire, therefore, necessitates not only explaining what it looks or feels like in the present, but also how it came to be what it is, the impact of the time wasted while enduring it, and the expression of the hope of a happy ending. In short, an outcast/e does not just occupy a contemporary oppressive physical state, but is also the product of a long, painful historical process of oppression and isolation.

This, however, does not prevent the outcast/e from holding on to the belief that outcasteness itself has a point of historical origin and, therefore, perhaps a future time of conclusion. Ambedkar declares: 'There was a time when the ancestors of the present day Untouchables were not Untouchables *vis-a-vis* the villagers but were merely Broken Men, no more and no less, and the only difference between them and the villagers was that they belonged to different tribes.'[14] There, however, remains a fundamental ambiguity. Has the outcast/e ever really been personally acquainted with a home, an environment, or a history apart from the one of total displacement that they have experienced? For many, there is no home, no other state, other than exclusion. There is indeed little hope of return, except through the struggles of visionaries, who fight for liberation: 'For ours is a battle not for wealth or power. It is a battle for freedom. It is the battle for the reclamation of human personality.'[15]

The temporal aspects of outcasteness are also painstakingly revealed in Kawamoto's book, *Buraku mondai towa nanika* (What is the Buraku Problem?), a collection of lectures delivered to students at Tsukuba University. The vast majority of this work is taken up in introducing and discussing the history of burakumin. In Kawamoto's view, comprehending the buraku problem is closely equated with ascertaining its past. A chronicle of pain, it is implicitly suggested, can only be understood by mapping out the forces that brought it into existence. People must comprehend the role of the past in the production of present anguish. For Kawamoto, ascertaining the reasons for the emergence of his plight is directly linked to being able to imagine a future without this form of suffering. He concludes his treatise by expressing a hope that modernity and its embedded equalizing agent, 'democracy', would facilitate the peaceful return of burakumin back to a common humanity.[16]

It is precisely because of the perceived weightiness of this temporal dimension of buraku discrimination that many scholars and buraku activists during the postwar period in Japan openly rejected the idea that the roots of buraku discrimination should be reduced simply to a matter of 'perception' (*kannen*). During the latter years of the Allied Occupation of Japan, the Marxist historian Inoue Kiyoshi criticized this kind of perspective and devised a class-based explanation which, while still explaining the way in which perception links to an outcast/e problem in Japan, reframed buraku difference as a historical problem of 'material' (*jittai*) disparity that needed to be overcome. Inoue isolated the root causes of buraku discrimination in what he termed as 'social status discrimination' (*mibun sabetsu*), which allegedly originated with the first sign of class difference in Japan during the ancient period. He further argued that it was only after the appearance of social status distinctions that 'outcast/e occupations' (*sengyō*) materialized, and that this discrimination had not disappeared because status distinctions prevented burakumin from joining the proletariat on an equal footing to engage in class struggle.[17] Inoue also suggested that historical restrictions on residency and occupation had combined with the problem of status to create the buraku problem and, therefore, their removal must be the first concrete step towards liberation.[18]

Based on Inoue's influential series of essays, historical accounts of Tokugawa outcaste groups began to proliferate during the early postwar period, describing the emergence of burakumin in the manner that has been outlined in detail in the previous chapter. Typically of medieval origin, late medieval outcasts were reorganized (*saihensei*) by warrior elites into fixed communities from around the middle of the sixteenth century onwards. Over the course of the Tokugawa period, the shogunate proceeded to issue discriminatory legislation designed to seal these communities into their respective outcaste fates. The result of these state-sponsored discriminatory acts was that during the eighteenth century, *eta* and *hinin* became outcastes within a strict system of social and legal status (mibunsei) akin to a caste system. This structure, often referred to as the shi–nō–kō–shō–*eta*–*hinin* (or 'warrior–peasant–artisan–merchant–tanner–beggar') system, saw the shogunate utilize a 'divide and conquer' (*bunretsu/bundan shihai*) strategy towards commoners. Peasants, for example, were encouraged to discriminate against people below them in status so that they would not need to vent their frustrations over the poor treatment meted out to them and heavy taxation levied on them on the warrior class above them. *Eta* and *hinin* languished at the bottom of this social system as the obvious target for harassment by the other, more numerous classes.

There was abundant historical evidence to support the claims of these scholars.[19] At the Tokugawa shogunate level, a succession of laws from the early eighteenth century onwards attempted to group undesirable elements together under the supervisory umbrella of the established groups of low social status: *eta* and *hinin*. However, the laws did not just find people guilty of certain crimes and seal them inside outcaste communities. They also increased levels of distinction among the outcaste groups themselves. Laws that amplified the public profile of the *eta* and *hinin* as social policing agents were also issued during the eighteenth century. Outcastes were given special powers not afforded to other sectors of the population. This power, however, was not conducive to social enhancement in the eyes of other members of society.

Postwar buraku activists like Asada Zennosuke, while readily acknowledging with Inoue that there were important historical root causes of buraku discrimination, preferred instead to focus intently on the early postwar conditions of buraku communities. Asada interpreted official inertia and indifference about the historical plight of the burakumin as well as the constant state refusal to actively strive for the removal of structural inequalities in postwar Japanese society as the true obstacle to overcoming buraku discrimination.[20] A plethora of postwar activists after Asada also argued along these lines.[21] More recent writers like Miyazaki Manabu continue to build on this model, arguing that buraku discrimination still persists in Japanese society and has merely changed its mode of existence.[22] Contemporary commentators argue that the burakumin continue to be alienated as a result of harsh discriminatory social attitudes based in segregationist ideologies as well as the resultant socio-economic structural impediments. Ideational and structural discrimination was strengthened through the development of a formal status system during the early modern era and the accumulative effects of social alienation in modernity only continue to make the lives of burakumin vulnerable and unstable. Burakumin, they insist, still remain one of the most disaffected groups in contemporary Japan.[23]

Formation of Early Modern 'Outcastes'

Empirical analysis of the manner in which the supposed early modern ancestors of burakumin—*eta* (and to some extent *hinin*)—emerged between the seventeenth and nineteenth centuries, however, reveals a complex process of marginalization that is somewhat at odds with this mainstream understanding of buraku discrimination. A close examination of the history of early modern outcaste groups, for example, suggests not a predominantly distinct people experiencing a unique form of discrimination, but rather a constellation of marginalized people undergoing a complex and ongoing process of reconstruction as 'outcastes' as a result of dynamic processes of social ordering often prompted by the Tokugawa authorities.

Empirical records suggest that there is little reason to suspect that membership of *eta* and *hinin* groups was ever completely stable or straightforward. Even at the level of Danzaemon (discussed in detail in Chapter 2), the name quickly became an institution with a representative head that was filled by people from different regions and backgrounds whose 'outcaste pedigrees' were complex and not always obvious. Danzaemon XI, for example, was born as the child of Danzaemon of Kawano in the province of Aki (Hiroshima); Danzaemon XII was the younger brother of Ōtomo Hikodayū from Shinano (Nagano); and Danzaemon XIII was the eldest son of Terada Rizaemon from the province of Settsu (Osaka / Hyōgo).[24]

There are numerous other examples too, which demonstrate that 'movement' was regularly the norm for members of the *eta* and *hinin* communities. Shogunate legislation, for example, expressly permitted *hinin* to become commoners if relatives of the person in question were persistent in their requests.[25] Extant records also suggest innumerable incidents of members of both *eta* and *hinin* communities absconding.[26] Moreover, shogunate legislation was constantly reproduced which censured *eta* and *hinin* for being indistinguishable from the rest of the population.[27] This last point is particularly critical. There was no 'natural' way of distinguishing between 'commoner' (*heinin*) and 'outcaste' (*eta-hinin-nado*) subjects in everyday life.

A close examination of the extant documentation in eastern Japan also reveals that the words *eta* and *hinin* referred to different groups on a regional level in Tokugawa Japan and probably did not achieve their currently assumed meanings of distinct outcaste groups until around the eighteenth century. Japanese scholars widely acknowledge that tanner communities in eastern Japan during the sixteenth and early seventeenth centuries, for example, were not even referred to as *eta*: they were called *kawazukuri* (literally 'leather makers').[28] It appears as if the label kawazukuri, moreover, was replaced by the terms kawata and *kawaya* over the course of the seventeenth century in eastern Japan (terms which simply imply people who work with leather).[29] Minegishi Kentarō also maintains that it was only from around the mid-seventeenth century onwards that Edo-based beggars (kojiki) came to be referred to as *hinin,* and kawata and kawaya as *eta.*[30]

In addition to the multiple changes in the labels used to refer to tanning groups in eastern Japan from the mid-sixteenth to the mid-seventeenth century, it is not altogether clear whether kawazukuri, kawaya, or kawata were actually universal objects of social discrimination in that region. Minegishi Kentarō argues that there is no reason to suspect that they were not.[31] One support for his idea is that separate cadastral registers (*kenchichō*) for kawata were sometimes produced at this time, suggesting the existence of a stigma. But Minegishi also demonstrates through his research (of these exact same registers) that all kawata in independent communities at this time appear to have engaged in agriculture and were not particularly poor (one wealthier kawata, for example, actually had five *genin* or menservants).[32] Moreover, the close relationship between leather-makers and elite warriors during the late sixteenth and early seventeenth centuries, evidenced in the direct lord–vassal style relationship between leaders of tanning cartels and influential warriors, may even lend support to the opposing argument.

From around the mid-seventeenth century onwards, a figure known as Danzaemon does appear to have begun to accumulate powers of governance over a number of groups of people including *eta* and *hinin* in relation to matters of a legal, jurisdictional, and disciplinary nature.[33] Edo authorities appear to have instigated this process by forcing certain punitive powers related to the torture and execution of non-warrior subjects on Danzaemon during the mid-seventeenth century. A man by the name of Danzaemon was apparently ordered, for example, to carry out the torture of 45 Christians in 1642.[34] Another revealing episode dated 1657 is found in a merchant's diary and involved Danzaemon and several other 'kawata'. Edo town elders ordered Danzaemon and some 'kawata' to build an embankment to be used in the beheading of several people found guilty of pickpocketing. Danzaemon and company declared that they had never before participated in such an activity and did not intend to start then. The town elders then attempted to sequester the help of other townsmen who also refused (and were subsequently beaten up). Eventually, Danzaemon and the other 'kawata' were denied access to the town market to sell their goods and it was only then that they reluctantly agreed to perform the task.[35]

A similar process can be seen to have occurred with *hinin* in eastern Japan. Francois Caron[36] noted in a diary entry for April 1636 that the authorities in Edo were rounding up local lepers, the blind, the lame, and the disabled, and placing those suspected of being Christians in detention camps.[37] Even though the grouping of the poor together seemed to have been a policy that was actively pursued by the Tokugawa shogunate from around this time, there is no evidence to suggest that the word *hinin* was used as a fixed term during the early part of the seventeenth century to refer to Edo's emerging poverty-stricken underclasses. Minegishi does point to one record from the mid-seventeenth century that includes the expression 'general of the poor' (*komokaburi taishō*)—but he refuses to link this to later *hinin* leaders like Kuruma Zenshichi.[38] *Hinin* communities with any degree of organization also probably only emerged in Edo during the second half of the seventeenth century.

By 1680, this situation had visibly begun to change. The famous 'dog shogun' Tokugawa Tsunayoshi issued an edict in that year to the *hinin gashira* (literally 'head of the *hinin*').[39] In it, he declared that there were many 'beggar *hinin*' in the city and that, forthwith, no such person would be permitted in the city. All *hinin* huts, moreover, had to be destroyed within three days.[40] The implication of this policy was that *hinin* leaders had to round up vagrants and the destitute, and force them to either live in *hinin* enclosures or to leave the metropolis. The *hinin* during this period, moreover, were not merely mobilized to police itinerants and vagrants. Records indicate that they were also marshalled to build and maintain institutions intending to care for (and maintain surveillance over) prisoners and the sick from around the same period onwards.[41] The *hinin* received stipends from the shogunate for these duties and they were also awarded *kanjin* or 'begging rights' that permitted them to walk around certain areas on auspicious occasions and bless residents in exchange for alms.[42]

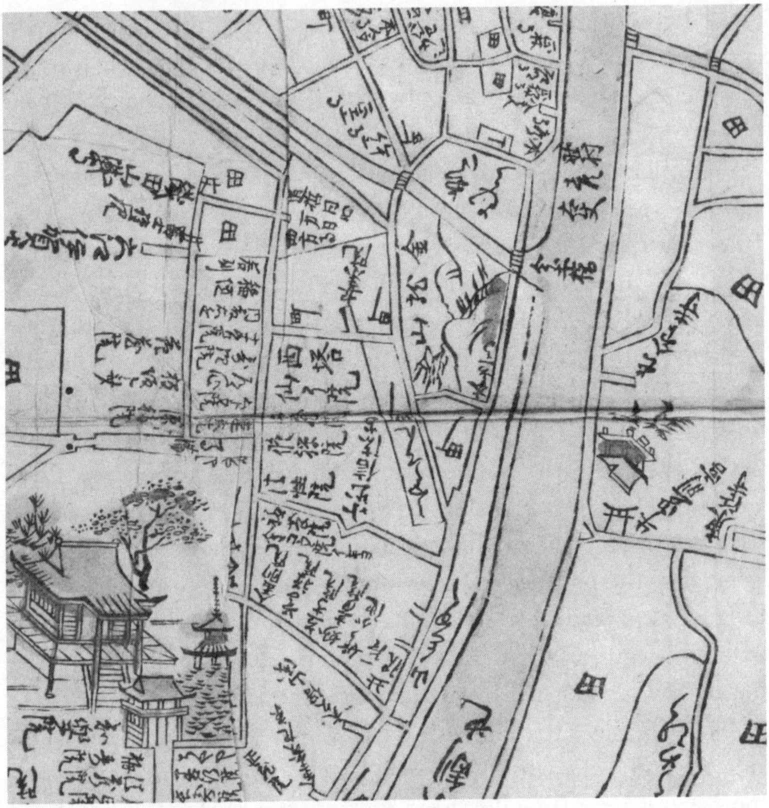

Map of Danzaemon and local area (1684)
(Source: *Tōhoku daigaku fuzoku toshokan kano bunko gazō* http://www2.library.tohoku.ac.jp/kano/ezu/edo/edo.html)

Maps of the area in Asakusa where the *eta* leader Danzaemon lived (written as 囲内, thought to be pronounced *kakoi-no-uchi*, and literally meaning 'inside the fence') confirm that there was a conceptual tightening of what constituted an impure subject between the seventeenth and nineteenth centuries. Examined over a 180-year period, these maps reveal changes in conceptions that took place over time in relation to this community. In an early map drawn by Yoshinaga Hayashi in 1680, for example, the area where Danzaemon lived was simply labelled as 'Imado Village'. In Hyoshiya Ichirobē's map, published four years later, the term '*eta* village' (*eta mura*) with the characters for *eta* written in *kana* (ゑ多→えた) was also used. In Ishikawa Ryūsen's map of 1710, however, the term '*eta* village' is employed with the Chinese characters meaning 'much pollution' (穢多). And while the *katakana* variants of エタ that reflects sound rather than ideographical meaning is still used in his map of 1748, the term '*eta* village' with the characters for 'much pollution' is used almost universally in maps of Edo by the early nineteenth century.[43]

Further evidence of a narrowing down of the meaning of the words *eta* and *hinin* can be found in the textual usages of these words. Extant literature reveals that they did not necessarily have a uniform meaning throughout the main islands of the archipelago during the late seventeenth and even early eighteenth centuries. During this period, they were just as likely to be adjectives or parts of a compound noun as to be words that referred to a specific type of 'outcaste'. Many interesting combinations of words can be found during the first half of the eighteenth century. Words like '*hinin*-peasant' (*hinin byakushō*), in particular, appear to be quite unusual when one attempts to imagine a fixed category of *eta* or *hinin*.[44] These kinds of ambiguities, however, tend to wane by mid-eighteenth century. Moreover, social standing became fixed in various ways—most commonly through legal discourse. *Eta* and *hinin* were ordered to undertake certain occupations, and were forced to live in certain areas, and these 'statuses' were subjected to a patriarchal form of hereditary succession.

Lives of Early Modern Outcastes

Extant documentation from the Tokugawa period also reveals the highly ambivalent status of individual members of early modern outcaste groups. Many leaders within these communities had considerable wealth and social position, suggesting that the idea of members of early modern *eta* and *hinin* groups being of universally low social status (i.e., 'outcast/es') may be somewhat misleading.

Regional *eta* leaders like the Suzuki family in Lower Wana Village, Musashi Province, produced elaborately detailed, colour maps in the early nineteenth century. These maps outlined a territory called 'the workplace' (*shokuba*) over which the local *eta* leader governed (the Suzuki household head actually refers to himself on one map as a *sōryō* or 'governor').[45] Constructing such elaborate maps was naturally an action that required not only considerable wealth and education, but also a positive self-awareness which runs contradictory to stereotypical ideas of an outcaste (i.e., poor, wretched, oppressed, excluded from society, constantly subject to discrimination, etc.). Maps such as the one given below suggest that *eta* leaders could have wealth, high levels of education, considerable social standing, self-confidence, and even 'pride'. *Eta* could be, in short, substantially different from the image of the outcast/e (senmin/hisabetsumin) found in the master narrative of buraku discrimination.

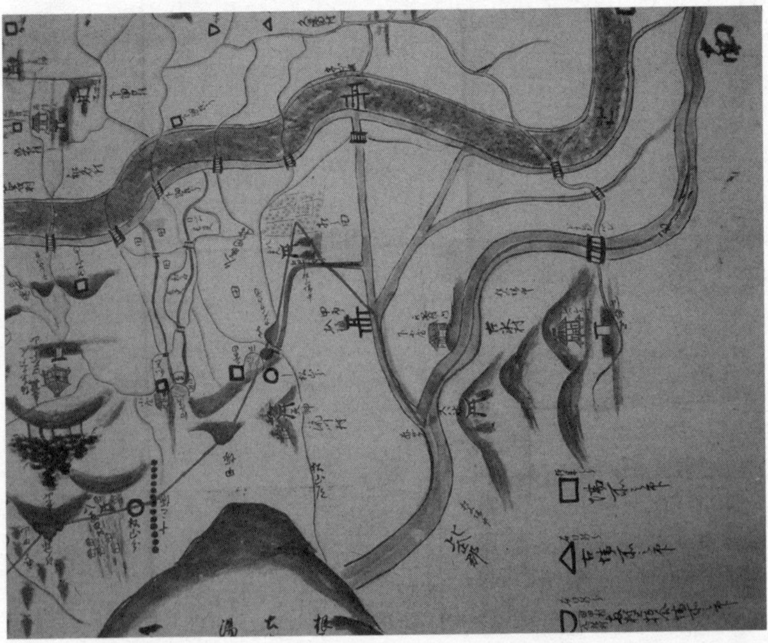

Portion of the 1823 Lower Wana Village workplace map
(Source: Saitama Prefectural Archives, *SKM*, #2068).

Other sources also hint at the inadequacy of the label outcast/e (senmin/hisabetsumin) used to describe people historically labelled as *eta*. Nakao Kenji has noted that *eta* in Tokugawa literature are, without exception, portrayed as 'wealthy'. *Hinin*, too, are characterized in some Tokugawa accounts as 'refined and elegant'.[46] Mase Kumiko, too, has stated that the status privileges awarded to Danzaemon were 'roughly equivalent to that of a small daimyo'.[47] In the case of Lower Wana Village, too, numerous examples of the development of a wealthy stratum of outcastes can be alluded to. One document, for instance, tells of a late eighteenth-century stage production (*hana shibai*) hosted by a local *eta* village leader in Musashi Province wherein guests were invited from all over the province and beyond (including important officials from Danzaemon's office). The performance appears to have been an elaborate scheme devised by one Danzaemon official and a local *eta* village head to line their pockets (supposedly for the purpose of erecting a shrine in the official's backyard). Nevertheless, this affair was scrupulously investigated, and the Suzuki family head temporarily imprisoned for his part in relaying rumours of the scheme to another Danzaemon official (with clearly less political clout).[48] This affair demonstrates, however, that staging such an elaborate event within the eastern Japanese outcaste community was entirely conceivable.

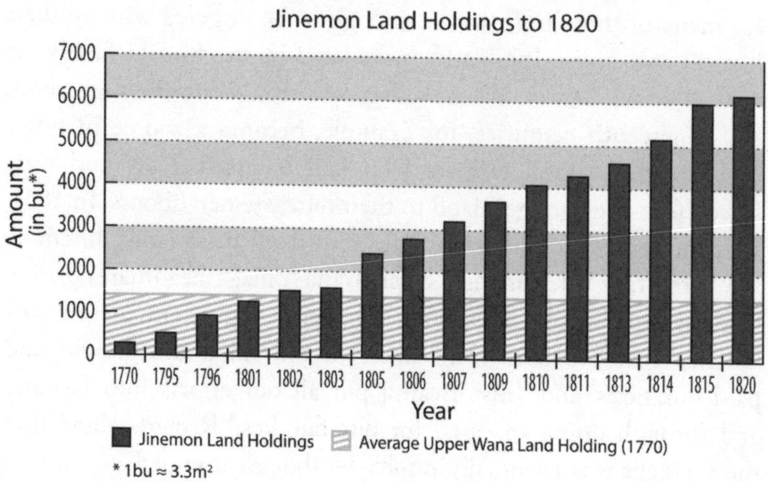

Source: SDKK, ed., *Suzuki-ke monjo: Saitama-ken buraku mondai kankei shiryōshū*, vol. 1 (Urawa: Saitama-ken Dōwa Kyōiku Kenkyū Kyōgikai, 1977, 178 [278], 187 [2806], 188 [2255], 189 [2256], 190 [2399])

Another striking example of the growing wealth of the leadership strata in the late Tokugawa *eta* village can be witnessed in the graph given above. Based on composite records, it gives a basic outline of the change in the amount of Suzuki family landholdings over a period of 150 years, set against the figure of average landholdings in Upper Wana Village (a peasant village) in 1770. From these figures, a striking change in the amount of total landholdings of the Suzuki family can be detected, demonstrating a pattern of emerging wealth amongst the leadership stratum in the village, particularly during the period 1770–1820 (a time, incidentally, when the Japanese status system, at least in terms of state legislation, was supposedly at its severest).[49] Once again, it seems reasonable to conclude that *eta* cannot all be portrayed merely as a group of downtrodden outcast/es (senmin/hisabetsumin).

Certainly representing all (or even the majority of) members of early modern *eta* communities as wealthy would be misleading, however. Many members of early modern *eta* communities were clearly impoverished. Individual records demonstrate that *eta* and *hinin* were, in fact, targets of severe acts of discrimination. When taken as a whole, moreover, extant archives paint a grim picture for many of those unfortunate enough to be targeted with epithets like *eta* and *hinin*. The land accumulated by the Suzuki family (as well as other Lower Wana Villagers) throughout the eighteenth and nineteenth centuries, for example, became a source of bitter resentment for local farmers who had incurred debts and were forced to mortgage their land to their outcaste neighbours. In 1861, farmers demanded the immediate return of 'their land'. Jin'emon, the hereditary title for the Lower Wana Village headman position held by the Suzuki household, rigorously argued in his village's defence that 'we have from times of old tilled the ground and paid our taxes' and '[historically] put all our efforts into farming and through doing so cared for our families.' Records show that the incident was eventually resolved—though it ended in a mixed (and extremely unfair) result for the Lower Wana community—with about half of the land being returned to the peasant community.[50]

The actions of neighbouring Upper Wana Village may, of course, have been motivated by jealousy or poverty rather than a disdain for *eta*. The idea that *eta* were not (and, therefore, should not be) farmers, however, clearly underpinned the dispute and heavily influenced the final outcome. The history of the residents of Lower Wana Village, therefore, was also undeniably a story of marginalized people struggling against discrimination.

Nonetheless, extant historical evidence is sufficient to demonstrate the inadequacy of the label outcast/e (senmin/hisabetsumin) to sufficiently explain the nature of *eta* (and *hinin*) in the eighteenth and nineteenth centuries. By the mid-nineteenth century, residents of Lower Wana Village had a strong identity as a farming collective and this identity was based in real agricultural practices. Some village leaders were even quite wealthy and well educated, enjoying late Tokugawa culture to an extent that was unfathomable even for the average peasant household. Poems, silkworm cultivation manuals, sophisticated onomatological explanations, and Sinological literature have also been found amongst the Suzuki family's documents, indicating a wealth and level of education that presumably surpassed many of the peasant communities nearby. Records of family wealth and assets were composed and sealed with instructions to descendants to carefully preserve them. Free time was spent, moreover, not only in work, but also in cultivating the mind and engaging in numerous social activities such as festivals within the wider community.

When Is an Outcaste an Outcast/e?

The application of the label outcast/e (senmin/hisabetsumin) to early modern *eta*, *hinin*, and contemporary burakumin poses not only empirical problems but also conceptual ones. The master narrative of buraku discrimination is built upon the assumption that premodern outcast/e villages and modern buraku communities are inextricably linked because specific families and geographical areas were subjected to the same discriminatory practices over time. As Hatanaka Toshiyuki notes, however, '"burakumin" do not exist objectively beyond historical periods' but are rather 'products of the social and political structure of each particular historical period.'[51] Put in another way, it is conceptually problematic to maintain that: the existence of burakumin predates, by many centuries, the actual emergence of the term itself; the methods and reasons for 'buraku discrimination' largely remain unchanged from one historical period to the next; and a fixed category of burakumin exists *a priori* to certain practices of discrimination.

In August 1999, I met Suzuki Mikio and his family, direct descendants of the village headmen introduced above from Lower Wana Village. I made the journey to Wana in Yoshimi township in order to discover more about the family who had made their ancestral history a matter of public record (Mikio's father, Shigeyuki, had donated most of his old family records to the Saitama Prefectural Archives in the early 1970s). My meeting with Suzuki and his family left quite an impression on me, but perhaps not for the reasons one might expect. The keen interest that Suzuki displayed in my 'foreign background', and the stories he related of his own journeys overseas probably signified the first 'irregularity' that occurred during our meeting. Another anomaly was that the words 'buraku' or 'burakumin' never entered into any of our discussions, or for that matter into conversations I had had with any other person living in or interested in Wana. This was true for members of the Yoshimi Town Office, the local branch of the Human Rights League, as well as the staff at the Saitama Prefectural Archive. In fact, the topic of the 'dōwa problem' only came up once, and that too in a rather transitory way, when I was asked to give a public address on 'human rights' (*jinken mondai*) at the Yoshimi Civic Centre. At that time, I agreed, upon request, to refrain from mentioning anything to do with 'burakumin'. The exact reasons for this plea for silence were not articulated, but upon much subsequent reading, research, and reflection, it can probably be attributed to an understandable attitude summed up in a popular Japanese saying related to the buraku problem: *nete iru ko o okosuna* (literally 'don't wake a sleeping child') or its English equivalent 'let sleeping dogs lie'.[52]

With such a mindset, however, I perceived it was also possible for some of the most obvious questions to remain untouched, and relegated to the realm of common sense. There was a danger, I thought, in assuming too much with regards to this sensitive issue. It seemed profitable to ask questions about buraku/outcast/e history that were simply assumed to be true. Is Suzuki Mikio really a burakumin? Is he an outcast/e (senmin/hisabetsumin)? Is the history of the Suzuki family outcast/e history? Have they experienced the same kind of discrimination over many generations?

At first glance, the answers to these questions seem straightforward enough. The available evidence points toward the affirmative in relation to all the four questions. Historical documentation, geographical location, and blood lineage all link the Suzuki family with the *eta* of the past and the 'buraku (or "dōwa") problem' of the present. Historical records demonstrate that the Suzuki family and other residents in Lower Wana Village were subject, on occasion, to quite disturbing discriminatory practices in the early modern era. They could, therefore, be considered as outcast/e. The issue of whether or not the Suzuki family have been subject to discriminatory treatment in recent times is questionable, but one can probably assume on the basis of articles printed in the Saitama Prefecture edition of the Liberation Newspaper (*Kaihō shinbun*) that discrimination is still present in that area of Japan, and that the Suzuki family may even have encountered it on occasion.

If one can categorically state that someone qualifies as a genuine burakumin, it must surely be Suzuki Mikio. The President of the Association for Research on Dōwa Education in Saitama Prefecture, Nagao Tomomi, wrote confidently in 1981 that the "Documents of the Suzuki Household" (*Suzuki-ke monjo*) were 'invaluable historical material in clarifying the history of burakumin in eastern Japan.'[53] In recent years too, the East Japan Buraku Liberation League (*Higashi nihon buraku kaihō kenkyūkai*) has published an article concerning field trips to Yoshimi to instruct others about the history of the burakumin.[54] These views are representative of mainstream ideas of buraku history and also reflect the official definitions of the buraku problem in government publications. The Division of the Promotion of Human Rights in the Saitama Prefectural Office, for example, explains the 'dōwa problem' as follows:

> The Dōwa problem has its origins between the end of the medieval period and the beginning of the early modern period, when the fiefal lords, who were the rulers at the time, in order to govern the people, created a system of status through political means. Even after the abolishment of this system, a cross-section of the population has encountered discrimination in connubial matters and employment simply because they were born or reside in Dōwa residential areas.[55]

On the basis of the above account, burakumin are, then, a 'cross-section of the population that have encountered discrimination' because 'they were born or reside in Dōwa residential areas'. With *eta* defined in historical reference works as the 'central outcast/e (senmin) stratum in the early modern period,' the association between burakumin and *eta* becomes immediately apparent in that they are linked through blood and place, and are both subject to the same discriminatory practices.[56] Although the premodern outcast/e groups to which the Suzuki family belonged were actually labelled as *eta*, there appears every justification for the President of the Association for Research on Dōwa Education in Saitama Prefecture to simply refer to the premodern Suzuki family as buraku'.[57] The answers to all the aforementioned questions then still appear to be in the affirmative. Suzuki Mikio is a burakumin and an outcast/e (senmin/hisabetsumin); and his family record comprises both buraku and outcast/e (senmin/hisabetsumin) history replete with a 'special' form of discrimination. Hesitation to fully support a view that the records of the Suzuki family constitute buraku history still seems warranted, however. The two key points in the Division of the Promotion of Human Rights explanation—that *eta* and burakumin are linked through blood and place, and are both subject to the same discriminatory practices—relies on the ideas of 'continuity' and 'similarity'. These ideas, however, are essentially both conceptual linkages that are made in order to tie disparate objects together. The decision to choose continuity over discontinuity and similarity over difference in this explanation is certainly based on a reasoned observation of historical and physical evidence. But it is not divorced from moral judgement, particularly in relation to the question of discrimination. The decision, moreover, goes against the judgement of scholarly experts like Noguchi Michihiko who caution that 'there is no commonly accepted standard upon which to define discrimination.'[58]

The word 'discrimination' (*sabetsu*), in the context within which it is used in the above explanation, has a purely negative connotation. It is an unwelcome word that is only uttered in the hope that all it represents will be eradicated. The fact that discrimination against burakumin is considered discrimination at all in the present is completely predicated upon the idea that this action is socially and morally reprehensible. Yet the idea that 'discrimination' against certain groups in society is wrong is a relatively new idea in Japan, at least in legal terms. The law that granted *eta* equality in 'status' (mibun) was only promulgated in 1871, and barely fifty years before that, the Tokugawa shogunate was actually warning *eta* and *hinin* groups through state legislation not to perform acts that went beyond their particular status limitations. There would seem to be, therefore, significant changes in institutional and social perceptions of what constitutes a marginalizing act in Japan that need to be understood first in order to properly narrate an outcaste history of discrimination.

In addition, the contemporary idea that buraku discrimination is wrong must logically lead to either of two conclusions—that the category of 'burakumin' should either be abolished or be clearly identified and respected. The explanation of the dōwa problem provided by the Division of the Promotion of Human Rights fails to comment on which is preferable, but my own experiences in Yoshimi indicated that the former course of action is regularly considered the most desirable in this area: 'sleeping children' should not be 'awakened'.[59] It is telling, moreover, that the residents of Yoshimi, including Suzuki Mikio, completely avoid identifying themselves as 'burakumin'. At the same time, however, and as will be seen in a subsequent chapter, many Japanese scholars and activists are also clearly supportive of the opposite idea that the buraku problem must be solved, not through silence, but through education. Burakumin are publicly identified for purposes of instruction against discrimination. In this way, the permanent dissolution of the buraku problem, perhaps somewhat ironically, is actively sought after through public pronouncement.

In order to entertain the idea of a resolution to buraku discrimination, however, it must first be possible for burakumin to cease being burakumin. There is a sense, therefore, in which burakumin cannot exist as an independent and firmly bounded category through time. 'Outcasteness' must be seen as an *a posteriori* imposition on human subjectivity that has been preserved historically to presumably serve some kind of political end. However, the idea that there is continuity and similarity between *eta* and buraku groups, even if it does start by assuming 'outcasteness' to be initially designated, fails to explain how an *a posteriori* imposition mysteriously becomes an *a priori* element in the subjectivity of the victim of these practices that is able to remain objectively stable in terms of both continuity and similarity over time.

Seen from this perspective, answers to questions like 'Is Suzuki Mikio a burakumin?', or 'Is Suzuki Mikio an outcast/e?', are clearly both affirmative and negative. Contemporary theory, however, first points to the answer 'no' because of the *a posteriori* origin of the notions of 'burakumin' and 'outcast/e', and the ease with which one may highlight the way discourse itself constructs 'buraku-ness' or 'outcasteness'. This is not to suggest, though, that reality itself has no impact on this discourse or this discourse on reality, for clearly the opposite is true. As Ernesto Laclau and Chantal Mouffe indicate in one of their earlier studies, the reduction of objects to discursive constructions has nothing to do with whether or not there is a world external to us. Rather, what is simply happening is our rejection of the claim that the world outside of us exists independently of or is untouched by discourse.[60] Ultimately, there can be no mistaking the role people play both in contemporary and historical society through discursive practices in the creation and recreation of people like Suzuki Mikio as either an 'outcaste' or 'burakumin'.

Discriminatory Actions and Narrative Sequences

A second conceptual problem within the master narrative of buraku discrimination and alluded to above lies with the problematical way in which the term 'discrimination' is often used. Discrimination is not simply an 'idea' (*kannen*) or a 'structure' (*jittai*) but rather a governing logic of human behaviour. Elizabeth Deeds Ermath in her discussion of postmodernism and Ferdinand de Saussure's philosophical contribution, points out that making distinctions is an act at the core of basic human linguistic activity: 'to read or understand even the simplest linguistic sequence is to recognize difference; it is to perform an incalculably complex and continuous act of differentiation.'[61]

Discrimination, in fact, has two different meanings (this is also true of the Japanese language equivalent *sabetsu*): the first an older and now less common use of the word that means 'differentiation' or 'discernment'; the second (and more commonly used sense of the word) implies an offensive act within an unequal power relationship between a perpetrator and a subject of discrimination.[62] In the first sense of the term, 'discrimination' can be understood as the most fundamental logic of human behaviour that governs speech, action, and thought. It is, in short, a 'natural act' (though this phrase is usually not considered applicable to the word in reference to its second meaning for this would suggest the inevitability and, therefore, a fatalistic 'acceptability' of the latter human action). The problem, however, is that while it is important to distinguish between these two usages, both meanings at their core essentially refer to an act of exclusion, which can be validly seen as a characteristic of human communicative behaviour evidenced in language use that constantly attempts to 'order' for purposes of survival. Irrespective of whether one 'differentiates' (the first meaning) or 'discriminates' (the second meaning) between things, the act always appear to occur within an unequal power relationship and, therefore, to be an expression of power. It does not really appear possible, moreover, to distinguish in any objective way between these two actions. Personal and collective moral and ethical considerations based on a firm belief in the universal equality of a common humanity would seem to be the only way to keep watch over the excesses of what may be quite reasonably defined as a foundational human behaviour.

Relating this discussion back to the Japanese context, the experience of many eighteenth-century *eta* and *hinin* communities in eastern Japan was that they were excluded from Tokugawa society through discriminatory actions found primarily in state legislation that encouraged the establishment of discriminatory social practices.[63] But as Herman Ooms has noted in his classic study of seventeenth-century village practice in Japan, *mura hachibu* (communal ostracism) was probably 'the best-known village-specific measure' of 'getting rid of undesirable community members' in the early Tokugawa era and included actions such as 'banishment, disinheritance, [and] stripping of "civic" status.'[64] This kind of social ostracism was not restricted to mainstream society, but also existed within the *eta* and *hinin* communities. One document in the Suzuki family documents dated 1794, for example, discusses how a *hinin* worker linked to Lower Wana Village got into a drunken altercation with a farmer, and ultimately had his head shaved and was banished from the 'workplace'.[65] Clear lines of distinction were drawn in early modern communities between those who were thought to 'belong' to a certain collectivity (whether real or imagined) and those who were not. Since both prejudicial practices linked to practices of 'mura hachibu' as well as discrimination against *eta* and *hinin* relied on the logic of cordon sanitaire, drawing an objective line of distinction between them is difficult.

The idea that buraku discrimination is a historically invariable action based on a false ideology of defilement and its related structural effects tends to misrepresent the phenomenon as capable of being something other than a basic contemporary discursive process of selection and ordering. Regardless of how powerful perceptions of a strengthening of discriminatory practices rooted in a particular ideology are, or the potency of the sensation that there is an increased repetitiveness of discriminatory acts against certain people over time, such judgements are ultimately based on an arbitrary privileging of certain links within historical sequential codes. Sequencing marginalizing events into a 'history of discrimination' is plainly a highly subjective practice. The accuracy of a narrative code of buraku discrimination is directly dependent on the idea of a neat correspondence between a discriminatory intention and a discriminatory act. Such an idea, in turn, rests on the assumption that perpetrators of marginalizing acts have a relatively unified subjectivity with a high level of self-awareness and that their actual intentions in acting in a particular way are not only decipherable but also collectively maintainable. Such a series of assumptions cannot seriously hold up to close scrutiny.

A better foundation for understanding discrimination locates it within a study of narratives rooted in experience that mobilize (and, in turn, are mobilized by) discourses to frame 'discriminatory actions' in certain ways.[66] Extant Tokugawa texts relating to *eta* and *hinin*, for example, are records of particular discriminatory actions. They are expressions of power found in human actions (such as speech acts) that are experienced and (sometimes) recorded by people who 'practise', 'experience', or 'witness them'. Narratives involving discrimination can be seen as attempts by people to communicate their actions or experiences to others and more often than not, reflect a posture of political struggle and resistance. The job of the historian is to 'mediate' between the past and the present: to examine particular historical narratives and ask questions about them on behalf of a contemporary audience. What does the narrative talk about? What is the relationship between the narrative and contemporary discourse? What is the relationship between this particular discriminatory action and other experiences recorded by the author? What kind of struggle is reflected in the narrative?

The identification of the existence of discriminatory actions and the ascertainment of their internal logics lies in the realm of phenomenology. Phenomenologists like David Carr, who have acknowledged many of the critiques of the modernist method, are helpful in establishing an experience-based approach to outcaste history. Carr argues that history consists of 'experience' and 'actions', which are sequenced together as a series of events that certain people live through and affect.[67] Many actions experienced by 'outcastes' will logically involve 'exclusivism' and 'differentiation' based upon the discursive practices of cordon sanitaire. Historians of marginalized groups isolate instances of cordon sanitaire in a body of texts and divide them according to who is narrating them: 'instigator', 'victim', and 'witness'.[68] They then examine them closely in order to ascertain their narrative style (letter, law, etc.) and content (subject matter, language, etc.). During the Tokugawa period, the most prevalent texts from the side of the 'instigator' are official documents like laws, legislation, and legal appeals. From the side of the victims, they are usually found in records kept by high *eta* officials such as Danzaemon and local village leaders. The terms 'instigator' and 'victim', however, should not belie the fact that the discursive practices of cordon sanitaire left to us in the form of narratives are not uni-directional but also signify a constantly recurring negotiation.

Ideational Aspects of Early Modern Outcaste History

The creation of a Tokugawa outcaste order was not simply a unilateral act of discriminatory policy that flowed out of the Edo City Magistrate's office and into the streets of the city or nearby villages. Intriguing methods were used in the creation of this order, and interestingly, a complicit role was played by *eta* leaders like Danzaemon. Many of the extant documents produced by Danzaemon in relation to the laws surrounding outcaste practices were officially formulated responses to questions posed by authorities like the Edo City Magistrate. From the laws and memoranda produced by Danzaemon, it is clear that he (the holder of the office at any one time) personally created quite specific and detailed regulations for the *eta* and *hinin* communities. The Edo Magistrate often accepted at face value Danzaemon's statements on the established practices of outcastes in Edo and the surrounding region. One particular tendency within Danzaemon documentation addressed to the various offices of the shogunate was the manipulation of the established logic of 'precedent' (*senrei/ zenrei*). This was arguably the most important cornerstone of Tokugawa law in all the various forms it took.[69]

There are multiple examples of Danzaemon informing the shogunate of the precedent with regard to his governing practices in eastern Japan. In 1719, for example, Danzaemon confirmed the correct procedures he needed to undertake for visiting the three magistrates of the shogunate.[70] Again, in 1725, Danzaemon submitted his household genealogy and summary of duties to the Bakufu.[71] In 1789, he reported on a crucifixion (including procedures undertaken) that occurred under his auspices in 1780.[72] In the same year, he issued a report discussing the possibility of 'unregistered commoners' (*mushuku*), who had been made *hinin* becoming 'commoners' (heinin).[73] This was a follow-up document to the one published the previous year that stipulated the clothing requirements of those under his jurisdiction involved in 'homeless hunting' (*mushuku-gari*).[74] In 1790 as well, a representative of Danzaemon reported on the habit of *hinin* (*teka*) tying their hair.[75] This was followed by a memo dated 1800 from Danzaemon pertaining to the status and activities of the *gōmune* (literally 'begging chest'), in which he recorded that they were not, in fact, under his jurisdiction, but were rather 'townsmen' (though as regards certain matters, they were under the jurisdiction of *hinin* leadership and, therefore, also subject to Danzaemon rule).[76]

It is clear through such examples that Danzaemon significantly contributed to the creation of his own leadership role at the apex of the Edo outcaste order by responding to shogunate queries in ways that expanded his jurisdiction over other members of the population. He did this while clarifying the distinction between outcastes and commoners. Admittedly, a straightforward compliance with shogunate requests for information or confirmation during the eighteenth century did not discount the possibility that Danzaemon sometimes yearned to resist the moves by the shogunate to increasingly define him in terms of his 'outcasteness'. It is unlikely, though, that the idea of open resistance to authority ever really crossed the mind of Danzaemon or other senior members of his bureaucracy at the time.

Records do survive, however, which indicate that Danzaemon played a more complicit part in the process of a personal accumulation of power and authority than he is normally credited with. He aspired, for example, to extend his power of governance by widening the scope with which he could wield power over his own subjects. This is an action best seen in his requests that others be severely punished; or that an increase in his executive powers over his own subjects be permitted by the authorities. The clearest example of this is witnessed in the early 1720s, during the period after Danzaemon successfully secured his position as head of the *hinin* in the eastern Japanese outcaste order. In 1724, the shogunate responded positively to a Danzaemon request to exile 226 *hinin* to a remote island, stating in its reply that it had ordered the exile 'as requested' (*danzaemon ainegai sōrō tōri konotabi entō mōshitsuke*).[77] Moreover, when Danzaemon asked for the death penalty for four *hinin* leaders that had attempted to stage a rebellion in the early 1720s, the City Magistrate granted this request too.[78]

This kind of action by Danzaemon continued throughout the eighteenth century. In 1743, he requested permission to tattoo *hinin* who had absconded and subsequently been recaptured, and the death penalty for those who ran away more than three times.[79] Likewise, in a Danzaemon response to a City Magistrate order to ensure that *hinin* were wearing the appropriate dress, he recorded an extended list of prohibited activities for *hinin* including: having skirting beams near the roof of their huts designed for show, having paper screen doors made from imported Chinese paper, and creating ranks amongst *hinin* based upon wealth. On the final point, Danzaemon explained that all *hinin* were 'ordinary *hinin*' (*minna hei-hinin*), with some of the reasoning behind the large body of restrictions placed on the *hinin* relying on the logic that it was not their 'established custom'.[80] In 1778 too, a Danzaemon official report was issued on the mobilization of *hinin* to drive off wild dogs from the execution fields in Shinagawa.[81] This was followed in 1794 by a request to the Magistrate to grant his application to exile one of the *eta* under his rule to an island off the coast of the mainland.[82] Exile was one of the strictest forms of punishment in

Tokugawa Japan apart from the death penalty, and it was probably requested partly as a sign to others under Danzaemon's jurisdiction that they should maintain unwavering obedience.

Unsurprisingly, the powers of Danzaemon markedly increased by the time the shogunate-inspired system of outcaste status had taken firm root at the beginning of the nineteenth century. In 1814, Danzaemon responded to a shogunate question about the limitations of the punishments he could impose on his subordinates.[83] Predictably, when questioned whether he was permitted to actually impose exile or banishments on subordinates, his answer was in the affirmative. In 1820 too, Danzaemon commented on the correct procedures for *hinin* leaders who needed to visit the Finance Commissioner's Offices.[84] This was followed in 1844 with a response to a request for information by the shogunate on how best to dispose of *hinin* who had drowned and whose bodies were floating in one of Edo's several rivers.[85]

In 1848, Danzaemon responded to an important question about the actual differences between *hinin* and *eta* duties. He acknowledged that when Danzaemon received a summons addressed to the most powerful *hinin* leader Kuruma Zenshichi, he did not dispatch any of his *eta* subordinates if the matters pertained to the *hinin* enclosure (*yoseba*) duties. But when matters from the various magistrates relating to investigations of *hinin* arose, the summons came directly to Danzaemon, who then led his subordinates out to investigate.[86] Three years later, an answer was once more solicited regarding jurisdiction, this time in relation to *eta* and *hinin* residing in rural areas. To this demand, Danzaemon stated that with respect to *eta* and *hinin* misdemeanours committed in rural areas under Daimyo or *hatamoto* (Tokugawa bannermen) rule, 'the appropriate papers… were burnt', but the documents that survived the fire indicate that these individuals too should be 'handed over to the *eta* heads of that region'. On the topic of the punishment of local *eta* heads, Danzaemon stated that in the event of there being only one village head, the leader was to be handed over to the appointed representative of the village. In the case that the *eta* and *hinin* were banished from the region, however, they would be handed over to a rural *eta* village head or *hinin* hut leader in another region. Furthermore, regarding court cases wherein these individuals appeal to local authorities against commoners, Danzaemon was in the habit of inquiring of each individual ruler whether these 'established procedures were acceptable'.[87]

Status negotiation, however, did not take place just at the level of Danzaemon. It was, rather, a common occurrence, often witnessed when people categorized under the labels *eta* and *hinin* responded to problems which arose from certain 'discriminatory acts' that were thought to target them. A pertinent example of this can be found in the following early nineteenth-century record. In 1812, members of a community in Edagō near Takaya Village in the Province of Tamba (present day Hyōgo prefecture) wrote a petition to the authorities concerning a sign erected by members of Takaya Village presumably directed at them, forbidding *eta-hinin* to enter the village. In response to this sign, members of the community wrote the following petition:

> We have been called by our Lord kawata. Those called *eta* do not engage in peasant work, do not own land, and do not have residences. Those people who live in rented accommodation throughout the wider village area, skin the hides of cattle, horses, deer, and other polluted animals are *eta*. We do skin the hides of dead cattle and horses, and while these are undoubtedly not the kind of activities peasants engage in, neither are we in our present capacity simply *eta* who engage only in knackery. This is a job we do alongside other activities.[88]

The community complained that any reference to them as *eta* was incorrect. It is clear from the above document, both from the description provided of *eta* (those who 'skin the hides of cattle, horses, deer, and other *polluted* animals') as well as the efforts that the community made to distance themselves from this label ('neither are we in our present capacity simply *eta* who engage *only* in knackery'), that the word *eta* was a potent epithet at the time that also described a reasonably tightly bound group of nearby 'outcastes'. While erecting a sign that forbade *eta* and *hinin* from entering the village, the neighbouring peasants had a clear idea of who they thought constituted *eta* and *hinin*. By taking offence at the sign, the 'kawata' demonstrated that they believed this discursive practice of cordon sanitaire was directed at them. These 'kawata' subsequently defined what they considered an *eta* to be (landless and houseless tanners) and argued that they did not fit this description and, therefore, the sign that was erected by the peasants that targeted them was incorrect and unjust.

This document demonstrates the way in which one community in Tokugawa Japan was subjected to a particular discursive practice of cordon sanitaire and how certain 'victims' then negotiated this action. Community members were physically restricted from entering another village because that community labelled them as *eta*. Interestingly though, the subjects of discrimination rejected the label 'eta' used by the neighbouring village. The targeted community adroitly highlighted the official label 'kawata' used by the ruling authority in relation to them to back up their appeal. This document shows a clear intent to circumvent the discriminatory action of a neighbouring peasant community by indicating the fundamental flaws in the logic of such an action and demonstrating the way the deed was actually in breach of the practices employed by the ruling authorities.

Another intriguing example of outcaste communities pursuing counter-hegemonic discursive practices in relation to official discriminatory discourse, but on a much grander scale, can be found in the research of Seiko Sugiyama. Focusing on the area in which the Suzuki family lived in Musashi Province (present day Saitama prefecture), Sugiyama demonstrates that labels like *eta* were never really adopted by the outcastes in rural areas in eastern Japan like Lower Wana Village. These communities, she observes, used far more neutral labels like *chōri* (literally 'official') [89] to refer to themselves if they used any labels of self-identification at all.[90] Sugiyama's research demonstrates the way in which local outcaste communities in eastern Japan refused discriminatory labels imposed on them not only in individual discriminatory incidents but also in undertaking wider social practices. *Eta* in eastern Japan preferred self-referential language that reflected their own distinctive ideas about their lives and occupations.

Clearly, *eta* and *hinin* were significantly defined in eastern Japan during the eighteenth and early nineteenth centuries through the processes of clarification and negotiation. The City Magistrate would request information about outcaste practices, and Danzaemon would respond in a way that largely defined *eta* and *hinin* as a visibly separate entity from the mainstream population. Danzaemon was careful to maximize the potential benefits that such a calculated response would provide. This process naturally cannot be seen as an entirely deliberate and calculated plot by a handful of outcaste officials in Edo to establish hegemonic power in a corner of the Tokugawa social complex. While it is clear that Danzaemon played a very instrumental role in the creation of his own position at the pinnacle of an eastern outcaste order, the shogunate in their masses of legislation and constant queries set the discursive limits of the dialogue about a 'commoner–outcaste' binary distinction. Discursive limits that were related to the emerging 'commoner–outcaste' binary, moreover, should be understood in the context of greater changes related to the nature of warrior governance and sovereignty (discussed further below). Danzaemon could only contest these limits upon pain of punishment.

Not all the distinguishing elements of the Edo outcaste order were simply created as selfish responses to shogunate inquiries by local outcaste leaders either. Nonetheless, an important theme still emerges in extant documents produced by Danzaemon and other outcaste communities in the eighteenth and nineteenth centuries. This theme is that the 'outcaste order' in eastern Japan was an important organ of the Tokugawa administrative machine but one that was in constant need of definition. The Edo outcaste order was not a naturally defined order, but a heavily constructed one. It demanded a good deal of perpetual mental callisthenics by those whose job it was to supervise and mobilize it.

Cordon Sanitaire within a Discursive History of Difference

On the basis of the arguments developed in this chapter, it becomes possible to reimagine *eta* and *hinin* as a diverse constellation of people who lived in disparate and largely independent regions throughout the Japanese archipelago during the early modern period and to whom certain offensive labels were applied. Their construction by state authorities and local communities as 'uncommon' (or 'outcastes') can be understood as an elaborate process of grouping together of what Michel Foucault called the 'non-observable', or, 'that which does not measure up to rule'.[91] In other words, rather than simply treating *eta* and *hinin* as fixed outcaste groups forced together through legislation and discriminatory social practices and remaining unchanged over time, they are more productively understood as people to whom certain discursive labels were applied (but which were also negotiated and resisted) within a politics orientated towards abnormalizing unconforming spaces. In one respect, it was never truly significant who specifically occupied these spaces: anybody could be associated through a process of naming. *Nado* (等) or 'et cetera' was a critical part of the legislative language used to define this unconforming space. *Eta* and *hinin*, over time, were merely made representative of these spaces of abnormality, perhaps because ordinariness was most recognizably policed and punished by their hand.

Historicizing the labels commonly thought to apply to early modern antecedents of burakumin reveals a process whereby the state (as well as other interlocutors) attempted to synthesize groups of people with unique, fluid, and divergent histories into homogenized masses of 'outcastes'. A close study of Tokugawa laws and legislation issued during this period reveals that the idea of an 'outcaste' (usually phrased in legal documents as '*eta*, *hinin*, etc.' [*eta–hinin*–nado]) actually developed in tandem with the idea of a 'commoner' (*heijin*/ heinin/ *shirōto*). Constructions of *eta–hinin* difference are, therefore, fruitfully understood as being linked to larger processes of social ordering related to other concerns such as urban drift and poverty (discussed earlier in the chapter), the bureaucratization of the warrior class, and the early formulations of what might be termed proto-nationalist thinking about the kinds of subjects who constituted a 'normal society'.[92] *Eta* and *hinin* were labels applied to constellations of people who were discursively excluded in a process that saw others attempt to achieve a firmer sense of belonging to a narrowly imagined polity.[93] What is usually generically referred to as 'buraku discrimination' in the early modern context, therefore, needs to be recognized as a historically distinct phenomenon.

One key feature of the emergence of *eta* and *hinin* groups during the late seventeenth/early eighteenth century concerned their links to new regimes of policing and social control. The Tokugawa shogunate was a regime built by soldiers who relied on military force and violence to secure a base of rule. The monopolization of the leather trade had taken place in eastern Japan during the sixteenth century, and Danzaemon had been awarded a dominant position in the manufacture of leather sometime later. As peace ensued during the second half of the seventeenth century, a partial separation of military and police powers occurred, with the latter powers being outsourced to the *eta* and *hinin* communities. The birth of the eighteenth-century 'outcaste order', therefore, was, at one level, a result of a late seventeenth-century policy of subcontracting administrative powers by warrior elites out to the *eta* and *hinin* communities in order to facilitate greater social cohesion. The idea of Tokugawa society being basically divided into 'commoner' and 'outcaste' spheres emerged several decades later (probably sometime after the early eighteenth century court case between Danzaemon and *hinin* leaders in Edo).[94] The legal decision to place a range of 'outcaste groups' under Danzaemon's rule unmistakably played an important role in promoting this kind of a polarized conceptual division of society.

Hardening notions of a 'commoner' (heinin) who constituted membership of a geographical and conceptual body called 'Japan' (*nihonkoku*) provided further impetus for imagining people who did not constitute part of this 'normal' entity. In the early seventeenth century, when the nature of the Japanese state was not clearly defined and the rulers appeared to be primarily interested in securing their own positions within society, relatively vague notions of 'noble' (*ki*) and 'base' (*sen*) were at the core of intellectual discourse on social belonging. Hayashi Razan (1583–1657), for example, wrote that

'Heaven is esteemed, earth is base; heaven is high, earth is low. Just as there is a difference between high and low, so too is there in people; indeed the ruler is esteemed and the vassal is base.'[95] By the early eighteenth century, however, the field of rule and the definition of the subject was becoming increasingly uniform. Ogyū Sorai (1666–1728), for example, wrote of 'iyashikimono' (base people), which incidentally included both prostitutes and kawaramono,[96] and it is in relation to these groups that he discussed the notion of 'heinin' (commoner). For Sorai, *iyashikimono* were base and immoral, and *heinin* were morally upright, had proper bloodlines, and were civilised (refined).[97] Sorai's discourse of 'outcastes' and 'commoners,' moreover, was located firmly within the context of a *nihonkoku* or 'Japanese state'—a notion scattered throughout the preceding sections of his work that appear to be predominantly centred on the city of Edo or the eastern states. *Nihonkoku* was a place being violently tugged apart at the seams by rapid and disturbing changes against which Sorai was desperately attempting to prescribe various countermeasures. Within this context, 'outcastes' were dangerous entities.[98]

'Commoner' (heinin) was by far the most common language of governance used in eighteenth-century Japan to refer to 'the people'. It was the term used by both intellectuals and rulers. The conglomerated expression *eta–hinin*–nado (*eta*, *hinin*, etc.) was often used in contradistinction to it and is, therefore, probably best translated as 'outcastes'. By the eighteenth century, people were increasingly defined in the popular and political imagination according to this narrowing definition of the field of rule and the binary existence of 'common' and 'outcaste' subjects. As the use of the character *hei* 平 illustrates, moreover, there was an increasing desire on the part of the warrior elites to document and dominate subjects within their territorial reach based on ideas of normality. *Eta* and *hinin* were invidious descriptors which lumped people who were considered abnormal by eighteenth century standards together as 'impure' and 'abnormal'. Certainly, these two signifiers were used in relation to people who, generally speaking, were not directly governed by samurai officials; often lived on untaxable land (*jochi*); and who generated a considerable part of their livelihood from non-agricultural activities related to dead animals, begging, or handling criminals. But more than words with fixed meanings that described certain groups, these labels also signified discourses of difference that underwent a conceptual tightening during the course of the eighteenth century.

While definitely capable of conveying a general sense of perceived deficiency, these terms did not really offer any hint at the real reasons behind their application. As such, they were, in another sense, 'empty signifiers' attached to vague social categories, which required constant clarification in the face of rapid and perpetual social change. In spite of the conceptual tightening that these terms experienced during the eighteenth century, moreover, a cross-sectional analysis of official documents during the 1760s and 1770s indicates that these official discourses of difference still tended to emit diverse messages. Some legislation continued to reinforce the idea that *eta* and *hinin* were 'subhuman' outcastes. Others, however, gave *eta* and *hinin* additional policing powers. Others still, unsure of the actual status of these groups, sought the advice of the *eta* leadership as to how they should best be defined.

The early modern binary discourse of commoner–outcaste, however, did not have a long life. As shown in Chapter 4, further changes in the notion of the 'commoner' emerged during the nineteenth century. The onset of modern ideas like 'nation' and 'citizen' brought about a major restructuring in the discursive formulation of social difference. Late Tokugawa and early Meiji rulers were soon forced to legislate against a commoner–outcaste discourse in an effort to unify the Japanese state in the face of a foreign threat and the collapse of internal civil order.

4

Modernity as Purgatory

Post-Meiji Discourses of Difference and the Formation of 'Buraku Culture'

In previous times, even as 'burakumin' were pushed to the outer extremities of society as uncivilised people they were nonetheless guaranteed a particular livelihood in exchange for this discrimination. In modernity, however, not only was this economic chance taken from them, but 'burakumin' were incorporated as the Emperor's subjects, as members of a national community rooted in the idea of 'one sovereign and his subjects'. This was the birth of 'new commoner-citizens' who joined the ranks of the other citizenry. In reality, however, they came to occupy the very lowest place in a transfer of oppression which saw those at the top of society weigh down those at the bottom. These people were really only transformed into 'foreign bodies' who became personal targets of discrimination. Without a doubt 'buraku' became a modern hell.

—Kang Sang-jung (2005)

It goes without saying that the buraku problem is a different kind of problem to that of ethnicity or sex; because 'burakumin' are overwhelmingly 'constructed' through the gaze of the Other no firm markers of them as 'burakumin' actually exist.

—Kurokawa Midori (1999)

Introduction

While I was at a trendy Italian restaurant in Shibuya with a group of Japanese cultural elites late in 2008, the topic of discussion turned to my research and my intended schedule for fieldwork in Tokyo. Cautiously informing my dinner partners of my plan to visit a 'former outcaste' community the following day, I was a little surprised to discover that a veil of silence did not immediately descend over the table. On the contrary, despite the well-documented taboo nature of this topic in Japan, what ensued was a surprisingly frank exchange of views about the nature of this 'problem' (the word 'buraku' was not used during the discussion except by me). My host for the evening informed me that he had descended from a long line of traditional performers in Tokyo and was quite knowledgeable about the ways in which the city had been transformed during the modern era. His father had revealed to him as a child, for example, the areas wherein members of 'these communities' lived and even the location of the specific houses that 'they owned and occupied'. Different merchant and artisan households were also apparently singled out for their questionable social status. One shop owner who specialized in the preparation and sale of horse meat was said to be 'one of them' (presumably because he engaged in butchery). Another dinner guest then responded that there was also a high profile and tremendously influential organization (an apparent reference to the Buraku Liberation League) in his native city of Fukuoka, which (purportedly) even the local police feared. He declared confidently with the nodding approval of some of the other guests that the areas where these organizations were located clearly signalled the whereabouts of these communities.

After considerable reflection upon the contents of this unexpected but intriguing dinner conversation, combined with the reading of critical literature, several modern dimensions of the 'buraku problem' that I had long been contemplating began to fall into place. I was again reminded through this exchange that while physical linkages between contemporary buraku communities and *eta* and *hinin* groups undoubtedly exist (my host's father presumably did not make up all the continuities he spoke about), nonetheless the idea that 'burakumin' constitute an old and relatively uniform outcast/e (senmin/hisabetsumin) community is also rooted in considerable circumstantial evidence and speculation (people were sometimes confidently identified as 'one of them' with little or no basis). Put in another way, modern understandings of 'burakumin' have relied on a principle of probabilistic association (or from a more critical perspective, distortion) whereby the existence of *some* historical connection in the modern era is usually treated as conclusive evidence of *comprehensive* continuity of Japan's outcast/e communities. Linkages between burakumin and premodern outcast/e groups do not merely exist objectively but are *made to exist* on the basis of assumptions of linkage. It is for this reason that scholars like Kang Sang-jung and Kurokawa Midori rightly place the words 'burakumin' and 'buraku' in single quotation marks when narrating this history.

The above dinner conversation, however, also revealed numerous other guiding principles that are clearly important in the development and articulation of 'buraku difference' in the post-Meiji era. A second recognizable principle is that of the 'homogenization of difference' (something more commonly associated in academic writing with processes of nation-building). The Japanese government, the general population, scholars, and activists themselves have, over time, tended to construct a relatively uniform image of a tightly bound outcast/e community known as 'burakumin'. A constellation of people and communities (for instance, people who engage in *a kind of* butchery, people who live in areas *near* BLL branches, etc.) have tended to be identified as belonging to the same outcast/e group.[1] Through this process, the real changes that took place in terms of who identified (or was identified) with social marginality in Japan and the processes whereby these people experienced that identification often become obscured. Marginalized people (including people who today are simply ascribed with the label 'burakumin') actually had unique, fluid, and often quite divergent histories. Despite the body of evidence that supports this view, however, 'outcast/e experience' is nonetheless usually characterized by strong uniformity and perhaps somewhat ironically little scope for difference.

A third principle closely related to the homogenization of difference is the 'time-lag effect'. This is to say that 'burakumin' have usually been understood as Japanese subjects stuck on the wrong side of an imaginary fault line between Japanese tradition and modernity. Just as Japan, until recent times, was often represented as 'not quite modern' and located within 'a historical trajectory derived from another's development',[2] 'burakumin', too, have frequently been imagined as being chained to the past—remnants of a backward feudal age upon which modernity's unsurpassed transformative powers have left little or no impression.[3] Just as the default setting for imagining Japan, its people, and its culture within modernity has usually involved a projected sense of relatively uniform timelessness and changelessness (concurrently believed to be under assault by new social forces), so too are the imagined peripheries of that very same nation, society, ethnicity, and culture envisaged as enduring and consistent in their backwardness. But whereas the Japanese nation, its dominant ethnic group, and interior culture are believed to display a fundamental resilience that permits retention of a core essence despite the onslaught of revolutionary change, modernity is ostensibly portrayed as universally failing 'burakumin'.

This prescribed uniform backwardness of the socially marginalized, though, is often regarded as exactly the same condition that necessitates the instigation of wholesale social change. The early Meiji state utilized it as evidence of the need to embark upon institutional change, which could lead to a more civilized and enlightened nationhood; later governments relied on it as a litmus test for the level of harmony that a diverse citizenry was achieving within the process of empire-building; and the socially marginalized themselves (people identified or who self-identified as 'Special Buraku' and subsequently 'burakumin') have consistently mobilized the idea during the twentieth century for its liberative potential—as a discourse that can build solidarity and consensus by revealing a common history of oppression, but which also functions as a springboard for social change by demonstrating social deficiencies that need to be addressed.

A fourth principle which helped define the contours of 'buraku' difference in the modern era can be termed as 'speciation' (or specialization). Modernity, while bringing with it egalitarian discourses and promises of emancipation, also had the opposite effect, increasing, as it did, the amount of signifiers available to rank and classify the socially marginalized. Traditional ways of ordering people were not removed as a result of the changes brought about by the Meiji Restoration and subsequent state-induced reforms but were often merely transformed. New ways of discriminating evolved through the infusion of modern technologies of discrimination so that often the outcaste condition only became more acute in modernity.[4] Older strategies for socially differentiating *eta* and *hinin* were transformed through modern regimes of social ordering like race, nation, and capital (as outlined briefly at the end of Chapter 2), resulting in complex hybrid structures of discrimination. The modern Japanese outcaste was no longer merely a member of a despised community who engaged in a certain occupation but became someone whose house was also overly conspicuous in a certain neighbourhood, who carried and spread the threat of disease, who possessed a warped character predisposed to criminal activity, and so on. To borrow Mark Morris' term, modern 'stigmata' frequently combined with traditional markers of difference to inspire new ways of constituting social outcastes and, therefore, preventing them from belonging in the post-Meiji period.[5] It is particularly in this sense that 'buraku' areas can be seen (in the words of Kang Sang-jung in the epigraph echoing Miyazaki Manabu) to have become a 'modern hell'.

A final principle important in the discursive construction of 'burakumin' in the modern era is perpetual recalibration (or in Kurokawa Midori's words 'constantly reconstructed signification'). 'Outcasteness' (or 'buraku-ness') is clearly not a permanent and static state but rather a dynamic and typically forced process, that is to say that outcasteness (or buraku-ness) is not a naturally defined condition, but (as Kurokawa intimates in the epigraph) a heavily constructed one that demands a good deal of perpetual mental callisthenics by those whose job it is to define, monitor, and mobilize difference. Rapid change disrupts the imagined social order, leaving one to rely on fuzzy individual and collective memories and subjective judgements to keep track of what one perceives to be irrevocable social difference. Scores of generic labels that referred to a general state of outcasteness in Japan (either owned by or applied to groups of people) were used in the modern era and the usage changed quite rapidly over time. Terms like *eta*, *hinin*, shinheimin, tokushu buraku, and burakumin, now commonly considered to only refer to one minority group that experienced a common history of discrimination, were used to signify a constantly changing notion of outcasteness defined in relation to an imagined dominant majority community ('Japanese nation', 'Japanese people', 'Japanese society', etc.). And as Tomotsune Tsutomu has pointed out, there is a certain 'catachrectic effect' embedded within signifiers like 'tokushu buraku': that is to say, they have a temporary and highly flexible meaning, which is regulated and manipulated to suit different political purposes.[6]

One last aspect of the dinner party conversation that needs to be mentioned here is the troubling practice of 'unnaming'.[7] The failure of any of my dinner acquaintances to actually name the subjects of social marginalization that they were talking about is an important reminder that 'burakumin' is a postwar discourse of difference (with roots in the prewar period), which was not only constructed and perpetually recalibrated over time but which has also been effectively silenced in many areas. Certainly this silence must be attributed, to some extent, to the activities of the targets of social discrimination themselves (the prewar Suiheisha and postwar BLL), who have, at times, waged quite bloody denunciation campaigns over issues of nomenclature. In this regard, 'burakumin' should also be seen as a discourse of resistance within a complex political struggle which has sought to break down the ways in which difference has been categorized and demonized in Japan, usually behind the veneer of a tantalizing and torturous rhetoric of social equality and freedom that is constantly promised but seldom realized.

This chapter, then, presents a history of the 'buraku problem' from the beginning of the Meiji period through to the early 1930s. It analyses the discourses of social difference that emerged in the writings of elites and intellectuals from the late Tokugawa period onwards and juxtaposes these emerging images of an increasingly uniform minority-like population against the real changes that actually occurred in the lives of the residents of former outcaste communities as well as other marginalized groups such as the urban poor. The adoption of this methodology makes it possible to demonstrate that despite historical continuities, large-scale change occurred in many areas to such as extent that the master narrative of buraku history really fails to retain much descriptive value. It also becomes evident that the twentieth century discourse of 'burakumin' followed no clearly determined linear path of development but rather emerged out of competing ideas about how best to characterize Japan's social margins during the period under examination. Social outcastes were constantly defined and redefined through fleeting 'commonsense ideas' about the nature of human associations, the historical development of societies, the existence of homogeneity within populations, and the importance of progress (in ways that usually integrated various combinations of the principles of probabilistic association, homogenization of difference, time-lag effects, speciation, and perpetual recalibration discussed above). The end-product of this complex discursive history of difference was the emergence of the idea of a reasonably well-defined group of marginalized subjects known as 'burakumin' during the early postwar period rooted in a premodern past with a body of shared memories and a sense of collective destiny.

Civilizing Social Frontiers

The 1871 Emancipation Edict is usually taken as one of the clearest evidences of the attempt by the Meiji state to dismantle the Tokugawa status system. The legislative act promised those legally defined as *eta* and *hinin* a life more ordinary, and in one sense, it initially created a feeling of a historical moment akin to a return from exile. The severed bond between outcaste body and communal place seemed to be re-established, and all space allegedly became equally accessible to every member of the Japanese nation-state. A number of measures were also adopted alongside the Edict to advance this course of action: commoner-citizens were permitted to take on surnames (1870); nobles and commoners were allowed to marry (1871); the sale of women into indentured prostitution was outlawed (1872); and the wearing of swords was prohibited (1876). The cumulative effect of these policies was to create an overwhelming impression that the new Meiji regime was carefully dismantling the Tokugawa status system in an attempt to build a more egalitarian society.

The Emancipation Edict certainly breathed life into the idea of the 'commoner-citizen' (heimin) but this category was clearly not designed for all members of society. The law was promulgated in a polity newly fashioned around the foundational principle of 'one sovereign and his subjects' (*ikkun banmin*). Since it was merely legislating for a union between 'commoners' and 'outcastes', the Edict did not involve the Emperor, the imperial court, and the aristocracy (former *daimyo*, court nobles, etc.), which comprised a large proportion of the leadership stratum. These people, like their historical forebears, existed above commoners, and as evidenced in documents like the peerage laws of 1871 and 1884, presided over the modernization of society from a thoroughly privileged position.[8] The Emperor, within the emerging modern Japanese state, operated in roughly three core capacities: as a political sovereign; as embodiment of the civilizational ideal; and as a symbolic marker of the Japanese ethnic nation (*minzoku kokka*). Given the Emperor's supreme position within the Meiji order, the Edict was predictably 'bestowed' on former outcaste communities, explained as a direct result of 'His imperial benevolence' (*ten'on*).[9] The former Tokugawa status system was, therefore, not destroyed by early Meiji legislation. It was merely recalibrated to match the new social conditions that the Meiji state faced in its pursuit of the development of a strong, modernized nation.

Critically important in the process of nation-building was the construction of a well-disciplined population that could meet the formidable challenges facing Japan during the latter half of the nineteenth century. From the state's perspective, it was imperative to foster a loyal and obedient population capable of displaying spontaneity and autonomy in their various productive capacities in order to help secure a level of civilizational parity with the West (and thereby revoke the unequal treaties that Japan had signed in mid-century upon threat of violence). At the same time, however, the new citizenry (especially 'former outcastes') were considered important resources, especially for the development of Japan's frontier regions and future colonies.[10]

The most important part of the process of constructing a well-disciplined citizenry was undoubtedly the creation and proliferation of policies and legislation that eliminated any potential impediments to Japan's endeavours to recreate itself as a modern civilization. Political elites began to act on numerous concerns during the early Meiji period, especially those that they believed encouraged Western observers to see Japan in an unfavourable light. As Takashi Fujitani has noted, for example, the state 'launched aggressive campaigns against mixed bathing, public nudity, and urinating in public' in Tokyo, arresting '2,091 people for nudity and 4,495 others for urinating in public' in 1876. In another prefecture, Fujitani continues, 'authorities prohibited a seemingly innocuous summer custom, daytime napping.'[11] But public nudity, urination and siestas were not the only causes for state consternation. Officials and intellectuals were also worried about the effect that problems such as the existence of *eta* and *hinin* communities in Japan might have on Japan's international standing. One conscientious official and budding author noted at the time, for example, that 'butchers' (*tosha*) were able to rise in social status in Western countries because 'civilization' (*bunmei kaika*) meant that poor people could become rich and the humble, lofty.[12]

Members of the foreign community in Japan were also having increasingly intimate contact with socially marginalized groups in Japan during the middle decades of the nineteenth century and their observations about the latter frequently filtered through into the pages of journals and books. Francis Hall,[13] an observer who was a member of the foreign community in Yokohama, included the following account of his encounter with an *eta* community in an 1860 diary entry:

> From the fishermen's quarter I went to the quarter occupied by the leather dressers. The houses were in a thick cluster with no apparent regularity of streets. A few hides were stretched and drying in the sun. There was nothing about this quarter to indicate any special poverty except a number of houses that were underground. A cellar was dug and over it a straw roof placed with a paper window in the floor. In the quarter generally the people were as well clad and looked as prosperous as other parts of Kanagawa. Some of these leather dressers are said to grow rich in their proscribed traffic. Persecuted they truly are, being forbidden to marry without their own guild, or to enter the houses of others. They are said to be particularly affected with ophthalmia, though this was not apparent in my walk.[14]

The idea that these communities were 'unsavoury elements' also emerged in some of the writings of Western observers around this time. Alfred East, for example, observed: 'I met with only one rude boy. He was dressed in broad stripes of blue and white. I think he belonged to a butcher.'[15] Christopher P. Hodgson, the officiating British consul at Nagasaki and Hakodate, also wrote assertively in a footnote in his volume: 'Tanners, a race despised in Japan, who live alone, and are not permitted to eat, drink, or talk with others than their own "caste".'[16]

Eager to remove any issue that could potentially detract from Japan's standing in the eyes of Western powers, the Meiji state promulgated the 1871 Edict and local governments quickly set about offering advice and admonishments to 'former outcastes' and 'new commoner-citizens' about how best to achieve equal standing with their fellow citizens. As Noah McCormack notes, however, designations like 'former outcaste' and 'new commoner' 'suggested that these people did not originally belong, but had different antecedents significant enough to be reflected in name.'[17]

An important part of this paradoxical process of exclusion and assimilation involved instructing 'former outcaste' communities to purify themselves and to eradicate 'old customs' that were believed to be preventing them from successfully entering the ranks of the commoner-citizen. One government directive, for example, read as follows: 'The name *eta* originally [indicates people who] have jobs requiring the handling of unclean things; [they] also do not like to worship the gods that ordinary people believe in… They do not seriously contemplate these things and the fact that they obscenely fraternise with commoners actually means that they are unable to escape the *eta* title. Herewith in regards to these matters, a cleansing ceremony will be held, and all people shall discreetly come forward regardless of their age, sex, and status and ask to undertake this purification.'[18] An ordinance from Ehime prefecture (introduced in Chapter 2) also instructed former outcastes to:

> Firstly, wash well both morning and evening, and clean up before slaughtering animals and handling hides. Pay caution to body odours and reform all behaviours which commoners consider unclean. For example, don't use hand towels as cleaners, toilet pans as pots, wash hands and feet in cooking pans, and neglect to wash your hands after defecating…[19]

It was not just 'former outcaste' settlements that were of concern to officials and other elites. Growing numbers of displaced subjects were moving in and out of established rural and urban communities and even beginning to construct their own temporary settlements as a result of the adverse effects of Japan's rapid social upheaval. McCormack notes that public intellectuals like Fukuzawa Yukichi began to express concern about a broader 'breed' (*shuzoku*) of poor people characterized by their 'lack of adherence to hygienic principles which constituted a major obstacle to civilization and progress.'[20] It was not just 'former outcaste' communities which were capable of reducing Japan's status in the eyes of Western countries, but also Japan's burgeoning urban centres which appeared uncivilized in comparison with their foreign counterparts. State officials, intellectuals and other literati began to engage in extensive and long-running debates about the problems associated with poor districts and their residents. These writings were marked by a conscious attempt to 'constitute a new kind of social solidarity, centred on the nation, through literary representations of shared national belonging.'[21]

However, regardless of how strenuously people (whether 'former outcastes' or the urban poor) tried to conform to the civilizational imperative of the Meiji government and local authorities, the general consensus was usually that they were doomed to failure. As Kurokawa indicates in relation to 'former outcaste' communities, numerous complaints found in newspapers of the time attested to their 'dirtiness', 'incapacity for courtesy and propriety', 'lamentable customs', and 'inability to reform because of obdurate traditions'.[22] Suggestions that 'former outcastes' could not achieve a true state of parity in civilizational terms with other Japanese citizens frequently became an impetus for many residents to attempt to modernize their own communities through the creation of facilities like schools. But these efforts also sometimes resulted in them becoming even stronger targets of social discrimination. Between 1871 and 1877 alone, for example, twenty-one incidents of social unrest directly linked to opposition to the Emancipation Edict and local reforms were recorded throughout Japan.[23]

Early Meiji Transformations in 'Former Outcaste' Communities

Policies and legislation devised during the early Meiji era tended to work together to homogenize all social differences into an easily manageable uniform category. Social differences, moreover, tended to be framed in a premodern idiom of social classification that preserved a sense of continuity between 'former outcaste' and modern disenfranchised communities. Historical records tend to suggest, however, that individual 'former outcaste' communities had unique, fluid, and often quite divergent fates in the modern era. Whether or not 'former outcaste' communities were located in urban or rural areas, the kinds of industries that residents were historically engaged in, the types of zoning practices that were employed in the post-Meiji era, and the kinds of government regulations that came to bear on the lives of people in specific localities, were all important factors that helped determine the modern character of neighbourhoods and their residential make-up. Also of great importance was the way in which each community dealt with the newly disenfranchised who began flowing into towns and cities as a result of modernization policies.

Beginning with eastern Japan, important changes occurred in 'former outcaste' communities in Edo (Tokyo) during the early Meiji period, particularly in the 'New Town' (Shinchō) area, where Danzaemon resided. Many of these changes came about as the result of policy and legislation issued at the level of either the Meiji government or the local municipal authorities. The state instigated a series of land reforms that had considerable effects on the residents of 'New Town' and other urban 'former outcaste' settlements. Maintaining 'New Town' as a separate quarter became administratively unnecessary with the promulgation of the Emancipation Edict in 1871 and the land upon which the community was built (previously *jochi* or 'non-taxable land') was returned to the state. It was then resold back to the previous landlords (totalling 205) with a subsequent 3% land tax levied on the property. In principle, most residents were able to purchase back the plots that they had been living on. On occasion, however, when former tenants were unable to do so, the land was subsequently sold to others.[24] Other interesting changes were also brought about in relation to administration and zoning in 'New Town'. Renamed as 'Kameoka' in 1871, the local system of governance reverted from a 'landlord system' (*nanushisei*) to an 'elder system' (*toshiyorisei*) and administratively became part of Tokyo's 69th ward. Further subdivided into three administrative divisions—Upper, Middle, and Lower Kameoka—the residence of Dan Naoki (the last of Danzaemon's post-Emancipation names) fell into the jurisdiction of Upper Kameoka. Interestingly, Dan Naoki was chosen as the representative town elder over his son Kennosuke, who was also nominated but eventually rejected because of his age.[25]

The emergence of new slum areas nearby also affected the modern fate of 'New Town'. Shiomi Sen'ichirō notes that there were at least two critical phases during the early Meiji period when large numbers of poor people flowed into Tokyo: immediately after the Meiji Restoration (1869–70); and during the Matsukata deflation in the mid-1880s. Particularly during the latter period, poor people—variously labelled as *kyūmin* (the destitute), *hinmin* (poor people), and *saimin* (the poor)—began to congregate in slum areas near railroad tracks, in marshlands, near graveyards and crematoriums, and on riverbanks and riverbeds. Three major slums emerged in the Tokyo region during the early Meiji period at Shinami, Samegahashi, and Mannenchō, and the residents of these slums included not only the unemployed but also people who engaged in a wide array of professions ranging from sewage disposal to carpentry. Small slum areas, however, also emerged at various locations throughout the city, including in Asakusa. The main slum area located there lay between 'New Town' and Senjū in an area known as Sanya.[26] The close proximity of this slum to a former *hinin* community undoubtedly facilitated some conceptual overlap, linking 'former outcastes' with modern social stigmata like poverty, disease, unemployment, day labour, and criminality. At the same time, however, the fact that the new slum area did not directly overlap with 'New Town' meant that attempts to dissociate that area with 'outcasteness' were relatively speedy and successful.

In western Japan, the impact of land reforms and zoning in both the 'former outcaste' communities and poverty-stricken areas was also conspicuous in cities like Osaka and Kyoto. The Meiji state was eager to encourage the construction of urban centres, which would neatly disjoin the rich from the poor, and, therefore contain, and eradicate some problems commonly associated with underprivileged areas, such as disease and sanitation. A range of building regulations were designed to limit and define housing in ways that would contribute to better living conditions and hygiene. The right to evict people from dwellings that failed to meet government standards was also reserved by the government. As a result, large numbers of people were moved to other locations, some of which included 'former outcaste' settlements. The relocation of large numbers of poor people to the area of Naniwa, for example, was a direct result of the tightening of regulations related to housing by the Osaka Metropolitan government.[27] Kyoto experienced an unusual path to modernity in that the Emperor and other court-related elites were forcibly moved to Tokyo after the Meiji Restoration. The economic base of the former capital was substantially weakened by this shift and substantial amounts of capital were allocated by the Meiji government to revive the local economy (though little was apparently done to help the plight of the city's poor). McCormack notes that in 1870, the total Kyoto population was listed as 382,049 people, out of which 9,176 residents were categorized as being of '*eta* status'. Almost half this number lived in a large 'former outcaste' area known as Yanagihara. A decline in traditional industries such as leatherwork and sandal-making, worsening economic conditions in the wider Kyoto area, and changes in government zoning led to a considerable migration of impoverished people into the area, over time. Neary notes that a survey dated 1886 'showed that fewer than one-third of the residents had been born there and over half regarded themselves as temporary residents.'[28] An 1896 census also revealed that 4,591 registered residents were living in the area along with 445 temporary residents.[29]

Former *eta* and *hinin* across Japan also experienced diverse fortunes with regard to occupation in the aftermath of the Restoration. In 1871, several months before the promulgation of the Emancipation Edict, a national law was passed permitting people to dispose of the carcasses of dead animals as they wished (*heigyūba katte shochihō*). Private entrepreneurs from the northeast region of the island of Honshū had already begun a profitable trade of transporting cattle for sale to the Tokyo/ Yokohama area in the 1860s and this led to a government attempt to regulate the livestock and meat industries immediately after the Restoration. Another motive for regulation lay in the fact that the state was now a major participant in these industries, establishing the Tsukiji Livestock Company in 1869, which included an abattoir as part of its infrastructure. This company, according to Shiomi, did not simply cater to the growing Western population in the greater Tokyo area but also supplied beef to an expanding domestic consumer market. The 1871 law that freed up the disposal of animal carcasses was, therefore, actually intended to break the *eta/hinin* monopoly on tanning and butchery and to allow operators (particularly the state-owned company) to dispose of the remains of slaughtered cattle in a manner of their own choosing.[30] Danzaemon predictably appealed against the new law but his protests were to no avail. However, it is also clear that not all 'former outcastes' opposed the loss of their occupational monopolies. Some communities used this legislation along with the Emancipation Edict as an opportunity to abandon the industries altogether. Kurokawa records, for example, that Shimoda Village in Osaka expressed thanks for the Edict in one official document and, thereafter, explicitly forbade its residents from 'handling dead cows and horses, diseased cattle, hoofed animals of any sort, or any kind of fur… and with regards to business, buying and selling any kind of shoe leather.'[31]

New government legislation also affected other industries in which Danzaemon and his subordinates (as well as other 'former outcaste' communities throughout Japan) had traditionally held monopolies. Monopoly rights in the sale of candle-wicks, for example, were subsequently surrendered. Official duties related to the policing of homeless persons who drifted into Tokyo were likewise relinquished during the early Meiji period. Danzaemon and *eta* and *hinin* under his charge had been responsible for policing 'vagrants' (*nobinin*; literally 'wild *hinin*') who drifted into Edo from predominantly regional areas for much of the latter half of the Tokugawa period. After the Restoration, however, and particularly following the turmoil of the brief civil war fought during the latter years of the 1860s, the number of drifters rose to an unprecedented level. This itinerant population not merely comprised agricultural producers who could no longer sustain themselves in rural areas, as had usually been the case before, but also included large numbers of samurai and merchants. These new assemblages of dispossessed persons congregated in vacant areas around the capital including the grounds of former daimyo mansions and the wider Edo castle grounds. The spread of contagious diseases within these new colonies became a pressing concern for the new Meiji government and it initially responded by rounding up the dispossessed and placing them in enclosures (just as the former Tokugawa shogunate had done when their policy of forced rural repatriation proved ineffective).[32]

The old facilities designed for these purposes—*yoseba* (stockades)—were clearly incapable of catering to the swelling numbers of the new poor (Ishikawajima only had a maximum capacity of around 300 persons).[33] Moreover, the old *hinin*-administered hospices (*tame*), which were used to house the sick and dying prisoners during the Tokugawa period, also had only limited capacities. The Meiji government replaced these latter institutions with new 'care facilities' (*kyūikusho*) built in the areas of Kōjimachi and Takanawa in 1868. Takanawa was specifically designed for people of low social status and was mooted as a direct replacement for the former *hinin* hospice. The task of looking after vagrants and the sick in this facility was also initially undertaken by Danzaemon and *hinin* under his charge.[34] Although the Takanawa facility was officially closed after the promulgation of the Edict in 1871, this apparently did not alter the fact that the sick and elderly continued to assemble in the building. Eventually, the Meiji state decided to rent the facility out to a private 'non-outcaste' citizen named Fukushima Kahē, who it appears continued to employ 'former outcastes' to look after the patients.[35]

The large *hinin* settlement in Asakusa (mentioned above) located near the Yoshiwara pleasure quarters and directly administered by Kuruma Zenshichi also remained in the same location for some time after the Restoration. As a response to the growing number of homeless people moving to Asakusa and the emergence of a slum area there, Tokyo city officials decided to build a new welfare facility called the *Yōikuin* on the grounds of the old temple Gokokuin in nearby Ueno. Former *hinin* who lived in Asakusa and other parts of Tokyo along with many other poor people were subsequently rounded up and sent there. As opposed to the former designation for vagrants—*nobinin*—the label *kyūmin* (the 'destitute') began to be used to refer to these displaced persons.[36]

Former facilities like the yoseba that were used to house 'wild *hinin*' during the Tokugawa period were initially built in response to the need for stabilizing a social status system under threat. But the new Meiji facilities operated according to a different logic—one governed by an emerging capitalist sentiment. Yōikuin was actually established by the Tokyo Meeting Hall run by a committee of officials that included entrepreneurs like Nishimura Shōzo (one of the first 'non-former outcaste' shoe manufacturers in Meiji Japan). Nishimura quickly realized the economic potential of this 'destitute' community as a source of labour and sent instructors from his shoe factory in Asakusa to the Yōikuin to teach its residents the art of cobbling. Such a response was significantly different from the way in which the Tokugawa shogunate had dealt with the problem of poverty. While the destitute in Tokugawa Japan were also rounded up and sent to labour camps during the latter half of the Tokugawa period, it was widely recognized that begging was a legitimate activity with strong religious associations and that it should be strictly regulated and policed rather than prohibited. As Shiomi notes, by banning mendicancy as a legitimate income-earning activity, the early Meiji state essentially began to treat all poor citizens as people not engaged in productive labour.[37]

Clearly, new legislation and government policies during the early Meiji period meant that residents of 'former outcaste' communities as a rule lost their monopoly on certain industries and, consequently, the basis for their economic livelihoods. At the same time, however, it also meant that residents of areas like 'New Town' were legally permitted to move freely from location to location, and occupation to occupation. Many individuals presumably chose this path of social mobility during the post-Meiji era. While communal ties of places like 'New Town' were undoubtedly strong for much of the Tokugawa period, early state policies basically worked to weaken communitarianism amongst members of 'former outcaste' settlements and social mobility was undoubtedly practised.[38]

However, while numerous people renounced their former outcaste status and identity in the new Japan, it is equally feasible that many also did not. In some areas, like the Kyoto district of Yanagihara discussed above, no amount of discontinuity, change and upheaval seemed to permit the residents of this area to leave the past behind.[39] Strong local convictions about the need for historical continuity, the nature of people, the desirability of certain occupations, and well-established collective practices of social memorization kept a firm hold on the present and continued to define the ways people identified with each other. In these kinds of areas, the residents undoubtedly continued to battle the harsh effects of modernization from the comfort and relative stability of the traditions and networks of their former communities. This identification, of course, was still rooted in the problematic practice of probabilistic association, for clearly, many members of this 'former outcaste' community did not have premodern ancestral links. But for communities like Yanagihara, the associations were strong enough to continue for multiple generations. Perhaps more frequently, however, close community ties formed during the Tokugawa period began to unravel after several generations, and the reality that many 'core residents' had drifted out of these 'problem areas' were widely recognized only after several decades had passed.

Social mobility by itself, however, offered no firm guarantee that discrimination rooted in premodern systems of classification would be eradicated. Modern 'outcaste areas' without clear premodern origins also emerged during the post-Meiji period and a myriad of different people became targets of social marginalization as a result. As mentioned above, Dan Naoki tried his hand at several leather businesses located outside the 'New Town' area during the early Meiji period. Such activity demonstrates that leather production was no longer subjected to the same geographical restrictions that it had experienced during the Tokugawa period and that different areas for leather work developed in the post-Meiji world. One such famous area in Tokyo was Kinegawa. Located in the Higashi Kuroda area, Kinegawa was an area that became famous for the production of pig leather, oil and animal fat only after the Restoration. It was originally selected as a prime location for tanning because it had ready access to a good water supply and was on a vacant lot located sufficiently far from the city so that smell and water pollution would have little impact on the surrounding communities.[40]

The area was originally called Katsushikano and was a former hunting ground of the Tokugawa shogunate. Historically, only a very small farming community and one tiny *hinin* settlement were located in the immediate vicinity. The *hinin* community was overseen by an individual called Kūbē and in 1800, the settlement consisted of a mere seven households. In 1868, moreover, in a list prepared by Danzaemon for the Meiji government, Kūbē is recorded as having 'absconded' (*kakeochi*) and his new replacement was simply listed as a certain Monjirō, a *hinin* hut leader living within the grounds of the Kōsaiji temple in the township of Sarue. It is unclear whether this individual even came to reside in the grounds of the old settlement and as Shiomi notes, there are few if any *hinin* colonies associated with modern buraku areas.[41] There is, therefore, no direct relationship between the location of this small *hinin* community and the development of a post-Meiji pig leather industry in the area.

Workers from Danzaemon's former settlement in 'New Town', people from other eastern Japanese 'former outcaste' communities, 'former outcastes' from western prefectures (particularly Shiga prefecture), as well as tanners from non-outcaste companies like the Sakuragumi, all came to be involved in leather work in Kinegawa.[42] It is easy to envisage a scenario in which many of the workers who came to the area during the early Meiji period at a time of rapid urbanization and industrialization were from 'former outcaste' communities around Japan. Information about the large number of factories sprouting in the area was doubtless spread by word of mouth and through familial networks, with the latter most likely being an important source of information for employers who were interested in expanding their workforces. A large number of the skilled labourers who entered this industry were, therefore, almost certainly from 'former outcaste' communities. At the same time, however, there is ample evidence to suggest that numerous people, who were not originally from 'commoner' communities, also gained employment and received training in the area.[43]

However, residents and workers in Kinegawa were clearly targets of discrimination. Traditional ideas about leatherworkers being socially contaminated as well as old taboos about the skinning and tanning of leather hides did not disappear in the early Meiji world. But discrimination against workers did not singularly rest on these factors alone. Kinegawa workers were also marginalized because they were perceived by others to be engaging in dead-end work that demanded little formal education and long hours. At the same time, however, it is clear that not all workers within the leather industry were uniformly discriminated against. The leather industry was a critical modern industry that supplied goods and products for both the military and the general population. In a country that boasted of a developmental slogan of 'rich country, strong army' (*fukoku kyōhei*), the leather industry (along with the rubber and steel industries) was an important and often lucrative industry, which offered those who generated wealth through it more than a measure of social standing in the wider community.[44] As Kurokawa notes, moreover, Kinegawa actually came to be held up as an ideal 'buraku' community in the 1910s, one that other areas were encouraged to emulate.[45]

While considerable continuity between 'former outcaste' settlements and modern 'buraku areas' in some regions should be acknowledged, it should also be clear through the above discussion that no straightforward link really exists in the transitional process from early modern outcaste communities to modern buraku communities. A wide range of people—wealthy and poor, influential and downtrodden, *eta*, *hinin*, performers, labourers and other assorted actors—came to be lumped together as one group called 'burakumin'. This process began early: the term *eta* was already being mobilized during the early Meiji period so it that it could refer both specifically to members of 'former outcaste' communities as well as other kinds of 'social undesirables'. Government orders such as 'Donations shall not be given to *eta and poverty-stricken people* [italics mine] for any reason if they enter the village', reveal a growing sense whereby any person or group perceived as a threat to the emerging social order became a potential candidate for the label.[46]

Towards a Specialization of Difference

Increasing preoccupation with 'Japanese ethnicity' is a phenomenon that can be dated back to the Tokugawa period (as discussed in Chapter 2). In the 1870s, however, this form of cultural fixation re-emerged with renewed intensity, partly as a result of the discovery of an ancient shell mound by the American scholar Edward Morse (1838–1925). The finding led to a plethora of works published on the historical origins of 'the Japanese'. Writings that discussed the foreign origins of Japan's 'former outcaste' community (drawing on premodern writings of the same orientation) also came into vogue at this time. As Kurokawa notes, terms like 'eta jinshu' (*eta* race) and 'shinheimin jinshu' (new commoner-citizen race) came into more frequent usage from around this time onwards.[47] Residents of the 'former outcaste' area Yanagihara discussed above were referred to, for example, as a 'special tribe' (*shuzoku*) in one publication. In another area, a proposal to merge a 'new commoner-citizen' settlement with a nearby village was rejected because the latter community claimed that the former 'had different customs and attitudes'.[48]

'Former outcastes' were increasingly portrayed during the subsequent decades of the late 1800s as a troubling social group with a strong degree of cohesion and whose difference was special and distinctive. An early evidence of such a perspective is found in the work of Fukuzawa Yukichi's student, Takahashi Yoshio, who compared 'former outcaste' groups to families with 'leprous bloodlines' in a discussion of genetic endowment.[49]

During the 1880s, the idea that 'new commoner-citizens' had 'barbaric customs' and were essentially 'obstinate' also gained popularity in publications such as newspapers (Kurokawa notes that one tabloid report even suggested that 'they' were building explosives).[50] Discourses that emphasized the absolute alterity of these people as essentially diseased and unhygienic bodies also became popular during this time. The idea that 'former outcastes' posed a variety of threats to the government and the well-being of the general population began to proliferate. Many 'former outcaste' communities were certainly adversely affected by the loss of their occupational monopoly and the deflationary economic policies of the 1880s, and poverty and disease were real issues for residents. But by including tags like 'shinheimin buraku' (new commoner-citizen area) after reports of cholera outbreaks in certain areas, newspapers helped contribute to a worsening perception of the attributes of these areas in the popular imagination.[51]

A growing link was also established between poverty, illness and a supposed lack of social morals. Writings tended to suggest that indolence and the lack of good hygiene were a direct result of a problem that ran much deeper: a failure of character. Those unable to observe the new civilizational standards of hygiene and cleanliness were considered to be failing in other broader areas of social conduct and were only one short step away from committing more scandalous crimes. Poverty was reconstituted as the result of a failure of people to help themselves by being diligent and productive. Late nineteenth century leaders in 'new commoner-citizen' areas, at this time, also became increasingly conscious of the penetrating gaze of outsiders who scrutinized their residents over matters of hygiene, cleanliness, and other 'good habits'.[52] These same leaders were keenly aware, moreover, that the accusatory stares of outsiders were not necessarily directed at them personally. Many community leaders, therefore, turned their attention inwards and linked the reasons for their discriminatory treatment at the hands of mainstream society to insufficient effort on the part of the residents to reform. The need for transformation of not only the physical environment of these communities but also the inner morality of residents was, therefore, propagated as a necessary precondition for the eradication of social discrimination.[53]

Reframing social difference within the language of the 'Other', however, was not just something that occurred in relation to 'former outcaste' communities. References to poverty and illness may have included mention of 'former outcastes' and 'new commoner-citizens' but that did not restrict the reference to them. As one mid-1880s report stated for example: 'With regards to this year's [1886] sudden jump in cholera outbreaks, the best solution is to gather up *all unclean people* in the one place and to set up a method whereby the towns and villages *where former eta and others live* are herewith the most hygienic [italics mine].'[54] As McCormack notes, moreover, it was also during this time that what he has labelled as 'ethnographies of urban poverty' began to be published in Japan. Particularly notable during the last decade of the nineteenth century, works such as Yokoyama Gennosuke's (1870–1915) *Nihon no kasō shakai* (Japan's

Lower Class Society, 1899) and Matsubara Iwagorō's (1866–1935) *Saianmoku no Tokyo* (In Darkest Tokyo, 1897) attempted to 'direct public attention at the poor, motivated by a desire to promote national solidarity and minimize social disharmony, and by the notion that the education and development of the poor was necessary for the progress of the country, as well as to prevent crime, disease and disorder.'[55] Works profoundly influenced by Social Darwinism and rooted firmly in increasingly rigid conceptions of ethnicity also addressed the issue of social marginalization in ways that tended to particularize difference.[56]

The Meiji state's response to a problem that was increasingly referred to in the language of 'buraku' (understood here in the broadest sense of 'former outcaste' areas, slums, and all other communities of socially marginalized persons) began in earnest during the early 1900s when the head of homeland security in the Ministry of Home Affairs, Arimatsu Hideyoshi, became governor of Mie prefecture. Arimatsu had joined the Ministry's Research Committee on Poverty in 1900 and his interest in the relationship between poverty and 'buraku areas' had begun around this time.[57] Arimatsu also inherited a policy of 'rural improvement' (*chi'iki kaizen*) from the former governor of the prefecture that was part of a larger national drive to improve social conditions in regional centres after the Russo–Japanese War (1904–05). Turning from national to social concerns after this costly war, the Meiji state's vision of what a 'good citizen' should look like became the subject of increased scrutiny as large-scale social unrest, including riots in the Tokyo suburb of Hibiya, rocked the nation. In a speech given to Shigō Village residents in 1906, for example, Arimatsu announced that while it was an extremely regrettable situation that people who performed military service and paid taxes like everyone else should be targeted by discrimination, it was 'unavoidable that the community be treated with suspicion because statistically this "buraku" had many criminals'.[58]

The leadership stratum of numerous regional 'special buraku' (tokushu buraku) communities (along with leaders like Arimatsu) also began to establish associations for working towards the improvement of local communities by bettering morals and behaviour. The League Association for the Improvement of Morals in Shizuoka prefecture and the Youth Society for Moral Development in Wakayama prefecture were all established around the same time.[59] The possible influence of socialism on 'special buraku' increasingly became a concern for national and local elites. The source of this concern was eventually 'confirmed' after the arrest of several people in 1910 with links to 'special buraku' for allegedly plotting to kill the Emperor.[60] The following year the government promptly set up incentive programmes for 'buraku' from the national treasury and ordered both branches of the Buddhist Honganji temple to work towards the improvement of 'the 800,000 people living in the 4000 or so special buraku'.[61]

In 1912, the *Yamato dōshikai* (Yamato Brotherhood Society) was established by powerful figures within a Nara 'special buraku' community and branches of the society were subsequently set up in Okayama, Izumo, Hiroshima, Kyoto and Mie in 1913. The movement was part of a perceived need to incorporate 'special buraku' into the Japanese nation and create an avenue for belonging in order to defuse the potential radicalization of these communities. A leading figure behind this movement, Matsui Shōgorō (1869-1931), was an imperial loyalist, and publications of the society like *Meiji no hikari* (Light of Meiji, 1912–1918) clearly centred around the key ideas of loyalty to the Emperor and the successful 'integration' (yūwa) of 'buraku' into Japanese society.[62] As Kurokawa notes, 'integration' was usually portrayed in publications as something that would come about as the result of a significant intellectual and industrious effort on the part of 'buraku' residents to attain levels of achievement in education and business on par with people in mainstream society.[63] As a consequence, 'buraku' communities were occasionally praised for successful efforts to improve themselves. On other occasions, however, suggestions were made that it would simply be easier for all parties concerned if 'these people' were to relocate to Japan's frontiers—Hokkaidō, Okinawa, or Korea—or even overseas because this was the easiest strategy for achieving liberation from discrimination.[64]

As can be witnessed through the newly emerging appellation 'special buraku', ideas of race continued to be a potent source for the specialization of difference around this time. While writing one of the first academic treatises on the 'special buraku' in 1913, Yanagita Kunio identified them as areas wherein unemployment, poor living conditions and poverty were rife—possibly because of racially divergent origins.[65] Yanagita placed this analysis in a narrative of 'outcast/e history', suggesting that the issue was a historical one. There were, however, considerable ambiguities in his perspective. He undermined historical continuity in this group by suggesting, for example, that 'there are today many kinds of people with very different economic conditions or social statuses who are to be found within the class called 'special buraku'.' The word 'special' in this document, too, was printed with the character signifying a meaning closer to race. Yanagita also compared '*eta* and other special buraku' indicating that he was aware that there was a 'non-*eta*' stream of 'special buraku'.[66] At the same time, though, he presented the buraku as a distinct and tightly bound social group with specific features.[67] Moreover, his work also made the suggestion that they were a 'class' of people whose labour could contribute significantly to Japan's modernization.[68]

In 1914, the national government established the *Teikoku kōdōkai* (Imperial Way Society) in response to these developments. Its two founding leaders were Itagaki Taisuke and Oe Taku, both famous for their activities related to the promotion of popular rights during the Meiji period. The Society pressed for the urgent resolution to the 'buraku' problem, which was perceived as a hindrance to Greater Japan's successful attainment of status as a first-rate imperial power, particularly after its annexation of Korea. Concerns about the independent establishment of self-help societies by residents in 'special buraku' communities were also voiced by leaders, who thought it best that these groups be absorbed into a national society.[69] From a state perspective, 'buraku' were increasingly conceived of as a recalcitrant social category threatening Japan's attainment of a more complete modernity. Kurokawa also notes that there was an attempt by state officials around this time to push for the adoption of the new label 'poor buraku' (*saimin buraku*) in place of 'special buraku' because of this growing concern.[70]

These concerns also led government officials in urban centres like Tokyo and Osaka to carry out statistical research in order to identify and reform all problem areas. As Mizuuchi Toshio notes, government surveys at this time were not restricted to 'former outcaste' areas but also included the residential areas of factory workers and day labourer districts.[71] It is clear that the term 'tokushu buraku' (特殊部落 'special buraku') did not necessarily refer singularly to a minority group that lived in a firm, bounded community at this time, but was rather a label with a 'catachrectic effect' used to refer to a constellation of people who lived in 'special areas'. One 1916 document produced at the request of the head of the medical department of an Osaka Leprosy Sanitarium (*Raibyō ryōyōjo*), for example, listed a total of 10,347 'special buraku' (using both variations of the word 'special' mentioned in Chapter 2) in 45 prefectures, which included former outcaste communities ('people formerly known as *eta*') as well as more generic groups like 'poor areas'.[72] The term was evidently applied to various social phenomena and not just 'former outcaste' communities. The 1922 Matogahama Incident further highlights this ambiguous aspect of the word. A *sanka* community[73] in Beppu (Kyūshū) was razed to the ground by local authorities on 25 March of that year because of an impending visit by the Emperor. Interestingly, one of the phrases used in some newspapers to describe the area (or community) in which this incident took place was 'buraku'.[74] In the 1910s and early 1920s, then, diverse groups qualified as 'buraku' without automatically having a clearly discernible 'outcaste pedigree' linked to early modern *eta* and *hinin* communities. At the time, 'burakumin' seemed to imply both 'people from special areas' (i.e., slums) as well as a distinct minority group with an outcast/e (senmin) heritage.

Government surveys of 'buraku' were doubtless designed to survey areas considered to be beds of criminality and possibly places of political resistance. The Rice Riots of 1918 seemed to further confirm the suspicions of both the government and elites who were demanding the immediate integration of 'special buraku' into Japanese society. Large numbers of people including residents from 116 'buraku' areas located in 22 different cities and prefectures participated in this large-scale disturbance and as a result, the government immediately moved to strengthen security measures in relation to these areas. The amount of money contributed from the 'Imperial Funds' allocated to 'buraku' areas was also increased and rhetoric was stepped up about all people being 'children of the Emperor'. 'Assimilation' (*dōka*), a principle also used in relation to colonial territories like Okinawa and Taiwan, became an important discourse for targeting 'buraku'. However, assimilation, said to be achievable within the context of a proper loyalty and respect for the Emperor, was clearly not possible for all members of Japanese society.

While the Japanese state had little problem embracing 'buraku' residents as citizens and soldiers during the Asia–Pacific War, and was clearly comfortable in expecting the same ultimate sacrifice from them as they did of every other citizen, discrimination against residents of these areas was apparently quite prolific in the military before the 1930s.[75] 'Buraku', in prewar Japanese society, were clearly incompatible with an Emperor considered to be a pure embodiment of the national polity. Another troubling evidence of this can be found in the modern transformation of the Hora 'buraku' community in Nara prefecture. This community was located at the base of a certain Mount Unebi, which in the modern era was 'identified' as the burial mound of the mythical emperor Jinmu. The village was forced to relocate en masse to a nearby stretch of land in 1917 after a national project designed to expand works on the fictional tomb was announced. The mass relocation was undoubtedly spurred on by a series of writings, which expressed outrage that a 'holy plot and sacred site' was 'subjected to such extreme desecration'.[76] While there is evidence that Hora was considered to be a 'former outcaste' village during the Tokugawa period, it is clear that the community really began to encounter sustained social discrimination after the realities of nation-building and emperor-centred politics took centre stage during the first quarter of the twentieth century.[77]

Formation of 'Buraku Culture'

A group of young radical activists centring around the figures of Saikō Mankichi, Komai Kisaku, and Sakamoto Sei'ichirō, who were opposed to the ideas of assimilation and self-improvement insisted upon by proponents of Yūwa policy, came together to form the All Japan Suiheisha Movement in 1922. They insisted on the right to a decent existence and the complete abolition of discrimination against 'special buraku'. On 3 March, at the first official meeting of the organization, an estimated 3000 people converged on the Okazaki Public Hall in Kyoto. Those in attendance heard the famous Suiheisha Declaration, a plea for all 'Tokushu burakumin' throughout the country to unite and 'be proud of being *Eta*'.[78]

The Suiheisha movement had multifaceted activist and conceptual origins. Saikō Mankichi (1895–1970), the central figure in the movement, was born in Minami Katsuragi-gun in Nara prefecture as the eldest son of a Pure Land Buddhist temple priest. He completed studies up to high school before dropping out and forming an association with Sakamoto Sei'ichirō (1892–1987). After recovering from a protracted illness, Saikō established the 'Black Tide Society' (*Kuroshiokai*) with Sakamoto and Komai Kisaku, and made plans to move to Celebes. In 1920, however, Sakamoto launched the 'Swallow Society' (*Tsubamekai*) and the group began participating in activities conducted by the Socialist Alliance. In 1921, after travelling to Kyoto to meet Sano Manabu, Saikō, along with Sakamoto and Komai, decided to establish the Suiheisha movement.[79]

Shiomi Sen'ichirō has argued that Sano Manabu was the actual father of 'Marxist buraku interpretation'. Sano's brief paper on the topic published in July 1921 contained many of the key interpretative concepts that would become so commonplace during the postwar era, particularly the idea of 'buraku' being a 'feudal remnant' (*zanshi*).[80] Sano, however, also incurred a considerable intellectual debt to a certain Kita Sadakichi (1871–1939). Kita, a historian, was the first scholar to openly reject the idea that people from 'special buraku' were 'foreign'. In 1919, he published a special edition of the journal *Minzoku to Rekishi* (Ethnicity and History), entitled the 'Research Edition of the Special Buraku' *(Tokushu buraku kenkyūgō)*. The bulletin contained the striking expression 'Tokushu buraku no kaihō' (liberation of the special buraku)—perhaps the earliest articulation of the idea of 'buraku liberation' in Japan. The insertion of the idea of 'liberation' in this volume was historic. It signalled an acceptance of 'special buraku' as places with a relatively unified and oppressed people in need of emancipation. Kita revealed both a conception of history as the basis for political action, and an assumption that assimilation into Japanese society was the desirable path of buraku liberation.[81]

Sano, following Kita, also framed the 'buraku problem' as a historical one and suggested that the path to 'special buraku' liberation lay in their ultimate assimilation into Japanese society. Arguing that the Meiji Restoration was an incomplete Bourgeois revolution, Sano pointed to the shortcomings of the Emancipation Edict of 1871 in challenging Tokugawa traditions of 'class policies' (*kaikyū seisaku*). He described the subsequent plans for liberation established by the government, philanthropists, and the organizations formed to deal with hygiene and youth, and their respective failure. Following the spirit (and language) of the Wilsonian principle, Sano argued that the first principle of buraku liberation had to be a struggle for independence (*jiritsuteki undō*).[82] Sano also emphasized the need to unify the proletariat through the eradication of outdated social beliefs. Activists like Saikō, Komai and Sakamoto devised their plans for political action by drawing on such interpretations. The Suiheisha Declaration of 1922 was, in fact, heavily influenced by Sano's 1921 piece on 'special buraku liberation'.[83] The conceptual models of buraku history, first outlined by Kita and further developed by Sano, were also thereafter frequently used among the increasingly active Suiheisha activists and intellectuals.

Other activists quickly joined the Suiheisha movement. Particularly important among them was Matsumoto Ji'ichirō (1887–1966), a person whom Miyazaki Manabu has labelled as the 'god of burakumin' (buraku no kamisama).[84] Born in the village of Kanehira in Kyushu in 1887, Matsumoto established an organization called the *Giyūdan* (Righteous Brotherhood) in opposition to the youth groups being organized by the government at the time in 1903. After spending three years wandering around China, he returned to Japan and built up his own arm of the family business. In 1921, in protest against the costs of a festival to honour a former warrior clan who reigned over the region, Matsumoto created the *Chikuzen kyūkakudan* (Chikuzen Region Protest Leather Group). He then responded to a call to join the Suiheisha movement by forming the All Kyūshū Suiheisha in 1923. The following year, he called for the resignation of Tokugawa Iesato and was arrested on allegations of plotting to murder him. In 1925, he was elected Chairman of the Suiheisha movement and remained a leading (and often controversial) figure of the buraku liberation movement until his death. Matsumoto was instrumental in re-establishing the movement during the postwar period and as a politician, he visited Australia, China and India—once even meeting B.R. Ambedkar, the foremost leader of the 'untouchables' at that time in India.

The establishment of the Suiheisha movement was certainly instrumental in helping to construct a more consolidated image of a group of scattered people, who had historically suffered a relatively uniform kind of discrimination. But this vision of 'special buraku' was certainly not necessarily subscribed to by all who participated in it. The idea of what constituted 'buraku' could still vary from place to place and person to person. In contrast to Kita's analysis that gave buraku discrimination a specific historical basis, some progressive sections of the Suiheisha movement suggested that there was no essential difference between the 'buraku problem' and the social inequality experienced by the lower classes. At the beginning of the 1930s, these branches of the Suiheisha movement put forward a case for the merger of the Suiheisha and labour movements. Other elements of the Suiheisha, however, completed disagreed. Many were already subscribing to the idea that 'special buraku' had a distinct historical legacy. Some, though, preferred to envisage the Suiheisha essentially as a radical union designed to protect the interests of the poor, underprivileged, and underrepresented.[85] Considerable numbers of activists during the prewar period also hinted at the universality of the buraku problem and the potential of linking movements such as the Suiheisha movement with similar ones in Korea and India.[86]

In stark contrast to this movement, organizations advocating policies of assimilation and integration (yūwa), also continued to proliferate, focusing intently on strategies for national reconciliation. The idea that increasing the overall wealth of 'buraku' areas while encouraging allegiance to the emperor and a belief in the mutual benefits which could be achieved through national devotion was a key focus of much of this activity. Organizations like the Mutual Love Association (*Dōaikai*), which was established in 1921 by an assistant professor at Tokyo University (and the son of a wealthy noble), Arima Yoriyasu, were unique in that they strongly advocated the idea that only 'buraku people' could really eradicate discrimination by organizing themselves together. The Association sponsored educational projects, land reclamation and work projects.[87] In 1925, the Central Yūwa Project Council (Chuō yūwa jigyō kyōkai) was also established to coordinate works aimed at improving 'buraku' areas at a national level. In 1927, however, the Teikoku kōdōkai and Dōaikai merged into the Central Yūwa Project Council, effectively signalling a government take-over of the Yūwa movement with the express aim of undercutting the radicalizing Suiheisha. Hiranuma Kichiro, a firm advocate of the principles of equality under the Emperor, became chairman of the movement. Under his leadership, the Central Yūwa Project Council 'was brought under strict central control and became one more part of the national mobilization policy.'[88]

Despite the obvious effect that the specialization of social difference in the form of 'buraku' had on socially marginalized people in Japanese society, there was, however, still no consensus or clear definition of what constituted 'buraku' in the early twentieth century. 'Special buraku', the term that emerged during the first quarter of the twentieth century to deal with this difference, was, more often than not, used in the sense of a distinctive 'area' or 'settlement' rather than in the sense of an area housing a well-defined former outcaste community. In numerous cases, these areas overlapped with the sites where historic outcaste communities had been located, but more importantly, the overlap was *assumed* through a process of probabilistic association. Poverty, low matriculation rates, criminality, and questionable hygiene were treated as the exclusive deficiencies of historic 'former outcaste' communities rather than as a shared characteristic of areas with low socio-economic status. Even during the period from the 1920s to the early 1940s, the word 'buraku' was being used to refer to rural farming communities, economic collectives, Russian settlers in Manchuria, clan groups in Korea, and tribal areas in New Guinea.[89] As early as in 1910, a newspaper tried to draw its readers' attention to this process of probabilistic association:

> The word "special buraku" simply means different to the lifestyles of ordinary folk and does not necessarily refer to communities known by the old label *eta*. That is just a literal interpretation. The real inference is that the unique condition of a non-mainstream lifestyle is immediately connected to old customary ideas remaining in people's heads and therefore is certain to awaken feelings of hatred and contempt.[90]

By the second quarter of the twentieth century, wider shifts linking 'special buraku' to premodern outcaste communities began to appear. In 1934, for example, Osatake Takeki published a well-known treatise entitled 'The Abolition of the Appellation "Special Buraku"'. In it, he argued that the 'the abolition of the appellation tokushu buraku—namely *Eta and Hinin*—is a large and praiseworthy event in the history of human rights *(jinken)*...' This paper, however, was basically a reproduction of a 1925 piece labelled 'The Abolition of the Appellations *Eta Hinin*', which at the time had not even made one reference to 'special buraku'.[91] It is interesting to note that Osatake's revision of the text and the inclusion of the new lexicon 'special buraku' coincided with the establishment of legislation for a 'buraku committee' by the National Suiheisha Standing Committee during the same year. Ian Neary has also described how the writer of the script for the movie *Fujin Sendara* (a 1934 film about 'outcast/es' in eastern Japan during the Tokugawa period)[92] responded to initial Suiheisha criticism by maintaining that he had portrayed the lives of *hinin*, and that the story had nothing to do with 'special buraku'. After a sustained denunciation campaign, the writer changed his mind: he eventually even expressed gratitude to the Suiheisha for making him examine the problem in depth.[93]

These examples hint at a small but growing consensus in terms of the way in which the problem of 'special buraku' came to be understood during the 1930s. The idea of 'special buraku' as a historical phenomenon emerged along with the increasing influence of dialectical materialist thought and positivism in prewar writing on history and in certain sectors of the Suiheisha movement. While noting a growing influence of Marxist texts on key Suiheisha activists like Asada Zennosuke in the late 1920s, Neary comments that the 1930 national Suiheisha conference, for example, 'was conducted almost entirely in terms which derived from Marxist sources.'[94] Relying on structures to understand society and human behaviour, and believing in the premise that certain phenomena can be objectively revealed as 'truth', some scholars and social activists came to articulate the existence of a unified, historically constant outcast/e group of 'burakumin', despite the fact that outside of their small circle, considerable interpretative diversity remained within understandings of 'special buraku'.

Although there was little clear sense of a 'buraku identity' during the prewar period, a handful of elite Marxist historians involved with a small group of former Suiheisha activists eventually succeeded in establishing a unified discourse on the physical and conceptual continuity of 'burakumin' during the early postwar period.[95] Inoue Kiyoshi's three-pronged explanation (*sanmi ittairon*) of the reasons for the emergence of buraku difference were particularly important, as they addressed not only the causal factors of the buraku problem that could be empirically investigated through historical research but also the potential areas that needed to be targeted by activists within the liberation movement to facilitate emancipation.[96] Historians and activists alike were undoubtedly unified by their belief that historical research could make sense of postwar Japanese society and was an indispensable tool for buraku liberation.[97]

Conclusion

Activists and historians clearly constituted a key driving force behind the move in the late 1910s and early 1920s to ascribe to 'special buraku' an interpretative framework that would serve to counter state-led attempts to create, identify, and particularize social difference in modern Japan. State- and media-propelled discourses of difference were reconfigured to become powerful discourses of resistance rooted in history, many of which laid the foundations for an understanding of the buraku problem that is still ubiquitous today. The emergence of these discourses of difference and resistance, moreover, was unmistakably influenced by ideas of emancipation and liberation (*kaihō*) that became increasingly important in Japan from the latter half of the nineteenth century onwards.

In the West, as Raymond Williams has noted, the idea of 'liberation' first came into usage in the English language in the middle of the fifteenth century and initially meant 'to set free' or 'release from', particularly in legal and administrative terms. In the twentieth century, the word was used in the names of groups that resisted fascism during World War II, and then in organizational titles dedicated to the armed overthrow of occupying powers or forces. The later use of liberation by the women's movement was linked to the activities of these political movements in the 1940s and 1950s. Closely associated with the history of the word 'liberation', moreover, was the notion of 'emancipation', frequently used in the nineteenth century, particularly in relation to the slave abolition movement. According to Williams, the discursive swing from emancipation to liberation in the early twentieth century marks an important shift away from ideas of the removal of disabilities or the granting of privileges among historical subjects to more active ideas of winning freedom and self-determination.[98]

Jan Nederveen Pieterse has further mapped the history of the idea of emancipation/liberation in the West, arguing that it was part of the language of the late eighteenth-century French Revolution and was tightly bound up in the political philosophy of the early nineteenth century. Early ideas of emancipation signalled a movement towards individual freedom and equality through a mobilization of collectivity and were closely interwoven with the idea of progress (of increasing equality).[99] Two important themes that emerged during the nineteenth century were the questions of the 'national' and the 'social', and these played an important role in delineating how emancipation was understood thereafter. Questions were raised about the extent to which emancipation could (or should) be realized within the framework of the collective and a national body. In the mid-nineteenth century, the 'social' became all-important but was eventually overshadowed in the latter half of the century by the 'national question'. The first half of the twentieth-century, however, saw the re-emergence of the 'social question', but firmly within the framework of the state. Emancipation, thereafter, became largely a discourse grounded in the idea of class, which became the centre of gravity in theory as well as in practice.[100] Pieterse also argues that while there have been differing ideas of emancipation within the competing traditions of liberalism and Marxism, there was a more natural affinity with ideas of liberation on the political Left. Emancipation has been closely linked with ideas of resistance, which 'is the default discourse of the Left, causally embedded in terms such as cultures of resistance.'[101]

Post-Meiji ideas of 'outcaste emancipation' as well as the subsequent construction of the idea of a unified body of 'buraku people' in need of liberation are productively understood within this framework.

There are, to be sure, considerable differences between the history of Anglophone notions of 'liberation' and 'emancipation', on one hand, and Japanese notions of *jiyū* ('liberty') and *kaihō* ('liberation'), on the other hand. The Sinologist Harriet Evans has usefully noted in her study of the employment of these same ideographs in Chinese, that there is a considerable difference between the etymology (and, therefore, meaning) of this word and the English word liberation. *Jiefang* (kaihō), she argues, 'had little to do with the notions of individual and personal rights inscribed in the Western humanist tradition... whereas liberation and liberty in English are etymologically the same... the Chinese words for liberation and liberty are contrastive.'[102] As the Chinese word for 'liberty' (*ziyou*) is the same as that used in Japanese (*jiyū*), Evan's call for a distinction between English and Chinese notions of liberation and liberty can reasonably be extended to the Japanese case as well. Notwithstanding this important difference, however, considerable correspondence between emancipatory movements in the West during the mid-nineteenth and early twentieth centuries, and during the immediate postwar era, and in Japan during these same periods can still be identified.

Assertions of 'liberty', a catchphrase within the Movement for Freedom and Popular Rights (*Jiyū minken undō*), was based on a claim that humans were born free with the right to participate equally in politics and was inspired by the writings of many Enlightenment philosophers. The basic aim of the Movement for Freedom and Popular Rights, moreover, can also be read in the light of Williams's definition of nineteenth-century emancipatory movements as an attempt to grant privileges to certain Japanese people. This movement developed immediately after the Emancipation Edict of 1871 that professed to remove the disabilities (particularly those resulted from labelling) of some subjects like *eta* and *hinin*. The Edict, moreover, was issued only eight years after the Emancipation Act concerning slaves in the United States, and the likely influence of the latter law on the former cannot be ignored. The emergence of the idea of 'buraku' in the early twentieth century and the subsequent development of Yūwa groups and the Suiheisha movement can also be interpreted as the re-emergence of a 'social question' in Japan within the framework of the state after a period of several decades of the dominance of the 'national question' culminating in the Russo–Japanese War.

The idea of 'buraku' emerged during a historical period marked by an increased prevalence of the notions of nation, race and capital. These ideas, combined with the unique set of circumstances that Japan and its citizenry faced during the latter half of the nineteenth century, led to an increased concern among the state and the public with domestic sociocultural difference, which was threatening to damage Japan's attempts at nation-building and expanding empire. Often borrowing the idioms surrounding historical practices of social marginalization, the idea of 'buraku' emerged through a complex process, which saw virtually all sociocultural differences framed as a special historical problem linked to the sociocultural backwardness of a distinctive group of people. Those subjected to these arbitrary attempts by the state and mainstream society to categorize and demonize all social differences in Japan, mobilized the idea of 'buraku' as a discourse of resistance and exploited the revolutionary potential of ideals such as collective class struggle and liberation. The social question in early twentieth century Japan, moreover, re-emerged within a polity that was firmly rooted in the foundational principle of 'one sovereign and his subjects'. This profoundly affected the way in which ideas of social difference and liberation from it were understood.

Relocating twentieth century notions of 'buraku' and 'burakumin' within a history of emancipation/liberation that has its roots in the Enlightenment, and a subsequent global process of suffusion, resistance and recalibration is important. These discourses are predicated upon logics such as 'dichotomic dimensions' and 'theories of ground', which according to Ernesto Laclau's persuasive argument, essentially rely on the neat binary division of the social into opposing forces and the idea of a 'radical chasm' that needs to be overcome by a complete break with the past.[103] While containing tremendous radical potential, 'buraku' and 'burakumin' also deceptively render into actuality things that have no real objective existence: they are simultaneously visions rooted in ideological perspectives with a distinctly modern flavour. The division of Japanese society into 'buraku' and 'mainstream', and the permeation of an idea that there is actually a 'real difference' that needs to be overcome is an idea that emerged during the post-Meiji/prewar era as a result of a range of historical actors (the Japanese government, the general population, scholars as well as 'buraku' activists) struggling over the question of what constituted a desirable society.

5

Walking to Liberty in Osaka

State, Community, and Burakumin in Postwar Japan

Introduction

What is the current state of the buraku liberation movement in Japan? How are burakumin conceiving of their struggle for emancipation in an era wherein government funding solely targeting them no longer officially exists? What kind of activism does Japan's largest buraku liberation organization, the Buraku Liberation League (BLL), currently engage in? This chapter argues that far from being dormant or in decline, buraku communities under the leadership of the BLL are energetically engaged in liberation activism. Facing an uphill battle to secure funding and declining youth membership, the BLL has reinvented itself over the last 15 years through the idea of 'human rights culture' (*jinken bunka*): a term popularized in the Plan of Action document authored for the United Nations Decade for Human Rights Education (1995–2004).[1] Perhaps the most striking example of BLL human rights cultural activism in Japan today is the Human Rights Museum, Liberty Osaka, located at the site inhabited by a historic outcaste community in Naniwa.

Human rights culture, however, is not merely a buraku concern. National and local governments also engage in 'human rights enlightenment activities' (*jinken keihatsu katsudō*) and 'human rights culture town development' (*jinken bunka machizukuri*) through the creation of posters, promotional videos, brochures, festivals, and monuments. National and local government participation in human rights culture discourse must be understood within the context of the particular postwar relationship forged between the state and the BLL. This relationship is defined by what Frank Upham once termed as 'bureaucratic legal informalism' whereby the national government has provided considerable financial support to buraku communities through organizations like the BLL for development projects but little or no endorsement for the enactment of official legalisation criminalizing buraku discrimination.[2] Although human rights culture is probably best conceived of as a joint activity conducted by the state and burakumin, human rights promotional materials produced at the levels of the national government, local community, and BLL, portray and articulate it in markedly different ways. Burakumin are currently engaged in what might best be termed as a 'human rights culture war'. While such a campaign from one perspective might appear 'soft', particularly when compared with more radical social movements, it can also be interpreted following Ian Neary as an effective BLL strategy to 'enforce benevolence' from the Japanese government.[3]

This chapter, then, through a comparative analysis of state, local community (focusing on the Osaka district of Naniwa), and BLL-centred cultural material related to the promotion of human rights, unearths the distinctive ways in which burakumin are conceiving of their historical struggle for liberation in contemporary Japan. Before analysing the different ways in which human rights culture is conceptualized at the state, community, and buraku levels, however, it is first important to understand more about the history of Naniwa and the role that the BLL has played there. The chapter will begin with an examination of the postwar history of state engagement with human rights at the national and local government levels, and analyse the question of how the BLL came to be involved in human rights debates and the reasons behind the emergence of a human rights culture discourse.

Background

Anglophone journalistic writing on the buraku problem frequently projects an outdated and, therefore, somewhat distorted view of contemporary life in former buraku (or dōwa) districts. Some writers, for example, still speak of 6,000 buraku settlements (or even 'slums') housing about three million burakumin. These accounts, in addition to the more obvious problem of being empirically dubious, tend to veer towards anachronism in their emphasis of a national buraku community that is affected by low matriculation and high unemployment rates.[4] Economic factors and social discrimination undoubtedly continue to influence the lives of many buraku communities today. A stroll through formerly affected areas, however, particularly urban sites, reveals the antiquated nature of these older accounts of the buraku problem. Many former buraku areas stand out conspicuously among the surrounding neighbourhoods precisely because of their impressive infrastructure and facilities.

The Human Rights and Taiko Drum Road (Naniwa, 2007). Photo: Timothy D. Amos

In recent times, moreover, buraku communities have been positively reinventing themselves through the idea of 'human rights culture' (jinken bunka). Human rights culture is, in fact, arguably the dominant trope of the contemporary buraku liberation movement. Human rights culture manifests itself in numerous ways. John Davis, for example, describes a traditional Japanese *Obon* festival (Buddhist Festival of the Dead) held in an Osaka buraku neighbourhood in the late 1990s. After describing what might best be characterized as a kind of fancy dress parade, Davis concludes, 'At the centre of all this fun, song, and dance is an important message: respect human rights. Human rights slogans are written on the platform from which the band performs; they are also written on the fans used by the dancers wearing costumes.'[5] 'Human Rights Cultural Festivals', moreover, are held in numerous other former dōwa (or buraku) districts such as Naniwa. The 2007 Naniwa Human Festival, for example, was a popular affair and included attractions such as a 'Get-In-Touch Market', an 'Exciting Movie Marathon', and an 'Experience Food Culture Corner'.[6]

Naniwa has been at the centre of buraku activism and identity politics, particularly since the split in the buraku liberation movement in the late 1960s (discussed below). As outlined in Chapter 2, Naniwa was the site of an early modern outcaste community involved in tanning and secondary leather work including the production of traditional taiko drums (according to one source, approximately 90 per cent of Japan's taiko drums are still made there). It is also home to a large Buraku Liberation and Human Rights Research Institute as well as a museum, Liberty Osaka, dominated by the Buraku Liberation League. Naniwa achieved its position as a focal point within the postwar buraku liberation movement as part of an intriguing power struggle by key activists, who eventually succeeded in shifting the centre of power away from Kyoto to Osaka.

The National Committee for Buraku Liberation (Buraku kaihō zenkoku i'inkai; hereafter NCBL) was originally established in Kyoto in 1946. The new name was employed instead of Suiheisha at the insistence of the noted Kyoto-born activist, Asada Zennosuke (1902–1983).[7] The debate about names, however, also reflected a wider dispute about whether the postwar liberation movement should aim to 'level society' or 'harmonize' (the literal meaning of Suiheisha) and thereby remove difference or 'liberate' buraku people. The Proclamation of the National Committee revealed a decision to follow the latter path but at the same time borrowed verbatim from the Suiheisha Proclamation of 1922, announcing the continuation of a half-century long struggle for buraku liberation against systemic military and police terror.[8]

The NCBL was established for the purpose of 'the complete liberation of the buraku masses', welcoming all prewar buraku organizational members regardless of political affiliation and offering full membership to buraku and non-buraku people alike. Politicians from diverse political backgrounds attended the Buraku Liberation People's Conference held in Kyoto the day following the NCBL's inauguration under the slogan 'liberation of oppressed people through the completion of democratic revolution'.[9] The NCBL experienced difficulty in mobilizing support for this postwar movement, however, with the inaugural meeting only attracting 240 participants nationwide in spite of the fact that travel had been paid for by the Committee.[10] Potential supporters may have been confused by the linkages of this new movement to the prewar Suiheisha, but it is more likely that little clear sense of 'buraku identity' actually existed during the early postwar period.

Morooka Sukeyuki notes that NCBL elitism during this period was an obstacle to its ability to invoke grassroots participation.[11] In 1947, it floated several intriguing policies aimed at 'buraku liberation', such as regaining a foothold in 'traditional buraku industries' like tanning as well as expanding cultural and welfare activities which would improve the physical and mental well-being of buraku residents.[12] Failing to attract popular support, however, the Committee decided in 1948 to clarify the direction of the organization by consulting with numerous academics including Hani Gorō, the noted Marxist historian and teacher of Marxist historian Inoue Kiyoshi (discussed in Chapters 3 and 4).[13] NCBL members like Asada appeared to have held the same faith as earlier Suiheisha activists such as Saikō Mankichi, believing that radical historians could best elucidate the truth about their oppression, providing them with the most powerful weapon in liberation activism.

The Buraku mondai kenkyūjo (Research Institute for the Buraku Problem; hereafter RIBP) was launched the same year in Kyoto as the research arm of the NCBL. It revolved around the figures of Asada and Inoue, who wished to recommence a movement dedicated to the advancement of outcast/e (senmin) issues that could draw on a surge in postwar emancipatory discourse. Initial members of the RIBP reminisced in later life that the institute, at the time of its establishment, was a 'salon with a mission' with a 'free' or 'liberating' atmosphere.[14] The RIBP Charter clearly designated 'buraku' as a 'remnant of the feudal system of social status', situating the institute very firmly within the interpretative framework of the prewar school of *kōzaha* Marxism.[15] The very first journal published by the institute in 1948, however, also suggested that the institute was equally committed to the ideal of objective social science research, assuring its readers that: 'When natural science shines its light on all of the darkness within nature's relationships, the eye of social science, with profound knowledge, will expose before all humanity all of the mysteries interwoven into societal relations.'[16] The second chapter of the RIBP's *Articles of Association of the Institute* also stated that the RIBP was primarily established as a place that would undertake 'academic investigation' (*gakujutsuteki chōsa*) contributing to 'buraku liberation'.[17]

The RIBP, however, was not in reality an independent research institute. It had an intimate relationship with the NCBL in terms of management, research, and book/journal publication and sales.[18] A survey of early RIBP publications also suggests that in many ways, it was merely acting as a mouthpiece for the NCBL, frequently and unapologetically publishing highly polemical writings by NCBL activists. The main body of work published within the institute during the early period after its inauguration clearly attempted to clarify the importance of the buraku problem within the larger context of a struggle for socialist democracy.

The first academic style treatises published on the buraku in the immediate postwar period were Matsumoto Ji'ichirō's 1948 volume

Buraku kaihō he no sanjūnen (Thirty Years of Buraku Liberation) and Kitahara Taisaku's 1950 work *Kutsujoku to kaihō no rekishi* (A History of Humiliation and Liberation).[19] Both these works were conscious attempts to instate kōzaha Marxism as the central explanatory narrative in the early postwar buraku liberation movement.[20] In these interpretations, 'buraku' were a 'feudal remnant' who persisted in spite of a revolution at the time of Meiji (an incomplete bourgeois revolution that witnessed events such as the Status Emancipation Edict of 1871). A resolution to this half revolution was still possible if the proletariat united and status distinctions within the working class were removed. In kōzaha historical interpretation, explanation, rationale for action, and the success of liberation were all supplied within one framework and this was obviously important for the NCBL, which (at least theoretically) was involved in activism.[21]

This kind of view also had detractors, however, most notably from within the NCBL itself. Kitahara Taisaku's work, in particular, came under heavy criticism from Takakuwa Suehide. In 1950, Takakuwa, a journalist and academic, wrote a critical article about the impact of a kōzaha faction line on buraku liberation, especially as supported by the former leftwing of the Suiheisha. Although evidently in favour of a dialectical materialist interpretation himself, Takakuwa targeted for review the historical interpretation of the buraku problem and debated the most realistic path for buraku liberation. Takakuwa challenged the view that the modern-day buraku were a tightly-bound historical community—a 'feudal remnant' that was not discarded at the time of the Meiji Restoration. He treated this as an unreflective adherence to an old party line that could possibly lead to a static and increasingly irrelevant path of liberation during the postwar period.

Kitahara responded to Takakuwa by calling his position a 'harmful opinion', but failed to summon up effective arguments capable of dismissing Takakuwa's suggestions that viewing the burakumin as a tightly bound historical minority group was ahistorical and that the kōzaha Marxists were actually creating a problem through this kind of interpretation. The challenge presented by Takakuwa to early postwar Marxist liberation theory was effectively killed, however, by the emergency of Inoue Kiyoshi's liberation theory in 1950. Inoue isolated the root causes of buraku discrimination in what he termed as 'social status discrimination' (*mibun sabetsu*), which allegedly originated with the first sign of class difference in Japan during the ancient period.[22]

Perhaps as a reward for the winning blow he was perceived to have given to Takakuwa in this debate, Inoue was appointed to the Central Committee of the NCBL in 1951 and commissioned with the responsibility of drafting policy for the buraku liberation movement, a position he held until 1963. During the same year that Inoue was appointed to this position, Asada Zennosuke led a group of activists in the NCBL on perhaps the most real 'denunciation' (kyūdan) campaign of the postwar period—the 'All Romance Incident'. In a story published in the magazine *All Romance* called 'Special Buraku', written by a Kyoto public servant, a Kyoto 'buraku area' (actually an area also with a large Zainichi Korean population referred to as 'buraku') was described as a place of poverty and crime, which led Asada to instigate a fiery denunciation campaign against the author and publisher for this 'discriminatory novel'.[23] This was immediately followed by a campaign against the Kyoto Municipal Government for their role in the 'reproduction… of discriminatory ideas about the buraku' through 'administrative stagnation'.[24]

It is clear that Inoue's theory of buraku liberation centring around the removal of material differences in residence and occupation in buraku areas had given Asada a great conceptual impetus for envisaging his own strategy of buraku liberation. Drawing on Inoue's theories, Asada began to stress the importance of viewing buraku discrimination through the realities of economic and social inequalities evidenced in poor living conditions. From this perspective, the only effective form of liberation came through political struggle by burakumin themselves to achieve parity in Japanese society. Asada was clearly interested only in a theory of liberation that would support his actual struggles against local, prefectural, and national governments for concrete policies that would improve the living standards of people living in buraku areas. Moreover, Asada, building on Inoue's work, took this one step further and began to claim that 'the everyday economic demands of burakumin themselves are a struggle against feudal social status relations.'[25]

Inoue's theory of buraku liberation that was not only able to explain in an intellectually sophisticated manner the root causes of the buraku problem but which also supported concrete plans for buraku liberation through demands for material improvement in buraku communities provided a neat platform for subsequent NCBL (renamed BLL in 1955) activism. Importantly, however, Inoue's emphasis on a buraku problem that was eventually going to be dissolved into class also created a perplexing dilemma for many buraku liberation activists. For those like Asada who were committed to the maintenance of a strong buraku identity, concepts of class and status seemed to disguise the true realities of buraku discrimination, which were symbolized by economic and political inequality targeting a minority. While this kind of tension would take more than a decade to fully emerge, it eventually did so in the context of the Culture, Health, and Welfare Assembly Hall Incident: an explosive struggle between Leftwing intellectuals and buraku activists over the appropriate response to the Japanese state's acknowledgement of the necessity to address their demands.

Special Measures and Internal Struggles

On 21 January 1966, Asada faced off against Fujitani Toshio outside the Culture, Health and Welfare Assembly Hall in Tanaka, Kyoto. Asada and Fujitani were very colourful characters. Both were born and raised in roughly the same area in Kyoto, but on different sides of the street. For Asada, born in the heart of the Tanaka buraku area in 1902, life had been characterized by a series of problems: poverty, discrimination, police harassment and violence. By the age of 25, he had had several run-ins with the law including a lengthy stint in prison, and an armed confrontation with the Yakuza (Japanese organized crime syndicate similar to the Mafia). Theoretically self-taught, Asada flirted with anarchism, Bolshevikism, Marxism, and fascist ideology during the years prior to 1945 and had been involved in the Suiheisha movement. In 1946, he became a founding member of the NCBL and slowly built a name for himself as one of the toughest buraku liberation activists in Japan. Fujitani, on the other hand, was a historian trained in Kyoto University and Director of the RIBP, but he was by no means an ivory tower academician. He had served a two-year stint in jail as a student for 'dangerous thought', collared as a result of the 1925 Peace Preservation Law. There was, moreover, no mistaking the postwar Marxist convictions of Fujitani. Stating publicly at his retirement that '15 August 1945 [the surrender date] was one of the happiest moments of his life', Fujitani dedicated his life to overcoming the 'buraku' and 'Emperor' problems—things he considered to be 'feudal remnants' in postwar Japanese society.

Asada and Fujitani stood at the outside entrance of the building that afternoon confronting each other for a number of reasons. During the previous year, Asada had been voted out of his position as Head of the Buraku Liberation League Kyoto Branch Committee (*Dōmei kyoto furen*), and bitterly unhappy with the decision, had decided to stage a *coup d'état*, establishing a new committee with himself as chairman. He then proceeded to forcibly take over the offices of the former Committee located in the Culture, Health, and Welfare Assembly Hall where the RIBP offices were also located. A day earlier, Fujitani and others in the RIBP were shocked to hear that Asada had, without any warning, suddenly declared the RIBP as a 'discriminatory research institute' in response to its weighted criticism of the 1965 findings of the Cabinet Dōwa Policy Council, of which Asada had been a key contributing member. Therefore, on that afternoon of 21 January, Fujitani confronted Asada and read out a carefully worded protest letter drafted earlier that day with the help of some of Japan's leading historians (also attached to the institute). When Fujitani attempted to hand over the letter to Asada, however, he was locked inside an Assembly Hall room, and the tense atmosphere was only diffused after the arrival of a patrol car. The occupation of this building by Asada and his breakaway faction, including the RIBP headquarters, was to last a remarkable 16 years.[26]

The RIBP, however, as mentioned above, was an institute of Asada's own creation, inaugurated in the Marxist historian Inoue Kiyoshi's lounge room in 1948.[27] Asada, moreover, was on the very first board of directors. What, then, had happened for Asada to so resoundingly reject it? The RIBP official histories unsurprisingly describe this incident purely as an internal BLL leadership struggle that spilled over into BLL–RIBP relations because Asada was evolving into a dictatorial leader, who cut off everyone who disagreed with him. Other commentators, however, suggest that the Socialist Party merely used Asada as a way to counter the influence of the Japanese Communist Party (JCP). It certainly appears from the comments Asada made at the time of the incident—'the Communists' (i.e. the RIBP) were 'making everything their own')—that he was consciously attempting to lessen the influence of the Communist Party on the buraku liberation movement. There were, however, perhaps more importantly, significant differences in the ways activists in the BLL and academics in the RIBP were envisaging the buraku problem and the best strategy for buraku liberation, which was visible right from the point of conception of the RIBP. Much of this difference can probably be explained by the way in which the different functions of the two organizations—activism versus research/education—altered the ways whereby the buraku problem and the correct course for liberation were defined.

For buraku activists like Asada Zennosuke, the reality of buraku discrimination from the beginning existed in society itself. While research was of importance in highlighting problems and school education was important for securing an easier path to liberation, it was really only social activism that was able to make people confront the real structural impediments that burakumin faced in their everyday lives. For influential researchers in the RIBP, however, scientific research, in particular historical science coupled with education, was considered as the primary tool capable of bringing about the removal of 'feudal difference' in contemporary Japanese society and producing true democratic equality. Scholars within the RIBP increasingly came to regard buraku discrimination as a result of feudal practices caused by backward thinking that persisted into modernity and which could be structurally altered through popular enlightenment. Proper education and knowledge themselves would lead to the social changes that buraku activists desired because they would foster the right class consciousness that would inevitably produce change. Capitalism, left to its own devices, would also presumably play an important role in eliminating remnants of feudal structures. For activists, however, buraku discrimination was becoming increasingly linked to the political and economic structures emerging within postwar Japanese society.

Certainly, the most divisive issue of the 1960s buraku liberation movement, embodied in the above incident with Asada and Fujitani, was the question of how the movement should respond to the government's position on the buraku problem. In 1965, the Japanese government released its findings in a document called the "The Report of the Dōwa Policy Council" (*Dōwa taisaku shingikai tōshin*). This report became the basis for subsequent government policy on the buraku problem, especially the Special Measures Law of 1969. In its findings, the report defined the buraku problem (referred to in the document as the 'dōwa mondai') as follows:

> The dōwa problem is an extremely serious and grave social problem whereby some groups of Japanese nationals are economically, socially, and culturally placed in a low social position through discrimination that originated in the social status structure formed during the historical developmental process of Japanese society; and have their fundamental human rights violated even in contemporary society, in particular, failing to have their civil rights and freedom fully protected, which are guaranteed to all people as the principles of modern society.[28]

This was a remarkable statement that summarized the contemporary realities of the buraku problem in one long sweeping sentence. The buraku problem was clearly interpreted by the Dōwa Policy Council as a problem that 'originated' in the premodern 'social status structure', and that persisted to the present in the form of a 'low social position'. The modern buraku problem, in this conception, was among 'Japanese nationals', and distinctions among nationals were considered contrary to the fundamental principals of 'human rights' that needed to be encoded in every modern society.[29] This report also became a key rationalization for the Special Measures Law of 1969 that lasted for 28 years and cost the Japanese taxpayer approximately 15 trillion yen.[30] The law was meant as a temporary bill that permitted the government to pour money into what it termed 'dōwa issues' (*dōwa mondai*), which meant, more often than not, the refurbishment of buraku districts, the construction of public housing, public works, cemeteries, community centres, and childcare facilities, and the setting up of anti-buraku discrimination educational programmes in problem areas. It also involved certain welfare measures including lower taxation rates and government scholarships. These laws were renewed until 2002, when finally a decision was made in the Lower House to allow them to expire.

Asada, along with a large number of other activists involved with the BLL, was convinced that the government bill should be seen as a positive development. Other groups, however, notably activists and scholars linked to the Communist Party, were not. With opinion over how best to react to the Special Measures legislation divided, the buraku liberation movement split into two, with the centre of power shifting to Osaka. In place of the RIBP, a rival research institute known as the Osaka Buraku Liberation Research Institute (*Osaka buraku kaihō kenkyūjo*) was newly established in Naniwa in 1969, declaring its primary objective as 'a plan for the complete abolition of buraku discrimination'.[31]

Material conditions in the targeted buraku areas like Naniwa began to improve visibly as the Special Measures legislation was implemented from that year onwards. At the time of the passing of the series of laws related to Dōwa Special Measures in 2002, material conditions had, in fact, improved to the extent that some buraku organizations supported the claim that the buraku issue had essentially been 'resolved'. *Zenkairen*,[32] for example, dissolved itself soon after the last Special Measures Law extension expired. For many in this group, the buraku problem had become, like an object in a museum, a thing of the past that should not be forgotten but also not permitted to dominate every waking moment. The BLL, however, continued to insist that an Anti-Buraku Discrimination Law was still essentially what was needed to end discrimination against burakumin. For these communities, certain aspects of the buraku problem, like discrimination against them because of their occupations in traditional industries like leatherwork, may have mostly become a thing of the past. Other factors, however, including prejudice against burakumin at school, or discriminatory marital practices, were still considered a thing of the present. All buraku organizations, though, tended to acknowledge that with improvements in literacy and matriculation rates as well as employment opportunities and living conditions arose the opportunity to consider the plight of other groups, who were often targeted by mainstream society for discrimination: groups such as Ainu (indigenous people of the northern islands of the Japanese archipelago), Koreans, women, and sexual minorities.

Liberty Osaka, which began its life as a BLL archive in 1985, is now the showpiece in a Naniwa cityscape, overflowing with material cultural products hinting at a distinctive cultural heritage. In Naniwa, almost every sign, poster, building, and activity seems to mention the words 'human rights'. It would appear, in fact, as if human rights culture is just other name for 'buraku culture'. Upon closer inspection, however, a simple equation of the two is misleading. Human rights festivals are not simply independent activities conducted by burakumin. The Naniwa Human Rights Cultural Centre (*Naniwa jinken bunka sentā*), which organizes the local festival, is officially a 'corporation' (*shadan hōjin*) staffed by Osaka public servants as well as local burakumin hired through affirmative action policies. Festivals, moreover, are linked to larger national government campaigns that seek to conduct public human rights awareness programmes throughout the Japanese archipelago through a network joining all the local municipal branches of the Ministry of Justice. Liberty Osaka, too, is officially a 'foundation' (*zaidan hōjin*) but listed as a local government facility by both the Osaka Prefectural Government and Osaka Municipal Government (90% of the funding, in fact, comes from local government). A picture begins to emerge, therefore, of a human rights culture that is not merely the concern of buraku liberation organizations such as the BLL. The state in Japan, at both the national and local government levels, is also deeply involved in its construction.

Towards 'Human Rights Culture'

Liberty Osaka explains its distinctiveness in the following way: 'While there are over 5,000 museums in Japan… there are few that aim to synthetically focus on human rights problems rooted in Japanese history and culture such as the buraku problem, and which contribute to the development of a culture rich in humanity and the permeation of a human rights philosophy through the collection and preservation of fieldwork data and public exhibitions.'[33] Perhaps contrary to these claims, however, Japan does now have quite a number of museums dedicated to human rights issues including the Fennikusu myūjiamu (Phoenix Museum, or the Sakai City Peace and Human Rights Museum; established 1988);[34] the Henomatsu jinken rekishikan (Henomatsu Human Rights Historical Museum; Sakai City);[35] the Suiheisha rekishikan (Suiheisha Historical Museum; established in Nara in 2002); and the Nara kenritsu dōwa mondai kankei shiryō sentā (Nara Prefectural Archive Related to Dōwa Issues; established in 1993). Many of these other museums were also founded by buraku organizations after the 1990s, often with substantial financial contributions from the state. All of these institutions are in some way dedicated to the remembrance of human rights struggles and all were institutions that originated as research centres or educational facilities to discuss the buraku problem. Liberty Osaka, however, probably began the initial push to memorialize the drive for human rights in Japan on the basis of activities of the buraku liberation movement.

Other organizations linked to buraku liberation also experienced name changes during the 1990s, which reflected their move to a concern for issues beyond the 'buraku issue' to matters related to *jinken* or 'human rights'. The Buraku kaihō kenkyūjo (Buraku Liberation Research Institute) became known as the Buraku kaihō jinken kenkyūjo (Buraku Liberation and Human Rights Research Institute) in 1998; and the Hyōgo Buraku kaihō kenkyūjo (Hyogo

Buraku Liberation Research Institute) changed its name to the Hyōgo Buraku kaihō jinken kenkyūjo (Hyogo Buraku Liberation and Human Rights Research Institute) in 2002. Interestingly, the Wakayama Buraku kaihō jinken kenkyūjo (Wakayama Buraku Liberation Human Rights Centre), founded in 1997, simply became the Wakayama jinken kenkyūjo (Wakayama Human Rights Centre) in 2002.

Other name changes have occurred too. In the area of education, for example, June Gordon has discussed the emergence of 'human rights education' in Japan: 'In the 1990s a shift in public perception and economic conservatism led to Government policy changes that could be considered more inclusive. *Dowa kyoiku* [sic], which had focused on addressing the educational disadvantage of *burakumin* children, became *Jinken kyoiku* [sic], or human rights education, and extended to issues of gender, disability and discrimination in general.'[36] This shift in the names and activities of buraku-related organizations in and around the 1990s deserves closer scrutiny. How can these recent changes in contemporary Japan related to buraku organizations be understood? Why have buraku organizations come to change their names to include words and phrases like 'peace' and 'human rights'?

Certainly, the role played by the BLL itself cannot be ignored. An understanding of the changing role of this organization emerges in recorded interviews conducted between a New Zealand researcher Ian Laidlaw and a representative of the organization in 2000. In the interviews, three phases of the twentieth-century buraku liberation movement are mentioned: the first period between 1922 and 1941; the second period from 1946 to 1985; and the third period from 1985 to the present. The period which is most relevant to the discussion here—the third period—was spoken about by the interviewee as having 'three major distinctive features'.

The first feature was the shift within activist circles from attempts to find 'a partial solution to the buraku problem' to a 'total solution'. This was driven by a belief that 'improving housing and going to high school alone' would not 'put an end to buraku discrimination', as well as a belief in the need for a 'Fundamental

Law for Buraku Liberation'. However, a total solution to the buraku problem also embodied the need for a kind of self-extinguishment, something which was obviously unacceptable for people who identified themselves as burakumin and who lived in buraku areas. Preserving a 'buraku culture', therefore, became critically important in the struggle for complete liberation. 'Buraku Liberation Cultural Festivals' were established in a desire to embody 'a movement to retain… traditional buraku culture' such as 'buraku songs, dances, foods and those kinds of things'. But buraku identity also needed to be shifted from one of victimhood and this was achieved through a new desire to 'participate actively in ending discrimination all across Japan and the world.' The shift to culture signals an opportunity for burakumin to think not only about the issue of buraku liberation but the equally important problem pertaining to the kind of emancipation that was desirable.

A second distinctive feature of the post-1985 movement related to the fact that the BLL no longer just wanted to 'improve the buraku areas, but also the areas surrounding the buraku' in addition to targeting forms of discrimination 'such as that against Korean residents of Japan and second-generation Koreans.' This involved the ambitious project of not 'only improving buraku areas, but also turning cities with buraku in them into cities that respect human rights.' The third major distinctive feature was the emergence of the idea of 'international responsibility'. This involved the establishment of organizations such as the International Movement Against All Forms of Discrimination and Racism (IMADR) in 1988 in order to join 'the struggle to end the problem of discrimination all around the world.' One concrete example of this kind of shift can be seen in the BLL's association with the US-based National Association for the Advancement of Colored People (NAACP) in the early 1980s. As part of the exchange between the NAACP and the BLL, it was discovered that some companies, which were engaged in discriminatory employment practices in Japan, were also causing problems overseas. This led to a realization that 'discrimination was occurring at an international level' and the notion that there was a need to 'work toward the elimination of discrimination together, as a joint international responsibility.' The attempt to link the buraku liberation movement to international human rights issues, however, was also partially a BLL response to the promulgation of international conventions on human rights. The International Convention on the Elimination of All Forms of Racial Discrimination, for example, was ratified in 1985, and became an important impetus for the movement.[37]

The BLL's perception of the reasons behind a shift in their focus understandably frames the process as a conscious effort on the part of burakumin leaders who, through an exercise of their own agency, affected changes in the movement. There exist, of course, different explanations, such as those offered by other buraku liberation organizations. One counterargument to explain a buraku preoccupation with the creation of a human rights culture was adopted by Zenkairen (mentioned above). Its members argued that the successful implementation of government policy (specifically the Dōwa Special Measures Law) during the previous decades succeeded in raising living standards and establishing a solid base for the creation of economic wealth in buraku areas. It became possible for burakumin to focus on the creation of a 'human rights culture' precisely because the vast majority of their historical concerns about material disparity had been addressed. The move to establish a human rights culture as part of a new buraku liberation politics in this view is nothing other than an acknowledgement on the part of buraku activists that a large part of the problem has basically been resolved. With the buraku problem now being an issue best described in the past tense in material terms, the argument follows that it is, in fact, quite apt that youth in the former buraku areas are leaving the movement in droves and older members of the BLL are building and working in museums. Debate about a human rights culture is merely a reflection that serious issues affecting burakumin are a thing of the past and the process of creating a new non-buraku identity has begun.[38]

Scholarly treatises written on the relationship between the Japanese state and the buraku liberation movement, however, raise questions about the validity of arguments that locate the reasons for a shift in postwar buraku discourse away from liberation to human rights in either a resourceful display of buraku agency or successful government policy. Frank Upham, for one, has famously suggested that civil society groups in Japan, especially burakumin, are, in fact, managed through a process of bureaucratic 'legal informality'.[39] By this he means that the state, through the adoption of informal negotiation style practices, dissuades civil rights groups from pushing for legal measures to address their concerns. When members of the buraku liberation movement like Asada Zennosuke advocated the adoption of the Special Measures Law in the 1960s, the state succeeded in depoliticizing the buraku liberation movement by encouraging activism based on joint initiatives between the state and civil rights groups (through the concentration of funds in communities in order to help them improve aesthetically and bestow on them additional facilities). By addressing buraku concerns in these relatively 'informal' or 'non-legal' ways, the state managed to defuse a potentially explosive political movement without having to make too many formal concessions. While Upham's text predates the entire shift to human rights culture debate in the buraku liberation movement, the fact that a human rights campaign is also strongly supported by local government and receives considerable national government backing supports Upham's thesis that this is just another case whereby the Japanese state has offered civil rights group funds to engage in 'soft activism' at the expense of more substantive political and legal reforms. This is not to argue, of course, that the state has everything its own way. In more recent times, Ian Neary has suggested that this kind of relationship—which he terms as 'neo-patriarchal'—has been skilfully manipulated by activists:

> The BLL used the democratic structure of postwar Japan to make demands on the State and thus "enforce benevolence", stressing the rights of the buraku communities to make claims on the State rather than insisting on policy that would guarantee liberties or immunities for individual burakumin. The human rights demanded by the BLL challenged power relations in Japan but provoked a benevolent response from the State.[40]

However, the relationship between burakumin and the state should not be oversimplified. Upham's general description of bureaucratic legal informality as a way to capture the overall mentality of the state (particularly the attitudes of Liberal Democratic Party [LDP] politicians and the national government bureaucracy but also to some extent local governments) and the way in which it engages with civil society groups is indeed apt on various levels. It should not be forgotten, however, that bureaucratic legal informality has also meant affirmative action in the area of public sector employment in Japan. Literally thousands of burakumin have been recruited into public service. Kyoto Municipality alone apparently hired 6,000 full-time 'buraku' public servants during the period of tenure of the Special Measures legislation.[41] And while the number of burakumin employed in Osaka is less clear, it is presumably even higher than Kyoto, with a total bureaucracy numbering close to 45,000 in 2005.[42]

In recent times, affirmative action policies adopted during the era of the Special Measures Policy have been censured by the media due to the public exposure of numerous cases of corruption involving members of buraku liberation movements, who apparently abused their positions of public trust. While corruption has, in fact, occurred at sometimes astonishing levels in local governments, particularly in western Japan, it cannot be forgotten that affirmative action also provided organizations like the BLL with opportunities to engage in a revolution from within. Affirmative action, perhaps the penultimate form of bureaucratic informalism, has meant that vast numbers of burakumin were subsumed into the state machinery. The boundaries between local government and organizations like the BLL have, therefore, become so blurred over time that it is often impossible to tell them apart. It is not readily apparent, for example, what the exact relationship is between Human Rights Cultural Centres and the BLL. Moreover, even museums like Liberty Osaka must, in one important sense, be thought of as public institutions. The strong presence of burakumin in local government in western Japan suggests that the old state versus civil society model that Upham applies is obsolete when one is analysing the buraku liberation movement from the late 1970s to the present.

Given the scale of affirmative action in the area of government employment in relation to the buraku problem in western Japan, it is perhaps unsurprising that Osaka is now a leading centre for human rights activism in Japan. It became one of the first municipal cities in Japan to respond positively to a call from the United Nations and create a plan of action for a Human Rights Education Decade in 1994. It is clear, too, that many of the major human rights events that took place during the 1990s in Osaka were organized in coordination with the BLL. As John Davis notes, the fact that the buraku issue plays a central role in human rights events is not 'fortuitous' but 'in many ways it is the product of efforts undertaken by the BLL and affiliated organizations.'[43] Local governments in western Japan were, in fact, extremely quick to engage with the new human rights discourse. HURIGHTS, a foundation established as a joint initiative with the BLL but largely sponsored by the Osaka Prefectural and Municipal governments, was established in 1994. The Osaka Liaison Committee for the UN Decade of Human Rights Education was also established at about the same time.

The national government, however, while being engaged in discussion about human rights from the time of the Universal Declaration of Human Rights in 1948, really appears to have engaged actively in human rights awareness campaigns only from the early 1980s onwards. By ratifying the International Covenant on Economic, Social and Cultural Rights and the International Covenant on Civil and Political Rights in 1979 (with some exclusions), the Japanese government attempted to send a message to the Japanese public as well as to the international community that it considered human rights issues important. There was, of course, a sense in which the government of Japan could not refuse to ratify such internationally recognized documents. During the late 1970s and early 1980s, Japan faced criticism from the international community for its stance towards refugees from Southeast Asia and 'domestic and foreign protest about its general neglect of human rights issues prompted the LDP to approve the decision to create a Human Rights Division in the [Human Rights Protection] Bureau in 1984 with a staff of ten.'[44] Facing continued criticism from the Human Rights Council of the UN, Japan also ratified the Refugee Covenant and the Protocol Relating to the Status of Refugees (October 1981 and January 1982) and the Convention on the Elimination of All Forms of Discrimination against Women (1985). There was, however, almost certainly an additional reason for signing these documents. By doing so, Japan would bolster its position in vying for a permanent seat on the United Nations Security Council. Ratifying these international treaties and demonstrating a concern for domestic human rights issues was perceived to be an important way of presenting the right image to the international community about the state of Japan's postwar democracy and its global leadership credentials.

At the time of the ratification of the International Covenants in 1979, activists within the buraku liberation movement were conscious of the fact that the Japanese government's aversion to legal measures could be challenged by bringing discussion of the ratification of the treaties into public view and linking them to buraku issues. The two covenants were, in fact, signed by the Japanese government on 30 May 1978 at precisely the same time that an extension of the Dōwa Special Measures Law was being discussed in parliament. At a Foreign Affairs Diet Committee meeting on 31 May 1979, moreover, just several weeks before the ratification of these covenants, the secretary of the BLL, Kamisugi Saichirō, took the opportunity to push for the creation of a domestic law on human rights:

> When we take into account the sheer breadth, definitive nature, and endless aspirations of the rights outlined in the International Human Rights Covenant, I think, at this historical juncture, we should establish a domestic law for Basic Law for Human Rights Protection in this country. I also think it is indispensable to create a proper organization such as a Committee for the Promotion of Human Rights to carry out this proposed law.[45]

The foray of BLL leaders into human rights identity politics in the late 1970s was a conscious attempt to adjust to changes in government policy and to redefine their yet unresolved political struggle in global terms, which could then potentially produce some positive effect on the policies of the Japanese state (for example, the extraction of a commitment to establish legislation which criminalized buraku discrimination). There is little doubt that bureaucratic legal informalism became increasingly difficult for the Japanese government to sustain with the ratification of international covenants and agreements related to human rights issues. This provided an impetus for the buraku liberation movement, placing it in a position of strength whereby the Japanese government would constantly be challenged to explain its decision not to draft and pass a bill that criminalized buraku discrimination. Moreover, buraku activists were quick to reinterpret their movement in the light of these documents. The buraku or dōwa problem rapidly, and quite consciously, became couched in the emergent global language of human rights. Moreover, as Ian Neary notes, the BLL was a prominent supporter of the campaign to ratify the UN Convention on the Elimination of all forms of Racial Discrimination (CERD) and it also 'made use of the UN structure in the summer of 1983 when it and the JCP supporting groups both sent representatives to attend the sessions of the Human Rights Committee in Geneva.'[46]

Another popular Japanese government catchphrase from around the same period was 'internationalization' (*kokusaika*). This, too, was mobilized in discussions surrounding the ratification of the aforementioned human rights covenants.[47] It was also mobilized by the buraku liberation movement, including in the Foreign Affairs Diet Committee Meetings held on 31 May 1979.[48] Initially a government discourse that attempted to account for trade friction as essentially a cultural phenomenon which needed to be addressed through the education of Japanese in overseas matters and a foreign audience in Japanese culture, internationalization over time gave momentum to the buraku liberation movement by encouraging its leaders to establish links with the United Nations and transnational human rights groups. It also provided the BLL with an opportunity to frame their movement in larger political discussions focusing on the need for increased 'international understanding' (*kokusai rikai*). Using government funding, the buraku liberation movement, under the banner of internationalization, established links with supranational organizations as well as transnational NGOs that ultimately came to help the BLL in pressurizing the Japanese government to address its human rights issues. The Japanese state's frequent attempts to sidestep appeals to legally address the political concerns of burakumin and their desire to establish informal structures to encourage buraku liberation became tools used against them as 'foreign pressure' (*gaiatsu*) came to bear on the government in the 1980s. The Japanese state could not very well obstruct the BLL's use of a discourse of their own creation because there was a need to demonstrate to the international community that Japan's commitment to 'democratic values' was genuine.

The move in the buraku liberation movement away from pure liberation ideology (*kaihō riron*) to human rights discourse should be seen as occurring within the above context. The BLL saw particular benefits in human rights and internationalization discourse during the 1980s. These discourses matched the needs of the movement whereby issues of material inequality were rapidly being addressed but discrimination against them continued to remain. With concerns about the possible end of the Special Measures legislation ever present, the BLL applied firmer pressure on the national government to establish more formal protective measures. The national government's response was, on the one hand, to try to take the wind out of the sails of the buraku liberation movement. A report produced in 1986–87 by the Consultative Committee for Measures Related to Regional Improvement (*Chi'iki kaizen taisaku kyōgikai*), for example, essentially blamed the evolving negative public image of the buraku liberation movement on internal corruption and adversarial measures like denunciation campaigns adopted by participant buraku organizations such as the BLL. Fujita Kei'ichi's extremely popular text *Dōwa wa kowai kō* (Thoughts on Why the Dōwa Problem is Scary) also further served to bring the buraku problem out into the public eye and to encourage criticism of the movement both from within and without.[49] On the other hand, the national government continued to renew the Special Measures legislation and to encourage local governments to invest money in the establishment of human rights organizations. The national government also established a Centre for Human Rights Affairs in 1987 in response to BLL pressure. Then, with the promulgation and ratification of the International Covenant on Economic, Social and Cultural Rights in 1989, the ground of confrontation between the state (at both the national and local government levels) and the buraku liberation movement became increasingly rooted in a struggle over human rights.

Chronologically speaking, the idea of engaging the state through human rights can probably be conceived of as a BLL strategy designed to alter the terms of reference in a struggle with a recalcitrant Japanese state and an unresponsive society. As John Davis has noted, 'the *dōwa* issue, ordinarily avoided by most' was 'recovered from the realm of the unmentionable when couched within the discourses of human rights and internationalization.'[50] Human rights cultural discourse was, however, simultaneously a product of state-sponsored discourse. The state can be seen, as Davis skilfully demonstrates, as attempting to depoliticize the discourse: constantly engaging in a struggle during this period to make human rights a personal issue between individuals rather than a legal issue between interest groups and the state demanding political and legal treatment. The material cultural products produced by the state at both the national and local levels during recent decades are clear expressions of this particular ethos.

State Human Rights Cultural Discourse

The national government celebrates 'Human Rights Week' from 4 to 10 December every year. The Human Rights Protection Agency explains that this week is a time for 'enlightenment activities aimed at the diffusion and elevation of thought respecting human rights.'[51] The Agency explains its choice of this day as relating back to the declaration by the United Nations in 1950 of 10 December as Human Rights Day. It has apparently celebrated this day ever since but regular activities have been included only in recent decades. The

59th Annual Human Rights Week had as its main theme 'Let's Cultivate a Human Rights Awareness of Each Person: Treasure a Sympathetic Heart and the Invaluableness of Life.' As part of this campaign, the Agency advocated the protection of human rights of women and children; respect for the elderly; a deeper understanding of the Ainu (an ethnic group historically located on the northern Japanese island of Hokkaido); a respect for the human rights of foreigners; the eradication of buraku discrimination; the eradication of prejudice against HIV sufferers, Hansen's Disease patients, recently released prisoners, people with different sexual orientations, and the homeless; the cessation of Internet abuse leading to human rights violations; and a deeper appreciation of the human rights abuses of the North Korean government.

The Human Rights Protection Agency attempts to achieve its goals through the initiation of several 'human rights enlightenment activities' (jinken keihatsu katsudō). In its promotional material, the Agency advertises a Human Rights Flower Movement and a National Creative Writing Contest for Junior High School Students. The Human Rights Flower Movement commenced in 1982 by targeting elementary schoolchildren. Seeds and roots are sent to elementary schools that endeavour to cultivate the flowers in class groups. The activity is meant to 'teach children the importance of cooperation and gratitude, enrich aesthetic sentiment, develop a kind and compassionate heart, and foster proper ways of thinking about human rights.' Once the flowers are fully grown, they are then given to parents or sent to retirement homes. Events are also held whereby people have opportunities to sketch the flowers or simply get together and appreciate them. These events, the Agency notes, are considered as ideal opportunities to 'diffuse and elevate thinking about respecting human rights.'

The National Creative Writing Contest for junior high school students began in 1981 as a way of getting these students to 'deepen their understanding of the importance of basic human rights' and 'develop a rich human rights sentiment through composition writing based on experiences in their everyday school and home lives.' In 2007, the Human Rights Protection Agency received 841,558 entries from over 7,000 schools. Interestingly, some 239,234 or approximately 30% of the children's entries related to *ijime* or schoolyard bullying (even though the problem was not mentioned in promotional material for Human Rights Week).

The Human Rights Protection Agency also attempts to heighten people's awareness of human rights through the development and publication of promotional material. In fact, two 'Human Rights Image Characters' were designed for the Agency by the famous writer and artist Yanase Takashi (the artist who created *Anpanman*, a popular cartoon series for young children). Their names are Human Rights Mamoru (a play here is made on the word *mamoru*, meaning both a boy's name as well as 'to keep' or 'protect') and Human Rights Ayumi (meaning both a girl's name as well as the word 'to walk' or 'tread'). The fringes of both the characters are fashioned by Yanase into the Chinese character *jin* meaning human, while the words *ken* are printed in English on their clothes. These characters have been mobilized by the national government in numerous ways. Life-size versions of the characters are employed to assist officials during visits by the public to the Ministry of Justice. They also visited the Prime Minister's Lodge during Junichirō Koizumi's tenure (apparently Koizumi became excited by their size and tried to push one of them over). Ice versions of the characters have been made for the Sapporo Snow Festival. A song entitled "Making the World a Happy Place", featuring both the characters, has also been penned by Yanase.

Another way whereby the Human Rights Protection Agency attempts to engage in 'enlightenment activities' is through the creation and circulation of posters. John Davis noted in his research on local government human rights posters that much of the material on human rights from the 1990s onwards appears to be 'soft' in the sense of making it a social concern of individuals rather than a legal matter for the state. This is, in fact, also true of recent national government campaign posters to some extent. In a campaign poster related to the eradication of buraku discrimination, for example, the message asks the reader: 'Is your heart awake?' Another poster states: 'Discrimination may well be the wall of the human heart.' The human heart is pictured as the precise location wherein buraku discrimination lurks.

Some posters, however, also tend to give off a slightly different message. The general poster on 'human rights abuses', for example, shows the picture of an injured person with an arrow pointing to a hospital and a person with a broken heart with an arrow pointing to a building with the characters 'Ministry of Justice'. The material dealing with North Korea, moreover, shows a person with the face covered over by a map of North Korea with the catchy copy stating: 'There are people shedding tears in Japan and North Korea.' The message here is that the State indeed plays a role in relation to human rights. The Japanese state provides care for victims of human rights violations. North Korea, on the other hand, perpetrates serious human rights abuses.

The Centre for Human Rights Affairs is another organization that 'supports and promotes education and public information on human rights.'[52] It was established in October 1987 as a Foundation under the auspices of the former Management and Coordination Agency designed to undertake activities as a central body for public information activities on the dōwa problem. Part of its activities also involves the creation of posters to generate greater public awareness about human rights issues. One 2007 poster entitled 'Communication' reveals a mother and a daughter smiling at each other with a catch copy in large print, which begins 'Hey Mum….' The poster then goes on to challenge parents by asking them if they are really listening when their children try to communicate with them or whether they are just simply too busy. The poster concludes by informing parents that the home is a 'small but important place for learning human rights' where they learn to value themselves and others. In this kind of poster, too, the home becomes the main setting for learning human rights. The right home environment will lead to the proper development of a human rights culture in Japan.

The Centre for Human Rights Affairs also has a promotional video on its homepage, advertising the problem of human rights and the role of the Centre. A female clown, presumably meant to symbolize an average unenlightened citizen, begins with a comment that she loves people who smile and cannot understand why there are so many people who suffer 'human rights abuses' (*jinken shingai*) and, therefore, cannot smile. Another female voice, an all-knowing voice presumably representing the Centre (and therefore the state), answers that it is basically because many people are 'disinterested' (*mukanshin*) in human rights. The female narrator then admonishes those who hold this view: it is precisely because we all have to deal with large numbers of people everyday that we cannot afford to say that 'human rights do not concern me'. This statement then leads the clown into a temporary state of enlightenment.

The narrator goes on to explain that a deeper understanding of human rights is required in present-day Japan, which is experiencing internationalization, the rapid spread of information, a declining birth rate, and aging. The narrator then informs the clown that the Centre is there to act as a 'helper'. The narrator explains the need for people to foster a 'human rights mentality' (*jinken kankaku*) and a 'human rights consciousness' (*jinken ishiki*). The clown is advised to think about various issues such as women's rights and the dōwa (buraku) problem from a 'human rights perspective' (*jinken shiten*). The clown then complains that the whole idea of human rights is a bit 'cumbersome' (*katagurushii*) and the female narrator attempts to console her. As one progresses through life, the voice explains, we meet an increasing number of different people with diverse attitudes and everyone's happiness can be secured only if all of us acknowledge and respect each other. Jinken, the narrator tells the clown, is something learnt at home, at school and the workplace, and everyone must learn to live life from a 'human rights perspective'.

Local Human Rights Cultural Discourse

Promotional material for the Naniwa Human Rights Cultural Centre, the institution primarily responsible for the extreme makeover that the community experienced over the last three decades, now confidently declares Naniwa as a place wherein Japanese citizens can have a firsthand 'encounter with human rights culture' (*jinken bunka to deai*). According to the present Deputy Director of the Centre, Arimoto Toshio, through a process of 'human rights culture town development' (jinken bunka machizukuri), potential visitors to Liberty Osaka can now develop a greater awareness of human rights by walking through the local area and acquainting themselves with the buraku problem before visiting the Museum to study a wider circle of groups engaged in a historical struggle for human rights.

Naniwa Human Rights Cultural Centre was established through a directive by the government in the early 1970s. Formerly known as the *Naniwa kaihō kaikan* (Naniwa Liberation Hall), this organization works closely with the Naniwa branch of the BLL to maintain local buraku communities and address a range of human rights and welfare issues. Although financially supported by the local government, it is perhaps best conceived of as a consortium consisting of local government officials, the BLL, community groups, and individual residents. Democratic decision-making in Human Rights Cultural Centres (twelve in total in the Osaka area) is important and the BLL and its members fully participate in its activities.

Promotional material for the Centre explains that it has a threefold purpose: consultation; education; and civil interaction. The Centre consults on a range of problems relating to welfare, education, and human rights, and ultimately aims for the 'independence' (*jiritsu*) of local citizens. Educational activities primarily relate to human rights awareness focusing on the buraku problem and there is a 'Naniwa Enlightenment Room' (*keihatsushitsu*) in the Centre itself that is designed for this purpose. Civil interaction activities include the aforementioned human rights festivals, which attempt to bring people both inside and outside the community together to interact with a proper 'human rights consciousness' (*jinken wo sonchō suru ishiki*).

The Centre is also primarily concerned with a human rights culture that relates to human rights awareness campaigns undertaken through a range of enlightenment activities. However, there are differences between the activities engaged in at this level and those at the national government level. Human rights culture at the national level appears to be envisaged as a futuristic place achieved through the proper enlightenment of citizenry. The Centre, however, is more intimately linked with the daily activities of the Naniwa community and, therefore, also associates human rights culture with the daily realities of buraku discrimination and the needs of community residents. What this means, in essence, is that for the Naniwa Human Rights Cultural Centre, human rights culture also assumes an additional meaning of 'the culture of everyday life' (*seikatsu bunka*). Human rights culture is not simply an ideal but something that visitors to the Naniwa area can experience firsthand.

The Centre serves as the starting point of a pedagogical journey into 'human rights culture' that has to be 'met with' or 'experienced'. As mentioned in Chapter 2, Arimoto Toshio, the museum official, spoke to me of the community of Naniwa as being a kind of 'field museum' that attempts to connect visitors to the town of Naniwa, its history and its people. As with the national government human rights campaigns, the metaphor of the home is used in material designed to discuss human rights culture in Naniwa too. Brochures and pamphlets designed to draw tourists to Naniwa speak of 'front doors' or 'entrance ways' (*genkan*) to the community. Perhaps unlike a house, however, this community is described as having three entrances—from north, east and west—but it is apparent through promotional material that the north entrance at Ashiharabashi Station is considered the real doorway to the community. It is here that visitors are informed that they will travel through various zones as they pass through the area. As one disembarks from the train, numerous signs and posters cautioning against discrimination, particularly through graffiti, become visible. Even before one passes through the station's turnstiles, it is possible to see several different local government posters and signs. Visitors to the areas are informed that they are currently in the 'concept zone'. And as one leaves the station, it is immediately clear why. The top of the local telephone box on the closest street corner to the station is fashioned into a drumhead. Such a spectacle invariably encourages the visitor to look for other drum-related paraphernalia. One soon discovers that the nearby bus shelter also boasts of benches with drum membranes as armrests. The walls of the bus shelter, too, contain replicas of the beautifully crafted ornaments, which were historically affixed to Japanese taiko drums. They are found alongside indecipherable musical scores hinting at a rich world of 'buraku culture' which exists beyond mere material objects. Even preschool children practise with taiko drums. Naniwa appears to be, to quote Anne Allison (drawing on Sigmund Freud), a place of 'polymorphous perversity', where material culture is creatively being reconstructed for a variety of purposes.[53]

At the Naniwa Human Rights Centre Museum, brochures inform the visitor that they are passing into the 'Taiko Drum Maker Zone', and the 'Spread throughout Society Zone'. The impressive road one travels on as they pass through these zones is called the 'human rights and taiko drum road' (*jinken/taiko rōdo*) and extraordinary landmarks proliferate along this self-professed path of liberty. The 1.5 km walk from Ashiharabashi Station down the main road to Liberty Osaka is purposely intended to be pedagogical. Signs and posters are scattered at reasonably regular intervals along the entire route to the museum: sometimes in bulletin boards protected by glass casing; sometimes blowing unprotected in the wind on rusting notice boards; and occasionally visible on small signs attached to stakes and hammered into the ground along the sides of the beautifully paved road. The 'Taiko Drum Example City Zone', which leads the visitor into Liberty Osaka, is also intended to be educational. Here one witnesses a variety of taiko drum performance statues.

What is interesting about the area around the Museum is that its components—Liberty Hall, Liberty Osaka, and the 'human rights and taiko drum road'—are uncontained. Liberty and human rights are not merely 'housed' or 'exhibited' in the Museum itself, and accessed for a fee. Rather, these important ideas seem to grow out and be sustained by the surrounding streets and parks. It is as if the area itself, through centuries of struggle, became fertile with liberty and human rights, that over time sprouted into modern parks and buildings. The impression Naniwa leaves is that it is not merely a place where Liberty Osaka is located, but a unique habitat revealing one important development within the evolution of human rights in Japan. The community itself is a manifestation of human rights culture and has become a pedagogical tool capable of instructing ordinary Japanese people about the importance of these issues.

After spending time at Liberty Osaka, the visitors are meant to pass through the 'Historical Road Zone', which leads them to the east entrance to the community at Imamiya Station. Just before leaving the community, however, the visitor passes Naniwa Park, which is a zone to itself: 'The Zone to Think about Human Rights Culture'. The park is fashioned into the outline of a historical Japanese house—itself home to a peculiar looking town clock. The signs point out that this park was originally the site of the home of a famous taiko drum maker. The message seems to be clear here too. Human rights culture in Naniwa is about non-burakumin learning of the plight of burakumin by witnessing their historical quandary firsthand and seeing the amazing way in which the community has been transformed. Human rights culture is something that exists in Naniwa and people can experience (*taiken*) it by visiting the community.

Liberty Osaka and Human Rights Culture

Liberty Osaka was reinvented as a museum in 1995 and underwent a major refurbishment in 2001. The current permanent exhibit installation opened in 2005 and occupies the first floor. Visitor information brochures reveal a detailed floor plan of the museum, which, like the temporary display room, is rectangular in shape, implying that the points of entry and exit to the museum are the same. The only detour options in the exhibit are short, dead-end corridors that provide new information, perhaps a little like footnotes, but which do not affect the main narrative within the exhibit itself. The limitations placed on movement within the exhibit help to establish interpretative boundaries. The path through the exhibit, as is often typical of museums, while meandering, is clearly designed so that all visitors are roughly exposed to the same story. Close attention, however, is also paid to the use of open space. The governing principle of the architectural construction is 'barrier-free'.

After watching a brief video in the guidance room located at the far left-hand corner of the museum, the visitor then has a choice of whether to enter the temporary display or proceed to the permanent exhibition. Upon entering the permanent exhibition, the visitor is greeted with a very small section, 'Corner One: Human Rights Today', the first of four such corners. A large screen broken into three sections runs a set of images on loop, which display the world hovering in the air above a city, presumably Osaka. In this room, visitors are asked to think about 'Human Rights in Japan and the World' through images of old documents labelled 'The Japanese Constitution' (*Nihonkoku kenpō*) and leaflets such as 'A Guide to Welfare' (*Seikatsu hogo no shiori*). Visitors are then introduced to a discussion of human rights such as the 'Right to Work' and the 'Right to Learn'. In a rather orthodox way, visitors are introduced to the idea that human beings are basically invested with inalienable human rights. However, there is also a radical pedagogy at work here. Younger visitors to the museum are encouraged to question sources of authority. One display states: 'Children are not under the rule (*shihai*) of adults, but rather they are individual subjects with the right to learn. We must not only lose all forms of human rights violations such as ijime and corporal punishment, but respect the will of children who are indeed individual subjects with the right to learn and acknowledge their views and choices.'[54]

Corner Two is entitled, 'Our Values and Discrimination', and it asks visitors to question 'commonsense ideas' (*jōshiki*) about what is important in life. The Corner's displays show how contemporary values towards things such as qualifications, citizenship, wealth, financial stability, cleanliness, and job security, while perhaps being important to modern people, all have rather short histories and have, in fact, been used in a negative fashion (made into a yardstick by which others have been measured and found wanting). The display contains colour reproductions of post-Meiji materials and shows how even supposedly modern Japanese values have been shaped by privileged ideas of race, civilization, and progress. The lack of material covering premodern Japan as well as wartime Japanese values is also conspicuous in the displays.

Perhaps the most powerful section of the entire Corner relates to the display representing a home setting. Like some of the national government's human rights campaigns, the suggestion is made that human rights can also begin at home. In a display meant to represent a side view of a house, ordinary everyday material products such as passports, Disney toys, and fashion magazines are displayed and linked to the information from the surrounding displays, which show the constructed nature of modern values that place importance on nationality or restrictive notions of beauty. As one passes by this display in order to move to the next section, however, visitors are confronted by a door to the house with a sign requesting them to open it. Upon pulling the door handle, one is confronted with a mirror with the words: 'What about you?'

Corner Three, called 'The Claims and Actions of Victims of Discrimination,' deals in a systematic fashion with the history and plight of Zainichi Koreans, Okinawans, Ainu, women, sexual minorities, HIV sufferers, the disabled, the homeless, burakumin and pollution victims. The meaning of the progression in the themes of the displays becomes conspicuous at this point. After being reminded that human beings are basically invested with inalienable human rights and that a dominant value system in society problematically assists in the construction of a commonsense understanding of what is considered normal, the discussion then moves to Japan's dominant minority groups. The message is clear: there are people in Japan who are being poorly treated because they do not conform to dominant social ideas of what is considered normal. Moreover, the central themes of each of the minority exhibits are unmistakable: Zainichi Koreans fight against fingerprinting; Okinawans against local discrimination and US occupation; Ainu against discriminatory assimilationist policy; women against discriminatory policies based on patriarchal systems of authority; and so on. Each exhibit reveals in stunning visual detail a political struggle by minority groups for legal rights in Japan in the face of strong social discrimination. The strong emphasis on political struggles for protective legal measures (on protests, court cases, etc.) sends out an unambiguous message that human rights culture exists not just individually but also collectively. Individually, it exists as a mentality that develops within members of minority groups when they struggle against state and social discrimination. Collectively, however, it is also manifested in the joint struggles of minority groups in their attempt to seek legal redress for their problems, which fosters a rich (and presumably better) civil society in Japan. Human rights culture, the exhibits suggest, needs to be transferred from minority to mainstream society, and the museum is an important pedagogical mechanism to facilitate the process.

It would appear that this interpretation of human rights culture has not been lost on local government representatives in charge of approving funding for the museum.[55] One part of the wall in the exhibit on women is dedicated to the discussion of so-called 'comfort women' (*ianfu*). Ota Kyōji, the Deputy Director of the museum and a high-ranking member of the BLL, mentioned in a private discussion that this particular display had sparked off quite an intense debate. Interest groups, politicians, and other persons involved in the examination of and approval of exhibit items and captions were hostile to its incorporation. Information about the display is also conspicuously absent in the official Japanese language Liberty Osaka exhibit guidebook (though it is contained in the English version). In the exhibit, a series of pictures drawn by former comfort women are displayed. One reads: 'A painting criticizing what the Japanese Army did to Korean Women During WWII.' There are, in fact, two paintings in this section. One is titled 'The Japanese Army Picking Pears' and has the following explanation in Japanese: 'A 1995 piece painted by Harmony Kang Deuk-Kyong who lived in Nanumu House near Seoul, Korea. The painting shows Japanese soldiers touching young Korean girls as if they were plucking unripe fruit from a tree.' The other is entitled 'The Angry Ghosts of Suicide Squads', depicting Harmony Kang Deuk-Kyong's experiences working in a Japanese aircraft factory as part of a 'Suicide Squad' at around the age of 15.

Corner Four of the museum, entitled 'Human Rights and You', is a section that provides numerous facilities including books, and audio-visual material to encourage visitors to further explore the material they have just witnessed in the form of testimonials. Members of the aforementioned minority groups move from being famous people involved in political struggle to everyday people who relate to visitors through video recordings a little about their own struggles to deal with real instances of social discrimination and asserting a minority identity.

The overall purpose of the permanent exhibit appears to be the creation of a narrative that is at the same time explanatory, rhetorical, and didactic: What did human rights mean for those who were denied human rights? How are our norms and values, which are taken for granted, related to discrimination? Do our habits and customs produce discrimination in new forms? These questions are explicitly raised for visitors to respond to and yet at the same time, there is an overarching sense that the museum curators have good answers to them already. It is entirely up to the visitor to search them out. This point is driven home further as visitors leave the museum. As one completes the loop that will lead them out from the museum, they encounter a study area and bookshop stacked with books and pamphlets from the Buraku Liberation Press.

Conclusion

Under the leadership of the BLL, burakumin are energetically engaged in liberation activism in contemporary Japan through the idea of 'human rights culture'. Liberty Osaka, located on the site inhabited by a historic outcaste community in Naniwa, is perhaps the most striking example of this activity. Human rights culture, however, is not merely a buraku concern. National and local governments also participate in human rights culture discourse and their interest in this issue must be understood through the unique relationship forged between the Japanese state and burakumin during the postwar period. Human rights culture is the product of a distinct struggle by burakumin both internally, as well as against national and local governments.

Human rights culture is clearly perceived differently at the national, community and BLL levels. At the national level, it is conceived of primarily as a futuristic place—as an ideal culture—which can only be achieved in Japan through appropriate tutelage. At this level, 'human rights enlightenment campaigns' (*jinken keihatsu katsudō*) are seen to play a pivotal role in the realization of this goal. Through government 'enlightenment campaigns', which reach into the home, school, and workplace, people's hearts and minds are refashioned through the attainment of proper perspectives. The ideas that national governments are actually involved in the perpetration of human rights abuses or, in fact, might have a moral responsibility to legislate against discrimination does not enter into its human rights cultural discourse (except, of course, when it comes to North Korea).

At the community level, though, human rights culture in Naniwa takes on another completely different aspect. Human rights culture at this level is more about educating non-burakumin about the Naniwa community. Human rights culture is not merely a futuristic place, but also a space shared by present-day residents. Human rights culture is shown to be embedded in the lives of people who have lived and continue to reside in the community. Yet in order to improve the visibility of this culture, and to give visitors some kind of clue as to how to understand it, the Centre, in league with the community, has devised a way whereby the cityscape itself can actually become a pedagogical tool for human rights culture.

The formulation of human rights culture found in Liberty Osaka exhibits differs quite significantly from that of the national government and local community. Terence M. Duffy has described Liberty Osaka as one of the first organizations in the world to truly embody what he provocatively terms 'Museums of Human Suffering'.[56] Museums in this discursive realm serve as powerful sites of social activism. Liberty Osaka, to borrow from Steven Dubin, performs the function of a 'site of persuasion… where social representations are constructed and public knowledge is produced.'[57] Museums are no longer places to simply find and study artefacts that can assist in research. Nor are museums, to quote Brian Durrans, simply the 'hegemonic devices of cultural elites or states'.[58] The exhibitions of Liberty Osaka construct cultures of human rights that emphasize the need for a liberation requiring enlightenment by challenging 'common sense' as well as the political and legal struggle of minorities against mainstream society. Liberty Osaka galvanizes the various strands of civil rights minority activism in Japan into an organized resistance against a state that frequently develops an acute allergic reaction to the very words 'multicultural' and 'multiethnic'.

Perhaps the metaphor of the home witnessed in a majority of the material discussed in this chapter best illustrates the differences between state and buraku perspectives on human rights culture. Both the state and the BLL envisage the home as an important learning place for human rights culture. Both speak of a need for people to nurture a 'human rights perspective'. For the state, however, human rights culture grows slowly in the context of a healthy nuclear family which, through state guidance, produces good Japanese citizens who recognize, accept, and negotiate difference (even if it is sometimes 'cumbersome'). For buraku activists within the Osaka Human Rights Museum, however, the home is represented as a site where assumptions of what constitutes normality are left unquestioned and perhaps even reinforced. It is only by opening the front door and moving out of the home that one will recognize real human rights culture, and the awakening that people require to understand human rights culture can begin with something as simple as looking in a mirror.

Finally, human rights cultural discourse from one perspective might legitimately be labelled as 'soft', particularly when compared to more radical forms of activism. Following Slavoj Žižek, human rights cultural discourse might be treated as a kind of 'moralistic depoliticization', whereby 'disappointed leftists' invest 'the thwarted excess of their political energy that cannot find satisfaction in the moderate changes within the system into the abstract, excessively rigid, moralizing stance.'[59] Yet Žižek, more recently, and in a slightly less pessimistic mode, has also argued that 'the properly cynical temptation' of reducing human rights discourse 'to a mere illusion' should be resisted. Instead of merely rendering buraku human rights cultural activists as 'docile cogs in the social machine', it is far more productive to examine the opposite process whereby buraku activists engage in human rights cultural discourse as a means of articulating their 'authentic' grievances.[60]

6
Narrating Buraku Experience in Contemporary Japan

Introduction

How far is it justifiable to challenge the way in which minority groups write about themselves? Henry Louis Gates, Jr, has argued that 'self-identification proves a condition for agency, for social change. And to benefit from such collective agency, we need to construct ourselves, just as the nation was constructed, just as the class was, just as *all* the furniture of the social universe was. It is utopian to think we can now disavow our social identity; there is no other one to take its place.'[1] One may think of several good reasons, particularly ethical ones, for agreeing with Gates's appeal for minorities to first be permitted to construct their identities before well-meaning (as well as sometimes not-so-well-meaning) intellectuals attempt to deconstruct them.

The problem, however, is that identity is not a category that can be simply 'constructed' and 'owned'. It is instead as was argued in previous chapters, a process of constant negotiation. It requires the use of conceptual tools and logics that predetermine the shape and texture of our visions of the world. The framework of buraku identity based on mainstream historical accounts, for example, is determined by firm structures, hard categories, traceable continuities, and rational causalities: all marks of a modernist, structuralist narrative. In this configuration, the burakumin are, from the outset, juxtaposed against a 'Japanese' or 'non-buraku' community. They are attributed a historical point of origin. Collective discrimination based upon religious or political ideology is designated as the primary cause of the emergence of their 'outcasteness'.

Such a vision of the world tends to make us lose sense of the burakumin existing, to borrow Kurokawa Midori's expression, 'between assimilation and differentiation'.[2] Burakumin, like all complex beings, do not neatly conform to any of our categories of explanation. And nonconformity is not a state that can be completely reduced to regret or acceptance. Like most explanations that aim to 'recreate', the mainstream structuralist narrative arbitrarily draws lines that cannot holistically capture the feelings, thoughts, and experiences of the subject of discrimination. Colour is taken away from the complex canvas of buraku life. We are made to see things in shades of black and white. And perhaps most troubling of all, this world vision frequently claims a 'truth' value for its interpreted subject matter, thereby injecting permanence and rigidity into its explanations.

True, history is also narrative, and narrative by its very nature is 'structuralist'. Historians cannot, therefore, completely evade their craft's predisposition to find certain shapes in their reconstructed version of the world. But certainly not all narratives need to be modernist, positivistic, or deterministic. Buraku or outcast/e (senmin/hisabetsumin) history does not have to be a narrative of the long history of the burakumin. We could instead choose to see it as personalized narratives that record real life struggles against discrimination. Narrative is not 'truth' in this vision, but rather a method of revealing one's values to the reader.

The example chosen to illustrate the points made here in relation to contemporary Japan is Uramoto Yoshifumi's 2003 publication *Edo/tokyo no hisabetsu buraku no rekishi*. As mentioned in an earlier chapter, Uramoto's story is somewhat unusual, because he is both a buraku activist and an accomplished historian, and was also the subject of a cruel campaign of buraku discrimination in Tokyo. Uramoto, in his book, links *eta* and *hinin* history in eastern Japan with his recent personal experience of buraku history, conceivably in order to demonstrate the way in which buraku history in eastern Japan developed and the role that history still plays in the buraku present. His history plainly plays a role in his negotiation of identity. From this reader's perspective, however, his narrative is equally instructive when read between the lines. It contains, I believe, a veiled appeal to the reader for understanding, and this provides an excellent starting point for understanding and possibly even reconceptualizing buraku and outcaste history.

Background

Let us return to an encounter I had detailed in the introductory chapter of this monograph. In May 2003, Uramoto Yoshifumi, a researcher and activist at the Tokyo headquarters of the Buraku Liberation League (BLL), received numerous packages in the mail marked 'pay on delivery' that he could not recall ordering. These were followed by dozens of handwritten postcards in Japanese, some of which contained clear death threats such as the following: 'For an eta, Uramoto Yoshifumi is pretty arrogant. I'll kill him.'[3] Discriminatory postcards were also sent to other people and organizations. One communication sent to the Tokyo Meat Market was particularly chilling: '[The name] Tokyo Meat Market has a pleasant ring to it, but you are really just a slaughter house. To the fucking eta who slaughter pigs.... At least you can eat pigs, it would help society more if we killed the eta. Let's start with Kumizaka and Matsuoka.'[4] A careful examination of the handwriting on the postcards suggested that they were in all probability written by the same person.

Uramoto's research, an important trigger for these abusive communications and violent threats, focused on providing detailed accounts of the rise of outcast/e groups (hisabetsumin) in premodern Japan such as *eta*, *hinin*, and gōmune.[5] The book which resulted from it was a fascinating history that traced the origins of the burakumin beginning with the period of Warring States (1470–1568) through to the early Meiji era (1868–1912). Uramoto discusses the central theme of his book in the following way:

> Since the 1980s, a number of lively debates have taken place concerning the form of the outcast/e (hisabetsumin) since the medieval period. Out of these debates, a narrative has emerged that expressly sees the outcast/e as one of the central figures of history and society, who undertakes important work during each historical period, and is not simply existing as someone who is 'discriminated against or oppressed'. As I was researching the outcast/es (hisabetsumin) of the early modern capital Edo, I thought just how well this kind of perspective fitted in with Edo's outcast/e population.[6]

Uramoto describes a shift in recent buraku historiography from seeing the premodern burakumin as 'discriminated against or oppressed' to being an invaluable part of premodern Japanese society, and he expresses strong agreement with this view.

Uramoto's view, however, contrasted starkly with mainstream Japanese society's treatment of outcast/e history during the celebration of the 400th year of Tokyo's founding in 2003. The absence of pedagogical and other information on premodern 'burakumin' during the 400-year anniversary celebrations of Tokyo became a primary motivation for Uramoto to embark upon his work. Uramoto argues that it is important to examine how and why Japanese society could not have developed in the way it did without outcast/e groups like *eta* and *hinin*. He reveals that these groups have assisted in key ways in the development of metropolises like Tokyo, besides, in a broader sense, contributing to Japanese society in general.[7]

Uramoto introduces the 'Mass Discriminatory Postcard Affair', as the incident is sometimes called in Japanese, in the last chapter of his book. He responded to the aforementioned attacks on him by stating in the Epilogue that they were, in fact, reflections of wider-reaching structural realities of discrimination targeting buraku people. Uramoto informed his readers that at one time, he was prepared to consider this act of discrimination as an isolated incident, but because he had encountered it several times throughout his life, he was forced to assume that it was part of a larger pattern of hate. In Uramoto's view, the disturbing incidents of discrimination targeting himself and other members of the buraku community were emblematic of the continued existence of a buraku problem in Japan, and indicative of a society that had not properly come to terms with one of its historical minorities.

Due to the subsequent efforts of the BLL Tokyo, a Tokyo bureaucrat and the Tokyo Metropolitan Police, a suspect was apprehended and charged with 'the intimidation of Uramoto Yoshifumi' on 19 October 2004.[8] The accused, in addition to admitting that he had sent letters of intimidation to Uramoto, also confessed to the police that he was responsible for sending menacing communications to over 400 individuals and groups between May 2003 and the time of his arrest. He had targeted sufferers of Hansen Disease, Zainichi Koreans, Nikkei Brazilians and Peruvians, and of course burakumin. Apparently, even on the morning of the day of his arrest, a postcard had arrived at Uramoto Yoshifumi's apartment with the following message: 'Oi, Uramoto Yoshifumi! Are you still living here in Tokyo as an *eta-hinin*? Hurry up and leave. If you don't, I will scatter Adachi Ward [Tokyo] with postcards letting people know where you are from.'[9] To further exacerbate the situation, a similar message appears to have gone to Uramoto's landlord and local residents in the area. It also seems that Uramoto had previously received letters from local residents urging him to move out before others began to think of their district as a 'buraku area'.[10]

According to information provided on the BLL Tokyo website, the person eventually convicted of intimidating Uramoto claimed in a statement made during the trial of the harasser that his actions had begun in jest, but after a while, he had convinced himself of the validity of his cause and persevered with the campaign. The assailant also apparently confessed to the police that reading a book critical of the BLL had been a motivating factor behind his actions. Documents related to the buraku problem were also found in his apartment.[11] It is clear then that the aggressor had some access to and a modicum of experience in reading buraku pedagogical materials. His discriminatory postcards were certainly littered with historical references. His assault on Uramoto made direct linkages to *eta* and *hinin*. In his handwritten memos, Uramoto and the employees at the Tokyo Meat Market were attacked for purportedly being outcastes (*eta*/*hinin*) incognito. According to the assailant, these men and women who claimed status as ordinary Japanese were basically members of old outcaste groups in disguise. He considered this as sufficient reason for acting with extreme prejudice towards them.

Anti-Buraku Structuralist Narratives

The discriminatory postcards addressed to Uramoto Yoshifumi labelled him as *eta* or *eta-hinin*—terms obviously meant as epithets. They were not, however, directed at Uramoto because he was a tanner or butcher, as was the case in some early nineteenth-century discriminatory texts addressed to *eta*. The fact that the *eta* worked with dead animals but Uramoto did not clearly provided an interpretative problem for the assailant. Allegations of occupational uncleanliness had to be directed elsewhere—to a place completely unrelated to Uramoto like the Tokyo Meat Works.[12] Interestingly, though, a postcard vilifying abattoir employees as *eta*, while still being a very serious matter, did not result in an indictment. The eventual charge laid against the malefactor was not that he threatened the Tokyo Meat Market (an organization that did not claim *eta-hinin* ancestry), but rather that he intimidated Uramoto Yoshifumi (who did). In his postcard to the meatworks, the perpetrator of these acts also reveals an awareness that his intended message would possibly be lost on its recipients. The names of two buraku activists as well as a death threat were subsequently added—presumably in an attempt to 'connect' the activities of the slaughterhouse to the buraku liberation movement.

The assailant's narrative of buraku history resembles some of the core aspects of the mainstream narrative of outcast/e (senmin/hisabetsumin) history presented in previous chapters: Uramoto is a burakumin; burakumin are *eta*; *eta* were butchers and tanners employed in 'impure' occupations and, therefore, treated as outcast/es; outcast/es are (or were considered) impure. However, there are problems associated with the borrowing of this narrative for the purpose of discrimination. Uramoto is an activist and a visible member of the BLL, a group which publicly owns and cherishes their history, and which argues that the burakumin are the descendants of the *eta-hinin*. But Uramoto is not a butcher or tanner. He is not engaged in an 'impure' profession. How can he then be an outcast/e (senmin/hisabetsumin)? And if Uramoto cannot be identified as an outcast/e, how can he then be impure? The accusation cannot be that Uramoto is a burakumin, because he is proud of that label. The charge, therefore, is that Uramoto is an *eta*, that *eta* are impure, and that because Uramoto takes pride in this history, he is 'arrogant'.

The perpetrator, in his discriminatory remonstrations, demanded that Uramoto accept his 'inferiority' upon threat of violence. Seen from this perspective, the 'Mass Discriminatory Postcard Affair' can be interpreted as a kind of social policing. Walter Benjamin has argued that 'a cause, however effective, becomes violent in the precise sense of the word, only when it bears on moral issues.'[13] What then is the moral issue at stake here? One hint can be found in the offender's postcards, wherein the terms 'national' (*kokumin*) and 'Japanese' (*nihonjin*) reveal a strong sense of normative purity.[14] The moral issue at stake here could be said to be the unacceptability of pluralistic identity in Japan. For the transgressor, Japan alone is interpreted as the indisputable source of a 'true' personal identity. It is entirely inconceivable that any other group could offer its members the same quality of existential meaning. This is especially the case for burakumin, who historically derived their livelihoods from fundamentally 'anti-Japanese' behaviour and practices.

Certainly, the perpetrator's attacks cannot be reduced simply to excessive nationalistic impulses. There are any number of reasons as to why he may have undertaken these actions. Nonetheless, a particular view of the Japanese past does appear to significantly contribute to his actions. David McCrone, drawing on the work of Ernest Renan, reminds us that 'getting history wrong is the precondition of nationalist history because it requires not only collective remembering but collective forgetting.'[15] For the convicted miscreant, his attack on the minorities (both social and ethnic) hinges upon his ability to invoke an image of an idealized Japanese nation with a majestic past, and social minorities that appear as obstacles or blights in that history. It also means conveniently forgetting the ways in which minorities historically contributed to, and were sacrificed for, the development of the Japanese nation.[16]

This distinctive view of buraku history is, however, not only a problem caused by the perpetrator's selective memory and his practice of national beautification but also emerges because of the way he conceives of history. For the perpetrator, historical time takes on the characteristics of a past that no longer exists, and a future that is yet to come. Cause and effect are strong, and the present is directly determined by the past. The passage of time serves to signify an accumulation of events and experiences that are arranged by the accused like shiny trophies in a display cabinet, which symbolize a glorious national past.

At one important level, the attacks on Uramoto and buraku history can thus be attributed to selective memory, historiographical perspective, and practices of valorization of actions/events in the past. Clearly, the assailant is the one that plays the pivotal role in the construction of a negative buraku past. His past is not merely unproblematic, objective truth or fact. The crushing weight he ascribes to a buraku past is the product of a particular kind of narrative, and, therefore, an imagination.[17] McCrone writes: 'History is not the dead weight of the past on the present, but the very means whereby identity is shaped in an active and ongoing fashion.'[18] What McCrone points to is a logically valid scepticism concerning structuralist narrative wherein the objective existence of a past dictates our position in the present (albeit to differing degrees). The accused created a negative ('impure') buraku past and present in order to be able to empower himself and define his own past and present as 'pure' and 'normal'.

Burakumin Creating Buraku History

One problem inherent in highlighting the constructed nature of history and focusing on questions of representation is that narrating the buraku past is also essential for people like Uramoto Yoshifumi for establishing meaningful identities for themselves. Just as the convicted assailant used national history as a tool to attack Uramoto, Uramoto's repossession of 'real' buraku history also signals a creative display of agency. There is a sense in which the proud ownership of buraku history signifies an unexpected twist and an incomprehensible action for those like the miscreant who wish to discriminate. Why would anyone *willingly* build their identity upon such a 'weak' foundation? Ownership of buraku history, moreover, challenges the hegemony of the idea of the desirability of mainstream identity. It indicates that there is nothing natural about this state, and that it can be rejected in favour of other categories of self-identification.

Burakumin often identify with their history in three discernible ways in present-day Japan: through victimhood, pride, and an appeal for national belonging. The term 'victimhood' means a conscious decision to mobilize past experiences of bigotry into a collective narrative that identifies and condemns discriminatory acts as part of a broader pattern of malevolent, prejudicial exploits perpetrated against a wider buraku community. 'Pride', on the other hand, refers to the victim choosing to exemplify the intrinsic value of the buraku community to which he belongs in order to demonstrate that it is, in fact, a collectivity of worth equivalent to that of 'the majority'. Finally, 'an appeal for national belonging' or 'inclusion' implies that while concrete differences may exist between the buraku community and the rest of mainstream society, these distinctions pale in the face of a common humanity, which, morally speaking, must be legally protected by the nation-state to which all Japanese naturally belong.

Uramoto's history of buraku in eastern Japan revolves around a combination of the second and third types of responses. He sees premodern 'buraku' as an invaluable part of historical Japanese society, and laments that mainstream society did not celebrate the contributions of these communities during the 400-year anniversary celebrations in Tokyo. But at the same time, in the epilogue to his book, Uramoto links his experience with a wider reality of discriminatory practice against burakumin: an action that falls under the first categorical response of victimhood. Clearly, Uramoto finds both positive and negative points in his identity as a burakumin; but he also identifies ways in which Japanese society needs to actively deepen its understanding of the buraku plight.

Uramoto's push for his own identity is, however, not without its problems. While each of the above responses is a valuable and readily comprehensible way of negotiating 'buraku-ness', importantly, each is also a reaction that contributes in a normative sense to a further delineation of a real, physical distinction between 'buraku' and 'majority' communities. This is a delineation which, while in some ways being desirable for Uramoto, may be unsuitable for others targeted by buraku discrimination (such as residents of the Yoshimi area discussed in Chapter 3). The first two responses are self-evident in this regard. They enter into a form of 'discursive negotiation' with those insisting upon the false and baseless idea that burakumin are utterly outcast/e in nature. However, while the condemnation of the violence of discriminatory acts or the depravity of a mainstream society that permits such ignorance is often a necessary and inevitable response, it also indulges the fantasy of 'real' buraku difference in the imaginings of the executors of buraku discrimination. This is also applicable to the act of enthusiastically appealing to a justifiable historical pride in a collective buraku history that is then permitted to become the basis for communal solidarity and political action. These responses may evoke a false societal perception of a need for 'dialogue' between buraku and non-buraku members of society in order to resolve problems. The 'majority' deceptively label the predicament of their own creation as a 'buraku problem', thereby implicitly suggesting that what really needs to be dealt with is something more than the actions of the perpetrator of a particular discriminatory act.

The third response too, of appealing to a common humanity that should be protected by the Japanese nation-state, outwardly promises to overcome the physical distinction between 'burakumin' and 'the majority', usually by emphasizing the all-inclusive category of 'Japanese', to which both the parties desire to belong. But it does not demonstrate how membership supposedly based on equality in this larger imagined community is either guaranteed or secure for 'late-comers' (those people who are portrayed as joining the community after the majority of society like 'former outcastes', 'new commoner-citizens', and more recently 'former buraku areas'). In fact, it is possible to argue, as scholars like Imanishi Hajime have done, that it was the modern nation-state that played a critical role in the marginalization of social minorities in Japan in the first place.[19]

In an important sense, these three responses engage in a disadvantageous dialogue, precisely because they thoughtfully and practically respond to 'discriminatory acts' as reflections of structural realities and also openly denounce them as such. The logic of debate and the parameters of discourse are predetermined by the executor of a prejudicial act. In order to successfully participate in this negotiation, the onus is placed on burakumin to disprove 'buraku difference' as existing as an *a priori* distinction, and they are similarly required to persuade both their assailants as well as mainstream society either of their similarity to the 'majority' or of their intrinsic worth to society in spite of their difference. For many 'majority' observers, who witness this lopsided negotiation, the arguments of the buraku community lack the power to persuade. There is little actual uniformity in buraku discrimination (not every 'majority' member engages in discriminatory acts and not every buraku community member experiences them); there are multiple reasons as to why burakumin should not feel pride in their history (the subscription of some Suiheisha leaders to ultranationalist ideas during the war years, the excesses of some of the postwar 'denunciation' campaigns, as well as recently documented cases of corruption); and there is a lot of ambiguity surrounding the ability of burakumin to commit to, and harmoniously participate in, a homogenous, unified Japanese society (many burakumin like Uramoto continue to make appeals to their identity as a distinct social minority).

Burakumin, though robustly disavowing in a number of ways the allegations that they are irrevocably different, cannot successfully and conclusively convince every observer of their absolute likeness. Moreover, by engaging in 'discursive negotiations' with people who are essentially ignorant of the realities of their lives, they also consequently rearticulate and reinforce as 'real' the imagined lines of their difference. Such an action permits difference between all human beings, which in reality pervades all corners of society, to become *the* dominant referent in the defining discourse of the buraku community.

This is not to say that Uramoto's response is not an important or effectual way of dealing with buraku discrimination. The decision of how to narrate 'outcaste history' must always be an intensely personal one. Uramoto's decision to narrate his history in the way he does is important because in this genuine response to buraku discrimination, which reveals both courage and conviction, he redirects our attention to a larger history of oppression. Uramoto's reaction, however, may also become problematic when his personal chronology of pain is contextualized within a shared 'buraku history', designed to mobilize popular support for a buraku movement, which collectively challenges the discursive and physical impositions of perpetrators of buraku discrimination. Responding to 'discriminatory events' in the way Uramoto does is clearly not an option for all members of the buraku community, and on occasion, his decision to adopt these kinds of responses may actually create difficulties for others (which, as noted in Chapter 2, he himself is the first to recognize).

Another significant problem relates to the sequencing of the narrative of buraku history. Uramoto's decision to link his buraku history in eastern Japan to his experiences is clearly an attempt to outline a history of buraku victimhood. By revealing his own painful experience, he is able to convincingly suggest the continuity of buraku history. But there is still considerable distance between *eta* and *hinin* history, on one hand, and his own experiences of discrimination, on the other. In order to strengthen these linkages, Uramoto must draw upon his own history of discrimination as a way of demonstrating a pattern of hate and hurt. What then are these other incidents that Uramoto experienced? One incident that he relates in his book (and cited in Chapter 1) centres around a problem created by one of his friends, who subscribed to a popular view that the buraku problem no longer existed in Tokyo. The friend refused to acknowledge Uramoto's existence as a member of the buraku community. This and other personal incidents suggested to Uramoto that buraku discrimination was widespread.

Other activists agree that Uramoto's most recent experience was representative of a widespread buraku discrimination rather than being exceptional. Journalist Saitō Kimio, for example, argued that the 'Mass Discriminatory Postcard Affair' was not simply an isolated event, but was instead part of wider discriminatory practices targeting burakumin. Saitō drew attention to the parallels between this incident and one that took place in Saitama Prefecture between the years 1993 and 1999 when a student from Keio University embarked upon a similar campaign of hate. Although Saitō stated that the former incident was probably the first time anonymous, malicious communications were sent to members of buraku organizations (indicating that he thought this earlier incident was the point of origin of these kinds of 'direct attacks' on burakumin), nonetheless he saw this incident as being reminiscent of a wider phenomenon of discrimination against burakumin.[20]

Uramoto and Saitō have linked 'separate' moments of discrimination together under the one umbrella of buraku history because their own bodies and experiences are the very receptacles of buraku discrimination. Uramoto's presence alone signifies the existence and continuity of 'buraku history'. Discrimination does not exist between individuals but rather in social relations, and society itself is a reflection of various material differences. Even if material differences dissipate, one can be assured that discrimination will simply appear in an alternative form. 'Personal experience' (*taiken*) plays a crucial part in identifying the continuity of buraku discrimination.

It is primarily experience, therefore, that enables Uramoto to tie the multiple fragments of personal discrimination into a single intelligible narrative of buraku history. However, it does not necessarily have to be one's own experience in order to qualify for inclusion in a sequential narrative. For Saitō, two vaguely similar incidents were linked together to demonstrate historical continuity. These incidents were linked together firstly because there were circumstantial similarities suggesting the emergence of a discriminatory practice, and secondly, because they had occurred in relatively close proximity to each other. The actions of the perpetrators and the experiences of the victims produced similarities that convinced the commentators that they were related within a wider sphere of discriminatory practice, and 'separate' incidents became 'connected' moments through knowledgeable interpretation based on firsthand experience.

The mainstream narrative of buraku history, while resolving some tensions for its 'owners', also creates additional ones. Some of these tensions are extremely complex. Burakumin appear, for example, as a 'hard' category for those that experience buraku discrimination, but they exist as an 'imagined' category (as a problem of perception) for others who do not have this experience. Depending on who is doing the talking, the 'truth' or the 'reality' of burakumin becomes a matter for debate. The consequences of such a dilemma are clear for people like Uramoto. The sting of social isolation and discrimination—the effect of cordon sanitaire—is not imagined. Each instance of inflicted pain is real. Burakumin are actual people who experience genuine pain. Firsthand experience, particularly of the negative and painful kind that produces wounds and scars, signals the undying truth of buraku history. For others though, the marks that supposedly distinguish burakumin from the rest of society (things like residential, occupational, or status-based difference) only exist because of a conscious decision to carefully demarcate (or accept the demarcation of) difference between the 'majority' and 'burakumin', and because of the existence of an emotional commitment invested in this distinction.

This situation is compounded by the fact that, from moment to moment, burakumin must oscillate between a set of unpredictable and circumstantial responses. Uramoto sometimes feels victimized, or proud, or experiences an urge to belong; and these feelings will naturally change between time and place. For some outsiders (even his friends), it is unclear, though, why Uramoto would choose to maintain a separate identity even if given a chance to merge with mainstream Japanese society. If the buraku problem is resolved in Tokyo (which many believe it is), then surely Uramoto's sense of 'buraku-ness' is imagined. The claim that burakumin constitute an imagined category, however, appears to Uramoto as a cruel tool of further ostracization, not liberation. His very existence is being negated. Other contemporary commentators like Miyazaki Manabu also argue that such talk arises from a society that continues to set the conditions for such a debate.[21] Just as the Japanese state and mainstream society breathe the burakumin into existence, suddenly everyone wishes to pretend that they no longer exist. The natural result of such a pressure to comply with a further discursive exile is a decision to draw upon personal experience and history: important tools that can 'prove' the existence and the continuity of the burakumin. Structural narrative and the mobilization of historical truth permit the past to continue to live with us in the present, thereby normatively ensuring a buraku identity.

Re-reading Uramoto's History

The decision to 'separate' or 'connect' historical moments into the one narrative of buraku history, and the choice of events to connect these moments, however, is ultimately an arbitrary decision based upon one's perception of reality and events; or on a collective decision that enables someone to privilege their interpretation as a hegemonic narrative. Buraku or 'outcaste history' does not exist as a stable entity that has a beginning (and end), moves through time, and is completely knowable objectively. While there is an element of truth in the assertions of historian–activists like Uramoto, who argue, from firsthand experience that it is, in fact, discriminatory events themselves that form the basis of buraku history and not their narration, it is also clear that 'history' and 'narration' are not simply self-evident or discoverable entities. People like Uramoto, who personally suffer buraku discrimination are, importantly, the subject narrators of their own experiences. But with regards to past *eta* discrimination, just like any other historian, they too are observers.

The above problems related to identification suggest a need to establish ways of responding to buraku discrimination which, while still being positive social and political statements, avoid the adoption of any of the 'constructed' categories employed by the perpetrators of the crimes, obliging all victims of buraku discrimination to relate their experiences in the same way, or that generate identity crises for those who are affected by them. This involves working out ways of conceptualizing burakumin other than as a 'fixed historical outcast/e group' or 'outcast/e remnant' continuous through time; as well as conceiving of buraku discrimination and buraku history in ways that establish a basis for narrative in the discriminatory events themselves.

Uramoto doubtless intended his narrative of buraku history to be read in a straightforward way. He writes mostly about premodern outcast/es and himself, and he obviously means to infer that they are the same minority group. The city of Tokyo in which Uramoto lives is introduced as a remarkable place with a rich history. A significant part of that history involves burakumin. But strangely enough, mainstream society still fails to recognize a buraku contribution to its creation. Buraku history, his text suggests, must be both taught and celebrated. However, Uramoto cautions that there are people who would use this same history maliciously. People must be taught accurate history that will become the basis for a proper understanding of Japanese society and the outcast/e problem.

There are difficulties, though, entailed in accepting Uramoto's history at face value. Problems relate to the factual basis upon which Uramoto narrates the history of Danzaemon, the outcaste leader of the *eta* and *hinin* who stood at the apex of early modern buraku history in eastern Japan. Although there is a large degree of consensus amongst Japanese academics concerning the history of Danzaemon, it is almost certainly problematic to relate the history of the Danzaemon as matter-of-factly as scholars do. Japanese scholars and buraku activists rarely note that the vast bulk of records used to reconstruct the pre-eighteenth-century history of Danzaemon were written during later periods, often during the late eighteenth or early nineteenth centuries.[22] The pre-eighteenth-century history of Danzaemon and the development of the eastern Japanese outcaste order are, therefore, predicated upon a large amount of conjecture, and are often built upon less than reliable primary sources.

But more significantly, Uramoto's description of his own experiences of discrimination and his linking of this narrative to the experiences of premodern *eta* groups is an action that blends personal experiences (subject narrator) and secondhand experiences of *eta* and *hinin* discrimination (observer narrator) into the one narrative. Uramoto's story of buraku history, therefore, while ostensibly being a unified narrative based on statements of historical fact, is actually, at an absolute minimum, built on what might be termed as a 'double narration'. Within this double narration, the reasons why Uramoto recounts his experiences of discrimination in 2003 significantly differ from the reasons why an eighteenth-century *eta* may have authored a particular document that he uses. Yet the documents written by the *eta* simply become threads of Uramoto's buraku history. Ultimately the most audible voice in Uramoto's text is his own.

The greatest significance of Uramoto's text for me, therefore, does not lie in its ability to present the reader with a 'true' historical reading of 'outcaste history' (though it certainly is one of the most complete historical accounts to date). The use of '*eta* documents' to narrate buraku history demonstrates how 'outcaste history' may be mobilized by buraku activists for the purposes of political identity in the present. Uramoto's narrative of buraku history does not merely lay the records of the past bare, revealing, in the process, a core history of chronological events that can explain a buraku present. Neither does it simply constitute an objective account of the way in which mainstream Japanese society has dealt with its 'outcastes'. It is, I propose, a story pieced together by using particular tools, identifiable logics, and the voices of others who may have experienced similar (yet nonetheless different) kinds of pain. I believe that the reader is ultimately being challenged to ask why Uramoto has authored his history in this particular way.

Uramoto's history can alternately be read as a valuable creation that relates important information about what he has experienced and what he considers to be important. His story of Danzaemon, and other outcast/es of medieval origins in eastern Japan, who struggled against all odds, finding themselves subjected to severe practices of discrimination, yet capable of contributing to the development of amazing metropolises like Tokyo, is clearly the product of someone who has himself suffered real experiences of discrimination. The history created by Uramoto can be read as an appeal by the narrator to comprehend the sufferings of people who have experienced actual incidences of exclusion in Japanese society. It is a petition to measure a chronicle of pain and a monologue of self-worth against what his readers believe in their hearts to be true and right. The origins of the buraku past are partly seen as reaching back into medieval times certainly because historical conjecture by Japan's most trustworthy academics suggests it to be so. But Uramoto also identifies with these 'outcastes' because their pain is familiar. He is seeking answers to his problems, and those with any degree of permanence or truth that might explain his predicament appear to be hidden in the dark recesses of the past. It is through Uramoto's discovery of other historical victims of past exclusion—the *eta*, *hinin*, and gōmune—and their amazing resilience in the face of oppressive state-sponsored discrimination that Uramoto finds hope. His pride in their history is, for his readers, a small window into the way Uramoto confronts discrimination and manages to initiate hope in even the most difficult of circumstances. As a reader or listener, when we read through Uramoto's history of the Tokyo burakumin, we are being urged, albeit indirectly, to understand him on his own terms with a measure of 'justice'.[23] In order to do this, and in spite of the fact that it may be a logical impossibility, we are being requested to switch between the roles of actor (Tokugawa 'outcaste'), narrator (Uramoto), and audience (ourselves), and to understand stories from each of these three perspectives in the hope that we may some day begin to relate to the idea of the burakumin as we relate to ourselves. In short,

Uramoto's book is an appeal to people from all walks of life to 'become burakumin'.[24]

Rather than simply reading Uramoto's history in the way he intended it to be read—as an expression of the objective facts surrounding events comprising buraku history—we can also understand 'outcaste history' from another perspective. It comprises defining moments (rather than merely as an objective, continuous, external category) narrated by people who identify themselves as burakumin. While the usefulness of piecing together of 'facts' in order to speak of a buraku history cannot be denied, the story of the Japanese outcaste should also be conceived of as the narration of discriminatory actions, which possess definitive possibilities for people who are historically defined by others as outcastes.

History and Liberation

While the need for self-articulation through historical narrative is clear, relying on mainstream structural history to 're-establish' the reality of a problem is also a precarious undertaking. A persistent and continuous collective history of the outcaste becomes a monument to the existence of the burakumin, and the decision to constantly rearticulate a history of difference means that a resolution of the buraku problem on the basis of ideas of assimilation becomes improbable. Silent mergers between separate units of collectivity depend heavily upon curbing open discussion of difference. Obviously not everyone hopes for quiet assimilation—Uramoto appears determined to create a buraku history, which represents a distinct category and which can become the basis for buraku identity. Yet as Watanabe Toshio notes, the buraku community is, in fact, split between those who would prefer quiet assimilation and those who support Uramoto's approach.[25] It would be ethically problematic, therefore, to try to establish a unified position on the issue on the basis of Uramoto's history. Nor does Uramoto himself appear to endorse this strategy in practice, a point confirmed by his utterance of 'wakaru kedone' (I understand of course) in the streets of Asakusa, when the issue of local residents 'coming out' was being discussed (see Chapter 2). Yet for Uramoto, remembering the past and vocally establishing a record for public remembrance is extremely important. From the very first instance, when he was discursively 'othered', the terse binary categories of 'burakumin' and 'non-burakumin' became vividly real. A personal connection was made between himself and those who have been subject to practices of 'othering' within the Japanese past.

However, while the discriminatory act of creating a 'sanitary cordon' that confirmed Uramoto in his 'buraku-ness' was real, the appeals to veracity behind the distinctions that produced the action were not. Albeit, Uramoto was 'different' to the accused, but no more different than anyone else; and certainly not different to the extent that there could ever be a sufficient basis to morally justify any act of violent exclusion towards him. There is thus justification for an argument whereby certain responses to discriminatory actions, while being entirely acceptable as individual narratives, become problematic when seen to possess elements that are coercive for other individuals and members of the wider community that they may impact. Particularly troubling are the reactions which articulate a response to discriminatory acts that reinforce the discourses at work behind them and that attempt to narrate more than one's own personal experiences of discrimination.[26] The 'Mass Discriminatory Postcard Affair', moreover, demonstrates that a 'buraku community' is not simply an objectively existing category, but a discourse of difference that threatens to be infused with life with the posting of a handful of malicious postcards. We are further reminded that it is also possible for this discourse to be propelled by members of the buraku community itself.

Another real problem with structuralist perceptions of buraku history is that there is a sense in which the burakumin do not constitute a firm, fixed entity with a long history defined by a specific kind of 'ahistorical' discrimination. What is, in fact, a very fluid idea is converted into a fixed one by the perpetrator, and those targeted by the attacks are expected to respond to them according to structuralist logic. One is forced into a corner where one has to decide whether or not one is a burakumin. But rather than just imagining burakumin as a derivative of materially existing discrimination that metamorphoses into different shapes during each historical period, it is possible to reconceive of it first as a discursive and physical imposition by a particular individual absent of a truth-value. It is an action that needs to be exposed as an act of violence that produces pain, which is replete with meaning. Those who experience these acts of violence may wish to respond to them by asking those who will listen to them to imagine how they would feel while experiencing discrimination imposed on them at the whim (and based on the fantasy) of others. In this imagining, outcaste history is about asking others to attempt to understand discriminatory acts from their perspective. For these people, buraku liberation does not have to mean political and social mobilization as a buraku community, but could instead entail attributing the meaning of burakumin that they want it to have and rejecting demands to respond to discursive impositions that imply the need to convince others of a sufficient level of 'normality'. This also means that these people should be permitted to challenge all readers or listeners whom they wish to engage, even if the latter include the perpetrators of such violence. It asks readers to switch between the roles of actor, narrator, and audience; and to attempt to understand stories from each of these three perspectives. In this way, each person can begin to try to relate to the victim as they would to themselves, without engaging in or accepting the logic of the perpetrator of a discriminatory act.

Narratives like the one that Uramoto has constructed not only require readers to familiarize themselves with a 'buraku problem' but also entail the existence of real life people who have actually experienced extreme forms of social marginalization. Readers who perhaps initially engage with such narratives as concerned individuals or professionals in an important sense become 'implicated' through their involvement. Although they may not be responsible for a 'buraku problem' in a strict legal sense, they become 'accessories after the fact' if they 'ignore the voices of those who seek redress for the continuing physical and mental effects of past injustice, or participate in the erasure of the memory of uncomfortable parts of history.'[27] What follows from this is not merely a strengthening of the human understanding of burakumin but an internalization of 'buraku-ness', which facilitates a critical engagement with issues of social difference from within.[28]

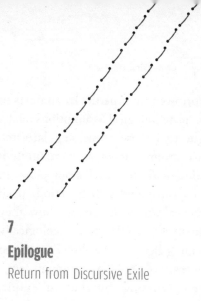

7
Epilogue
Return from Discursive Exile

Japan's largest minority group, burakumin, are generally understood to constitute a group descended from premodern outcast/e (senmin/hisabetsumin) groups, who engaged primarily in tanning and leatherwork and who were discriminated against by mainstream society. A close scrutiny of this master narrative, however, reveals considerable empirical, conceptual and ideational factors, which indicate that 'burakumin' need to be understood as a far more recent and equivocal construction. The argument posited in this book is that 'burakumin' is best understood as a particular modern discourse of difference that needs to be contextualized within a larger history of people on the Japanese archipelago wrestling with the question of how best to accommodate social diversity.

Certainly terms like *eta*, *hinin*, shinheimin, tokushu buraku and burakumin are not merely discourses of difference. They are important labels that have been applied to real people subjected to actual practices of discrimination and marginalization. The decision to interpret all these labels as referring to groups who form part of a long, largely continuous buraku history, however, is not simply rooted in an objective, chronological ordering of the available facts. It is a conscious decision on the part of the narrator to frame the problem of social difference in a particular light by using conceptual tools borrowed from particular contexts or ideologies, and rooted in certain epistemological assumptions related to how the world works. To argue that these terms singularly refer to a specific historical minority group known as burakumin is, therefore, to disregard the lexical and structural ambiguities that surround them. Each referent clearly abides by a period-specific 'grammar' and 'system of reference' which determines how they function hononymically, euphemistically, epithetically, neologically and catachrestically.

Shedding light on the discursive aspects of the buraku problem helps reveal how burakumin are, in fact, highly ambiguous bodies. By deconstructing 'burakumin' empirically and conceptually, and by incorporating the ideational aspects of the problem, one can identify them as the most recent avatar in a succession of temporally imagined social outcaste communities that are defined and bound together in the modern era through marginalizing discourses of difference rooted in the ways in which the 'Japanese' have thought about themselves, their language, and their culture. It also becomes clear that 'burakumin', while being the dominant way in which social difference has been articulated in twentieth century Japan, is not the only way. 'Burakumin' has largely been ignored as a term of reference by both the state and society, particularly during the postwar period. The state has opted for the term 'dōwa residents' (dōwa chiku jūmin) to frame this social difference, an idea rooted firmly in the notion of the supremacy of national integration. Mainstream society, on the other hand, has generally opted for silence on the issue, choosing to 'unname' those it rejects as being socially different. The dominant perception of the absolute desirability of homogeneity has served to stigmatize social incompatibility to the point that all conflict is seen as not only unproductive but undesirable.

Locating the discourse of 'burakumin' within a larger history of how social difference has been articulated on the Japanese archipelago helps cast the issue in a new light. The dominant ideologies mobilized in the construction of social difference in Japan and the ways in which they have changed over time gain greater visibility. Each historical period plainly has its own context and mechanisms for the creation of outcastes through the practice of cordon sanitaire. The dominant ideologies at work in the construction of social difference in Japan have certainly not remained constant over time but have undergone numerous complex changes. The emergence of outcastes in the form of *eta* and *hinin* in eastern Japan, for example, was closely linked with the emerging ideas of state and citizenry during the late seventeenth/early eighteenth century. *Eta* and *hinin* constituted one outcome of a process in which Tokugawa rulers attempted to assert control over the population. They emerged as part of a discourse emphasizing the binary distinction of 'commoner–outcaste' linked to a new regime of policing and social control.

With the promulgation of the Emancipation Edict in August 1871, however, and a host of other new laws and regulations passed by the Meiji government, the social world, formerly articulated through a 'commoner–outcaste' discourse in the eighteenth century, altered again. In some cases, former *eta* village elite were able to be neatly slotted into leadership positions in the new Meiji political administration. In the case of many others though, the changes seemed to work against them. Emancipation was not accompanied by any significant protective measures, and the fundamental mechanisms of inclusion/exclusion that lay at the heart of the premodern social order were not addressed but merely transformed. The discriminatory idea of a 'commoner-citizen' emerged as the foundational logic of civil order in a strong, centralizing Japanese nation-state from the mid-nineteenth century onwards. The logics behind these new practices of cordon sanitaire, however, were vastly different from the old ones. National, racial, and capitalist modes of thought featured prominently in post-Meiji discursive formulations of social difference and the experience of alienation by both 'former outcaste' communities and the newly marginalized urban poor was striking in both its complexity and intensity. Social outcastes in the modern era were constantly defined and redefined by the state, media, intellectuals, and various other actors through subscription to fleeting commonsense ideas about the nature of human associations, the historical development of societies, the existence of homogeneity within populations, and the importance of progress (in ways which usually emphasized the 'probable association' of diverse groups of people subjected to socially marginalizing practices and their uniform backwardness and particularity).

However, 'special buraku' (the discursive precursor to 'burakumin'), emerging out of this complex array of discourses of difference designed to estrange and particularize social difference in Japan, simultaneously became a discourse of resistance. As Ian Neary has noted, 'Active protest against discrimination first emerged at the start of the twentieth century when a small group of *burakumin* made the initial, tentative suggestions that they should be treated as equals.'[1] 'Buraku' was, to a large extent, a discourse of resistance that came to be articulated in the twentieth century, heavily reliant on the emergence of 'liberal thought' in Japan.[2] 'Modern' or 'progressive' thinking based on liberal ideas closely linked with the project of modernity in the West enabled the outcast/e (senmin/hisabetsumin) in the form of 'buraku' to be articulated in that particular way.[3] 'Buraku' was a powerful response to a state and society fixated with national and social cohesion. It was a discourse of resistance that arose in direct response to an increasingly dominant vision of difference that saw it as completely alien. But at the same time, it could not help but share some of the logic and interpretative tendencies of the discourses it resisted. Continuity between *eta*, *hinin*, shinheimin, tokushu buraku, and burakumin was claimed and evidence that some families and areas were subjected to real practices of discrimination and marginalization over a long period of time was taken as evidence that all 'buraku people' had experienced history in this same way. As a result, the real changes that took place in terms of both who was identified (or self-identified) as a social outcaste in Japan and how they experienced that identification also became obscured.

'Buraku' became a dominant discourse related to social difference in Japan precisely because of the constant remonstrations of activists and academics, who objected to the ways in which they were being socially framed and marginalized. It was, to a large extent, the direct result of the ideational struggle of various actors to resist a simple caricature of their difference. Through a thorough theorization of 'their struggle', they succeeded in transforming the particularization of their difference at the hands of the state and society into a radical struggle of resistance, achieving a sense of empowerment and liberation. The emergence of twentieth-century ideas of 'special buraku' and 'burakumin' were, therefore, closely linked to a growing awareness amongst intellectuals, political activists, and educated members of the poorer communities, of the project of modernization itself, and the structures in place that both permitted and restricted the accumulation of power and capital. Particularly, in the early associations linked to the Suiheisha movement, there was a growing articulation of what it was to 'discriminate', an increased ability through the prevalence of meta-historical narratives to identify discrimination within a historical context, and a burgeoning understanding of the powerful potential of social movements to invoke real change when a front of solidarity was maintained. Marxian understandings of the buraku as a feudal remnant that remained as a result of an incomplete revolution at the time of Meiji became dominant because, as Neary argues, 'it was the only theoretical framework that could both explain the persistence of the *Buraku* problem and suggest a way forward.'[4]

The truth of the theoretical framework supplied by Marxism was, of course, challenged both from inside and outside the movement during both the prewar and postwar periods. Even in the prewar social movements, there had been considerable numbers of people who hinted at the universality of the buraku problem and the potential of linking movements such as the Suiheisha movement with similar ones in Korea and India.[5] During the later years of the Occupation, too, scholars such as Takakuwa Suehide challenged the mainstream Marxist interpretation of buraku history based on a kōzaha perspective that had begun to emerge in the mid-1930s.[6] Takakuwa, to some extent, attempted to build upon these earlier understandings of the contemporary buraku problem. This was possible because at the very beginning of the buraku movement in the early twentieth century, there were some who envisaged the buraku problem as a phenomenon whereby certain members of the working class were subjected to forms of discrimination by drawing upon false ideologies that could be resolved with an enlightened and united proletariat. As Neary also notes, not a few activists in the early twentieth century before the domination of the buraku movement by radicals simply envisaged their organization as essentially a radical union designed to protect the interests of the poor, underprivileged, and underrepresented.[7]

No doubt, these radical unions could exist with a difference. It is true that certain areas of poor people with links (in some cases, considerable overlaps) to premodern outcaste groups were discriminated against by mainstream society because of their ancestry. But it is also clear that they were discriminated against because they were poor. The yardsticks of the 'modern citizen'—hygiene, education, civic-mindedness, wealth, etc—were constantly being applied to them and they were persistently found wanting. Just as it is not surprising that many Japanese looked to antiquity and the Japanese past as a source of inspiration for imagining the beauty and potential of the Japanese present in the eighteenth century, so too is it not surprising that the ranks of the poor in a modernizing Japan were also spoken about and described in historical language. The modern pauper could be labelled as *eta*, not only because some members of poverty-stricken communities were direct descendants of premodern outcastes, but because it was a language of the not-too-distant past that was still fresh in the memories of many people and nostalgia for premodern forms of exclusive communitarianism waxed strong in a society so riven by change. It was also because legal emancipation from the language used to describe historical outcastes had meant so much to those who had been forced to bear the labels. Words like *eta*, therefore, were not only used in relation to the descendants of premodern outcaste groups, but were also epithets that expelled the 'poor citizen' from belonging to the modern Japanese nation. It is clear, too, that the word 'buraku' was conversely used to refer to people other than premodern *eta* or *hinin* groups. The targets of these words, through their utterance, became second-class citizens, and their strong reactions to these acts of discrimination demonstrate a fervent desire on their part to belong to the society and polity from which they were excluded. The remarkable statement 'The time has come for us to take pride in ourselves as *eta*', a key catchphrase for self-identification amongst many participants in the Suiheisha movement, demonstrates how some people were able to use the discursive impositions of others to empower a movement that could evoke meaningful changes in their lives.[8]

Inevitably though, utterances designed as epithets to demonstrate inferiority were also accepted by many as having truth in them. This was, to some extent, inevitable given the fact that the victims had all the 'signs' of inferiority, particularly when examined collectively. Communal solidarity amongst 'buraku residents' conversely became a vital and effective means of combating mass discrimination and protecting people who were ill-equipped to protect themselves. But at the same time, the decision by leaders of the prewar 'buraku' social movements, a large number of whom had access to capital, power, and radical world visions, to mobilize around allegations of 'outcasteness', also sometimes permitted scattered and often isolated acts of discrimination to be narrated into a systematic and organized 'truthful' phenomenon, whereby a Japanese majority discriminated against a clearly defined buraku minority. Often, the intellectual tools with which the leaders of this movement mobilized the poor and articulated their cause, were poorly understood, and were predisposed to finding hard, fixed categories and systematic discrimination in every context that one examined. Yet it must be remembered that not all intellectuals, even during the turbulent era of the 1930s, believed in the story of a continuous buraku history, with roots in antiquity and continuity through to the present. As shown in Chapter 4, the writer of the script for the movie *Fujin Sendara* only acknowledged the link between *hinin* and buraku after substantial amounts of ideational persuasion.

The larger question looms, of course, as to whether there are any similarities at all in the ideologies used over time to construct social difference in Japan. Are the appeals to the prevalence of the concept of 'pollution' (kegare), for example, evident not only in the master narrative of burakumin but also in the historical discourses used to frame social difference, really all that misleading? Certainly, to suggest that ancient ideologies play no part in the construction of modern discourses of difference would be plainly inadmissible. At the same time, however, it is clear that ideological imperatives do not remain constant over time. It is not, therefore, the similarity in ideology that is important in the framing of social difference but rather the universality of the main function of discourse itself. To articulate is to differentiate and to engage in a violent but inescapable act that draws firm lines of distinction. What is particularly reprehensible about 'buraku discrimination' (defined throughout this book as the practice of cordon sanitaire) is that the discourses in question attempt to chisel a line of distinction on actual human subjects in a way that presents them as both temporally and spatially permanently distinct entities. While in essence, it is nothing more than a label or epithet, this discourse of difference is ascribed the status of an unchanging designation which brazenly mobilizes the social practices it engenders and germinates as concrete evidence, which justifies its existence as an 'objective descriptor'.

Finally, it is useful here to return once more to the comparative aspects of the buraku problem. For those interested in a basic empirical comparison of the structural effects of discrimination in Japan and India, certain observations can be tentatively made on the points at which the 'buraku' and 'dalit' problems might possibly converge and deviate. At the most general of levels, the geographical distribution of historical outcaste communities in these two countries would appear to be very different. Research on historical 'dalit populations' suggests that they were widely scattered throughout the subcontinent.[9] In Japan, however, the oldest outcaste areas were plainly concentrated in the western (kansai) region and a strong correlation can be demonstrated between the physical proximity of a given occupational community and the seat of the Imperial throne. Many *eta* and *hinin* communities in eastern Japan, however, plainly have a different historical trajectory, and their historical circumstances need to be interrogated in relation to the establishment of warrior rule. Recent research also suggests that the idea of 'pollution' (*kegare*) may not have been prevalent in the northeastern region of Japan.[10]

Another important difference between the 'dalit' and 'buraku' experience would appear to be the duration of stratification observed in both contexts. Gail Omvedt has argued, for example, that 'closed-group formation and purity–pollution hierarchies' in India most likely had their origins in Dravidian culture.[11] Buraku history, however, is usually treated as a phenomenon with ancient conceptual origins but with physical origins, which probably go no further back than the eleventh or twelfth centuries. The differing durations of the caste histories of both countries might be identified as another important factor that helped to determine the degree of stratification observed in each society as well as the intensity in the forms it took. Ōyama Kyōhei's recent work on medieval Japan as a 'loose caste' society is an important attempt to conceptualize this kind of difference.[12] Moreover, the number of 'Scheduled Castes' in India in the 2001 census was listed as over 166 million, comprising 17% of the total population.[13] Clearly, no such level of intense stratification can be evidenced on the Japanese archipelago, with the upmost figure of 'burakumin' usually listed at around 3 million, comprising less than 2.5% of the population (see Chapter 5). The intensity of caste distinction is, therefore, considerably dissimilar between these two contexts, with the types of discrimination experienced by both 'dalit' and 'buraku' communities also diverging to a considerable extent.[14]

A strong case might be made, therefore, for claiming that 'dalit' and 'buraku' experiences do not provide grounds for the best immediate comparison. A contrast between burakumin and Korea's *paekjong* (白丁), for example, may be more productive in some respects. Meaning 'common people', paekjong are generally considered to have roots quite similar to burakumin, usually linked to the breaking of strict Buddhist prohibitions of the eating of meat. paekjong, like burakumin, moreover, are commonly considered to have become cemented in their outcaste fates due to discriminatory state legislation, which emerged during Korea's late medieval/early modern period. From around that time onwards, members of these communities were forced to live in fixed places, engage in certain occupations, and observe strict endogamous practices. Paekjong, as was also the case for burakumin, assumed a number of rights and privileges during this period, which ensured that they earned a living. The primary occupations reserved for them were basketry, butchering, leatherworking, and straw sandal-making, and they were also later forced to serve as executioners. Paekjong were also supposedly liberated through the Kabo Reform of 1894, but as was the case in Japan, legal equality did not lead to liberation from discrimination. Beginning in the late nineteenth and early twentieth centuries, paekjong, like burakumin, actively began to resist social discrimination which targeted them. Coming under Japanese colonial rule at this time, however, the emerging social movements were heavily influenced by wealthy or educated paekjong as well as non-paekjong social activists, which restricted the radical dimensions of the emerging *Hyongpyongsa* (Association for an Equitable Society) movement, which began in 1923.[15]

Yet as Daniel Botsman notes, 'the very fact that English language scholarship of the Tokugawa period routinely refers to groups who were subject to discrimination (被差別民), such as the *eta* and *hinin*, using the term "outcaste" is a clear indicator of the general sense in which "caste" continues to be seen as relevant to an understanding of pre-Meiji Japan.'[16] Moreover, drawing on the work of Ōyama and Sekine Yasumasa, Botsman examines the list of tasks that were considered 'toRil' (tasks that carried religious or ceremonial significance) in an outcaste group in a village in Tamil Nadu (drumming, disposing of dead animal carcasses, grave digging, relaying messages, and village guard duties) and observes that 'these are very much the same kind of duties commonly associated with different groups of *hisabetsumin* [outcastes] in the Tokugawa period'.[17] At the most basic level, then, there is a need to further comparative work between dalits and burakumin because members of these groups were subject to discriminatory treatment while undertaking strikingly similar occupations and duties.

The possibilities for cross-cultural comparison lie in many areas but here I would like to suggest a few points. Following the work of George Hart, for example, Omvedt suggests that the real emergence of strict hierarchies in the early caste system emerge when brahmins 'picked up concepts of purity/pollution from the indigenous Dravidians and then exaggerated them to maintain their own superiority'.[18] Hart's work, according to Omvedt, saw 'extreme Hindu oppression of women… as deriving from Dravidian traditions that attributed a sacred power to women that was dangerous if uncontrolled by patriarchal bondage'.[19] Interesting parallels can be made here with early life on the Japanese archipelago, which Chinese sources indicate had a system of religious matriarchs. The role played by early brahmins and Japanese Emperors in refashioning social relations in their attempts to construct a political symbolics that would underpin their attempts at state-building is clearly an excellent ground for comparison and contrast.

Oyama's suggestive work on kinship and ritual in medieval India and Japan, which has already been noted, also offers useful ground for comparative enquiry. Moreover, Omvedt's definition of caste—'the endogamous principles and practices that constitute the jatis, the purity–pollution behaviour rules and occupational tasks governing the relations of hierarchy and exploitation existing among them, are the practices and rules that constitute the caste system'[20]—would appear to have much in common with theories of status being developed in Japan. Tsukada Takashi has recently suggested, for example, that early modern 'status groups' (*mibunteki shūdan*) must first be understood as groups which were formed through the promulgation of rules and laws that attempted to define them in certain ways. To this, though, Tsukada adds that these groups were not only defined through law but they also actively interpreted social constraints in ways (often beneficial to themselves) at the level of everyday life (*jisseikatsu reberu*) based on certain retrievable logics. Tsukada emphasizes, however, that official ideologies were also mobilized during particular periods to further subordinate these groups.[21] While Tsukada does not promote precisely the same methodology for the investigation of caste as Omvedt, it is clear that Tsukada's framework for understanding status has a lot of resonance with this important work on caste.

There are, however, also obvious points of departure in the historical records of both countries. The role of Buddhism in both societies, for example, as well as the historical role it is generally perceived to have played in caste formation, is different in important respects. Buddhism in the Japanese context was mobilized by historical elites in ancient, medieval, and early modern Japanese societies, and more often than not, became further justification for the inability of certain social groups within Japanese society to achieve even a minimal degree of social acceptability. Pure Land Buddhism did become a popular system of belief among medieval (and later early modern) outcaste groups precisely because of its promise that all people were capable of enlightenment and salvation, and in this sense, it can be read as an ideology which promoted resistance. Yet at the same time, Buddhism in Japan continued to operate as a discriminatory belief system that attested to the 'untouchability' of certain groups within premodern Japanese society, particularly those related to certain occupations that dealt with the 'polluting' effects of death. In this sense, Japanese Buddhism is clearly important at an emotional, psychological, and institutional level in facilitating a kind of social belonging among all members of society, but mass subscription to it and later state manipulation of it, particularly during the early modern period, also inadvertently became an important mechanism, which helped to assist in the continual marginalization of certain groups within society.

Another obvious point of difference relates to the colonial experiences of both countries. Daniel Botsman, drawing on the work of Nicholas Dirks, has suggested that the hand of colonial powers in the creation of caste in India provides an important hint for Japanologists in understanding the ways the modern idea of premodern Japan as a status society developed in the post-Meiji world.[22] The fact that Japan and India have very different colonial histories and relationships to imperialism, however, seems to provide the most salient demonstration of the point of departure of 'caste thinking' in both contexts. In the case of colonial India, as Omvedt points out, the British provide an important counterpoint in the struggles for dalits to achieve liberation from their plight. In the

Japanese context, however, appeals were certainly made to Western civilization and liberal conceptions of society during the early Meiji period as an important counterweight to 'caste thinking', but ultimately these appeals proved ineffectual in terms of real politics. It is only the emergence of Marxism that provides a consistent intellectual and political strategy to mainstream conceptions of caste. Omvedt's descriptions of the way Marxism helped define the dalit movement in India have countless parallels in the Japanese context, making it perhaps the most useful area for cross-cultural comparison. There are also, to be sure, several differences. The second wave of Marxism that Omvedt describes as occurring in India from the 1970s onwards would appear to be conspicuously absent in the Japanese context. The enormous economic leap forward by Japan during the postwar period, as well as the enormous amount of energies dedicated to the relationship between buraku organizations and the state from that time onwards, is an important point of departure in the comparison of both contexts.

While these kinds of international comparisons of master narratives of descent-based difference are undoubtedly important, the central agenda of this book has been to explore the assertion that burakumin and *eta* are better seen as discourses of difference. It is in this area that I believe numerous productive possibilities for future comparative analysis exist. The central dilemma of buraku studies, perhaps best expressed by Hatanaka Toshiyuki who writes that '"buraku" and "burakumin" are illusions—they don't exist but simultaneously they are realities—they have a clear existence. To exist but at the same time not to… that is "buraku" and "burakumin"',[23] is a sentiment reflected somewhat in the writings of key dalit thinkers like Gangadhar Pantawane. Pantawane writes, for example: 'To me, dalit is not a caste. He is a man exploited by the social and economic traditions of this country. He does not believe in God, Rebirth, Soul, Holy books teaching separatism, Fate and Heaven because they have made him a slave. He does believe in humanism. Dalit is a symbol of change and revolution.'[24] This kind of perspective hinting at the discursive origins of dalit difference is fertile terrain for the cross-fertilization of ideas between the buraku and dalit liberation movements. Both 'dalit' and 'buraku' are clearly discourses that have relied heavily upon ideas of historical continuity and uniformity to secure a modicum of freedom for the affected people from state and social discrimination throughout the twentieth century. But the changing conditions of the twenty-first century signal that it may be time for 'burakumin' to re-embrace the forgotten internal revolutionary potential embedded in the politics of nomenclature. The latent power of the label to frame the temporality and in-betweenness of all people who have faced a discursive exile rooted in social differences on the Japanese archipelago is precisely the force that can again assist in expanding its meaning to include a myriad other globally disenfranchised social groups.

The above intellectuals also point to the way in which the structures we impose on the past and our current problems are insufficient, but meaningful histories (particularly meaningful to those that live them) need them. The Marxian perspective, which has informed the master narrative of buraku history, subjected to considerable critique in this book has been popular and prevalent precisely because it has been meaningful to those that have lived and breathed it, and because it has provided concrete strategies for political and social responses to discrimination. 'Truth', in a modernist sense, only ever really exists in its entirety: an ideal so impossible in human terms that most often, we filter what we see or believe through terse binary relationships assuming it to be the balance struck between two opposing points. Yet from another perspective, seemingly anomalous points that appear diametrically opposed to one another may actually be viewed as being quite harmonious.[25] This means for the purposes of this study that there is space in the 'modern' for 'postmodern critique' (and vice versa); there is room for the 'real' alongside the 'constructed'; and there is scope for diversity and conflict to reside within human subjectivity.[26] These dichotomous subjects may appear contradictory, but, in fact, they are merely 'antiphonies', meaning that they exist and play out alongside each other, and are privileged at different points in time and by different people. The point of 'antiphonies' is that generally they are arranged to achieve a sense of balance or symmetry, an instinct that appeals to many of our modern human sensibilities. Just as a majority of the human bodies enjoy symmetry, many of our intellectual endeavours also strive for the same ideal.

The central 'antiphony' of this book has been the desire to strike a balance between the conflicting ideas of the 'constructed' and 'real' nature of burakumin. When we deal with an issue as complex as the buraku problem, effective narration demands that we speak with certainty about solid instances of discrimination that may be morally critiqued. The modernist approach to this moral obligation has been to establish methodologies that speak of 'truth', and use hard facts that allegedly speak for themselves. But for those who worry about the oppressive nature of such a problematic dictum, and are convinced that there is ample room for uncertainty in the sciences of man, there is little choice but to attempt to 'right the scales' through intellectual endeavours. This book, therefore, might be considered as an attempt to rethink the boundaries of buraku history, the lives of Tokugawa *eta* and *hinin* groups, and the category of the outcast/e (senmin/hisabetsumin) in Japan. It is my view, which I think is abundantly clear in this book, that there is not one gospel when it comes to that past. The one that we have been subject to in Japanese outcaste history should ideally be supplemented with other perspectives, which are permitted in the future to grow and develop in different ways that add to an explanatory richness in the field.

Notes

Acknowledgements

[1] http://epress.lib.uts.edu.au/ojs/index.php/portal/article/view/76. Last accessed 1 October 2010.

[2] 155–71: http://www.informaworld.com/openurl?genre=article&issn=1037-1397&volume=27&issue=2&spage=155. Last accessed 1 October 2010.

Chapter 1

[1] For recent discussions on the issue of terminology, see Alastair McLauchlan, *Prejudice and Discrimination in Japan: The Buraku Issue* (Lewiston, N.Y.: Edwin Mellen Press, 2004), ii–iii; Noah McCormack, "Prejudice and Nationalization: On the 'Buraku' Problem, 1868–1912" (PhD, The Australian National University, 2002), 7.

[2] In certain places, like the northeast corner of the main Japanese island of Honshū, the word 'buraku' does not really connote a 'special community' targeted by discrimination. In many areas in the Japanese archipelago, however, particularly in the western areas of Honshū around the cities of Kyoto, Osaka, and Kobe, the terms 'buraku' and 'burakumin' are generally recognized as referents to people whose ancestors historically engaged in various occupations related to tanning, leatherwork, execution, burial, and the like.

[3] This was basically a law that aimed to disarm the peasantry and it was instrumental in creating a firmer distinction between warrior and peasant in the late sixteenth century. See, for example, Kaihō Shuppansha, ed. *Buraku mondai: shiryo to kaisetsu* [The Buraku Problem: Historical Records and Commentaries] Osaka: Kaihō Shuppansha, 1993), 162.

[4] Gerald Groemer has advocated the adoption of the label 'outcast' for medieval groups and 'outcaste' for their early modern counterparts in an attempt to

demonstrate sensitivity to the research findings of postwar Japanese historians who have tended to emphasize the relative fluidity of the social conditions of medieval marginalized groups. While this basic labelling practice is also adhered to in the following pages, these terms are also in need of more discussion. This will follow later in the chapter along with a basic outline of the other ways in which they will be employed in this monograph. Gerald Groemer, "The Creation of the Edo Outcaste Order", *The Journal of Japanese Studies* 27, no. 2 (2001): 264.

5 *Pax Tokugawa* is a term that refers to the peace that settled over Japan after the Tokugawa political consolidation finally brought hundred years of constant warfare to an end. Daniel Botsman used the term to refer to the domestic political accommodations and class structures put into place by the Tokugawa regime that resulted in a prolonged period of internal peace. See Daniel V. Botsman, *Punishment and Power in the Making of Modern Japan* (Princeton; Oxford: Princeton University Press, 2005), 86.

6 For a selection in Japanese, see Harada Tomohiko, *Hisabetsu buraku no rekishi* [Buraku History], vol. 34, Asahi sensho (Tokyo: Asahi Shinbunsha, 1975); Kawamoto Yoshikazu, *Buraku mondai towa nanika* [What is the Buraku Problem?] (Tokyo: San'ichi Shobō, 1994); Kobayashi Shigeru, *Hisabetsu buraku no rekishi* [Buraku History] (Tokyo: Akashi Shoten, 1988). For some English language versions of this narrative, see Mikiso Hane, *Peasants, Rebels, Women, and Outcastes: The Underside of Modern Japan*, 2nd ed. (Oxford: Rowman & Littleford, 2003), 138–71.; Robert C. Christopher, *The Japanese Mind: The Goliath Explained* (New York: Linden Press/Simon & Schuster, 1983), 44–45; Jacob Meerman, "The Mobility of Japan's Burakumin: Militant Advocacy and Government Response", in *Boundaries of Clan and Colour: Transnational Comparisons of Inter Group Disparity*, eds. William A. Darity and Ashwini Deshpande (New York: Routledge, 2003), 131–34; Ian Neary, *Political Protest and Social Control in Pre-War Japan: The Origins of Buraku Liberation* (Manchester: Manchester University Press, 1989), 12–29; Ian Neary, "Burakumin at the End of History", *Social Research* 70, 1 (2003): 269–71; Buraku kaihō kenkyūjo, ed. *The Reality of Buraku Discrimination in Japan* (Osaka: Buraku Kaiho Kenkyusho [sic], 1994), 2–16.

7 Yoshio Sugimoto, for example, drawing on the work of John Davis, has suggested 'that three different categories exist among burakumin': people with blood relational ties to premodern outcaste groups and who live in buraku areas; people with blood relational ties but who do not currently reside in buraku areas; and people without blood ties who moved to buraku areas after the Meiji Restoration. See Yoshio Sugimoto, *An Introduction to Japanese Society*, 2nd edn. (Cambridge: Cambridge University Press, 2003), 192.

8 'Tokushu buraku' was the common term used to refer to people often thought

to be the descendants of former outcaste communities in the prewar period, particularly from the 1910s through to the 1930s.

9 Suzuki Ryō, for example, has discussed this problem in *Suiheisha sōritsu no kenkyū* [Research on the Establishment of the Suiheisha] (Kyoto: Buraku Mondai Kenkyūjo, 2005), 12–13.

10 McLauchlan, *Prejudice and Discrimination in Japan: The Buraku Issue,* 13, 25.

11 Ibid., 25; Hatanaka Toshiyuki, *'Burakushi' no owari* [The End of Buraku History] (Kyoto: Kamogawa Shuppan, 1995), 47–60.

12 Neary, *Political Protest and Social Control in Pre-War Japan: The Origins of Buraku Liberation*, 34.

13 McCormack, "Prejudice and Nationalization: On the 'Buraku' Problem, 1868-1912", 180–84, 232–33, 300, 13; Noah McCormack, "Making Modern Urban Order: Towards Popular Mobilisation", *Japanese Studies* 22, no. 3 (2002): 271.

14 John B. Cornell, "Individual Mobility and Group Membership: The Case of the Burakumin", in *Aspects of Social Change in Modern Japan*, ed. R.P. Dore (Princeton: Princeton University Press, 1967), 345.

15 For example, see, Buraku Liberation League, "What is Buraku Discrimination?"; available at http://www.bll.gr.jp/eng.html

16 Sōmusho, "Gyōsei kanri / sōgō chōsei hakusho (heisei 10 nen)" [White Paper on Administrative Management and Comprehensive Regulation (1998)]; available at http://www.soumu.go.jp/soumu/hokoku10.htm

17 For the intriguing debates between William Wetherall and the Buraku Liberation League concerning the buraku population issue, see the section beginning with William Wetherall, "Outcastes of History: Ferro-Concrete Monuments to Discrimination"; available at http://members.jcom.home.ne.jp/yosha/minorities/Murakoshi_1986_buraku_today_FEER.html#letters

18 Chong-do Hah and Christopher C. Lapp have summarized the problem of census records as follows: 'The Tokugawa era status was last recorded in the Koseki records in 1872. These records are the so-called Jinshin Census, which differentiated between "New Commoners" and "Commoners". The term, "New Commoners", referred to a person who had legally become a commoner as a result of the 1871 *Eta* Emancipation Decree. Companies and schools were usually reluctant to hire people whose Koseki registered their ancestors as *eta* or "New Commoners", and thus the modern-day burakumin had to maintain their lowly position. Furthermore, families would investigate their children's prospective spouses in much the same way as companies and other institutions investigated their prospective employees. For reasons of prejudice, the ordinary Japanese would shun anyone of *eta* background for fear of "contaminating" their lineage… In the latter half of January 1969, the Ministry of Justice closed all pre-twentieth century records, including the 1872 census. One high-ranking national prosecutor of Japan stated that access to the old records can only be

gained through court order, then only under extraordinary circumstances, such as settlements of estates or other such litigation. He also noted that penalties were stiff for unauthorized use of the records.' Hah and Lapp, "Japanese Politics of Equality in Transition: The Case of the Burakumin", *Asian Survey* 18, no. 5 (May 1978), 498–99.

19 In my own research, I received permission to see only ten of the fifteen 'designated documents' (*shitei monjo*) related to outcaste communities at Saitama Prefectural Archives in 2003. After a one-month wait, I was informed by archive officials that some of the documents I had applied to see were sealed in envelopes when they first entered the archives and would never be opened.

20 Harada Tomohiko and Yoshio Tanaka, *Tōhoku hokuetsu hisabetsu burakushi kenkyū* [Historical Research on the Buraku of Northeastern and Northwestern Japan] (Akashi Shoten, 1981).

21 This is an old problem. While some members of the early Suiheisha movement, for example, could trace their ancestry back to Tokugawa outcaste communities, others, including influential activists and writers like Takahashi Sadaki, claimed a 'special buraku' pedigree despite considerable evidence that suggested otherwise. The basic argument in Takahashi's case comes down to whether one believes the buraku activist Kimura Kei'ichirō's reminiscent account of what Takahashi purportedly told him about his family background and the falsification of ancestral documentation purporting his family to be 'samurai' in origin. For an intriguing discussion of the problem surrounding Takahashi's birth, see Nakamura Fukuji, *Yūwa undōshi kenkyū* [Research on the Yūwa Movement] (Kyoto: Buraku Mondai Kenkyūjo, 1988), 227–30. See also Imanishi Hajime, "Kindai nihon no chi'iki shakai to buraku sabetsu", [Rural Society and Buraku Discrimination in Modern Japan] *Buraku kaihō* no. 470 (June 2000): 97–98; Shiomi Sen'ichirō, *Datsu-ideorogii no burakushi: jubaku ga tokete rekishi ga mieru* [Buraku History Without Ideology: Improving Historical Visibility Through the Breaking of Spells] (Tokyo: Ningen Shuppan, 2005), 19–20.

22 Gerald Groemer, "The Creation of the Edo Outcaste Order", 264; David Howell, *Geographies of Identity in Nineteenth-Century Japan* (Berkeley: University of California Press, 2005), 25, 208.

23 As scholars like Judith Butler and John Lie remind us, extracting hope by playing with concepts deeply touched by time (in this case the simple addition or subtraction of a vowel), while a fundamental and necessary component of any act of resistance, should also be undertaken reflexively. Judith Butler, "Afterword: After Loss, What Then?", in *Loss: The Politics of Mourning*, eds. David L. Eng, et al. (Berkeley: University of California Press, 2003), 468; John Lie, 'Narratives of exile and the search for homeland in contemporary Japanese Korean writings', in *Constructing Nationhood in Modern East Asia*, eds. Kai-wing Chow, Kevin M. Doak and Poshek Fu (The University of Michigan Press, Ann Arbor, 2001), 353.

[24] Timothy D. Amos, "Portrait of a Tokugawa Outcaste Village", *East Asian History* 32/33 (June 2006/December 2007), 83–108. See Chapter 2 for more on this family.

[25] Hatanaka Toshiyuki, *'Burakushi' wo tou* [Questioning 'Buraku History'] (Kobe: Hyōgo Buraku Mondai Kenkyūjo, 1993), 143.

[26] While Kurokawa makes this point on the basis of a far more detailed analysis and still tends to focus on the overall historical continuity of burakumin rather than on the changes she examines, her research nonetheless reveals in intriguing detail the way terms like *eta*, *hinin*, and burakumin are period-specific and, therefore, quite conceptually different. Kurokawa Midori, *Ika to dōka no aida* [Between Differentiation and Assimilation] (Tokyo: Aoki Shoten, 1999).

[27] Zainichi Koreans are long-time Korean residents of Japan and make up the country's largest ethnic minority.

[28] Mark Morris makes this point far more eloquently as follows: '…the islands of abject discrimination associated with *burakumin* status offer little solid ground on which to found an identity.' "Passing: Paradoxes of Alterity in *The Broken Commandment*", in *Representing the Other in Modern Japanese Literature: a Critical Approach*, eds. Rachael Hutchinson and Mark Williams (London: Routledge, 2006), 138.

[29] See, for example, the article related to 'Descent-based discrimination' on the website of the Japan-based International Movement Against all forms of Discrimination and Racism (IMADR); available at http://imadr.org/descent/

[30] Uesugi Satoshi, for example, has written a fascinating history of the meaning of the *nado* or 'etcetera' found in the Emancipation Edict. He shows how, regionally, it actually referred to a range of diverse groups considered to be of 'outcaste status'. Uesugi Satoshi, *Tennōsei to buraku sabetsu: buraku sabetsu wa naze aru no ka* [The Emperor System and Buraku Discrimination: Why is there Buraku Discrimination?] (Tokyo: San'ichi Shinsho, 1990), 63–73.

[31] Hatanaka Toshiyuki, *'Kawata' to heijin: kinsei mibun shakai ron* ['Kawata' and Commoners: Early Modern Status Society Theory] (Kyoto: Kamogawa Shuppan, 1997), 109–68.

[32] One of the most intriguing examples I have come across is the story of Yura. In 1831, a 33-year old woman called Yura, listed as the sister of Shine, who was the wife of a commoner town official in the sixth precinct in Edo, was apparently leading a 'dissipated life' and refused to heed the advice of her parents and relatives. She was sent to live with her relative Shōemon, but he purportedly could not tolerate her behaviour either. Her family subsequently disowned her and she went to live in Lower Wana Village with the Suzuki family as an '*eta*'. See Saitama-ken Dōwa Kyōiku Kenkyū Kyōgikai (hereafter SDKK), ed., *Suzuki-ke monjo: saitama-ken buraku mondai kankei shiryōshū* [The Documents of the House of Suzuki: Collection of Historical Sources Related

to the Buraku Problem in Saitama Prefecture], 5 vols., vol. 1 (Urawa-shi: Saitama-ken Dōwa Kyōiku Kenkyū Kyōgikai, 1977–1979), 118 [82]. There are two numbering systems for the documents contained in the published version of the *Suzuki-ke monjo*. The first number '118' represents the number in the published series and [82] refers to the number that is used in the official index used for the *Suzuki-ke monjo* (*SKM*) at the Saitama Prefectural Archives. Saitama kenritsu urawa toshokan monjokan, ed., *Musashi no kuni yokomi gun wana mura suzuki-ke monjo mokuroku* [Documents Index for the Suzuki Household, Wana Village, Yokomi County, Musashi Province] (Urawa: Saitama Kenritsu Toshokan, 1975).

33 See, for example, Nakao Kenji, *Edo no danzaemon: hisabetsuminshū ni kunrin shita 'kashira'* [Edo's Danzaemon: Sovereign 'Head' of Outcastes] (Tokyo: San'ichi Shobō, 1996), 180–82. This issue is also addressed in detail in Chapter 4.

34 *Suiheisha* is an abbreviation of *Zenkoku suiheisha* or 'The National Great Levellers' Society', an autonomous movement started in 1922 by buraku activists for the abolition of buraku discrimination and universal liberation, and dissolved in 1942. The Suiheisha Declaration is a famous document that outlined the platform for future struggles against discrimination by people who were identified as 'former outcastes'. Kurokawa Midori, *Tsukurikaerareru shirushi: nihon kindai / hisabetsu buraku / mainoriti* [Reconstructed Symbols: Modern Japan, Buraku, Minorities] (Osaka: Buraku Kaihō / Jinken Kenkyūjo, 2004), 114–16, 68, 85. See also Chapter 4.

35 Miyazaki Manabu, *et al.*, eds., *'Dōwa riken no shinsō' no shinsō: nani ga riaru ya!*. [The Real Truth Behind the 'Truth of Dōwa Concessions': So you think that's real?!] (Osaka; Tokyo: Kaihō Shuppansha, 2003), 32–34, 36.

36 Edwin O. Reischauer and Albert M. Craig, *Japan, Tradition & Transformation* (Sydney: Allen & Unwin, 1979) 206.

37 Maeda elaborates on his early educational experiences in a piece entitled *Wa ga kyōshi wa haha nari* [My Teacher was my Mother], originally published in the February 1986 edition of the journal *Kaihō kyōiku* (Liberation Education). This is also found in his collection *The Sun Will Rise Again*. Maeda Katsumasa, "Taiyō ga mata noboru: ningen wa tōtoi" (1991).

38 Ibid.

39 Uramoto Yoshifumi, *Edo/Tokyo no hisabetsu buraku no rekishi: danzaemon to hisabetsu minshū* [The History of Buraku in Edo/Tokyo: Danzaemon and Outcastes] (Tokyo: Akashi Shoten, 2003), 234. This book is based on a revised collection of the essays that Uramoto submitted to the *Kaihō shinbun* during that year. The same incident is also recorded in the following volume, though Uramoto's anonymity is preserved in it. Buraku kaihō/jinken seisaku kakuritsu yōkyū chuō jikkō i'inkai, *2004 ban zenkoku no aitsugu sabetsu jiken* [2004 Edition Successive Discriminatory Incidents in Japan] (Osaka: Kaihō Shuppansha, 2004), 22–48.

[40] BLL Tokyo, *Tonai no dōmei intaku ni tairyō no sabetsu tegami/ hagaki ga* [Mass Discriminatory Letters and Postcards Sent to Innercity (Buraku Liberation) League Employee]; available at http://www.asahi-net.or.jp/~mg5s-hsgw/sabetu/hagaki/hagaki1.html.

[41] Uramoto, *Edo/Tokyo no hisabetsu buraku no rekishi: danzaemon to hisabetsu minshū* [The History of Buraku in Edo/Tokyo: Danzaemon and Outcastes], 235.

[42] Yuko Okubo, "'Visible' Minorities And 'Invisible' Minorities: An Ethnographic Study of Multicultural Education and the Production of Ethnic 'Others' In Japan" (PhD, University of California, Berkeley, 2005).

[43] Terazono Atsushi, *Dare mo kakanakatta 'buraku'* [The 'Buraku' No One Writes About] (Kyoto: Kamogawa Shuppan, 1997); Terazono Atsushi, "*'Shinjitsu' wo kakusu 'ryōshin' no hōdō: asahi shinbunsha, iwanami shoten*", [Conscientious News That Hides the Truth: Asahi Newspaper, Iwanami Books] in *Dōwa riken no shinsō* [The Truth Behind Dōwa Concessions], ed. Ichinomiya Yoshinari, Terazono Atsushi, and Gurūpu K21 (Tokyo: Takarajimasha, 2003), Terazono Atsushi, Yoshinari Ichinomiya, and Gurūpu K21, *Dōwa riken no shinsō: masumedia ga mokusatsu shitekita sengōshi saigō no tabū*, [The Truth Behind Dōwa Concessions: The Final Taboo Erased from Postwar History by the Media] Vol. 29, Bessatsu Takarajima Real (Tokyo: Takarajimasha, 2003).

[44] The Buraku Liberation League still claims '200,000 members nationwide'. Buraku kaihō dōmei, "Sasayama Jiken Shiryōshitsu [Records Room for the Sasayama Case]: Supplementary Report to the Fourth Periodic Report by the Government of Japan"; available at http://www.bll.gr.jp/sayama/s-sayam-counte.html

[45] A neat differentiation between 'social' and 'biological' is certainly difficult. These categories often merged in the popular imaginary, particularly from the mid-nineteenth to the mid-twentieth centuries, with biological distinction frequently being mobilized as an explanation for social difference.

[46] For more on the historical emergence of the discourse of 'tokushu buraku', consult Tomotsune Tsutomu, "*Meijiki buraku mondai no gensetsu ni tsuite*', [Regarding Meiji Discourse on the Buraku Problem] in *Kindai no toshi no arikata to Buraku mondai*, [The State of Modern Cities and the Buraku Problem] ed. by Zenkoku burakushi kenkyū kōryūkai. (Osaka: Kaihō Shuppansha, 1998), 59–79.

[47] For an in-depth discussion from this perspective, see my "Binding Burakumin: Marxist Historiography and the Narration of Difference in Japan", *Japanese Studies* 27, no. 2 (2007), 155–71.

[48] Vera Mackie, "Embodiment, Citizenship, and Social Policy in Contemporary Japan", in *Family and Social Policy in Japan: Anthropological Approaches*, ed. Roger Goodman (Cambridge: Cambridge University Press, 2003), 203.

[49] This argument, though leading to different conclusions, has some resonances with the views presented by Yoshida Tomoya, Haraguchi Takahiro, and Fujiwara Hiroshi. Yoshida Tomoya has argued that an 'exclusionary instinct

towards the other' is included in the human organism as well as in the very idea of community. Haraguchi Takahiro has labelled 'buraku discrimination' a 'communal illusion' (*kyōdō gensō*). Fujiwara Hiroshi suggests that the idea that the burakumin are a 'communal illusion' is slightly problematic and simply labels them an 'illusion' (*gensō*). Haraguchi Takahiro, "Buraku sabetsu to kyōdōsei", [Buraku Discrimination and Communitarianism] in *'Burakumin' towa nanika* [What are 'Burakumin'?], ed. Fujita Kei'ichi (Kyoto: Aunsha, 1998), 87. Yoshida Tomoya, "Buraku mondai wa naze owaranai noka", [Why Doesn't the Buraku Problem End?] *Gendai shisō* 27, no. 2 (1999): 74–75. Fujiwara Hiroshi, *Shōchō tennosei to buraku gensō: shūen e no tojō ni te* [The Symbolic Emperor System and the Buraku Illusion: On the Way to the End] (Tokyo: San'ichi Shobō, 1993), 10–15.

50 It is possible to point to any number of theoretical works that speak of history as 'narrative'. One of the most popular proponents of this view in Japanese studies is Sakai Naoki. Refer to, for example, Chapter 5 on the political function of the 'narrative called history' (*rekishi to iu katari*) and the imperial system and modernity in Sakai Naoki, *Shisan sareru nihongo/nihonjin: 'nihon' no rekishi – chiseiteki haichi* [The Stillbirth of the Japanese: The Geopolitical Locus of 'Japanese' History] (Tokyo: Shinyokusha, 1996), 127–45. Sakai writes, for instance, that 'history is a practice narrated (or lied about) in the present with a statement of qualifications relating to the past.' (128).

51 The well-known author Shiomi Sen'ichirō, who has written extensively on premodern outcast/e groups in eastern Japan, reached similar conclusions in an interesting piece on language and discrimination. Sen'ichiro Shiomi, *Shinpen gengo to sabetsu* [New Edition of Language and Discrimination] (Tokyo: Shinsensha, 1990). Shiomi writes: 'Expressions [*hyōgen*] that don't rely on discriminatory structures are for the reader a pipe-dream—a fabrication.... Ironically, regardless of what kind of expression it is, through tracing back over discrimination, we reinforce the reality of discrimination, and we take on the responsibility of educating about discrimination. Of course, pointing out the unfairness of real discrimination and taking on the role of advocating anti-discrimination is also [a form of] expression. But even in that case, the author must begin by tracing back over the realities of discrimination, identifying discrimination in places where it has hereto not been articulated; and then at the point where the realities of discrimination have been gouged out to a depth previously unattained, the expressions we adopt achieve the paradox of creating a sharp fissure in the structures of discrimination of the recipient [of that knowledge]' (12).

52 This perspective has its origins in the influential work by Benedict Anderson, *Imagined Communities: Reflections on the Origin and Spread of Nationalism* (London: Verso, 1996). See the following texts for earlier applications of this

idea to the buraku problem. Hatanaka Toshiyuki, "'Hitokukuri' to 'Hitorihitori'," ['People' and 'Person'] in *'Burakumin' towa nanika* [What are 'Burakumin'?], ed. Fujita Kei'ichi (Kyoto: Aunsha, 1998), 13; McCormack, "Prejudice and Nationalization: On the 'Buraku' Problem, 1868–1912", 4; Kurokawa, *Tsukurikaerareru shirushi: nihon kindai / hisabetsu buraku / mainoriti*, 52–53.

53 One of the classic statements along these lines is George A. De Vos's Minority Rights Group Report, first published in March 1971, which includes the following statement: 'We are all becoming familiar with the fact that present-day European and American societies continue to be afflicted with a racialist tendency which they exercise with varying degrees of subtlety. Japanese racialism, as extended towards outsiders, was a disquieting discovery to the peoples of South-east Asia during the brief military ascendancies of the Japanese during World War II. What is less known in the West is the secret shame felt by many Japanese about the discriminatory treatment of two million of their own population segregated in supposedly "different" or "special" communities (Tokushu Buraku)…. The irony of the Japanese situation is that the "racialism" there is a form of *caste feeling* [italics mine] based on a mythology of different "racial" origins that have no basis in fact.' George De Vos, *Japan's Outcastes: The Problem of the Burakumin* (London: Minority Rights Group, 1971), 3–4.

54 Harada Tomohiko suggested multiple reasons as to why the Japanese and Indian outcast/es should be considered fundamentally different entities. He writes, for example, of the influence of Confucian thought, the way outcast/es were predominantly victims of political manoeuvrings, and the relationship between the buraku problem and the Pure Land Sect of Buddhism (*Jōdō shinshū*) in the Japanese context. Harada Tomohiko, *Sabetsu to buraku: shūkyō to buraku sabetsu wo megutte* [Discrimination and Buraku: Regarding Religion and Buraku Discrimination] (Tokyo: San'ichi Shinshō, 1984), 19–22.

55 Joan R. Piggott, *The Emergence of Japanese Kingship* (Stanford: Stanford University Press, 1997), 59–60.

56 Burakumin have, on many occasions, sought to forge solidarity with dalits and other groups targeted by 'descent-based' discrimination by emphasizing the commonalities that exist between caste, racial, and status groups. One such important occasion was the 2001 World Conference against Racism in Durban. The BLL, moreover, continues to conceptualize buraku history in terms of caste, stating on its official website that burakumin were historically a 'caste-like minority amongst the ethnic Japanese'. BLHRRI, *What is Buraku Discrimination?*; available at http://www.bll.gr.jp/eng.html.

57 Louis Dumont, *Homo Hierarchicus: The Caste System and Its Implications*, Rev. English edn. (Chicago: The University Of Chicago Press, 1980).

58 For more on the comparative aspects of the buraku problem vis-à-vis India, see Kotani Hiroyuki,"Mibunsei ni okeru hisen gainen to kegare ishiki: indo to nihon no hikaku wo tōshite", [Outcaste Notions and Pollution Consciousness

in Social Status Systems: Comparing India and Japan] in *Kokkazō, shakaizō no henbō: gendai rekishigaku no seika to kadai* [Changes in Images of State and Society: The Achievements and Problems of Contemporary Historical Scholarship], ed. Rekishigaku Kenkyūkai (Tokyo: Aoki Shoten, 2003), 147–60; Teraki Nobuaki, "Buraku no rekishi wo indo no hisabetsu kāsuto to hikaku shinagara kangaeru". [Thinking about Buraku History through a Comparison with India] *Kenkyūjo tsūshin* 300 (August 2003); available at http://blhrri.org/info/koza/koza_0068.htm.

59 Yamada Yoshio, ed. *Konjaku monogatari* [Tales of Old and New], 102 vols., vol. 22, *Nihon Koten Bungaku Taikei* [Compendium of Classic Japanese Literature] (Tokyo: Iwanami Shoten, 1959), 130.

60 The word kiyome (literally 'purifier') was used rather loosely in the medieval period, often interchangeably with the term *eta*. Kawashima Masao, "Kiyome", in *Buraku mondai jinken jiten* [Buraku Problem and Human Rights Dictionary], ed. *Buraku kaihō jinken kenkyūjo* (Osaka: Kaihō Shuppansha, 2001), 249; Teraki Nobuaki, "Buraku no rekishi: zenkindai", [Premodern Buraku History] in *Buraku mondai jinken jiten*, 941.

61 For an easy-to-read quotation of this passage and an interesting discussion on the relation between meat and pollution, see Tsujimoto Masanori, *Buraku sabetsu no kongen ni aru mono: kawa to niku no kegare (sono 2)* [At the Root of Buraku Discrimination: Pollution over Leather and Meat] [online]. Tokyo *Jinken Keihatsu Kigyō Renrakukai*, June 2005; available at http://www.jinken-net.com/test/hiroba/hiroba0502.html.

62 Quoted in Kuroda Toshio, *Nihon chūsei no kokka to shūkyō* [The Medieval Japanese State and Religion] (Tokyo: Iwanami Shoten, 1975), 380. Kawaramono were basically poor people who lived in cities during the medieval period. They were named kawaramono apparently because when people came to live in the city because of famines, plagues, or other reasons, they lived in dry riverbeds that were non-taxable lands. During the Muromachi period, people called kawaramono were also involved in landscape gardening and some had skills that were said to be second to none. During the Edo period, kawaramono involved in entertainment were called 'dry river-bed beggars' and often discriminated against. Takeuchi Rizō and Mitsutoshi Takayanagi, *Kadokawa nihonshi jiten* (Tokyo: Kadokawa Shoten, 1994), 226. The linkages between all these terms is explained further in Chapter 2.

63 Harada Tomohiko, ed. *Hennen sabetsushi shiryō shūsei* [Chronological Compendium of Historical Sources Related to Discrimination], 21 vols., vol. 8 (Tokyo: San'ichi Shobō, 1987), 73.

64 Wakita Osamu, "Kawara makimono", ed. *Burakushi no saihakken* [Rediscovering Buraku History] (Osaka: Buraku Kaihō Kenkyūjo, 1996), 130–36.

65 As Noah McCormack observes, however, some outcaste communities did

begin to associate their historical origins with these places, particularly in the nineteenth century. McCormack, "Prejudice and Nationalization: On the 'Buraku' Problem, 1868–1912", 94.

Chapter 2

1 Herman Ooms, *Tokugawa Ideology: Early Constructs, 1570–1680* (Princeton: Princeton University Press, 1985), 4.

2 For explanations on the *toraijin*, *emishi*, *hayato*, and runaway peasants as well as other marginalized groups in the ancient period, see Sasahara Kazuo, *Nihonshi kenkyū* [Japanese Historical Research] (Tokyo: Yamakawa Shuppansha, 1977), 22, 43, 58–59, 74. For a concise history of twentieth century mainstream academic thought on the ancient slave system, see Yoshida Akira, "Doreisei", [The Slavery System] in *Kokushi daijiten* [Japanese History Dictionary], ed. Kokushi daijiten henshū iinkai. Vol. 10 (Tokyo: Yoshikawa Kōbunkan, 1989), 483–86.

3 For a brief introductory discussion in English on slaves during the ancient period, consult Kozo Yamamura, "The Decline of the Ritsuryo System: Hypotheses on Economic and Institutional Change", *Journal of Japanese Studies* 1, no. 1 (Autumn 1974), 30–37.

4 The ritsuryō period (*ritsuryō jidai*) is generally delineated as the period from the mid-seventh to the tenth centuries. Ibid., 34–35.

5 Buraku kaihō kenkyūjo, ed., *Buraku mondai jiten* [Buraku Problem Dictionary] (Osaka: Buraku Kaihō Kenkyūjo, 1986), 500–01.

6 Sasahara, *Nihonshi kenkyū*, 73.

7 Buraku kaihō kenkyūjo, ed., *Buraku mondai jiten*, 815–16.

8 One pedagogical buraku text designed for children that was written in the early 1960s adopted this view, debating the position and meaning of storage huts in villages occupied by primeval man, which apparently reflected the first signs of wealth accumulation and, therefore, social difference in Japanese society. Buraku Mondai Kenkyūjo, ed., *Yasashii buraku no rekishi* [Buraku History Made Simple] (Kyoto: Buraku mondai kenkyūjo, 1961), 18–21.

9 Ishiwatari Shin'ichirō, *Nihon kodai kokka to buraku no kigen* [The Ancient Japanese State and Buraku Origins] (Tokyo: San'ichi Shobō, 1994), 164; Yamanaka Yorimasa, *Hisabetsumin to sono buraku no okori to rekishi* [Outcastes and the Origins and History of Buraku] (Tokyo: Kokusho Kankōkai, 1999), 2.

10 Yamanaka, ibid.,14.

11 Amino Yoshihiko presents an interesting perspective on this point. He argues that the fundamental distinctions during the ancient period were between 'good people' and 'base people', as well as between the 'human' and the 'supernatural'. The latter distinction, he argues, was to become the more pronounced of the two during the medieval period. Amino Yoshihiko, *Nihon no rekishi wo yominaosu*

(sei) [Re-Reading Japanese History]. Chikuma Purimā Bukkusu, vol. 50 (Tokyo: Chikuma Shobō, 1991), 83–85.

12 Some obvious examples of historians who have subscribed to the medieval origins theory are Hayashiya Tatsusaburō, Watanabe Hiroshi, and Uesugi Satoshi. Hayashiya, in one of his earlier works, famously used the word 'buraku' in reference to medieval outcasts. Watanabe also subscribed to a late ancient/early medieval origin theory; and recently Uesugi has also drawn up a theory of medieval origins that differs only slightly from Watanabe's original thesis. Hayashiya Tatsusaburō, "Chūseihen", [Medieval Section] in *Buraku no rekishi to kaihō undō* [Buraku History and the Liberation Movement], ed. Buraku mondai kenkyūjo. (Kyoto: Buraku Mondai Kenkyūjo, 1954): 57–89; Uesugi, *Tennōsei to buraku sabetsu*, 37; Watanabe Hiroshi, *Mikaihō buraku no shiteki kenkyū: kishū o chūshin toshite* [Historical Research on the Yet-to-be-Liberated Buraku: Focusing on the Wakayama/Mie Region] (Tokyo: Yoshikawa Kōbunkan, 1963).

13 The word *fukashoku* is a direct modern Japanese translation of the English word 'untouchability' and is borrowed from studies of Indian caste.

14 Harada, *Hisabetsu buraku no rekishi*, 81. Wakita Osamu, Teraki Nobuaki, and Minegishi Kentarō have also used the terms 'ryūdōsei' in their explanations. Teraki, "Buraku no rekishi: zenkindai", 941; Wakita Osamu, *Burakushi ni kangaeru* [Thinking Through Buraku History] (Kyoto: Buraku Mondai Kenkyūjo, 1996), 22. Minegishi Kentarō, *Kindai ni nokotta shūzokuteki sabetsu*, [Modern Remnants of Customary Discrimination] vol. 5, *Hyūman bukkuretto* (Kobe: Hyōgo Buraku Mondai Kenkyūjo, 1990), 64.

15 Minegishi Kentarō, *Kinsei hisabetsuminshi no kenkyū* [Research on Early Modern Outcaste History] (Tokyo: Azekura Shobō, 1996), 313.

16 Kitagawa Tadahiko, "Chūsei geinō", [Medieval Entertainers] in *Burakushi yōgo jiten* [Dictionary of Buraku Historical Terms], eds. Kobayashi Shigeru, et al. (Tokyo: Kashiwa Shobō, 1985), 212–13; Miura Kei'ichi, "Chūsei senmin", [Medieval Outcasts] in *Burakushi yōgo jiten*, eds. Kobayashi Shigeru, et al. (Tokyo: Kashiwa Shobō, 1985), 213–15.

17 *Shuku* (literally 'dwelling') lived mainly in the Kinai region: in Kii, Iga, Ōmi, Ise, Tamba, Harima, and Awaji. They appear more often in medieval records than *eta*. In the Kamakura period, people referred to as *shuku hinin* appear in literature. They were involved in religious purification, in arresting criminals, and caring for beggars and lepers. A *hinin shuku* (*hinin* residence) had a hierarchy of *chōri* (chief priest in the chūsei period/chief *eta* in the Edo period), *chōri-no-geza* (assistant priests), *kobōshi* (sweepers/gardeners/broom- and Japanese sandal-makers), and *wakakobōshi* (apprentice kobōshi). Rites for the dead were undertaken at each of the *shuku* in Yamato. It is generally thought that temples and shrines took people who had lost the means for supporting themselves and made them undertake cleaning, purification, and policing duties. *Shuku*

belonged to temples and shrines as well as the *kebi'ishinochō* (Kyōtō Criminal Prosecutor's Office) in Yamato. The *shuku* of different regions were closely linked in a *hon–matsu* (head lodge–branch lodge) relationship. For a good discussion of the *shuku* see CDI, ed., *Kyoto shomin seikatsushi* [Everyday Life History of the Kyoto Common People] (Tokyo: Kashima Kenkyū Shuppankai, 1973), 56. Yanagita Kunio writes that compared with a marginalized group called the *hachiya* or 'pot-beaters', the distribution of *shuku* was very small, and limited to areas around Yamato, Kawachi, and Settsu. Yanagita also mentions that some *shuku* members like Nakano Yoshio were able to amass great amounts of wealth. Yanagita Kunio, *Teihon Yanagita Kunio shū* [Works of Yanagita Kunio (Standard Edition)], vol. 9, (Tokyo: Chikuma Shobō, 1962), 385.

18 The word *kawata* first appears in primary records in 1430. Initially, *kawata* did not refer to any particular social status: it was merely the professional name for people engaged in leatherwork. It is argued that this word became discriminatory after it was written in the land cadastral records to distinguish between agricultural and non-agricultural producers. Takeuchi and Takayanagi, *Kadokawa nihonshi jiten*, 118, 214.

19 *Hōmen* were servants belonging to the Kyōtō Criminal Prosecutor's Office. Usually they had served prison sentences and were mobilized to undertake investigative and prisoner escort duties after their release. Ibid., 867–68.

20 See, for example, discussions by Fujimoto Seijirō and Miura Kei'ichi on the history of Shima Village (Kansai), its medieval origins, and the way it was reorganized as an outcaste settlement during the Tokugawa period. Fujimoto Seijirō, ed., *Izumi no kuni kawata mura shihai monjo: azukari shōya no kiroku* [Documents Related to the Governance of a Kawata Village in Izumi Province: Records of a Subordinate Village Official], 2 vols., vol. 1, *Seibundō shiryō sōsho* (Osaka: Seibundō Shuppan, 1998), 3–11; Miura Kei'ichi, *Nihon chūsei senminshi no kenkyū* [Research on Medieval Japanese Outcaste History] (Kyoto: Buraku Mondai Kenkyūjo, 1990).

21 Miura, "Chūsei senmin", 214. Kuroda Toshio, perhaps one of the most influential Japanese scholars on medieval outcast groups (alongside Amino Yoshihiko), posited a slightly different view. Kuroda treated all the low status groups as falling under the category of *hinin*, a term he believed was less of a fixed status and more like a generic term during the medieval period. Kuroda separated the medieval outcasts into subgroups within the *hinin* category into those that were criminals (hōmen and *gokushū*); those that were poor and sick (*kojiki*, *sakanomono*, etc.); those who were entertainers (*shōmonji*, *etoki*, *kugurishi*, etc.); those with a religious and/or entertainment function (*biwa hōshi*, *hōka*, *sensubanzai*, etc.); those who were mendicant priests (*hijiri*); and those at the bottom end of the social strata (kiyome, kawaramono, *eta*, etc.) involved in 'impure' work. Kuroda Toshio, *Nihon chūsei no kokka to shūkyō*, 351–98.

22 There is also the problem that people labelled as *kawarajin* ('riverbed-people') are found to be performing tanning activities in Kyoto in early eleventh century records. Teraki, "Buraku no rekishi", 941.

23 Teraki states that the 'mainstream interpretation' (*tsūsetsu*) of burakumin origins is the 'early modern political origins theory' (*kinsei seiji kigen setsu*). Teraki Nobuaki, "Buraku no kigen", [Buraku Origins] in *Buraku mondai jinken jiten*, 939. One such document that is used to demonstrate the political hand of the Sengoku warrior lords in the 'creation' of the burakumin is found in Minegishi Kentarō's research. Minegishi, *Kinsei hisabetsuminshi no kenkyū*, 239.

24 Tsukada Takashi, *Kinsei nihon mibunsei no kenkyū* [Research on the Early Modern Japanese Status System] (Kobe: Hyōgo Buraku Mondai Kenkyūjo, 1987), 51. Tsukada attempts to resolve the chicken-and-egg-style debate related to buraku origins. Policies were put in place during the late medieval period that clearly may be read as 'political constructions' of outcaste groups. However, he argues that it cannot be denied that groups called *chōri* or *kawata* existed before these policies were even conceived. While scholars and activists like Okamoto Ryōichi and Fujiwara Hiroshi have emphasized the difference between medieval and early modern outcast/es, others like Saitō Yōichi and Ōishi Shinzaburō stress the continuity that can be seen to exist between the groups. They, therefore, tend to be in agreement with Tsukada's suggestion that the 'roots' of outcast/e groups actually go back further into history. Okamoto Ryōichi, *Osaka no sesō* [Osaka Social Conditions] (Suita: Mainichi Hōsō, 1973), 263; Saitō Yōichi and Ōishi Shinzaburō, *Mibun sabetsu shakai no shinjitsu* [The Truth About Social Status Discrimination Societies] (Tokyo: Kōdansha Gendai Shinsho, 1995); Fujiwara, *Shōchō tennōsei to buraku gensō: shūen e no tojō ni te*, 13.

25 Sasahara, *Nihonshi kenkyū*, 242. See also Arai Kōjirō, *Kinsei senmin shakai no kiso kōzō* [The Basic Structure of Early Modern Outcaste Society] (Tokyo: Akashi Shoten, 1987), 4-6; Teraki, "Buraku no kigen", 939.

26 Minegishi, *Kinsei hisabetsuminshi no kenkyū*, 239.

27 Tamamuro Fumio, "Shūmon ninbetsu aratame chō", [Temple Population Registers] "Terauke seidō" [Temple Registration System]; Wakita Osamu, "Mibunsei: kinsei", [Status System: Early Modern Japan] in *Buraku mondai jinken jiten*, 485, 701–02, 1016; Teraki, "Buraku no rekishi: zenkindai", 941.

28 Kawashima Masao, "Eta"; Teraki Nobuaki, "Sabetsu jōmoku kyohi tōsō" [The Struggle to Protest Discriminatory Labels] in *Buraku mondai jinken jiten*, 94–96, 391; Teraki, "Buraku no kigen", 940; Wakita, "Mibunsei: kinsei", 1016.

29 Kodama Kōta, et al., *Nihon no rekishi* [Japanese History] (Tokyo: Yamakawa Shuppansha, 1991), 123. Texts written for academic consumption, however, state that the 'warrior–farmer–artisan–merchant' model was an ideal type and found no real expression in reality in Tokugawa society. On this point, the works of Asao Naohiro are particularly useful. See, for example, Asao Naohiro, "'Mibun'

shakai no rikai", [Understanding 'Social Status' Society] in *Nihon rekishi no naka no hisabetsumin* [Outcastes in Japanese History], ed. Nara jinken/buraku kaihō kenkyūjo (Nara: Nara Jinken / Buraku Kaihō Kenkyūjo, 2001), 71–100.

30 Teraki, "Sabetsu jōmoku kyohi tōsō", 391.

31 For an excellent English language introduction to Danzaemon, consult Groemer, "The Creation of the Edo Outcaste Order", 263–94. For a concise summary of each of the periods of Danzaemon rule, see Nakao, *Edo no danzaemon: hisabetsu minshu ni kunrin shita 'kashira'*; Shiomi Sen'ichirō, *Danzaemon to sono jidai* [Danzaemon and His Times] (Tokyo: Kawade Shobō Shinsha, 2008) is also a useful introductory text.

32 Hane, *Peasants, Rebels, Women, and Outcastes*, 142.

33 Since words such as 'empire' (*kōkoku*) were used in political discourse as early as the late 1860s in discussions related to outcaste emancipation, it is the view here that translating the term heimin 平民 as 'commoner-citizen' is not too great a leap in logic. See, for example, Osatake Takeki, *Meiji yonnen senshō haishi fukoku no kenkyū* [Research on the 1871 Edict to Abolish Discriminatory Labels] (Tokyo: Hihyōsha, 1999), 64–65.

34 Kurokawa, *Tsukurikaerareru shirushi: nihon kindai/hisabetsu buraku/mainoriti*, 12–18, 24–25.

35 Ibid., 76–80.

36 Ibid., 66–67.

37 Nakamura Fukuji describes the Yūwa (integration) movement as a specific government organisational response to the grassroots Rice Riots uprising of 1918 that was interpreted as signalling the failure of the previous government policy of local improvement *(kaizen seisaku)*. Nakamura, *Yūwa undōshi kenkyū* [Yūwa Movement Research] (Kyoto: Buraku Mondai Kenkyūjo, 1988), 6. Mahara Tetsuo explains the Yūwa movement as a social front inspired by both the landed and wealthier sectors of the buraku community as well as the Japanese government. It began in the Meiji period and pushed for the improvement of buraku conditions so that these communities could be successfully assimilated into Japanese society. Mahara Tetsuo, *Suihei undō no rekishi* [History of the Suiheisha Movement] (Kyoto: Buraku Mondai Kenkyūjo, 1992), 4. For more on these groups, consult Kurokawa, ibid., 114–16, 168, 185.

38 Denunciation or kyūdan is the way in which burakumin in both the Suiheisha movement and the postwar Buraku Liberation League (BLL) have traditionally tackled buraku discrimination. It involves confronting the person/s responsible for a discriminatory action and convincing them of their need to: (1) admit to their wrongdoing; (2) issue an apology; and (3) express a commitment to help eliminate future discrimination in Japanese society. It is a practice that has sometimes led to grave excesses including violent confrontations, but is still an officially endorsed policy of the Buraku Liberation and Human

Rights Research Institute (*Buraku kaihō jinken kenkyūjo* – the current name for the former *Buraku kaihō kenkyūjo*). For the Buraku Liberation and Human Rights Research Institute's statement on 'denunciation', see http://www.blhrri.org/blhrri_e/blhrri/q&a.htm#What%20is%20Denunciation? For a dated but nonetheless insightful article on a particularly violent 'denunciation' campaign in Japan in the 1970s, see Thomas P. Rohlen, "Violence at Yoka High School: the Implications for Japanese Coalition Politics of the Confrontation between the Communist Party and the Buraku Liberation League", *Asian Survey* 16, no. 7 (July 1976).

39 'Administrative struggle' refers to a political strategy adopted by the National Committee for Buraku Liberation from the early postwar period. It originated with the activities of early postwar activists like Asada Zennosuke, who were inspired by Marxist liberation theory. In 1952, Asada led a group of activists from the Committee on perhaps the most real 'denunciation' campaign of the postwar period – the '*All Romance* Incident'. See Chapter 5; also Asada Zennosuke, *Sabetsu to tatakaitsuzukete* [Continually Fighting Against Discrimination], vol. 145, Asahi sensho (Tokyo: Asahi Shinbunsha, 1979), 169.

40 Kurokawa, *Tsukurikaerareru shirushi: nihon kindai/hisabetsu buraku/mainoriti*, 196–201, 208–10. The word dōwa literally means 'harmony' and is an abbreviation of the term *dōwa yūwa*, which has the approximate meaning of 'brotherly harmony', and refers to assimilation. The term dōwa is most commonly associated with the terms dōwa kyōiku (dōwa education), *dōwa chiku* (dōwa residential area), and *dōwa mondai* (dōwa problem), and is the official government term for the word buraku. For a discussion of the term dōwa, consult the entry, Akisada Yoshikazu, 'Dōwa', in *Buraku mondai jinken jiten*, 721. For an interesting introduction to the problem of censorship and the word buraku, see James Sterngold, "Ideas & Trends; Fear of Phrases", *The New York Times*, 18 December 1994. For a more scholarly introduction that contextualizes the issue in broader terms, see Nanette Gottlieb, "Discriminatory Language in Japan: Burakumin, the Disabled and Women", *Asian Studies Review* 22, no. 2 (June) (1998), 157–73.

41 The Indian and Japanese Constitutions stand in stark contrast to each other on the point of the criminalization of 'descent-based' discrimination. Articles 14, 15, 17, and 46 of the 1950 Indian Constitution abolished and criminalized caste-based discrimination and legislated for the promotion of educational and economic interests of 'Scheduled Castes and Scheduled Tribes'. Article 14 of the 1947 Japanese Constitution, however, only provided for the equality of all people under the law and while ordering the abolition of 'discrimination in political, economic or social relations because of race, creed, sex, social status or family origin' did not outline any punitive measures against the continuation of these practices.

42 The foundational elements of the post-Meiji narrative of buraku history can be found in a number of sources but the most succinct and easily accessible

version is found from Chapter 2 onwards in Neary, *Political Protest and Social Control in Pre-War Japan: The Origins of Buraku Liberation*. Also consult Hane, *Peasants, Rebels, Women, and Outcastes*, 143–71. For the last point, see Kurokawa, *Tsukurikaerareru shirushi: nihon kindai/hisabetsu buraku / mainoriti*, 211–13.

43 Honda Yutaka, *Edo no hinin: burakushi kenkyū no kadai* [The Hinin of Edo: Problems in Buraku Historical Research] (Tokyo: San'ichi Shobō, 1992), 5–7.

44 McCormack, *Prejudice and Nationalization: on the Buraku Problem, 1868–1912*, 300; McCormack, "Making Modern Urban Order: Towards Popular Mobilisation", 257–72.

45 Some of my initial research on this topic can be found in Timothy D. Amos, "Outcaste or Internal Exile? Ambiguous Bodies in the Making of Modern Japan", *Portal*, vol. 2, no.1, 2005; available at http://epress.lib.uts.edu.au/journals/portal/.

46 Hirota Masaki, ed., *Sabetsu no shosō* [Various Aspects of Discrimination], vol. 22, *Nihon kindai shisō taikei* [Modern Japanese Thought Series] (Tokyo: Iwanami Shoten, 1990), 69.

47 Ibid., 70–71; SDKK, ed., *Suzuki-ke monjo: saitama-ken buraku mondai kankei shiryōshū*, vol. 1, 25 [318].

48 "Dannaiki mibun hikiage ikken", [Incident Related to Dan Naiki's (Danzaemon) Elevation in Status] in *Nihon shomin seikatsu shiryō shūsei* [Compendium of Historical Sources on the Everyday Life of Japan's Common People], 30 vols., vol. 14, edited by Harada Tomohiko and Kobayashi Hiroshi. (Tokyo: San'ichi Shobō, 1971), 473; Hatanaka Toshiyuki, "Mibun hikiage to shūmei jokyo: 'Dannaiki mibun hikiage ikken' no saikentō", [Status Elevation and Eradication of Epithets: Re-examining the Incident Related to Dan Naiki's (Danzaemon) Elevation in Status] *Ritsumeikan gengo bunka kenkyū* 90 (November 2007), 205–06.

49 Ibid.; Hirota, ed., *Sabetsu no shosō*, 70–71.

50 On the importance of these elements of early modern 'status' (*mibun*) consult, for example, Wakita, *Burakushi ni kangaeru*, 20–30, 35–38, 156–157.

51 Hirota, ed., ibid., 71–72.

52 Ibid., 81–82.

53 For recent Japanese works related to the Emancipation Edict, see Osatake, *Meiji yonnen senshō haishi fukoku no kenkyū*.

54 Ibid., 64–65.

55 Ibid., 66–67.

56 Hirota, ed., ibid., 79.

57 Ibid., 83–84.

58 *M-kemonjo*, No. 11, Saitama Prefectural Archives. The documents that figure in these few paragraphs labelled *M-kemonjo* [The Documents of the House

of M] were gathered from the Saitama Prefectural Archives during fieldwork in 2003. These documents are 'designated documents' (*shitei bunsho*), and are restricted because of their sensitive nature and because they contain the surnames of persons that may still live in the community. Subsequently, names of documents, places, and people have all been replaced with pseudonyms to ensure the protection of the privacy of the descendants of these individuals.

59 Ibid. This document supports Imanishi Hajime's research conclusion that the leadership strata of *eta* communities were sometimes subsumed into the Meiji government bureaucracy after the Emancipation Edict in western Japan. Imanishi, "Kindai nihon no chi'iki shakai to buraku sabetsu", 26–27. See also my "Outcaste or Internal Exile? Ambiguous Bodies in the Making of Modern Japan".

60 *M-kemonjo*, No. 14, Saitama Prefectural Archives.

61 Arai Kōjirō recorded rumours that Danzaemon's descendants possibly moved to either the northeastern cities of Utsunomiya or Sendai. Miyatake Toshimasa states that Danzaemon (Dan Naiki/Dan Naoki) died in the 1880s and was buried in the city of Kobe. Arai Kōjirō, "Toshi senmin gyōseishi no kiso kōsatsu: tokyo no hisabetsu buraku to 'gōmune' buraku no baai", [Rudimentary Reflections on Urban Outcaste Administrative History: The Case of Tokyo and Gōmune Buraku] *Tōyō hōgaku* 11 no. 4 (1969), 106; Miyatake Toshimasa, "Tokyo-to danzaemon kakoinai-ato: danzaemon to edo no hisabetsumin (burakushi yukari no chi)", [The Remains of the Danzaemon Settlement in Tokyo: Danzaemon and Edo's Outcastes (Places Related to Buraku History)] *Buraku kaihō* no. 555 (2005), 22–25.

62 Carol Gluck, "Japan's Modernities, 1850s–1990s", in *Asia in Western and World History*, eds. Embree, Ainslie T. and Carol Gluck (Armonk, N.Y.: M.E. Sharpe, 1997), 574.

63 Murata Munejiro, *Tokyo chiri enkaku-shi* [Record of the Geographical History of Tokyo] (Tokyo: Inagaki Josaburo, 1890), 422–23.

64 Ijino-no-Genō, *Ijin no genkō* [Words and Deeds of Great Men] (Tokyo: Daigakukan, 1900), 131–32.

65 Arai, "Toshi senmin gyōseishi no kiso kōsatsu: tokyo no hisabetsu buraku to 'gōmune' buraku no baai", 86.

66 Hatanaka, *'Burakushi' no owari*, 176–87. Arguing that these groups are 'statuses', Hatanaka, however, also continues to ascribe to them a position as pure, objectively existing categories that have a point of origin and an end. The case for Kurokawa Midori is also quite similar. Kurokawa, while subscribing to the idea of the premodern and modern outcast/e as distinctive status-based phenomena, also argues for the continuity of 'discrimination' (*kegare ishiki*), albeit in a more limited sense, from the premodern period into the present. Kurokawa, *Tsukurikaerareru shirushi: nihon kindai / hisabetsu buraku / mainoriti*, 17–20.

[67] The emergence of ideas like 'a society outside society' (*shakaigai no shakai*), which have been used to explain premodern outcast/es from the Meiji period, is a good evidence of this. See Kobayashi Takehiro's entry "Shakaigai no shakai eta hinin" in *Buraku mondai jinken jiten*, 448. However, this is not always the case. Amino Yoshihiko is one researcher who has developed a far more complex view of Japan and the problems related to simplistic notions of Japanese identity than the one outlined here. Consult Amino Yoshihiko, "Deconstructing Japan", *East Asian Studies*, no. 3 (1992), 121–42; Amino Yoshihiko, "Nihon chūsei ni okeru sabetsu no shosō", [Various Aspects of Discrimination in Medieval Japan] in *Nihon rekishi no naka no hisabetsumin*, 9–35.

[68] Hatanaka, *'Burakushi' wo tou*, 110.

[69] S. Anand mentions a similar problem in relation to dalits and caste in India. He writes: 'As many foreigners ask: how do we know who is from which caste when everyone looks alike? It is this apparent invisibilization of the debilitating hierarchies of caste, and the ability of elite Indians to claim victimhood as one-time subjects of colonial racism, that help elide the question of caste.' Yet Anand also comments that 'Indians practising caste do know how to place the other person's caste within minutes of a meeting or conversation. Surnames, accents, food habits, place of origin or residence and other personal preferences are giveaways. Yet, the intractability of caste for an international audience persists.' "Caste and the World", *The Hindu*, 24 May 2009, available from http://www.hindu.com/mag/2009/05/24/stories/2009052450180500.htm

[70] Taiko are Japanese drums in the shape of barrels. They come in various sizes and styles. Leather is usually spread over one or both ends of the barrel to form the drum-head. Taiko were historically used on diverse occasions including in Shinto rituals and during warfare. During the early modern period, the task of affixing drum heads was often assumed by *eta*/kawata groups.

[71] Sugita Genpaku, "Rantō Kotohajime", [Dawn of Western Science] in *Koten Nihon Bungaku Taikei*, eds. Kodaka Toshirō and Matsumura Akira (Tokyo: Iwanami Shoten, 1964), 469–553. (All translations are my own but were cross-checked against the 1969 English translation: *Dawn of Western Science in Japan: Rangaku kotohajime*, trans. by Matsumoto Ryōzō and Ei'ichi Kiyo'oka (Tokyo: Hokuseido Press, 1969).

[72] Sugita, "Rantō Kotohajime", 490–91.

[73] For more on this process, consult 'Naniwa buraku no rekishi' hensan i'inkai, ed., *Watanabe/Nishihama/Naniwa: Naniwa buraku no rekishi* [Watanabe/Nishihama/Naniwa: History of Naniwa's Buraku] (Osaka: Kaihō Shuppansha, 1997), 3–6.

[74] Hatanaka, *'Kawata' to heijin: kinsei mibun shakai ron*, 109–68.

[75] Interestingly, only about 40–50% of the people living in buraku areas in Osaka today are believed to claim a status as burakumin. See, for example, Osaka

Prefectural Government, "Dōwa Taisaku Kankei Shiryō" [Sources Related to Dōwa Measures]; available from http://www.pref.osaka.jp/osaka-pref/jinken/measure/kunidowa /d1_2.html.

76 Originally the Eishō Elementary School was called the Western Greater Union Precinct 23 School in 1872. For the history of this school, consult 'Naniwa buraku no rekishi' hensan i'inkai, ed. *Watanabe/Nishihama/Naniwa: Naniwa buraku no rekishi*, 50–54.

77 Harry D. Harootunian, *Things Seen and Unseen: Discourse and Ideology in Tokugawa Nativism* (Chicago: University of Chicago Press, 1988), 8.

78 Sakai, *Shisan Sareru Nihongo/Nihonjin*, 211–13.

79 McCormack, "Making Modern Urban Order: Towards Popular Mobilisation", 257–72. As Susan Burns has noted too, the disintegration of premodern forms of leper communities in the early Meiji years was quickly followed by the establishment of modern institutions that were designed to clean up after social outcastes that were 'dirtying the streets'. Susan L. Burns, "From 'Leper Villages' to Leprosaria: Public Health, Nationalism and the Culture of Exclusion in Japan", in *Isolation: Places and Practices of Exclusion*, eds. Carolyn Strange and Alison Bashford (London, New York: Routledge, 2003), 107–08.

80 Yamanouchi Yasushi writes of the 'second-class citizen' formed in the twentieth century who created problems for 'political integration' but nevertheless fell outside the definition of the 'ideal citizen'. Yasushi Yasunouchi, "Total War and Social Integration: A Methodological Introduction", in *Total War and 'Modernization'*, eds. Yasushi Yasunouchi, et al., *Cornell East Asia Series* 100 (Ithaca, New York: East Asia Program Cornell University, 1998), 2–3. Kurokawa Midori has also used this term (*nijū no kokumin*) in her work. Kurokawa, *Tsukurikaerareru shirushi: nihon kindai / hisabetsu buraku / mainoriti*, 40–41.

81 "Zenchūdan", [Conversations on Good] found in Okiura Kazuteru, *Suihei: hito no yo ni hikari are* [Levellers: Let there be Light in the World of Man] (Tokyo: Shakai Hyōronsha, 1991), 20.

82 "Tōsenpuron", [Discourse of an Eastern Hermit] found in Okiura Kazuteru, *Suihei: hito no yo ni hikari are*, 44–45.

83 "Eta ni tsuite no jinruigakuteki chōsa", [Anthropological Survey Concerning Eta] found in Okiura Kazuteru, *Suihei: hito no yo ni hikari are*, 88.

84 "Tokushu burakumin to sōjō", [Special Buraku People and Rioting] in *Kindai burakushi shiryō shūsei* [Compilation of Historical Documents Relating to Modern Buraku History], eds., Watanabe Tōru et al. Vol. 8. Tokyo: Sanichi Shobō, 1985, 263–64.

85 Kurokawa, *Tsukurikaerareru shirushi: nihon kindai/hisabetsu buraku/mainoriti.*

86 Interestingly, the word 'kawa' in Japanese refers to both leather and a river, and was thus written both ways. This suggests that the term 'kawata' was simultaneously a spatial and geographical referent.

87 This term is translated as 'Residents of Dōwa Residential Districts'. For a discussion of the term dōwa consult, Akisada, "Dōwa", 721.

88 In the prewar period, particularly during the 1920s and 1930s, 'special buraku' were occasionally referred to as *hiappaku buraku* or 'oppressed buraku' by activists. Scholars and intellectuals striving for 'buraku' liberation in the early postwar period often referred to 'buraku' with the label *mikaihō buraku* or 'yet-to-be-liberated buraku'. Similarly it is possible to offend burakumin today by referring to them simply as 'burakumin' in Japanese. The more respectful term is the one Uramoto used during his tour of Imado: hisabetsu buraku or 'buraku who-are-discriminated-against'.

Chapter 3

1 For one of the most lucid discussions of buraku discrimination in recent years, see Watanabe Toshio, "Burakushi no tenkan", [Changes in Buraku History] *Gendai shisō* [Contemporary Thought] 27, no. 2 (1999), 32.

2 The idea of cordon sanitaire employed here is taken from B.R. Ambedkar's *The Untouchables: Who Were They and Why They Became Untouchables*. New Delhi: Amrit Book Company, 1948. The definitive study on pollution and contamination is Mary Douglas' *Purity and Danger: An Analysis of Concepts of Pollution and Taboo* (London: Routledge & Kegan Paul, 1966).

3 For arguments along these lines in English, see Leslie D. Alldritt, *The Burakumin: The Complicity of Japanese Buddhism in Oppression and an Opportunity for Liberation* (2000); available at http://jbe.gold.ac.uk/7/alldritt001.html.

4 The expression 'fear and loathing' is taken from Amino Yoshihiko's classic work *Nihon no rekishi wo yominaosu*, 79.

5 See, for example, works such as Kotani Hiroyuki, "Ajia kindai ni okeru sabetsu no mekanizumu: indo wo sozai toshite", [Discriminatory Mechanisms in Modern Asia: Focusing on India] In *Ima naze sabetsu wo tou ka* [Why is it Important to Question Discrimination Now?], edited by Kan Takayuki. (Tokyo: Akashi Shoten, 1985); Noguchi Michihiko, "Sabetsu", [Discrimination] Buraku kaihō jinken kenkyūjo (Osaka: Kaihō Shuppansha, 2001), 386–87.

6 Minegishi, *Kindai ni nokotta shūzokuteki sabetsu*, 4.

7 Kurokawa, *Ika to dōka no aida*, 29.

8 Watanabe, "Burakushi no tenkan", 33; Kurokawa, *Tsukurikaerareru shirushi: nihon kindai / hisabetsu buraku / mainoriti*, 227.

9 See, for example, Kitaguchi Suehiro, "Aratana buraku chimei sōkan", [New Buraku Residence Lists] *Gendai kokusai jinken kō* [Thoughts on Contemporary International Human Rights]. No. 66 (March 2006) Available at http://www.hurights.or.jp/newsletter/J_NL/066/01.html; Watanabe, "Burakushi no tenkan", 33.

10 Quoted in S. Anand, "Caste on the Couch: Do Brahminical Ideologies Permeate Indian Psychological Theory?" *Himal*, 24 April 2003; available at http://www.countercurrents.org/dalit-anand24403.htm.

[11] Ambedkar, *The Untouchables: Who Were They and Why They Became Untouchables*, 22.

[12] Kawamoto, *Buraku mondai towa nanika*, 13–14. For another account of buraku discrimination in English, read the life story of Kariya Ryuichi. Kariya Ryuichi, "The Confidence to Live! Experiencing the Buraku Liberation Movement", in *Diversity in Japanese Culture and Language*, eds. John C. Maher and Gavnor Macdonald (London: Kegan Paul International, 1995). Yamashita Tsutomu's recent autobiography is also insightful. Yamashita Tsutomu, *Hisabetsu buraku no waga hansei* [My Life in a Buraku] (Tokyo: Heibonsha, 2004).

[13] Ambedkar, *The Untouchables: Who Were They and Why They Became Untouchables*, vii.

[14] Ibid., 34.

[15] Ambedkar spoke these words in 1942 at a meeting of the All-India Depressed Classes Association. Quoted in Debjani Ganguly, *Caste, Colonialism and Counter-modernity: Notes on a Postcolonial Hermeneutics of Caste.* (New York: Routledge, 2005), 160.

[16] Kawamoto, *Buraku mondai towa nanika*, 237.

[17] Inoue Kiyoshi, "Buraku kaihō riron to burakushi no kadai", [Buraku Liberation Theory and Issues in Buraku History] in *Sengo buraku mondai ronshū: kaihō riron I* [An Anthology of Writings on the Postwar Buraku Problem Vol. 1], ed. BMK 1 (Kyoto: Buraku Mondai Kenkyūjo, 1998), 76–85.

[18] For more on this, see my "Binding Burakumin: Marxist Historiography and the Narration of Difference in Japan", 155–71. See also Chapter 5 of this book.

[19] For a detailed index of documents containing references to outcast/es in Japanese history, see Harada Tomohiko ed., *Hennen sabetsushi shiryō shūsei* [Chronological Compilation of Historical Documents on Discrimination], 21 vols. (Tokyo: San'ichi Shobō, 1984–1995).

[20] Asada Zennosuke, *Sabetsu to tatakaitsuzukete*, 169.

[21] For a selection of writings on buraku discrimination along these lines see Harada, *Hisabetsu buraku no rekishi*, 297; Kobayashi *Hisabetsu buraku no rekishi*, 152.

[22] Miyazaki, et al., eds., *'Dōwa riken no shinsō' no shinsō: nani ga riaru ya!*, 32.

[23] Miyazaki, ibid., 31-36; Uesugi, *Tennōsei to buraku sabetsu: Buraku sabetsu wa naze aru no ka*, 4–5.

[24] The family background of Danzaemon XIII is particularly complex. His grandmother on his father's side and his grandfather on his mother's side were born into outcaste communities in Settsu and Kyoto but the backgrounds of his other grandparents are somewhat unclear. Nakao, *Edo no danzaemon: hisabetsu minshū ni kunrin shita 'kashira'*, 54–56, 60.

[25] Saitama-ken, ed., *Shinpen saitama-kenshi shiryōhen* [New History of Saitama Prefecture: Historical Sources], vol. 14, *Saitama-kenshi* (Urawa: Saitama-ken, 1991), 225–26.

[26] In 1781, for example, the shogunate gave instructions on what to do in the case of *eta* and *hinin* who absconded. Harada Tomohiko, ed., *Hennen sabetsushi shiryō shūsei* [Chronological Compilation of Historical Documents on Discrimination], 21 vols., vol. 10 (Tokyo: San'ichi Shobō, 1988), 523. In 1786, too, the shogunate ordered the sub-village organizational unit of the *gonin gumi* of each village not to permit vagrants to stay in their village overnight. Rural communities were constantly cautioned about this throughout the eighteenth century, but the difference with this law was that *eta* and *hinin* were also included in the list of vagrants, suggesting that they had also become increasingly mobile. Harada Tomohiko, ed., *Hennen sabetsushi shiryō shūsei* [Chronological Compilation of Historical Documents on Discrimination], 21 vols., vol. 11 (Tokyo: San'ichi Shobō, 1988), 175.

[27] See, for example, the various shogunate and domain edicts dated 1722, 1734, 1735, 1737, 1738, 1743, 1771, 1778, and 1780 in the series Harada ed., *Hennen sabetsushi shiryō shūsei.*

[28] Minegishi, *Kinsei hisabetsuminshi no kenkyū*, 17; Tsukada, *Kinsei nihon mibunsei no kenkyū*, 49.

[29] Minegishi, ibid., 22, 30–31. The word *toji* (屠児) or 'butcher' can also be found in references to the very earliest seventeenth century Shogunate legislation. Harada Tomohiko, ed., *Hennen sabetsushi shiryō shūsei* [Chronological Compilation of Historical Documents on Discrimination], 21 vols., vol. 6 (Tokyo: San'ichi Shobō, 1987), 54.

[30] Minegishi, ibid., 36–37.

[31] Ibid., 22.

[32] Ibid., 29–31.

[33] Ibid., 24–27. For a concise history of this process see Gerald Groemer, "The Creation of the Edo Outcaste Order", 276–80.

[34] Minegishi, *Kinsei hisabetsuminshi no kenkyū*, 28-29. Interestingly, Danzaemon's name, written throughout most of the eighteenth century as 弾左衛門, is recorded in this merchant diary entry of 1642 as 談左衛門, suggesting the possibility that it may have been a different person.

[35] Ibid., 33–35. The word 'kawata' is placed in single parentheses here because Minegishi Kentarō notes that this word may have been penned in next to Danzaemon's name on the original document at a later date.

[36] Francois Caron (1600–1673). Caron was born into a French family in Brussels. He joined the Dutch East India Company, and served on one of the Company's ships as a cook's assistant. In 1619, he jumped ship in Hirado, throwing himself at the mercy of the Dutch trading post there. In 1639, he was appointed director of the trading post, and though he was banished from Japan in 1641 by order of the Shōgunate, he continued to hold key posts in the Company, and in his later years, became a director of the French East India Company.

[37] Ibid., 32.

[38] Ibid., 38. Kuruma Zenshichi was the official title given to the head of the largest *hinin* community in Edo. It was a hereditary post. There were actually four (at one stage five) *hinin* leaders who emerged in the Greater Edo area during the latter half of the Tokugawa period: Kuruma Zenshichi (Asakusa), Matsuemon (Shinagawa), Zensaburō (Fukagawa), and Kubē (Sasaki). Very little is known about the origins of these communities except that after the Great Meireki Fire (1657), a sizable parcel of land next to the famous pleasure quarters (the Yoshiwara) was given to Kuruma Zenshichi and a large *hinin* community was built there. Interestingly though, Zenshichi's '*hinin* community' is referred to in Hyoshiya Ichirobē's 1684 map simply as 'beggar village' (*kojiki mura*). Tohoku University Library, *Kano bunko gazō* [Images from the Kano Collection]; available at http://www2.library.tohoku.ac.jp/kano/ezu/edo/edo.html

[39] Tokugawa Tsunayoshi was Japan's fifth Tokugawa shogun and was given the nickname 'dog shogun' because of a law he promulgated which forbade people from harming dogs. For a recent work in English on this interesting ruler, consult Beatrice Bodart-Bailey, *The Dog Shogun: The Personality and Policies of Tokugawa Tsunayoshi* (Honolulu: University of Hawai'i Press, 2007).

[40] Harada Tomohiko, ed., *Hennen sabetsushi shiryō shūsei* [Chronological Compilation of Historical Documents on Discrimination], 21 vols., vol. 7 (Tokyo: San'ichi Shobō, 1987), 259.

[41] Ibid., 340–44, 589–90. These documents are dated 1687 and 1701.

[42] Minegishi, *Kinsei hisabetsuminshi no kenkyū*, 40–41.

[43] All these maps are available online through the East Asia Library at the University of California, Berkeley. The 1684 map is also available online at the Tohoku University's digital Kanō collection at Tohoku University Library, *Kano bunko gazō*.

[44] Harada Tomohiko, ed., *Hennen sabetsushi shiryō shūsei*, vol. 8, 296. Note also other early eighteenth-century phrases that are equally problematic: '*eta* bounty hunter' (*eta meakashi*), '*eta* hut' (*eta goya*), '*hinin* bounty hunter' (*hinin meakashi*), and 'beggar *hinin*' (*kojiki hinin*). These expressions are dated 1713, 1719, 1724, and 1733, respectively. Ibid., 222, 321, 457; Harada Tomohiko, ed., *Hennen sabetsushi shiryō shūsei* [Chronological Compilation of Historical Documents on Discrimination], 21 vols., vol. 9 (Tokyo: San'ichi Shobō, 1987), 262.

[45] For more on this map and the concept of the 'workplace', see Amos, "Portrait of a Tokugawa Outcaste Village"; Howell, *Geographies of Identity in Nineteenth-Century Japan*, 37–38.

[46] Nakao Kenji, *Edo jidai no sabetsu gainen: kinsei no sabetsu wo dō toraeruka* [Discriminatory Notions in the Edo Period: How Should We Understood Early Modern Discrimination?] (Tokyo: San'ichi Shobō, 1997), 12, 57. Early modern

outcastes were, in some cases, clearly able to amass great sums of wealth, to the point wherein they were even capable of funding activities that threatened the very fabric of the Tokugawa social order. Records exist, for example, of *eta* involving themselves in large-scale social rebellions. We see in other records too such as the *Edo masago rokujūchō* (1748–1764) gossip concerning *eta* and *gōmune* leaders who, with bands of followers, were supposed to have revelled in the prostitute's quarters in Osaka for seven months consecutively. The *Tenmeikimon kanseikimon* in 1782 also relates an incident whereby an *eta* supposedly loaned a domain lord a large sum of money. The *Daijinmaikōshō* (1804) suggests that a big spender in the Yoshiwara pleasure quarters was an *eta* from Osaka. Moreover, the *Sejikenbunroku* (1816) speaks of outcastes from the Osaka area that had amassed great wealth, treasures, and even concubines.

47 Mase Kumiko, "Hisabetsu shūdan to chōtei / bakufu", Outcaste Groups and the Imperial Court/Shogunate] in *Iwanami kōza: tennō to ōken wo kangaeru* [Iwanami Lectures: Thinking About the Emperor and Imperial Power], eds. Amino Yoshihiko, et al. 7 (Tokyo: Iwanami Shoten, 2002), 139.

48 SDKK, ed., *Suzuki-ke monjo: Saitama-ken buraku mondai kankei shiryōshū* [The Documents of the House of Suzuki: Collection of Historical Sources Related to the Buraku Problem in Saitama Prefecture], 5 vols., vol. 3 (Urawa-shi: Saitama-ken Dōwa Kyōiku Kenkyū Kyōgikai, 1977–1979), 613 [817].

49 Urabe Manabu has argued that the Suzuki family began a pharmaceutical business in 1784 and it was probably the wealth generated from this enterprise that enabled them to buy large portions of land. Urabe Manabu, "Bushū shimo wana chōri no shitchi ukemodoshi hantai tōsō", [The Oppositional Struggle by Outcastes in Lower Wana Village in Musashi Province to the Return of Mortgaged Landm] in *Buraku no seikatsushi* [The Everyday Life History of Buraku], ed. Buraku mondai kenkyūjo (Kyoto: Buraku Mondai Kenkyūjo, 1988), 225–30.

50 SKDKK, *Saitama dōwa kyōiku sankō shiryō: suzuki-ke monjo kaisetsu* [The Documents of the House of Suzuki: Collection of Historical Sources Related to the Buraku Problem in Saitama Prefecture] (Urawa: Saitama-ken Dōwa Kyōiku Kenkyū Kyōgikai, 1981), 35–42; Fujita Genji, "Saitama-ken," [Saitama Prefecture] in *Buraku mondai jinken jiten*, 366.

51 Hatanaka, *'Burakushi' wo tou*, 143.

52 For an old but still very interesting discussion by Harada Tomohiko, one of Japan's foremost twentieth century historians, on the pedagogical problem of silence versus vocality with regard to the buraku problem, refer to Harada Tomohiko, "Buraku mondai no honshitsu to kadai", [The True Nature and Problems Surrounding the Buraku Problem] *Buraku kaihō* no. 1 (October 1968), 16–31.

53 SDKK, ed., *Saitama dōwa kyōiku sankō shiryō: suzuki-ke monjo kaisetsu*, 1.

54 Ishida Tadashi, "Bushū yokomi-gun shimo yoshimi wo aruku", [Walking Lower Yoshimi in Yokomi County, Musashi Province] *Ashita wo hiraku*, no. 36 (December 2000), 5–19.

55 Saitama kenchō sōmubu jinken suishinka, *Dōwa mondai* [The Dōwa Problem]; available at http://www.pref.saitama.lg.jp/A01/BI00/contents/4.html.

56 Takeuchi and Takayanagi, *Kadokawa nihonshi jiten*, 118.

57 SDKK, ed., *Saitama dōwa kyōiku sankō shiryō: suzuki-ke monjo kaisetsu*, 7. This link is also made by Fujita Genji. Fujita, "Saitama-ken", 366.

58 Noguchi, "Sabetsu", 386.

59 Professor Patricia Steinhoff of the University of Hawai'i suggested to me in a private communication that attitudes towards public affirmation of one's 'buraku-ness' should probably be understood as differences between the stances of different buraku-related organizations, whose influence may differ from region to region. This point is also brought out in Matsuoka Tōru's interview with Kobayashi Yoshinori in his famous Manga *Gōmanizumu sengen sabetsuron supesharu* [Declaration of Arrogance: Special Version on Discrimination] (Tokyo: Gentosha, 1998).

60 Ernesto Laclau and Chantal Mouffe, *Hegemony and Socialist Strategy: Towards a Radical Democratic Politics*. Second Edition. (London: Verso, 2001), 108.

61 Elizabeth Deeds Ermath, "Postmodernism", in *Routledge Encyclopaedia of Social Science*, ed. E. Craig (London: Routledge, 1998); available at http://www.rep.routledge.com/article/N044SECT2.

62 This point is made or alluded to in numerous referential works including Noguchi, "Sabetsu", 386–87; Hamashita Akira, et al., eds, *Shakaigaku shōjiten* [Concise Dictionary of Sociology] (Tokyo: Yūhikaku, 2005), 211.

63 Herman Ooms, *Tokugawa Village Practice: Class, Status, Power, Law* (Berkeley: University of California Press, 1996), 216. The discriminatory legislation of the centralizing Tokugawa state (labelled as 'state racism' by Herman Ooms), as Daniel Botsman points out, cannot be the end of the story of eighteenth century outcaste history. It is problematic to simply assume that a thing called 'racism' analogous to the Western concept existed in early modern Japan. Botsman, *Punishment and Power in the Making of Modern Japan*, 244–45.

64 Ooms, ibid., 216.

65 SDKK, ed., *Suzuki-ke monjo: Saitama-ken buraku mondai kankei shiryōshū*, vol. 1, 239 [116].

66 Joan W. Scott has argued along similar lines: 'Writing is reproduction, transmission—the communication of knowledge gained through (visual, visceral) experience". Joan W. Scott, "The Evidence of Experience", *Critical Inquiry* 17:4 (Summer 1991), 776.

67 David Carr, *Time, Narrative, and History* (Bloomington, Indianapolis: Indiana University Press, 1986), 54. It is through attempts to witness the effects of

discourse and ideology on our historical subjects (and ourselves) that we become better able to produce narratives which make sense of the worlds that are external to our historical subjects and ourselves. As Carr also notes, discourses themselves are informed by experiences in the real world. While the relationship between discourse and reality is problematic and irretrievable in an absolute sense, 'constructed' and 'experiential' relationships clearly do go together to form historical events (49).

68 Discourses can, of course, be identified in specific texts ('positioned discourses') as well as in a wider reading of society ('social discourses'). Historians can examine discourses of difference either within specific texts that demonstrate the ways in which ideas like *eta* and *hinin* are used and how individual meanings diverge during a particular period; or by searching for 'social discourses' found in large numbers of narratives, which suggest the ways in which 'positioned discourses' are part of more comprehensive historical changes.

69 For an excellent discussion of the importance of the idea of precedent in ruler–peasant relations, see Chapter 4 "Perceptions of Commerce, History, and Politics" in Anne Walthall, *Social Protest and Popular Culture in Eighteenth-Century Japan* (Tucson: The University of Arizona Press, 1986), 72–95.

70 Nakao Kenji, ed., *Danzaemon kankei shiryōshū: kyūbakufu hikitsugisho* [Collection of Documents Related to Danzaemon: Transmitted Documents of the Former Bakufu], 3 vols., vol. 1 (Osaka: Buraku Kaihō Kenkyūjo, 1995), 29.

71 Nakao, ibid., 24–29; Harada, ed., *Hennen sabetsushi shiryō shūsei*, vol. 8, 511–94.

72 Nakao, ibid., 76–79.

73 Ibid., 98–99.

74 Ibid., 98.

75 Ibid., 207–08.

76 Ibid., 198–99.

77 Harada, ed., *Hennen sabetsushi shiryō shūsei*, vol. 8, 455–56.

78 SDKK, ed., *Suzuki-ke monjo: saitama-ken buraku mondai kankei shiryōshū*, 5 vols., vol. 1, 138 [2103].

79 Nakao, *Danzaemon kankei shiryō shū*, vol. 1, 35–36. The ruling by the Edo City Magistrates Ishikawa Masatomo, Governor of Tosa (period in office was 1738–1744) and Shima Yoshimasa, Lord of Nagato (period in office was 1740–1746) also concludes with 'Danzaemon uttaeide sōrō tōri ni mōshi tsuke shikaru beki to zonji tatematsuri sōrō' (translated approximately as 'We think we should order in the way the Danzaemon has petitioned').

80 Ibid., 210–11.

81 Nakao Kenji, *Danzaemon kankei shiryōshū: kyūbakufu hikitsugisho* [Collection of Documents Related to Danzaemon: Transmitted Documents of the Former Bakufu], 3 vols., vol. 2 (Osaka: Buraku Kaihō Kenkyūjo, 1995), 4.

82 Nakao, *Danzaemon kankei shiryō shū*, vol. 1, 261–62.

[83] Harada Tomohiko, ed., *Hennen sabetsushi shiryō shūsei* [Chronological Compilation of Historical Documents on Discrimination], 21 vols., vol. 12 (Tokyo: San'ichi Shobō, 1988), 414–15; Nakao, *Danzaemon kankei shiryō shū*, vol. 1, 597.

[84] Nakao, *Danzaemon kankei shiryōshū*, vol. 2, 34–35.

[85] Ibid., 39–40.

[86] Ibid., vol.1, 487.

[87] Ibid., 546–47.

[88] Document quoted in Hatanaka Toshiyuki, *Mibun/sabetsu/aidentitī: 'burakushi' wa bohyō to naruka* [Status, discrimination, identity: Will 'Buraku history' become a grave post?] (Kyoto: Kamogawa Shuppan, 2004), 63–64.

[89] In the 1871 version of Ōishi Kyūkei's *Jikata hanreiroku* [Explanatory Notes on Village Life], Danzaemon is said to have described the word *eta* as having 'popular origins' (*sewa*) and asserts that his proper status designation should be 'chōri' (32). Historical evidence suggests that many people officially designated as '*eta*' during the Tokugawa period like Danzaemon far preferred the term 'chōri'. Based on Danzaemon's obvious distaste for the label 'eta', replacing the term altogether with 'chōri' seems advisable. I have resisted such a move in this book for several reasons, however. The terms *eta* and *hinin* are clearly the dominant ones found in extant historical documentation related to these groups. These were officially sanctioned and publicly recognized status markers and are found in most laws and legislation pertaining to these groups throughout the second half of the Tokugawa period. As such, they are terms of considerable historical importance and retain an important communicative value for contemporary readers. They remind us that a demonstration of historical agency on the part of certain marginalized peoples in Tokugawa Japan (in this case, an act of discursive resistance by the appropriation of labels) was necessary precisely because of the deeply entrenched regimes of state-sponsored social hatred that enveloped the lives of the members of these groups.

[90] Sugiyama Seiko, "Kinsei kantō ni okeru 'hisabetsu buraku' no mibun kōshō ni tsuite: suzuki-ke monjo yori", [Regarding the Status Labels of the 'Buraku' in Early Modern Kantō: From the Documents of the House of Suzuki] *Minshūshi kenkyū*, no. 26 (1984): 8, 18.

[91] Michel Foucault, *Discipline and Punish: The Birth of the Prison* (London: Penguin Books, 1977), 178.

[92] This perspective features particularly prominently in the work of Imanishi Hajime. See, for example, Imanishi Hajime, "Kindai nihon no kokumin kokka to buraku mondai", [The Modern Japanese Nation-State and the Buraku Problem] in *Burakushi kenkyū: buraku minshū / kokumin kokka to suihei undō* [Buraku Historical Research: Burakumin, Nation-State, and the Levellers' Movement], ed. Zenkoku burakushi kenkyū kōryūkai. Vol. 3 (Osaka: Kaihō Shuppansha, 1999), 82–83.

93 For a similar argument in Japanese, see Imanishi Hajime, *Bunmei kaika to sabetsu* [Enlightenment and Discrimination] (Tokyo: Yoshikawa Kōbunkan, 2001), 8–9.

94 For more on this court case, see Groemer, "The Creation of the Edo Outcaste Order", 276–77.

95 For an abbreviated and annotated version of this work with notes, see Okiura Kazuteru, *Suihei: hito no yo ni hikari are* [Levellers: Let there be Light in the World of Man] (Tokyo: Shakai Hyōronsha, 1991), 12–13.

96 The term *kawaramono* is often considered to be an alternative name for *eta* but Hatanaka Toshiyuki has recently argued that it may be a separate 'status'. Hatanaka Toshiyuki, "'Eta' 'hinin' towa dare no koto nanoka", [Who does 'eta' and 'hinin' refer to?] in *Datsujōshiki no buraku mondai* [The Buraku Problem Minus The Common Sense], ed. Takeshi Asaji, et.al. (Kyoto: Kamogawa Shuppan, 1998), 211–19.

97 Okiura, *Suihei: hito no yo ni hikari are*, 16.

98 Ibid.

Chapter 4

1 As John H. Davis has pointed out, moreover, certain districts and people are also sometimes mistakenly identified as 'buraku' and 'burakumin'. John H. Davis, "Blurring the Boundaries of the Buraku (min)", in *Globalization and Social Change in Contemporary Japan*, eds. J. S. Eades, et al. (Melbourne: Trans Pacific Press, 2000), 111–13.

2 Harry Harootunian, *Overcome by Modernity: History, Culture, and Community in Interwar Japan* (Princeton and Oxford: Princeton University Press, 2000), xvi.

3 This point struck home particularly vividly in the context of the above dinner conversation because the interlocutors themselves were actors engaged in an old performing art, which had successfully managed to negotiate its 'premodern-ness' in the modern era.

4 This point is well-made by Zygmunt Bauman who writes: 'The production of "human waste", or more correctly wasted humans (the "excessive and redundant", that is the population of those who either could not or were not wished to be recognized or allowed to stay), is an inevitable outcome of modernization, and an inseparable accompaniment of modernity. It is an inescapable part of *order-building* [sic] (each order casts some parts of the extant population as "out of place", "unfit", or "undesirable") and of *economic progress* [sic] (that cannot proceed without degrading and devaluing the previously effective modes of "making a living" and, therefore, cannot but deprive their practitioners of their livelihood).' Zygmunt Bauman, *Wasted Lives: Modernity and its Outcasts* (Cambridge: Polity Press, 2004), 5.

[5] Morris, "Passing: Paradoxes of Alterity in The Broken Commandment", 133.

[6] Tomotsune Tsutomu, "Nakagami Kenji and the Buraku Issue in Postwar Japan", *Inter-Asia Cultural Studies*, vol. 4, no. 2 (2003): 228.

[7] Debra Walker King writes about this practice as follows: 'Unnaming occurs when a name phrase, name or nickname *replaces* [sic] the original designator, forcing it from the text entirely; when an epithet, or other pejorative name, functions as the primary signifier for a character; or when a sense of namelessness, nullification, or a loss of historicity dominates either a name's deep talk [discourses existing beneath the text] or a character's subject position within a text.' Debra Walker King, *Deep Talk: Reading African-American Literary Names* (Charlottesville: University of Virginia Press, 1998), 92.

[8] Article 8 of the 1884 peerage law stated that 'The household registry and social status [*mibun*] of nobles shall be administered by the Imperial Household Ministry.' For an interesting interpretation of the link between the buraku problem and the modern peerage system, see Hatanaka, *'Burakushi' no owari*, 206–09.

[9] Kurokawa, *Ika to dōka no aida*, 24.

[10] For a lucid introduction to the problem of mobilizing outcastes to settle Japan's frontiers, see Noah McCormack, "Buraku Immigration in the Meiji Era—Other Ways to Become 'Japanese",' *East Asian History*, no. 23 (June 2002): 87–101.

[11] Takashi Fujitani, "Inventing, Forgetting, Remembering: Toward a Historical Ethnography of the Nation-State", in *Cultural Nationalism in East Asia: Representation and Identity*, edited by Harumi Befu (Berkeley: Institute of East Asian Studies, University of California, 1993), 99.

[12] This quote, taken from the Meiji bureaucrat and author, Nishimura Kanefumi (1832–1896), is found in Kurokawa, *Ika to dōka no aida*, 39.

[13] Francis Hall (1822–1902). A New York book dealer who went to Japan to collect material for a book, and served as a correspondent for the *New York Tribune*. Lived in Japan (predominantly Yokohama/Kanagawa) through the years 1859–1866.

[14] Francis Hall, *Japan Through American Eyes 1859-1866: The Journal of Francis Hall Kanagawa and Yokohama* (Princeton: Princeton University Press, 1992), 154–55.

[15] Alfred East, *A British Artist in Meiji Japan* (Brighton: In Print, 1991), 44.

[16] Christopher Pemberton Hodgson, *A Residence in Nagasaki and Hakodate in 1859-1860; With an account of Japan generally; With a series of letters on Japan by his wife* (London: R. Bentley, 1861), 196.

[17] Noah McCormack, "From Alien to Backward: Reconceptualizing Difference in Modern Japan", *Ritsumeikan gengo bunka kenkyū* 17 no.3 (2006), 214.

[18] Kurokawa, *Ika to dōka no aida*, 27.

[19] Also found in Ibid., 29.

20 McCormack, "Making Modern Urban Order: Towards Popular Mobilisation", 269–70.

21 Noah McCormack, "Civilising the Urban Other: Poverty as a National Problem", *Ritsumeikan Annual Review of International Studies* vol. 6 (2007), 31.

22 Kurokawa, *Ika to dōka no aida*, 36.

23 Ibid., 37.

24 Shiomi, *Danzaemon to sono jidai*, 122.

25 Ibid., 121–25.

26 Ibid., 131–32.

27 McCormack, "Making Modern Urban Order: Towards Popular Mobilisation", 262–63.

28 Neary, *Political Protest and Social Control in Pre-War Japan*, 34.

29 McCormack, ibid., 268.

30 Shiomi, *Danzaemon to sono jidai*, 117–18.

31 Kurokawa, *Ika to dōka no aida*, 31.

32 Shiomi, ibid., 99–111.

33 For recent work in English on these facilities, see Botsman, *Punishment and Power in the Making of Modern Japan*, 61–69, 100–04.

34 Shiomi, ibid., 112–13.

35 Ibid., 127.

36 Ibid., 127–28.

37 Ibid., 128–30.

38 Ibid., 126.

39 One of the most important local elites in the Yanagihara district, Sukarada Gihē (1832–1893), was born into the household of the hereditary *eta* village officials and was elected to the position of village head after the Meiji Restoration, a position he held until the 1890s. It is clear that Yanagihara as a whole was an area that had a well-established reputation as a 'former outcaste' area, and officials like Sakurada felt obliged to spend considerable amounts of their own personal wealth to 'improve the local area and counter prejudices against its residents'. Such activities included the establishment of local newspapers to address the lack of education among residents, and distributing food and clothes to needy residents. McCormack, "Making Modern Urban Order: Towards Popular Mobilisation", 269–70.

40 Kinegawa enkakushi kenkyūkai, ed., *Kinegawa chiku no ayumi sengo hen* [The Postwar History of Kinegawa] (Tokyo: Gendai Kikakushitsu, 2005).

41 Shiomi, *Danzaemon to sono jidai*, 126.

42 Kinegawa enkakushi kenkyūkai, ed., *Kinegawa chiku no ayumi sengo hen*, 13–14.

43 Ibid., 24.

[44] Ibid., 14, 23–24.

[45] Kurokawa, *Ika to dōka no aida*, 105.

[46] Quoted in Kurokawa, ibid., 33–34.

[47] Ibid., 41.

[48] Ibid., 54.

[49] Ibid., 44.

[50] Ibid., 50.

[51] Ibid., 51.

[52] By the late 1880s, the idea of 'former outcastes' had faded somewhat into the background and the language of 'new commoner-citizens' tended to dominate discourse on socially marginalized groups with purportedly ancient pedigrees. Ibid., 46–47, 56.

[53] Ibid., 57.

[54] Ibid., 52.

[55] McCormack, "Civilising the Urban Other: Poverty as a National Problem," 31.

[56] Fujino Yutaka, "Hisabetsu buraku," [Buraku] in *Iwanami kōza nihon tsūshi* [Iwanami History of Japan], eds. Asao Naohiro, et al. Vol. 18 (Tokyo: Iwanami Shoten, 1994), 140–41.

[57] Kurokawa, ibid., 74.

[58] Quoted in ibid., 75. The most famous piece of literature on the 'former outcaste' problem, 'The Broken Commandment' (*Hakai*), was also published during this year. As René Andersson notes, 'While Shimazaki Tōson (1872–1943) was not the first writer to bring burakumin and their situation to the Japanese readership… his *Hakai* is clearly the single most important work to date in the genre of burakumin literature.' The novel tells the story of Segawa Ushimatsu, a schoolteacher working in the northwestern prefecture of Nagano. Ushimatsu is heavily burdened by the fact that he must, under strict orders from his father, conceal his real identity as a 'former outcaste'. The novel concludes with him moving to the United States and purportedly realizing the possibility of a normal life. René Andersson, *Burakumin and Shimazaki Tōson's Hakai: Images of Discrimination in Modern Japanese Literature* (Lund, Sweden: Department of East Asian Languages, Lund University, 2000), 10.

[59] Kurokawa, ibid., 60.

[60] Ibid., 92.

[61] Ibid., 93.

[62] Ibid., 95–107.

[63] Ibid., 105.

[64] Ibid., 98.

[65] As Ueda Masaaki notes, Yanagita's early position on the possible foreign origins of the 'special buraku' was ambivalent. Ueda Masaaki, *Kita Sadakichi*

[Kita Sadakichi], vol. 5, Nihon minzoku bunka taikei (Tokyo: Kōdansha, 1978), 34.

66 Yanagita Kunio, "Iwayuru tokushu buraku no shurui", [Concerning the So-called Race of Special Buraku] *in Suihei: hito no yo ni hikari are* [Levellers: Let there be Light in the World of Man], edited by Okiura Kazuteru. (Tokyo: Shakai Hyōronsha, 1991), 108, 111.

67 Ibid., 107.

68 Ibid., 111. Yanagita concluded his treatise by stating that many buraku produced large economic surpluses and grew rich, suggesting that the 'productive aspects' of the buraku problem should be carefully monitored by government officials. Yanagita's concern with productivity displays a close correlation with other discourses prevalent at the time, which highlighted the supposed physical defects of 'buraku' residents, especially in relation to their sexual organs and menstruation cycles. For more on this, see Kurokawa, *Ika to dōka no aida*, 78, 94.

69 Ibid., 110–11.

70 Ibid., 96–97.

71 Mizuuchi Toshio, "The Historical Transformation of Poverty, Discrimination, and Urban Policy in Japanese City: The Case of Osaka", in *Representing Local Places and Raising Voices from Below*, edited by Toshio Mizuuchi. (Osaka: Osaka City University, 2003), 15.

72 Matsushita Tatsuhito, 'Taishōki no sabetsu chōsa shiryō ga mitsukaru'; available at http://blhrri.org/topics/topics_0087.html

73 Sanka refers to an organized body of people in Japan who are not engaged in agriculture and are nomadic without a fixed address. See Tatsuta Hiroyuki, "Sanka", [Mountain Nomads] in *Yashi yobina jiten* [Dictionary of Names for Marginalized Groups], ed. Tatsuta Hiroyuki (Hiroshima: Menmehei Shuppan, 1998), 426.

74 Photocopies of some of these newspaper articles can be found at Hansenbyō kaifuku kanja to furusato wo musubu [Joining Together Recovering Hansen Disease Patients and Their Communities of Origin], *Oita to hansenbyō no rekishi* [The History of Hansen's Disease in Oita Prefecture]; available at http://www.geocities.jp/furusatohp/panerurten/oita/matogahama.html.

75 For the first point see Kurokawa, ibid., 17. Kitahara Taisaku, the well-known postwar buraku activist, is perhaps best known for presenting a petition regarding 'buraku' discrimination in the army directly to the Shōwa Emperor, an action which earned him a one-year prison sentence. The petition was delivered in November 1927 and part of it reads as follows: 'The discrimination and contempt displayed toward members of the special buraku in the armed forces is as severe as the conditions that prevail under feudalism. Frequently disputes are touched off by discriminatory actions. The attitude of the authorities who

deal with these disputes indicates a complete absence of sincerity toward the victims of discrimination. Instead they behave oppressively toward us.' Hane, *Peasants, Rebels, Women, and Outcastes*, 169. A copy of this petition in Japanese can be found in Nadamoto Masahisa, "Buraku kaihō ni han tennōsei wa muyō", [Anti-Imperial Sentiment is not Necessary for Buraku Liberation] *Momento* no. 12 (April 2003), 8.

[76] Buraku kaihō dōmei nara-ken rengōkai Okubo shibu, ed., *Kyōku ni taezaru koto ni kō shite: tennō (sei) ni yoru hora buraku kyōsei idō* [Defying the Inability of Others to Resist Fear: The Forced Migration of the Hora Community at the Hands of the Imperial Institution] (Nara: Ikeda Shuppan Insatsusha, no date), 5.

[77] For work on this community, see ibid. Despite the twentieth century relocation of the community, Hora was identified as a buraku area under the Dōwa Special Measures legislation established in the 1960s.

[78] Neary, *Political Protest and Social Control in Pre-War Japan,* 226.

[79] Kurokawa, *Tsukurikaerareru shirushi: nihon kindai / hisabetsu buraku / mainoriti,* 111–19.

[80] Shiomi, *Datsu-ideorogii no burakushi: jubaku ga tokete rekishi ga mieru,* 108–10.

[81] Kita Sadakichi, "Minzoku to rekishi (tokushu buraku kenkyūgō) hakkan no ji", [Ethnicity and History (Research Edition on Special Buraku): Publisher's Introduction] found in Okiura Kazuteru, *Suihei: hito no yo ni hikari are* [Levellers: Let there be Light in the World of Man] (Tokyo: Shakai Hyōronsha, 1991), 121–26.

[82] Sano Manabu, "Suiheisha sōritsu hakkisha: yoki hi no tame ni", [The Movers Behind the Establishment of the Suiheisha: For a Better Day] in *Suihei: hito no yo ni hikari are* [Levellers: Let there be Light in the World of Man], edited by Okiura Kazuteru. (Tokyo: Shakai Hyōronsha, 1991): 173–74.

[83] As Shiomi Sen'ichirō notes, Saikō Bankichi's 'Suiheisha Declaration' actually reproduced verbatim Sano's section on the 'Principles of Liberation'. Shiomi Sen'ichirō, *Datsu-ideorogii no burakushi: jubaku ga tokete rekishi ga mieru,* 105.

[84] Miyazaki Manabu, *Kindai no naraku* [The Modern Purgatory] (Tokyo: Gentōsha Autorō Bunko, 2005), 52.

[85] Neary, *Political Protest and Social Control in Pre-War Japan,* 157–59. Also Kurokawa, *Tsukurikaerareru shirushi: nihon kindai / hisabetsu buraku / mainoriti,* 130–31.

[86] Neary, ibid., 82–83.

[87] Ibid., 101.

[88] Ibid., 103.

[89] A survey of the titles of books published at this time confirms this point. See, for example, Baba Kōzō, *Nōson buraku no shidō* [Guides for Agricultural Settlements]. Tokyo: Ōnuki Shobō, 1942; Roba-to Li-fuman, *Kyōsan buraku*

no kenkyū [A Study of Communal Settlements]. Translated by Ōtaku Sōichi. Tokyo: Shinchōsha, 1927; Fukuda Shinsei, *Hokuman no roshiyajin buraku* [Russian Settlements in Northern Manchurian]. Tokyo: Tama Shobō, 1942; Zenshō Eisuke, *Chōsen no seishi to dōzoku buraku* [Korean Family Names and Tribal Settlements] (Tokyo: Zenshō Eisuke, 1940); M. Mi-do, *Manusu-zoku no seitai kenkyū*: *Nyūginea suigō buraku no jūmin* [Ecology of the Manus: Residents of the Water Settlement in New Guinea]. Translated by Kaneko Shigetaka (Tokyo: Okakura Shobō, 1940).

90 Quoted in Kurokawa, *Ika to dōka no aida*, 88.

91 Osatake, *Meiji yonnen senshō haishi fukoku no kenkyū*, 94.

92 "The *Buraku mondai/suihei undō shiryō shūsei*" (Buraku Problem / Collection of Leveler's Movement Documents) lists this film's title as *Fujin Mandala* not *Fujin Sendara*. See Watanabe Tōru and Akisada Yoshikazu, eds, *Buraku mondai / suihei undō shiryō shūsei*, vol. 3. (Tokyo: Shōin, 1974), 240.

93 Neary, ibid., 201.

94 Ibid., 154.

95 Amos, "Binding Burakumin: Marxist Historiography and the Narration of Difference in Japan". Also consult Chapter 5 of this book.

96 For an explanation of Inoue's ideas, see Chapter 3.

97 Nakao Kenji's assessment of this period is as follows: 'Buraku history had to be a bloody history of struggle towards liberation that won out against this misery: this was the basic stance of buraku history in the 1950s.' Nakao Kenji, "Burakushi no kakko, genzai, mirai", [The Past, Present, and Future of Buraku History] in *Datsujōshiki no buraku mondai* [The Buraku Problem Minus The Common Sense], eds. Asaji Takeshi, et al. (Kyoto: Kamogawa Shuppan, 1998), 31.

98 Raymond Williams, *Keywords: A Vocabulary of Culture and Society* (London: Fontana Press, 1976), 181–83.

99 Jan Nederveen Pieterse, "Emancipations, Modern and Postmodern", in *Emancipations, Modern and Postmodern*, ed. Jan Nederveen Pieterse (London: Sage, 1992), 7.

100 Ibid., 18.

101 Ibid., 11.

102 Harriet Evans, "The Language of Liberation: Gender and Jiefang in Early Chinese Communist Party Discourse", *Intersections*, no. 1 (September 1998): para. 10. http://wwwsshe.murdoch.edu.au/intersections/back_issues/harriet.html.

103 Ernesto Laclau, "Beyond Emancipation", in *Emancipations, Modern and Postmodern*, ed. Jan Nederveen Pieterse (London: Sage Publications, 1992), 121–22.

Chapter 5

1 "United Nations Decade for Human Rights Education, Osaka Prefectural Government Plan of Action: Creating an affluent human rights culture – From Learning to Action"; available at http://www.pref.osaka.jp/jinken/measure/jinken/kouki10.htm

2 Frank Upham, *Law and Social Change in Postwar Japan* (Cambridge: Harvard University Press, 1987), 22.

3 Ian Neary, *Human Rights in Japan, South Korea and Taiwan* (London: Routledge, 2002), 42.

4 See, for example, "Settlement development through linking people. A case of Kitagata Project in Japan", *Habitat International Coalition*; available at http://www.hic-net.org/document.asp?PID=102; Sunil Sethi, "You can't wish away reservation", *Business Standard*, 22 April 2006; "Burakumin - Current Numbers, Terminology, Historical origins, End of feudal era, Postwar situation, Burakumin rights movement"; available at http://encyclopedia.stateuniversity.com/pages/3395/Burakumin.html.

5 John H. Davis, "Challenging the State, Embracing the Nation: An Ethnographic Analysis of Human Rights in Japanese Society". PhD, Stanford University, 2002, 98.

6 *Zaidan hōjin osaka-shi jinken kyōkai* [Osaka Municipal Human Rights Foundation]; available at http://www.ochra.or.jp/event/2007_03/naniwa_070308.html

7 Morooka Sukeyuki, *Sengo buraku kaihō ronsōshi* [History of Postwar Buraku Liberation Debates], 4 vols., vol. 1. (Tokyo: Tsuge Shobō, 1980), 31.

8 Ibid., 28.

9 Buraku kaihō kenkyūjo, ed., *Zenkoku taikai undō hōshin* [National Committee Conference Campaign Policy]. 3 vols, vol. 1. (Osaka: Kaihō Shuppansha, 1980), 2–3.

10 Morooka, ibid., 24.

11 Ibid., 91.

12 Buraku kaihō kenkyūjo, ed., *Zenkoku taikai undō hōshin.*, 6–10.

13 Buraku mondai kenkyūjo, ed., *Buraku mondai kenkyūjo 50 nen no ayumi* [Research Institute for the Buraku Problem: 50 years of history] (Kyoto: Buraku Mondai Kenkyūjo Shuppanbu, 1998), 101.

14 Ibid., 6–7.

15 In the 1920s, a debate emerged between two Marxist factions in Japan—the kōzaha (lecture faction) and the *rōnōha* (farmer's faction)—over the nature of Japanese capitalism. The former faction argued that Japanese capitalism was semi-feudal and required a subsequent revolution apart from the one that took place at the time of Meiji, whereas the latter faction argued that a bourgeois revolution had in fact taken place at the time of Meiji. It was the kōzaha

factional view of history that dominated much of postwar Japanese Marxian historiography. From this perspective, the contemporary buraku minority were seen as a feudal remnant, and only able to be liberated from discrimination through a future unification of the proletariat. Takeuchi and Takayanagi, *Kadokawa nihonshi jiten*, 333, 742.

16 Quoted in Buraku mondai kenkyūjo, ed., *Buraku mondai kenkyūjo 50 nen no ayumi*, 15.

17 Buraku mondai kenkyūjo, *Shakai hōjin buraku mondai kenkyūjo teikan* [The Charter of the Buraku mondai kenkyūjo Foundation]; available at http://www.burakken.jp/cgi/file/1065076993__1027402929__teikan.html.

18 Asada Zennosuke, *Asada zennosuke zenkiroku: sabetsu to tatakaitsuzukete* [The Complete Records of Asada Zennosuke: Continuing to Fight Discrimination], vol. 22 (Kyoto: Asada Kyōiku Zaidan, 1995), 59.

19 It is widely acknowledged that *Buraku kaihō he no sanjūnen* was actually written by Asada Zennosuke and Matsumoto's name was used only to attract readership. Morooka, *Sengo buraku kaihō ronsōshi*, 121.

20 Ibid., 128, 131.

21 As Ian Neary argues, Marxism appeared to be the only theoretical framework that could both explain the persistence of the buraku problem and suggest a way forward. Neary, *Political Protest and Social Control in Prewar Japan*, 219, 221.

22 For more on this, see Chapter 2.

23 Tōjō Takashi, *Ima buraku mondai towa* [What is the Buraku Problem Today?] (Kyoto: Buraku Mondai Kenkyūjo, 1998), 32–33.

24 Asada, *Sabetsu to tatakaitsuzukete*, 169.

25 Ibid., 167–68.

26 Buraku mondai kenkyūjo, ed., *Buraku mondai kenkyūjo 50 nen no ayumi*, 42–43.

27 Asada Zennosuke, et al., "Sengo buraku kaihō undo no riron", [Postwar Buraku Liberation Movement Theory] *Buraku kaihō*, no. 100 (April 1977): 24.

28 Found in Teraki Nobuaki, *Kinsei mibun to hisabetsumin no shosō: 'burakushi no minaoshi' no tojō kara* [Early Modern Status and Various Aspects of Outcastes: Amidst 'Buraku History Revisionism'] (Osaka: Kaihō Shuppansha, 2000), 11.

29 Komatsu Katsumi has noted that this document demonstrates the 'limitations' of Japanese attitudes towards human rights in the mid-1960s, treating the buraku problem as one concerning Japanese nationals and not all citizens/residents that comprised Japanese society. Komatsu Katsumi, "Fukuzawa yukichi 'manazashi' kara uki testuj ō 'manazashi' he", [From a Fukuzawa Yukichi to an Uki Tetsujō 'standard'] in *Datsujōshiki no buraku mondai* [The Buraku Problem Minus The

Common Sense], eds. Asaji Takeshi, et al. (Kyoto: Kamogawa Shuppan, 1998), 21.

30 Yamashita Tsutomu, "Nijū isseiki wo mokuzen ni shite: fushime wo mukaeta buraku kaihō undō no genjō", [The Realities of the Buraku Liberation Movement at the Turn of the 21st Century:] *Gendai shisō* [Contemporary Thought] 27, no. 2 (1999): 64. This figure is quoted as 16 trillion yen in Yoshida, "Buraku mondai wa naze owaranai noka", 82.

31 *Shakai hōjin buraku kaihō jinken kenkyūjo teikan* [The Charter of the Buraku Liberation and Human Rights Research Institute Foundation]; available at http://www.blhrri.org/blhrri/about/teikan.htm

32 The 'All Japan Federation of Buraku Liberation Movements', formed in the late 1960s by BLL activists linked to the Communist Party and who were purged due to their opposition to the Special Measures legislation. It was formerly Japan's second biggest buraku liberation organization but was formally disbanded in 2004.

33 "Setsuritsu mokuteki to kihon rinen"; available at http://www.liberty.or.jp/cp_pf/index.html

34 *Henomatsu jinken rekishikan* [Henomatsu Human Rights Historical Museum]; available at http://www.city.sakai.osaka.jp/fureai/henomatsu/index.html

35 "Sakai City Peace and Human Rights Museum"; available at http://www.city.sakai.osaka.jp/city/info/_jinken/index.html

36 June A. Gordon, "From Liberation to Human Rights: Challenges for Teachers of the Burakumin in Japan", *Race Ethnicity and Education* 9: 2 (2006), 187.

37 Ian Laidlaw, "Interview with T_, of the Buraku Liberation League and Human Rights Research Centre"; available at http://www.geocities.com/gaijindo4dan/BLHRRI.html

38 See, for example, Zenkoku Chi'iki Jinken Undō Sōrengō, "What is Braku [sic] Problem?"; available at http://homepage3.nifty.com/zjr/english.html

39 Upham, *Law and Social Change in Postwar Japan*, 22.

40 Neary, *Human Rights in Japan, South Korea and Taiwan*, 42.

41 This figure is found in Terazono Atsushi, "Ubawareta jinjiken to baibai sareta saiyōwaku (ge): 'Dōwa' toiu yamai (4)" (Stolen Human Resource Rights and Brokered Employment Systems: The 'Disease' of Dōwa), *Mariido* (*Dōwa Gyōsei Obuzaabaa*) (July 2008) 156; available at http://muhajirin.com/almarid/text/156.html (accessed July 2009).

42 "Kenshō: Osaka-shi shokuin kōgu mondai" (Investigative Report: The Problem Surrounding the Preferential Treatment of Osaka Municipal Personnel), *Sankei Shinbun*, 2 February 2005.

43 Davis, "Challenging the State, Embracing the Nation: An Ethnographic Analysis of Human Rights in Japanese Society", 167.

44 Neary, *Human Rights in Japan, South Korea and Taiwan*, 34.

[45] Gaimu I'inkai, 14 gō, 31/05/1979, 52.

[46] Neary, *Human Rights in Japan, South Korea and Taiwan*, 41.

[47] Gaimu I'inkai, 14 gō, 31/05/1979, 54; Gaimu I'inkai, 9 gō, 07/05/1979, 10.

[48] Gaimu I'inkai, 14 gō, 31/05/1979, 81.

[49] Fujita Kei'ichi, *Buraku wa kowai kō* [Thoughts on Why the Dōwa Problem is Scary] (Osaka: Aunsha, 1987).

[50] Davis, "Challenging the State, Embracing the Nation: An Ethnographic Analysis of Human Rights in Japanese Society", 166.

[51] All the information about the Human Rights Protection Agency in the following section is found in *Jinken yōgokyoku* [The Human Rights Protection Agency]; available at http://www.moj.go.jp/JINKEN.

[52] All the information about The Centre for Human Rights Affairs in the following section is found on the website http://www.jinken.or.jp/index-en.html.

[53] Anne Allison, *Millenial Monsters: Japanese Toys and the Global Imagination* (Berkeley: University of California Press, 2006), 11–12.

[54] Osaka jinken hakubutsukan, ed., *Osaka jinken hakubutsukan sōgō tenji zuroku: watashi ga mukiau nihon shakai no sabetsu to jinken* [A Pictorial Record of the General Exhibits at the Osaka Human Rights Museum: The Discrimination I Face in Japanese Society and Human Rights] (Osaka: Osaka Jinken Hakubutsukan, 2006), 13.

[55] A stark reminder of this occurred during the writing of this monograph. A change of government at the prefectural level in Osaka led to the incumbent governor freezing all future funding for Liberty Osaka, thereby placing the future of the institution in doubt.

[56] Terence M. Duffy, "Museums of 'Human Suffering' and the Struggle for Human Rights", in *Museum Studies: An Anthology of Contexts*, ed. Bettina Messias Carbonell. (Malden: Blackwell Publishing, 2004), 117.

[57] Steven C. Dubin, "Incivilities in Civil(-ized) Places: Culture Wars in Comparative Perspective", *A Companion to Museum Studies*, ed. Sharon Macdonald. (Malden, MA: Blackwell, 2006), 478.

[58] B. Durrans (1992), "Behind the Scenes: Museums and Selective Criticism", *Anthropology Today* 8 (4): 11.

[59] Slavoj Žižek, "Human Rights and its Discontents", 16 November 1999. Available at http://www.egs.edu/faculty/zizek/zizek-human-rights-and-its-discontents.html

[60] Slavoj Žižek, "Against Human Rights", *New Left Review* 34 (July–August 2005): 130.

Chapter 6

[1] Henry Louis Gates, Jr, "The Master's Pieces: On Canon Formation and the Afro-American Tradition", in *The Bounds of Race: Perspectives on Hegemony and*

Resistance, ed. Dominick LaCapra (Ithaca; London: Cornell University Press, 1991) 33.

2 Kurokawa, *Ika to dōka no aida*.

3 Uramoto, *Edo/tokyo no hisabetsu buraku no rekishi: danzaemon to hisabetsu minshū*, 234. This book is based on a revised collection of the essays that Uramoto submitted to the *Kaihō shinbun* during that year. The same incident is also recorded in the following volume, though Uramoto's anonymity is preserved in it. Buraku kaihō/jinken seisaku kakuritsu yōkyū chuō jikkō i'inkai, *2004 ban zenkoku no aitsugu sabetsu jiken*, 22–48.

4 Found in Miyazaki, et al., eds., *'Dōwa riken no shinsō' no shinsō: nani ga riaru ya!*. 117. Also available on the Buraku Liberation League, Tokyo website at http://www.asahi-net.or.jp/~mg5s-hsgw/sabetu/hagaki/h_sinsou.html. Kumizaka and Matsuoka refer to Kumizaka Shigeyuki and Matsuoka Tōru from the Central Headquarters of the Buraku Liberation League in Kyoto.

5 *Gōmune* are street performers of the Tokugawa period. They earned a living by performing on street corners, in temple grounds, and in public spaces. They paid taxes to a *gōmune* head, who gave them official permission to perform.

6 Uramoto, *Edo/Tokyo no hisabetsu buraku no rekishi: danzaemon to hisabetsu minshū*, 233.

7 Ibid., 232.

8 Hasegawa Yutaka and Morimoto Hidehiko, "Kyōhaku: buraku kaihō dōmei no shokuin ni kyōhaku hagaki okuru mushoku no otoko taihō - keishichō asakusashō", [Intimidation: An Unemployed Man is Arrested for the Intimidation of a Buraku Liberation League Employee – Asakusa Police] *Mainichi shinbun* [Mainichi Newspaper], 20 October 2004.

9 BLL Tokyo, *'Renzoku/tairyō sabetsu hagaki jiken' yōgisha taihō* ['Mass Discriminatory Postcard Affair' Suspect Arrested]; available from http://www.asahi-net.or.jp/~mg5s-hsgw/sabetu/hagaki/hagaki07.html.

10 Ibid.

11 BLL Tokyo, *'Sabetsu hagaki jiken' yōgisha ga kiso* ['Discriminatory Postcard Incident' Suspect Indicted]; available at http://www.asahi-net.or.jp/~mg5s-hsgw/sabetu/hagaki/hagaki08.html.

12 The Tokyo Meat Works, which was established in 1966, has 94 employees, and records an annual turnover in excess of one billion Australian dollars. Statistics found at http://www.tmmc.co.jp/saiyo.htm.

13 Walter Benjamin, "Critique of Violence", *Deconstruction: A Reader*, ed. Martin McQuillan (Edinburgh: Edinburgh University Press, 2000), 62.

14 Miyazaki, et al., eds., *'Dōwa riken no shinsō' no shinsō: nani ga riaru ya!*, 117–19.

15 David McCrone, *The Sociology of Nationalism* (London, New York: Routledge, 1998), 44.

[16] This is a position that can be replicated, of course, by members of the social minorities too. Within narratives relating to the struggle of the burakumin against mainstream Japanese society, there is, as Suginohara Juichi indicates, often a view that 'everyone except burakumin are discriminators'. Suginohara Juichi, *Buraku kaihō no 'kyōko riron' hihan* [Criticism of the 'Firm Theory' of Buraku Liberation] (Kyoto: Buraku Mondai Kenkyūjo, 1999), 10.

[17] Even if a clear link exists through familial genealogy from the Tokugawa period outcaste to the present-day burakumin and a strong case can be made for historical continuity, such a perspective means that we lose grip on our justification to link people or categories through time or through blood. Michel Foucault was one of those who cautioned that we must 'free historical chronologies and successive orderings from all forms of progressive perspective', and the historian of Japan, Daniel Botsman quite accurately points out that it did not appear useful for Foucault to link groups on a time-line of development, not because this is an utterly impossible scenario, but because attention would be torn away from explanation of how something *happened* to how something *progressed* over time. Indeed, it is through a questioning of the notions of time and the commonsense acceptance of causality that we begin to witness some of the more complex problems of the mainstream view of outcast/e history. Daniel V. Botsman, "Politics and Power in the Tokugawa Period", *East Asian Studies*, no. 3 (1992): 2; Michel Foucault, *Power/ Knowledge* (Hassocks: Harvester Press, 1980), 49–50.

[18] McCrone, *The Sociology of Nationalism*, 63.

[19] Imanishi, "Kindai nihon no kokumin kokka to buraku mondai", 82–83.

[20] Miyazaki, et al., eds., *'Dōwa riken no shinsō' no shinsō: nani ga riaru ya!*, 120.

[21] Ibid., 36.

[22] The following records are usually listed as the main primary sources on the pre-eighteenth century history of Danzaemon: *Ochiboshū* (1728), *Bukō nenpyō* (1850), *Bunsei jisha machikata kakiage* (1829), *Kōgei shiryō* (1878), *Edo sunago* (1732), *Morisada mankō* (1837–53), *Kiyū shōran* (1830), and *Kyūbakufu hikitsugisho* (eighteenth century). As can be seen, most of the records are dated post-eighteenth century. Many records too, though perhaps dating back to the seventeenth century in their original forms, are only extant as second-hand copies due to a number of circumstances such as fire or multiple editing. This suggests that many of the records relating to pre-eighteenth century Danzaemon history are less than reliable.

[23] This is also alluded to by Iris Marion Young who writes from the perspective of the idea of 'justice': 'While everyday discourse about justice certainly makes claims, these are not theorems to be demonstrated in a self-enclosed system. They are instead calls, pleas, claims *upon* some people by others. Rational reflection on justice begins in a hearing, in heeding a call, rather than in asserting and

mastering a state of affairs, however ideal.' Iris Marion Young, *Justice and the Politics of Difference* (Princeton: Princeton University Press, 1990) 5.

24 Clearly, it is difficult if not a logical impossibility to carry out such a request. Yet it is arguably what many people attempt to do in everyday practice. And most importantly, while risking the threat of being labelled as overly idealistic, I believe it is an important prescription for a world that too often seeks to retaliate against violent acts. The view put forward here is in some ways similar to what Judith Butler has argued in her treatise on imagining alternative ways of responding to violence: an essay written in response to the 11 September 2001 bombings and subsequent US reactions. Butler attempts to establish a theoretical basis for seeing human actions both individually and collectively. She writes: 'The body implies mortality, vulnerability, agency: the skin and the flesh expose us to the gaze of others, but also to touch, and to violence, and bodies put us at risk of becoming the agency and instrument of all these as well. Although we struggle for rights over our own bodies, the very bodies for which we struggle are not quite ever our own. The body has its invariably public dimension. Constituted as a social phenomenon in the public sphere, my body is and is not mine. Given over from the start to the world of others, it bears their imprint, is formed within the crucible of social life; only later, and with some uncertainty, do I lay claim to my body as my own, if, in fact, I ever do.' As Butler goes on to argue 'we are something other than "autonomous" in such a condition, but that does not mean that we are merged or without boundaries.' Her point is that within this conception of history, from the perspective of our bodies, 'we cannot represent ourselves as merely bounded beings' and therefore matters such as violence and loss—central themes in premodern outcaste and buraku history—can and should, in this conception, become matters for 'we'. Judith Butler, *Precarious Life: The Powers of Mourning and Violence* (London, New York: Verso, 2004), 26–28.

25 Watanabe, "Burakushi no tenkan", 49. There may, of course, be other positions in addition to Uramoto's and the 'silent assimilation' option that members of the buraku community might choose to adopt, which are not explored here.

26 Noah McCormack also relates this idea in his discussion of the Local Improvement Campaigns (*chihō kairyō undō*) intended to improve buraku areas in the early twentieth century: 'Reform, which was problematic in that it involved tacit acknowledgement of the validity of practices of inclusion and exclusion based on the attainment of certain standards and norms, was a process wherein those on the social margins acquired the conviction that they had valid nationalist claims upon the Japanese state. Their claims were recognized by the state, in the form of budgetary allocations and reform programs. And in turn, those official responses would have the effect of strengthening the "national" attachment of "*buraku*" residents.' McCormack, "Prejudice and Nationalization: on the 'Buraku' Problem, 1868–1912", 307. Hatanaka Toshiyuki also makes a

similar point concerning Cathy Freeman's comment about her ancestors after winning a gold medal at the 1997 World Athletics Championship in Athens. Freeman had made comments to reporters such as 'I am such a proud indigenous Australian', and 'I take my role model very seriously...I have never really had a horrible experience of racial discrimination. (But) history, the way my ancestors were treated, is what I have gained strength from.' Japanese newspapers had subsequently run stories quoting Freeman as saying that 'I have pride in my people. I feel the strength of my ancestors inside me.' 'Furīman senjutsu no shōri: joshi yon-hyaku hatsu v 97 sekai rikujō', [Freeman's Victorious Strategy: A First in the Women's 400 Metres at the 1997 World Athletics Championship] *Asahi shinbun* [Asahi Newspaper], 6 August 1997. "A Proud Champion", *The Canberra Times*, 8 August 1997; Adrian Warner, "Athletics-Freeman becomes first aboriginal to win world title", *Reuter News*, 4 August 1997. Hatanaka argues that because he has never experienced the phenomenon of 'gaining strength from ancestors', it does not mean that he can deny the fact that Freeman did. However, he goes on to argue that in this complex issue relating to Aboriginal identity, there is an important sense wherein it was not necessarily because Freeman was 'born aboriginal' that she felt the strength of her ancestors, but because she was 'raised as an aboriginal', hence pointing at the constructed element within the identities of minority groups. Hatanaka, "'Hitokukuri' to 'Hitorihitori",' 15.

27 Tessa Morris-Suzuki, "Remembering War, Making Peace: History, Truth, and Reconciliation in East Asia", in *Thinking Peace Making Peace*, edited by Barry Hindess and Margaret Jolly, (Canberra: Academy of the Social Sciences in Australia, 2001), 59.

28 I owe much of this perspective to Geremie Barmé's provocative essay, "On New Sinology"; available at http://rspas.anu.edu.au/pah/chinaheritageproject/newsinology/.

Chapter 7

1 Neary, *Political Protest and Social Control in Pre-War Japan: the Origins of Buraku Liberation*, 217.

2 As Noah McCormack rightly points out, this should not only be seen as a process of 'borrowing', but also as a 'more thorough application of the Confucian notion of a universal human nature'. McCormack, "Prejudice and Nationalization: on the 'Buraku' Problem, 1868–1912", 118.

3 Sumida Ichirō introduced a very important and closely related discussion on the question of the 'naming' of the buraku. Sumida discusses the dilemma of dōwa education whereby a teacher can answer yes to the student's questions of whether a buraku area and buraku discrimination really exist, but cannot answer affirmatively to the question about who the buraku people are. Sumida alludes to the idea that whether or not buraku children choose to identify themselves

is essentially a matter for the individual. Sumida Ichirō, "Ima naze, kamuauto nanoka", [Why Must We Come-out Now?] in *'Burakumin' towa nanika* [What is 'Burakumin'?], ed. Fujita Kei'ichi (Kyoto: Aunsha, 1998) 43–45.

4 Neary, *Political Protest*, 219, 221. John B. Cornell in 1967 explained this process well: 'By being in fact thwarted in their effort to remove the barriers to free interaction in the society, the burakumin have developed a conscientious of kind, a community of purpose throughout the country which solidifies "caste" unity and which thereby increases the gulf separating them from *ippan* majority society. To achieve their avowed goal of complete assimilation, they have brought upon themselves in the last forty to fifty years a sharper delineation of the boundaries of the group through nationwide action and collective political action.' Cornell, "Individual Mobility and Group Membership: The Case of the Burakumin", 339–40.

5 Neary, *Political Protest*, 82–83.

6 Amos, "Binding Burakumin: Marxist Historiography and the Narration of Difference in Japan". See also Chapter 4 of this book.

7 Neary, *Political Protest*, 157–59. Also Kurokawa, *Tsukurikaerareru shirushi: nihon kindai/ hisabetsu buraku/ mainoriti*, 130–31.

8 Kurokawa, *Tsukurikaerareru shirushi: nihon kindai/ hisabetsu buraku/ mainoriti*, 120.

9 Gail Omvedt, *Dalits and the Democratic Revolution: Dr. Ambedkar and the Dalit movement in Colonial India* (New Delhi: Sage Publications, 1994).

10 Ōtō Osamu, *Nihon kinsei no seishi to sōsō / bosei* (Life-and-Death, Funeral Rites and Grave Systems in Early Modern Japan). Unpublished paper presented at the Death and Dying in Early Modern Japan Workshop at the National University of Singapore, 25 September 2009.

11 Omvedt, *Dalits and the Democratic Revolution*, 35.

12 Ōyama Kyohei, *Yuruyakana kāsuto shakai: chūsei nihon* (The Loose Caste Society: Medieval Japan) (Tokyo: Asekura Shobō, 2003).

13 *Census of India: Scheduled Castes & Scheduled Tribes Population*, Registrar General & Census Commissioner, India. Available at http://www.censusindia.gov.in/Census_Data_2001/India_at_Glance/scst.aspx; accessed on 29 September 2009.

14 There are scores of reports and official documents that indicate that even today dalits are segregated in Indian villages with substantial Hindu populations. Despite being legally banned since 1947, 'untouchability' receives religious sanction as dalit-untouchables cannot enter mainstream Hindu temples and face obstacles in renting houses in cities. Dalits, moreover, are not supposed to own property or draw water from a common village well. If dalits defy these social rules in rural India, they face physical violence, even death. Justice, moreover, is often denied to people who face this violence and oppression. According

to official statistics, everyday two dalits are murdered through caste conflict in India and three dalit women are raped. Massacres and lynching are also common. Many of the crimes committed against dalits also go unreported. For an account of atrocities on dalits in contemporary India, see Anand Teltumbde, *Khairlanji: A Strange and Bitter Crop* (New Delhi: Navayana, 2008).

15 Ian Neary, "The Paekjong and the Hyongpyongsa: The Untouchables of Korea and Their Struggle for Liberation". *Immigrants and Minorities* 6:2 (1987): 117–50.

16 Daniel Botsman, *Caste, Status, and the Possibilities of Comparative History*, 10. Unpublished paper presented at the *Kokusai enza 'kinsei mibun shakai no hikakushi'* (International Roundtable on 'The Comparative History of Early Modern Status Societies') at Osaka City University, 19 July 2009.

17 Ibid., 10.

18 Omvedt, *Dalits and the Democratic Revolution*, 35.

19 Ibid., 35.

20 Ibid., 30.

21 Tsukada Takashi, *Kinsei Osaka no mibunteki shūen: mondai teiki wo kanete* (Status Marginality in Early Modern Osaka and Related Issues), 15. Unpublished paper presented at the *Kokusai enza 'kinsei mibun shakai no hikakushi'* (International Roundtable on 'The Comparative History of Early Modern Status Societies') at Osaka City University, 19 July 2009.

22 Botsman, *Caste, Status, and the Possibilities of Comparative History*, 18–19.

23 Hatanaka, *Mibun/sabetsu/aidentitī: 'burakushi' wa bohyō to naruka*, 16.

24 Quoted in Ganguly, *Caste, Colonialism and Counter-modernity: Notes on a Postcolonial Hermeneutics of Caste*, 132.

25 It is for this reason that we must arguably maintain a tension between things and the ways in which they are represented, and here we may find useful ideas such as David Bebbington's concept of idealism and positivism lying as complementary to each other. Bebbington, quoting Raymond Aron, argues that, 'The complexity of the world of history...corresponds to a pluralist anthropology.' David Bebbington, *Patterns in History* (Leicester: Inter-Varsity Press, 1979), 160–61.

26 The concept of 'truthfulness' as opposed to 'truth' is found in Tessa Morris-Suzuki, *The Past Within Us: Media, Memory, History* (London: Verso, 2005). Applied to this context, this means an acceptance of a conflicting process by which the 'outcaste' is both reconstructed and real. Through this, the view is retained that a myriad of epistemological factors, working constantly in nature at all times, generate an image for us. In this sense, outcastes are dually constructed, but when 'truthfully' constructed at the contemporary level, they start resembling a form that the subjects who lived and breathed would be more likely to recognize themselves.

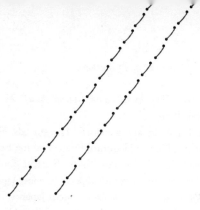

Bibliography

Unpublished Primary Sources

Ōishi, Kyūkei. *Kaisei hotei jikata hanreiroku* [Revised and Expanded Edition of *Explanatory Notes on Village Life*]: Unknown, 1871, in the possession of the National Diet Library, Tokyo.

Suzuki-ke monjo [The Documents of the House of Suzuki], in the possession of Saitama Prefectural Archives, Saitama.

'M'- ke monjo [The Documents of the House of M], in the possession of Saitama Prefectural Archives, Saitama.

Published Primary Sources

Buraku kaihō kenkyūjo, ed. *Zenkoku taikai undō hōshin* [National Committee Conference Campaign Policy]. 3 vols. Vol. 1. Osaka: Kaihō Shuppansha, 1980.

Harada, Tomohiko, ed. *Hennen sabetsushi shiryō shūsei* [Chronological Compendium of Historical Sources Related to Discrimination]. 21 vols. Vol. 6. Tokyo: San'ichi Shobō, 1987.

———, ed. *Hennen sabetsushi shiryō shūsei*. 21 vols. Vol. 7. Tokyo: San'ichi Shobō, 1987.

———, ed. *Hennen sabetsushi shiryō shūsei*. 21 vols. Vol. 8. Tokyo: San'ichi Shobō, 1987.

———, ed. *Hennen sabetsushi shiryō shūsei*. 21 vols. Vol. 9. Tokyo: San'ichi Shobō, 1987.

———, ed. *Hennen sabetsushi shiryō shūsei*. 21 vols. Vol. 10. Tokyo: San'ichi Shobō, 1988.

———, ed. *Hennen sabetsushi shiryō shūsei*. 21 vols. Vol. 11. Tokyo: San'ichi Shobō, 1988.

———, ed. *Hennen sabetsushi shiryō shūsei.* 21 vols. Vol. 12. Tokyo: San'ichi Shobō, 1988.

Harada, Tomohiko and Kobayashi Hiroshi, eds. *Nihon shomin seikatsu shiryō shūsei* [Compendium of Historical Sources on the Everyday Life of Japan's Common People], 30 vols., vol. 14. Tokyo: San'ichi Shobō, 1971.

Hirota, Masaki, ed. *Sabetsu no shosō* [Various Aspects of Discrimination]. Vol. 22 of *Nihon kindai shisō taikei* [Modern Japanese Thought Series], edited by Katō Shūichi. Tokyo: Iwanami Shoten, 1990.

Nakao, Kenji. *Danzaemon kankei shiryōshū: kyūbakufu hikitsugisho* [Collection of Documents Related to Danzaemon: Transmitted Documents of the Former Bakufu]. 3 vols. Vol. 1. Osaka: Buraku Kaihō Kenkyūjo, 1995.

———. *Danzaemon kankei shiryōshū: kyūbakufu hikitsugisho.* 3 vols. Vol. 2. Osaka: Buraku Kaihō Kenkyūjo, 1995.

Saitama-ken, ed. *Shinpen saitama-kenshi shiryō hen* [New History of Saitama Prefecture: Historical Sources] . Vol. 14 of *Saitama-kenshi*, edited by Saitama-ken. Urawa: Saitama-ken, 1991.

Sugita, Genpaku. "Rantō Kotohajime [Dawn of Western Science]." In *Koten Nihon Bungaku Taikei* [Series of Classical Japanese Works], edited by Toshirō Kodaka and Matsumura Akira. Tokyo: Iwanami Shoten, 1964: 469–553.

Saitama dōwa kyōiku kyōgikai, ed. *Saitama dōwa kyōiku sankō shiryō: suzuki-ke monjo kaisetsu* [Referential Documents for Dōwa Education in Saitama: Explanatory Notes for the Documents of the House of Suzuki]. Urawa: Saitama-ken Dōwa Kyōiku Kenkyū Kyōgikai, 1981.

———, ed. *Suzuki-ke monjo: saitama-ken buraku mondai kankei shiryōshū* [The Documents of the House of Suzuki: Collection of Historical Sources Related to the Buraku Problem in Saitama Prefecture]. 5 vols. Vol. 1. Urawa: Saitama-ken Dōwa Kyōiku Kenkyū Kyōgikai, 1977.

———, ed. *Suzuki-ke monjo: saitama-ken buraku mondai kankei shiryōshū.* 5 vols. Vol. 3. Urawa-shi: Saitama-ken dowa Kyōiku Kenkyū Kyōgikai, 1978.

Watanabe Tōru, et al., eds, *Kindai burakushi shiryō shūsei* [Compilation of Historical Documents Relating to Modern Buraku History], Vol. 8. Tokyo: San'ichi Shobō, 1985.

Watanabe, Tōru and Akisada Yoshikazu, eds, *Buraku mondai / suihei undō shiryō shūsei* [Buraku Problem / Collection of Leveller's Movement Documents]. 5 vols. Vol. 3. Tokyo: Shōin, 1974.

Yamada, Yoshio, ed. *Konjaku monogatari* [Tales of Old and New]. Edited by Ichinosuke Takagi. 102 vols. Vol. 22, Nihon koten bungaku taikei. Tokyo: Iwanami Shoten, 1959.

Digital Archival Material

Hyoshiya Ichirobē. 1684, *Ōedo zenzu* [Map of Greater Edo], found in the digital Kanō collection at Tohoku University Library, Sendai (http://www2.library.tohoku.ac.jp/kano/ezu/edo/edo.html)

Gaimu I'inkai [Records of the House of Representatives Foreign Policy Committee], nos. 9–14 (07/05/1979–31/05/1979), *Kokkai Kaigiroku* [Proceedings of the National Diet of Japan].

Published Secondary Sources

Allison, Anne. *Millennial Monsters: Japanese Toys and the Global Imagination.* Berkeley: University of California Press, 2006.

Ambedkar, Bhimrao Ramji. *The Untouchables: Who Were They and Why They Became Untouchables.* New Delhi: Amrit Book Company, 1948.

Amino, Yoshihiko. *Nihon no rekishi wo yominaosu (sei)* [Re-Reading Japanese History]. vol. 50, *Chikuma Purimā Bukkusu.* Tokyo: Chikuma Shobō, 1991.

———. "Deconstructing Japan." *East Asian Studies* no. 3 (1992): 121–42.

———. "Nihon chūsei ni okeru sabetsu no shosō [Various Aspects of Discrimination in Medieval Japan]." In *Nihon rekishi no naka no hisabetsumin* [Outcastes in Japanese History], edited by Nara jinken/buraku kaihō kenkyūjo. Nara: Nara Jinken/Buraku Kaihō Kenkyūjo, 2001: 9–35.

Amos, Timothy D. "Outcaste or Internal Exile? Ambiguous bodies in the Making of Modern Japan," *Portal* 2:1 (2005). Available at http://epress.lib.uts.edu.au/journals/portal/

———. "Portrait of a Tokugawa Outcaste Community." *East Asian History* 32/33, (June 2006 / December 2007): 83–108.

———. "Binding Burakumin: Marxist Historiography and the Narration of Difference in Japan," *Japanese Studies* 27: 2 (2007): 155–71.

Anderson, Benedict. *Imagined Communities: Reflections on the Origin and Spread of Nationalism.* London: Verso, 1996.

Andersson, René. *Burakumin and Shimazaki Tōson's Hakai: Images of Discrimination in Modern Japanese Literature.* Lund, Sweden: Dept. of East Asian Languages, Lund University, 2000.

Arai, Kōjirō. "Toshi senmin gyōseishi no kiso kōsatsu: tokyo no hisabetsu buraku to 'gōmune' buraku no baai [Rudimentary Reflections on Urban Outcaste Administrative History: The Case of Tokyo and Gōmune Buraku]." *Tōyō hōgaku* 11 no. 4 (1969): 83–115.

———. *Kinsei senmin shakai no kiso kōzō* [The Basic Structure of Early Modern Outcaste Society]. Tokyo: Akashi Shoten, 1987.

Asada, Zennosuke. *Asada zennosuke zenkiroku: sabetsu to tatakaitsuzukete* [The Complete Records of Asada Zennosuke: Continuing to Fight Discrimination]. Vol. 22. Kyoto: Asada Kyōiku Zaidan, 1995.

———. *Sabetsu to tatakaitsuzukete* [Continuing to Fight Discrimination]. Vol. 145, *Asahi sensho.* Tokyo: Asahi Shinbunsha, 1979.

Asada, Zennosuke, et al., "Sengo buraku kaihō undō no riron [Postwar Buraku Liberation Movement Theory]," *Buraku kaihō*, no. 100 (April 1977): 24.

Asao, Naohiro. "'Mibun' shakai no rikai [Understanding 'Social Status' Society]." In *Nihon rekishi no naka no hisabetsumin* [Outcastes in Japanese History], edited by Nara jinken / buraku kaihō kenkyūjo. Nara: Nara Jinken/Buraku Kaihō Kenkyūjo, 2001: 71–100.

Bauman, Zygmunt. *Wasted Lives: Modernity and its Outcasts*. Cambridge: Polity Press, 2004.

Bebbington, David. *Patterns in History*. Leicester: Inter-Varsity Press, 1979.

Benjamin, Walter. "Critique of Violence." In *Deconstruction: A Reader*, edited by Martin McQuillan. Edinburgh: Edinburgh University Press, 2000: 62–70.

Bodart-Bailey, Beatrice. *The Dog Shogun: The Personality and Policies of Tokugawa Tsunayoshi*. Honolulu: University of Hawai'i Press, 2007.

Botsman, Daniel V. "Politics and Power in the Tokugawa Period." *East Asian Studies* no. 3 (1992): 1–32.

———. *Punishment and Power in the Making of Modern Japan*. Princeton; Oxford: Princeton University Press, 2005.

———. "Caste, Status, and the Possibilities of Comparative History." Unpublished paper presented at the *Kokusai enza 'kinsei mibun shakai no hikakushi'* [International Roundtable on 'The Comparative History of Early Modern Status Societies'] at Osaka City University, 19 July 2009.

Buraku kaihō kenkyūjo, ed. *The Reality of Buraku Discrimination in Japan*. Osaka: Buraku kaihō kenkyūjo, 1994.

———, ed. *Buraku mondai jiten* [Buraku Problem Dictionary]. Osaka: Buraku Kaihō Kenkyūjo, 1986.

Buraku kaihō dōmei nara-ken rengōkai okubo shibu, ed., *Kyōku ni taezaru koto ni kō shite: tennō (sei) ni yoru Hora buraku kyōsei idō* [Defying the Inability of Others to Resist Fear: The Forced Migration of the Hora Community at the Hands of the Imperial Institution]. Nara: Ikeda Shuppan Insatsusha, no date.

Buraku kaihō/jinken seisaku kakuritsu yōkyū chuō jikkō i'inkai. *2004 ban zenkoku no aitsugu sabetsu jiken* [2004 Edition Successive Discriminatory Incidents in Japan]. Osaka: Kaihō Shuppansha, 2004.

Buraku mondai kenkyūjo, ed. *Yasashii buraku no rekishi* [Buraku History Made Simple]. Kyoto: Buraku Mondai Kenkyūjo, 1961.

———, ed. *Buraku mondai kenkyūjo: 50 nen no ayumi* [Research Institute for the Buraku Problem: 50 years of history]. Kyoto: Buraku Mondai Kenkyūjo, 1998.

Burns, Susan L. "From 'Leper Villages' to Leprosaria: Public Health, Nationalism and the Culture of Exclusion in Japan." In *Isolation: Places and Practices of Exclusion*, edited by Carolyn Strange and Alison Bashford. London; New York: Routledge, 2003: 104–18.

Butler, Judith. "Afterword: After Loss, What Then?" In *Loss: The Politics of Mourning*, edited by David L. Eng, et al. Berkeley: University of California Press, 2003: 467–73.

———. *Precarious Life: The Powers of Mourning and Violence*. London; New York: Verso, 2004.

Carr, David. *Time, Narrative, and History*. Bloomington; Indianapolis: Indiana University Press, 1986.

CDI, ed. *Kyoto shomin seikatsushi* [Everyday Life History of the Kyoto Common People]. Tokyo: Kashima Kenkyūjo Shuppankai, 1973.

Christopher, Robert C. *The Japanese Mind: The Goliath Explained*. New York: Linden Press/Simon & Schuster, 1983.

Cornell, John B. "Individual Mobility and Group Membership: The Case of the Burakumin." In *Aspects of Social Change in Modern Japan*, edited by R.P. Dore. Princeton: Princeton University Press, 1967: 337–72.

Davis, John H. "Blurring the Boundaries of the Buraku (min)." In *Globalization and Social Change in Contemporary Japan*, edited by J.S. Eades, et al. Melbourne: Trans Pacific Press, 2000: 110–22.

———. "Challenging the State, Embracing the Nation: An Ethnographic Analysis of Human Rights in Japanese Society." PhD, Stanford University, 2002.

De Vos, George. *Japan's Outcastes: The Problem of the Burakumin*. London: Minority Rights Group, 1971.

Douglas, Mary. *Purity and Danger: An Analysis of Concepts of Pollution and Taboo*. London: Routledge & Kegan Paul, 1966.

Dubin, Steven C. "Incivilities in Civil(-ized) Places: Culture Wars in Comparative Perspective." In *A Companion to Museum Studies*, edited by Sharon Macdonald. Malden, MA: Blackwell, 2006: 477–93.

Duffy, Terence M. "Museums of 'Human Suffering' and the Struggle for Human Rights," in *Museum Studies: An Anthology of Contexts*, ed. Bettina Messias Carbonell. Malden: Blackwell Publishing, 2004, 117–22.

Dumont, Louis. *Homo Hierarchicus: The Caste System and Its Implications*. Revised Edition. Chicago: The University Of Chicago Press, 1980.

Durrans, Brian (1992), "Behind the Scenes: Museums and Selective Criticism." *Anthropology Today*, Vol. 8, no. 4 (August 1992): 11–15.

East, Alfred. *A British Artist in Meiji Japan*. Brighton: In Print, 1991.

Evans, Harriet. "The Language of Liberation: Gender and Jiefang in Early Chinese Communist Party Discourse," *Intersections*, no. 1 (September 1998). Available at http://wwwsshe.murdoch.edu.au/intersections/back_issues/harriet.html.

Foucault, Michel. *Discipline and Punish: The Birth of the Prison* (London: Penguin Books, 1977).

———. *Power/ Knowledge*. Hassocks: Harvester Press, 1980.

Fujino, Yutaka. "Hisabetsu buraku [Buraku]." In *Iwanami kōza nihon tsūshi* [Iwanami History of Japan], edited by Asao Naohiro, et al. Vol.18. Tokyo: Iwanami Shoten, 1994: 135–67.

Fujimoto, Seijirō, ed. *Izumi no kuni kawata mura shihai monjo: azukari shoya no kiroku jōkan* [Documents Related to the Governance of a Kawata Village in Izumi Province: Records of a Subordinate Village Official]. 2 vols. vol. 1, *Seibundō shiryō sōsho*. Osaka: Seibundō Shuppan, 1998.

Fujita, Kei'ichi. *Dōwa wa kowai kō* [Thoughts on Why the Dōwa Problem is Scary]. Kyoto: Aunsha, 1987.

Fujitani, Takashi. "Inventing, Forgetting, Remembering: Toward a Historical Ethnography of the Nation-State." In *Cultural Nationalism in East Asia: Representation and Identity*, edited by Harumi Befu. Berkeley: Institute of East Asian Studies, University of California, 1993: 77–106.

Fujiwara, Hiroshi. *Shōchō tennōsei to buraku gensō: shūen e no tojō ni te* [The Symbolic Emperor System and the Buraku Illusion: On the Way to the End]. Tokyo: San'ichi Shobō, 1993.

Ganguly, Debjani. *Caste, Colonialism and Counter-modernity: Notes on a Postcolonial Hermeneutics of Caste.* New York: Routledge, 2005.

Gates, Henry Louis, Jr. "The Master's Pieces: On Canon Formation and the Afro-American Tradition." In *The Bounds of Race: Perspectives on Hegemony and Resistance*, edited by Dominick LaCapra. Ithaca; London: Cornell University Press, 1991: 17–38.

Gluck, Carol. "Japan's Modernities, 1850s–1990s." In *Asia in Western and World History*, edited by Ainslie T. Embree and Carol Gluck. Armonk, New York: M.E. Sharpe, 1997: 561–93.

Gordon, June A. "From Liberation to Human Rights: Challenges for Teachers of the Burakumin in Japan." *Race Ethnicity and Education* 9 no. 2 (July 2006): 183–202

Gottlieb, Nanette. "Discriminatory Language in Japan: Burakumin, the Disabled and Women." *Asian Studies Review* 22 no. 2 (June 1998): 157–73.

Groemer, Gerald. "The Creation of the Edo Outcaste Order." *The Journal of Japanese Studies* 27 no. 2 (2001): 263–94.

Hah, Chong-do and Christopher C. Lapp, "Japanese Politics of Equality in Transition: The Case of the Burakumin." *Asian Survey* 18:5 (May, 1978): 498–99.

Hall, Francis. *Japan Through American Eyes 1859–1866: The Journal of Francis Hall Kanagawa and Yokohama*. Princeton: Princeton University Press, 1992.

Hane, Mikiso. *Peasants, Rebels, Women, and Outcastes: The Underside of Modern Japan*. 2nd ed. Lanham; Boulder; New York; Oxford: Rowman & Littleford, 2003.

Harada, Tomohiko. "Buraku mondai no honshitsu to kadai [The True Nature and Problems Surrounding the Buraku Problem]." *Buraku kaihō* no. 1 (October 1968): 16–31.

———. *Hisabetsu buraku no rekishi* [Buraku History]. Vol. 34, *Asahi sensho*. Tokyo: Asahi Shinbunsha, 1975.

———. *Sabetsu to buraku: shūkyō to buraku sabetsu wo megutte* [Discrimination and Buraku: Regarding Religion and Buraku Discrimination]. Tokyo: San'ichi Shinsho, 1984.

Harada, Tomohiko, ed. *Hennen sabetsushi shiryō shūsei* [Chronological Compendium of Historical Sources Related to Discrimination]. 21 vols. Tokyo: San'ichi Shobō, 1984–95.

Harada, Tomohiko, and Yoshio Tanaka. *Tōhoku hokuetsu hisabetsu burakushi kenkyū* [Historical Research on the Buraku of Northeastern and Northwestern Japan]. Tokyo: Akashi Shoten, 1981.

Haraguchi, Takahiro. "Buraku sabetsu to kyōdōsei [Buraku Discrimination and Communitarianism]." In *'Burakumin' towa nanika* [What are 'Burakumin'?], edited by Fujita Kei'ichi. Kyoto: Aunsha, 1998: 75–107.

Harootunian, Harry D. *Things Seen and Unseen: Discourse and Ideology in Tokugawa Nativism*. Chicago: University of Chicago Press, 1988.

———. *Overcome by Modernity: History, Culture, and Community in Interwar Japan*. Princeton and Oxford: Princeton University Press, 2000.

Hatanaka, Toshiyuki. *'Burakushi' wo tou* [Questioning 'Buraku History']. Kobe: Hyōgo Buraku Mondai Kenkyūjo, 1993.

———. *'Burakushi' no owari* [The End of Buraku History]. Kyoto: Kamogawa Shuppan, 1995.

———. *'Kawata' to heijin: kinsei mibun shakairon* ['Kawata' and Commoners: Early Modern Status Society Theory]. Kyoto: Kamogawa Shuppan, 1997.

———. "'Eta' 'hinin' towa dare no koto nanoka [Who does 'eta' and 'hinin' refer to?]." In *Datsujōshiki no buraku mondai* [The Buraku Problem Minus The Common Sense], edited by Asaji Takeshi, et al. Kyoto: Kamogawa Shuppan, 1998: 211–19.

———. "'Hitokukuri' to 'Hitorihitori' ['People' and 'Person']." In *'Burakumin' towa nanika* [What are 'Burakumin'?], edited by Fujita Kei'ichi. Kyoto: Aunsha, 1998: 11–35.

———. *Mibun / sabetsu / aidentitī: 'burakushi' wa bohyō to naruka* [Status, discrimination, identity: will 'Buraku history' become a grave post?]. Kyoto: Kamogawa Shuppan, 2004.

———. "Mibun hikiage to shūmei jokyo: 'Dannaiki mibun hikiage ikken' no saikentō [Status Elevation and Eradication of Epithets: Re-examining the Incident Related to Dan Naiki's (Danzaemon) Elevation in Status]." *Ritsumeikan Gengo Bunka Kenkyū* 90 (November 2007): 200–20.

Hayashiya, Tatsusaburō. "Chūseihen [Medieval Section]." In *Buraku no rekishi to kaihō undō* [Buraku History and the Liberation Movement], edited by Buraku mondai kenkyūjo. Kyoto: Buraku mondai kenkyūjo, 1954: 57–89.

Hoashi, Banri. "Tōsenpuron [Discourse of an Eastern Hermit]." In Okiura Kazuteru, ed., *Suihei: hito no yo ni hikari are* [Levellers: Let there be Light in the World of Man]. Tokyo: Shakai Hyōronsha, 1991: 44–45.

Hodgson, Christopher Pemberton. *A Residence in Nagasaki and Hakodate in 1859-1860; With an account of Japan generally; With a series of letters on Japan by his wife.* London: R. Bentley, 1861.

Honda, Yutaka. *Edo no hinin: burakushi kenkyū no kadai* [The Hinin of Edo: Problems in Buraku Historical Research]. Tokyo: San'ichi Shobō, 1992.

Howell, David L. *Geographies of Identity in Nineteenth-Century Japan.* Berkeley: University of California Press, 2005.

Ijino-no-Genō. *Ijin no genkō* [Words and Deeds of Great Men]. Tokyo: Daigakukan, 1900.

Imanishi, Hajime. "Kindai nihon no kokumin kokka to buraku mondai [The Modern Japanese Nation-State and the Buraku Problem]." In *Burakushi kenkyū: buraku minshū / kokumin kokka to suihei undō* [Buraku Historical Research: Burakumin, Nation-State, and the Levellers' Movement], edited by Zenkoku burakushi kenkyū kōryūkai. No. 3. Osaka: Kaihō Shuppansha, 1999: 82–107.

———. "Kindai nihon no chi'iki shakai to buraku sabetsu [Rural Society and Buraku Discrimination in Modern Japan]." *Buraku kaihō* no. 470 (June 2000): 24–31.

———. *Bunmei kaika to sabetsu* [Enlightenment and Discrimination]. Vol. 127 of *Rekishi bunka raiburarī.* Tokyo: Yoshikawa Kōbunkan, 2001.

Inoue, Kiyoshi. "Buraku kaihō riron to burakushi no kadai [Buraku Liberation Theory and Issues in Buraku History]." In *Sengo buraku mondai ronshū: kaihō riron I* [An Anthology of Writings on the Postwar Buraku Problem Vol. 1], edited by Buraku mondai kenkyūjo. Vol. 1. Kyoto: Buraku Mondai Kenkyūjo, 1998: 76–85.

Ishida, Tadashi. "Bushū yokomi-gun shimo yoshimi wo aruku [Walking Lower Yoshimi in Yokomi County, Musashi Province]." *Ashita wo hiraku* no. 36 (December 2000): 5–19.

Ishiwatari, Shin'ichirō. *Nihon kodai kokka to buraku no kigen* [The Ancient Japanese State and Buraku Origins]. Tokyo: San'ichi Shobō, 1994.

Kang Sang-jung, "Aratana 'kusamura' wo motomete [Towards a New 'Thick Grass']," in Miyazaki Manabu, *Kindai no naraku* [The Modern Purgatory]. Tokyo: Gentōsha Autorō Bunko, 2005: 478–84.

Kaihō Shuppansha, ed. *Buraku mondai: shiryō to kaisetsu* [The Buraku Problem: Historical Records and Commentaries]. Osaka: Kaihō Shuppansha, 1993.

Kariya, Ryūichi. "The Confidence to Live! Experiencing the Buraku Liberation Movement." In *Diversity in Japanese Culture and Language*, edited by John C. Maher and Gavnor Macdonald. London; New York: Kegan Paul International, 1995: 178–201.

Kawamoto, Yoshikazu. *Buraku mondai towa nanika* [What is the Buraku Problem?]. Tokyo: San'ichi Shobō, 1994.

Kinegawa enkakushi kenkyūkai, ed., *Kinegawa chiku no ayumi sengo hen* [The Postwar History of Kinegawa]. Tokyo: Gendai Kikakushitsu, 2005.

King, Debra Walker. *Deep Talk: Reading African-American Literary Names.* Charlottesville: University of Virginia Press, 1998.

Kita, Sadakichi. "Minzoku to rekishi (tokushu buraku kenkyūgō) hakkan no ji [Ethnicity and History (Research Edition on Special Buraku): Publisher's Introduction]." In Okiura Kazuteru, ed., *Suihei: hito no yo ni hikari are* [Levellers: Let there be Light in the World of Man]. Tokyo: Shakai Hyōronsha, 1991: 121–26.

Kobayashi, Shigeru. *Hisabetsu buraku no rekishi* [Buraku History]. Tokyo: Akashi Shoten, 1988.

Kobayashi, Yoshinori. *Gōmanizumu sengen sabetsuron supesharu* [Declaration of Arrogance: Special Version on Discrimination]. Tokyo: Gentosha, 1998.

Kodama, Kōta, et al. *Nihon no rekishi* [Japanese History]. Tokyo: Yamakawa Shuppansha, 1991.

Komatsu, Katsumi. "Fukuzawa yukichi 'manazashi' kara ueki tetsujō 'manazashi' he [From a Fukuzawa Yukichi to an Uki Tetsujō 'Standard']." In *Datsujōshiki no buraku mondai* [The Buraku Problem Minus The Common Sense], edited by Asaji Takeshi, et al. Kyoto: Kamogawa Shuppan, 1998: 20–28.

Kotani, Hiroyuki. "Ajia kindai ni okeru sabetsu no mekanizumu: indo wo sozai toshite [Discriminatory Mechanisms in Modern Asia: Focusing on India]." In *Ima naze sabetsu wo tou ka* [Why is it Important to Question Discrimination Now?], edited by Kan Takayuki. Tokyo: Akashi Shoten, 1985:

———. "Mibunsei ni okeru hisen gainen to kegare ishiki: indo to nihon no hikaku wo tōshite [Outcaste Notions and Pollution Consciousness in Social Status Systems: Comparing India and Japan]." In *Kokkazō, shakaizō no henbō: gendai rekishigaku no seika to kadai* [Changes in Images of State and Society: The Achievements and Problems of Contemporary Historical Scholarship], edited by Rekishigaku kenkyūkai. Tokyo: Aoki Shoten, 2003: 147–60.

Kuroda, Toshio. *Nihon chūsei no kokka to shūkyō* [The Medieval Japanese State and Religion]. Tokyo: Iwanami Shoten, 1975.

Kurokawa, Midori. *Ika to dōka no aida* [Between Differentiation and Assimilation]. Tokyo: Aoki Shoten, 1999.

———. *Tsukurikaerareru shirushi: nihon kindai / hisabetsu buraku / mainoriti* [Reconstructed Symbols: Modern Japan, Buraku, Minorities]. Osaka: Buraku Kaihō / Jinken Kenkyūjo, 2004.

Laclau, Ernesto, and Chantal Mouffe. *Hegemony and Socialist Strategy: Towards a Radical Democratic Politics.* Second Edition. London: Verso, 2001.

Laclau, Ernesto. "Beyond Emancipation." In *Emancipations, Modern and Postmodern*, edited by Jan Nederveen Pieterse. London; Newbury Park; New Delhi: Sage Publications, 1992: 121–37.

Lie, John. "Narratives of exile and the search for homeland in contemporary Japanese Korean writings.' in *Constructing Nationhood in Modern East Asia*, edited by Kai-wing Chow, Kevin M. Doak and Poshek Fu. The University of Michigan Press, Ann Arbor, 2001: 343–58.

Mackie, Vera. "Embodiment, Citizenship, and Social Policy in Contemporary Japan." In *Family and Social Policy in Japan: Anthropological Approaches*, edited by Roger Goodman. Cambridge: Cambridge University Press, 2003: 200–29.

Maeda, Katsumasa. "Taiyō ga mata noboru: ningen wa tōtoi [The Sun Will Rise Again]." Self-Published.1991.

Mahara, Tetsuo. *Suihei undō no rekishi* [History of the Suiheisha Movement]. Kyoto: Buraku Mondai Kenkyūjo, 1992.

Mase, Kumiko. "Hisabetsu shūdan to chōtei/bakufu [Outcaste Groups and the Imperial Court/Shogunate]." In *Iwanami kōza: tennō to ōken wo kangaeru* [Iwanami Lectures: Thinking About the Emperor and Imperial Power], edited by Amino Yoshihiko, et al. Vol. 7. Tokyo: Iwanami Shoten, 2002: 139–67.

McCormack, Noah. "Prejudice and Nationalization: on the 'Buraku' Problem, 1868-1912." PhD, The Australian National University, 2002.

———. "Making Modern Urban Order: Towards Popular Mobilisation." *Japanese Studies* 22 no. 3 (2002): 257–72.

———. "Buraku Immigration in the Meiji Era—Other Ways to Become 'Japanese'," *East Asian History*, no. 23 (June 2002): 87–108.

———. "From Alien to Backward: Reconceptualizing Difference in Modern Japan," *Ritsumeikan gengo bunka kenkyū* 17 no.3 (2006): 209–22.

———. "Civilising the Urban Other: Poverty as a National Problem." *Ritsumeikan Annual Review of International Studies* 6 (2007): 21–43.

McCrone, David. *The Sociology of Nationalism*. London; New York: Routledge, 1998.

McLauchlan, Alastair. *Prejudice and Discrimination in Japan: The Buraku Issue*. Lewiston, N.Y.: Edwin Mellen Press, 2004.

Meerman, Jacob. "The Mobility of Japan's Burakumin: Militant Advocacy and Government Response." In *Boundaries of Clan and Colour: Transnational Comparisons of Inter-Group Disparity*, edited by William A. Darity and Ashwini Deshpande. New York: Routledge, 2003: 130–51.

Minegishi, Kentarō. *Kindai ni nokotta shūzokuteki sabetsu* [Modern Remnants of Customary Discrimination]. Vol. 5, *Hyūman bukkuretto*. Kobe: Hyōgo Buraku Mondai Kenkyūjo, 1990.

———. *Kinsei hisabetsuminshi no kenkyū* [Research on Early Modern Outcaste History]. Tokyo: Azekura Shobō, 1996.

Miura, Kei'ichi. *Nihon chūsei senminshi no kenkyū* [Research on Medieval Japanese Outcaste History]. Kyoto: Buraku Mondai Kenkyūjo, 1990.

Miyatake, Toshimasa. "Tokyo-to danzaemon kakoinai-ato: danzaemon to edo no hisabetsumin (burakushi yukari no chi) [The Remains of the Danzaemon Settlement in Tokyo: Danzaemon and Edo's Outcastes (Places Related to Buraku History)]," *Buraku kaihō* no. 555 (2005): 22–25.

Miyazaki, Manabu. *Kindai no naraku* [The Modern Purgatory]. Tokyo: Gentōsha Autorō Bunkō, 2005.

Miyazaki, Manabu, et al. *'Dōwa riken no shinsō' no shinsō: nani ga riaru ya!* [The Real Truth Behind the 'Truth of Dōwa Concessions': So you think that's real?!]. Osaka; Tokyo: Kaihō Shuppansha, 2003.

Mizuuchi, Toshio. "The Historical Transformation of Poverty, Discrimination, and Urban Policy in Japanese City: The Case of Osaka." In *Representing Local Places and Raising Voices from Below*, edited by Toshio Mizuuchi. Osaka: Osaka City University, 2003: 12–30.

Morooka, Sukeyuki. *Sengo buraku kaihō ronsōshi* [History of Postwar Buraku Liberation Debates]. 4 vols. vol. 1. Tokyo: Tsuge Shobō, 1980.

Morris, Mark. "Passing: Paradoxes of Alterity in *The Broken Commandment*." In *Representing the Other in Modern Japanese Literature: a Critical Approach*, edited by Rachael Hutchinson and Mark Williams. New York; London: Routledge, 2006: 127–44.

Morris-Suzuki, Tessa. "Remembering War, Making Peace: History, Truth, and Reconciliation in East Asia." In *Thinking Peace Making Peace*, edited by Barry Hindess and Margaret Jolly. Canberra: Academy of the Social Sciences in Australia, 2001: 56–63.

———. *The Past Within Us: Media, Memory, History*. London; New York: Verso, 2005.

Murata, Munejiro. *Tokyo chiri enkaku-shi* [Record of the Geographical History of Tokyo]. Tokyo: Inagaki Jōsaburō, 1890.

Nadamoto, Masahisa. "Buraku kaihō ni han tennōsei wa muyō [Anti-Imperial Sentiment is not Necessary for Buraku Liberation]." *Momento* no. 12 (April 2003): 1–14.

Nakamura, Fukuji. *Yūwa undōshi kenkyū* [Yūwa Movement Research]. Kyoto: Buraku Mondai Kenkyūjo, 1988.

Nakao, Kenji. *Edo no danzaemon: hisabetsu minshū ni kunrin shita 'kashira'* [Edo's Danzaemon: Sovereign 'Head' of Outcastes]. Tokyo: San'ichi Shobō, 1996.

———. *Edo jidai no sabetsu gainen: kinsei no sabetsu wo dō toraeruka* [Discriminatory Notions in the Edo Period: How Should We Understand Early Modern Discrimination?]. Tokyo: San'ichi Shobō, 1997.

———. "Burakushi no kakko, genzai, mirai [The Past, Present, and Future of Buraku History]." In *Datsujōshiki no buraku mondai* [The Buraku Problem Minus The Common Sense], edited by Asaji Takeshi, et al. Kyoto: Kamogawa Shuppan, 1998: 29–35.

'Naniwa buraku no rekishi' hensan i'inkai, ed., *Watanabe / Nishihama/Naniwa: Naniwa buraku no rekishi* [Watanabe/Nishihama/Naniwa: History of Naniwa's Buraku]. Osaka: Kaihō Shuppansha, 1997.

Neary, Ian. "The Paekjong and the Hyongpyongsa: The Untouchables of Korea and Their Struggle for Liberation." *Immigrants and Minorities* 6:2 (1987): 117–50.

———. *Political Protest and Social Control in Pre-War Japan: The Origins of Buraku Liberation*. Manchester: Manchester University Press, 1989.

———. *Human Rights in Japan, South Korea and Taiwan*. London: Routledge, 2002.

———."Burakumin at the End of History." *Social Research* 70 no. 1 (Spring 2003): 269–94.

Okamoto, Ryoichi. *Osaka no sesō* [Osaka Social Conditions]. Suita: Mainichi Hōsō, 1973.

Okiura, Kazuteru. *Suihei: hito no yo ni hikari are* [Levellers: Let there be Light in the World of Man]. Tokyo: Shakai Hyōronsha, 1991.

Okubo, Yuko. "'Visible' Minorities and 'Invisible' Minorities: An Ethnographic Study of Multicultural Education and the Production of Ethnic 'Others' In Japan." PhD, University of California, Berkeley, 2005.

Omvedt, Gail. *Dalits and the Democratic Revolution: Dr. Ambedkar and the Dalit movement in Colonial India*. New Delhi: Sage Publications, 1994.

Ooms, Herman. *Tokugawa Ideology: Early Constructs, 1570-1680*. Princeton: Princeton University Press, 1985.

———. *Tokugawa Village Practice: Class, Status, Power, Law*. Berkeley: University of California Press, 1996.

Osaka jinken hakubutsukan, ed., *Osaka jinken hakubutsukan sōgō tenji zuroku: watashi ga mukiau nihon shakai no sabetsu to jinken* [A Pictorial Record of the General Exhibits at the Osaka Human Rights Museum: The Discrimination I Face in Japanese Society and Human Rights]. Osaka: Osaka Jinken Hakubutsukan, 2006.

Osatake, Takeki. "Eta hinin shōgō haishi mondai no keika [Background to the Abolition of the Appellations Eta Hinin]" *Minzoku to rekishi* 2 no. 5 (1919): 545–47.

———. *Meiji yonnen senshō haishi fukoku no kenkyū* [Research on the 1871 Edict to Abolish Discriminatory Labels]. Tokyo: Hihyōsha, 1999.

Ōtō, Osamu, *Nihon kinsei no seishi to sōsō/bosei* [Life-and-Death, Funeral Rites and Grave Systems in Early Modern Japan]. Unpublished paper presented at the Death and Dying in Early Modern Japan Workshop at the National University of Singapore, 25 September 2009.

Ōyama, Kyohei, *Yuruyakana kāsuto shakai: chūsei nihon* [The Loose Caste Society: Medieval Japan]. Tokyo: Asekura Shobō, 2003.

Pieterse, Jan Nederveen. "Emancipations, Modern and Postmodern." In *Emancipations, Modern and Postmodern*, edited by Jan Nederveen Pieterse. London; Newbury Park; New Delhi: Sage Publications, 1992: 5–41.

Piggott, Joan R. *The Emergence of Japanese Kingship*. Stanford: Stanford University Press, 1997.

Reischauer, Edwin O., and Albert M. Craig. *Japan, Tradition & Transformation*. Sydney: G. Allen & Unwin, 1979.

Rohlen, Thomas P. "Violence at Yoka High School: The Implications for Japanese Coalition Politics of the Confrontation between the Communist Party and the Buraku Liberation League." *Asian Survey* 16 no. 7 (July 1976): 682–99.

Saitama kenritsu urawa toshokan monjokan, ed., *Musashi no kuni yokomi gun wana mura suzuki-ke monjo mokuroku* [Documents Index for the Suzuki Household, Wana Village, Yokomi County, Musashi Province]. Urawa: Saitama Kenritsu Toshokan, 1975.

Saitō, Yōichi, and Ōishi Shinzaburō. *Mibun sabetsu shakai no shinjitsu* [The Truth About Social Status Discrimination Societies]. Tokyo: Kōdansha Gendai Shinsho, 1995.

Sakai, Naoki. *Shisan sareru nihongo/nihonjin: 'nihon' no rekishi-chiseiteki haichi* [The Stillbirth of the Japanese: The Geopolitical Locus of 'Japanese' History]. Tokyo: Shinyokusha, 1996.

Sano, Manabu. "Suiheisha sōritsu hakkisha: yoki hi no tame ni [The Movers Behind the Establishment of the Suiheisha: For a Better Day]." In *Suihei: hito no yo ni hikari are*. [Levellers: Let there be Light in the World of Man], edited by Okiura Kazuteru. Tokyo: Shakai Hyōronsha, 1991: 173–74.

Sasahara, Kazuo. *Nihonshi kenkyū* [Japanese Historical Research]. Tokyo: Yamakawa Shuppansha, 1977.

Scott, Joan W. "The Evidence of Experience." *Critical Inquiry* 17:4 (Summer 1991): 776–97.

Shiomi, Sen'ichirō. *Danzaemon to sono jidai* [Danzaemon and His Times]. Tokyo: Kawade Shobō Shinsha, 2008.

———. *Datsu-ideorogii no burakushi: jubaku ga tokete rekishi ga mieru* [Buraku History Without Ideology: Improving Historical Visibility Through the Breaking of Spells]. Tokyo: Ningen Shuppan, 2005.

———. *Shinpen gengō to sabetsu* [New Edition of Language and Discrimination]. Tokyo: Shinsensha, 1990.

Sugimoto, Yoshio. *An Introduction to Japanese Society*. Cambridge: Cambridge University Press, 1997.

Suginohara, Juichi. *Buraku kaihō no 'kyōko riron' hihan* [Criticism of the 'Firm Theory' of Buraku Liberation]. Kyoto: Buraku Mondai Kenkyūjo, 1999.

Sugiyama, Seiko. "Kinsei kantō ni okeru 'hisabetsu buraku' no mibun kōshō ni tsuite: suzuki-ke monjo yori [Regarding the Status Labels of the 'Buraku' in Early Modern Kantō: From the Documents of the House of Suzuki].” *Minshūshi kenkyū* no. 26 (1984): 1–18.

Sumida, Ichirō. “Ima naze, kamuauto nanoka [Why Must We Come-out Now?].” In *‘Burakumin’ towa nanika* [What is ‘Burakumin’?], edited by Fujita Kei’ichi. Kyoto: Aunsha, 1998: 37–74.

Suzuki, Ryō. *Suiheisha sōritsu no kenkyū* [Research on the Establishment of the Suiheisha]. Kyoto: Buraku Mondai Kenkyūjo, 2005.

Takeuchi, Rizō, and Mitsutoshi Takayanagi. *Kadokawa nihonshi jiten* [Kadokawa Japanese History Dictionary]. Tokyo: Kadokawa Shoten, 1994.

Teltumbde, Anand. *Khairlanji: A Strange and Bitter Crop*. New Delhi: Navayana, 2008.

Teraki, Nobuaki. *Kinsei mibun to hisabetsumin no shosō: ‘burakushi no minaoshi’ no tojō kara* [Early Modern Status and Various Aspects of Outcastes: Amidst ‘Buraku History Revisionism’]. Osaka: Kaihō Shuppansha, 2000.

Terazono, Atsushi. *Dare mo kakanakatta ‘Buraku’* [The ‘buraku’ No One Writes About]. Kyoto: Kamogawa Shuppan, 1997.

———. “‘Shinjitsu’ wo kakusu ‘ryōshin’ no hōdō: asahi shinbunsha, iwanami shoten [Conscientious News That Hides the Truth: Asahi Newspaper, Iwanami Books].” In *Dōwa riken no shinsō: ‘undō dantai’ no akutoku wo sasaeta TV, shinbun, bunkajin no tsumi* [The Truth Behind Dōwa Concessions: The Sins of Television Stations, Newspapers, and Cultural Elites Who Support the Vices of the ‘Movement Groups’], edited by Ichinomiya Yoshinari, et al. Vol. 3. Tokyo: Takarajimasha, 2003: 68–80.

Terazono, Atsushi, Yoshinari Ichinomiya, and Gurūpu K21. *Dōwa riken no shinsō: masumedia ga mokusatsu shitekita sengoshi saigō no tabū* [The Truth Behind Dōwa Concessions: The Final Taboo Erased from Postwar History by the Media]. Vol. 29, Bessatsu Takarajima Real. Tokyo: Takarajimasha, 2003.

Tomotsune, Tsutomu. “Meijiki buraku mondai no gensetsu ni tsuite [Regarding Meiji Discourse on the Buraku Problem].” In *Kindai no toshi no arikata to buraku mondai* [The State of Modern Cities and the Buraku Problem], ed. by Zenkoku burakushi kenkyū kōryūkai. Osaka: Kaihō Shuppansha, 1998: 59–79.

———. “Nakagami Kenji and the Buraku Issue in Postwar Japan.” *Inter-Asia Cultural Studies* 4, no. 2 (2003): 220–31.

Tōjō, Takashi, *Ima buraku mondai towa* [What is the Buraku Problem Today?]. Kyoto: Buraku Mondai Kenkyūjo, 1998.

Tsukada, Takashi. *Kinsei nihon mibunsei no kenkyū* [Research on the Early Modern Japanese Status System]. Kobe: Hyōgo Buraku Mondai Kenkyūjo, 1987.

———. *Kinsei Osaka no mibunteki shūen: mondai teiki wo kanete* [Status Marginality in Early Modern Osaka and Related Issues]. Unpublished paper presented at the *Kokusai enza ‘kinsei mibun shakai no hikakushi’* [International Roundtable on 'The Comparative History of Early Modern Status Societies'] at Osaka City University, 19 July 2009.

Ueda, Masaaki. *Kita Sadakichi* [Kita Sadakichi]. Tokyo: Kōdansha, 1978.

Uesugi, Satoshi. *Tennōsei to buraku sabetsu: buraku sabetsu wa naze aru no ka* [The Imperial Institution and Buraku Discrimination: Why is there Buraku Discrimination?]. Tokyo: San'ichi Shinsho, 1990.

Upham, Frank. *Law and Social Change in Postwar Japan*. Cambridge, Mass.; London: Harvard University Press, 1987.

Urabe, Manabu. "Bushū shimo wana chōri no shitchi ukemodoshi hantai tōsō [The Oppositional Struggle by Outcastes in Lower Wana Village in Musashi Province to the Return of Mortgaged Land]." In *Buraku no seikatsushi* [The Everyday Life History of Buraku], edited by Buraku mondai kenkyūjo. Kyoto: Buraku Mondai Kenkyūjo, 1988: 225–30.

Uramoto, Yoshifumi. *Edo / tokyo no hisabetsu buraku no rekishi: danzaemon to hisabetsu minshū* [The History of Buraku in Edo/Tokyo: Danzaemon and Outcastes]. Tokyo: Akashi Shoten, 2003.

Wakita, Osamu. "Kawara Makimono [Kawara Hand Scrolls] ." In *Burakushi no saihakken* [Rediscovering Buraku History], edited by Buraku kaihō kenkyūjo, 130–36. Osaka: Buraku Kaihō Kenkyūjo, 1996.

———. *Burakushi ni kangaeru* [Thinking Through Buraku History]. Kyoto: Buraku Mondai Kenkyūjo, 1996.

Walthall, Anne. *Social Protest and Popular Culture in Eighteenth-Century Japan*. Tucson: The University of Arizona Press, 1986.

Watanabe, Hiroshi. *Mikaihō buraku no shiteki kenkyū: kishū o chūshin toshite* [Historical Research on the Yet-to-be-Liberated Buraku: Focusing on the Wakayama/Mie Region]. Tokyo: Yoshikawa Kōbunkan, 1963.

Watanabe, Toshio. "Burakushi no tenkan [Changes in Buraku History]." *Gendai shisō* 27 no. 2 (1999): 32–51.

Williams, Raymond. *Keywords: A Vocabulary of Culture and Society*. London: Fontana Press, 1976.

Yamamura, Kozo. "The Decline of the Ritsuryo System: Hypotheses on Economic and Institutional Change." *Journal of Japanese Studies* 1 no. 1 (Autumn, 1974): 3–37.

Yamanaka, Yorimasa. *Hisabetsumin to sono buraku no okori to rekishi* [Outcastes and the Origins and History of Buraku]. Tokyo: Kokusho Kankōkai, 1999.

Yamashita, Tsutomu. "Nijū isseiki wo mokuzen ni shite: yakeme wo mukaeta buraku kaihō undō no genjō [The Realities of the Buraku Liberation Movement at the Turn of the 21st Century]." *Gendai shisō* 27 no. 2 (1999): 64–72.

———. *Hisabetsu buraku no waga hansei* [My Life in a Buraku]. Tokyo: Heibonsha, 2004.

Yanagita, Kunio. *Teihon yanagita kunio shū* [Works of Yanagita Kunio (Standard Edition)]. vol.9. Tokyo: Chikuma Shobō, 1962.

———. "Iwayuru tokushu buraku no shurui [Concerning the So-called Race of Special Buraku] ." In Okiura Kazuteru, ed., *Suihei: hito no yo ni hikari are* [Levellers: Let there be Light in the World of Man]. Tokyo: Shakai Hyōronsha, 1991: 105–18.

Yasunouchi, Yasushi. "Total War and Social Integration: A Methodological Introduction." In *Total War and 'Modernization'*, edited by Yasunouchi Yasushi, et al. *Cornell East Asia Series*, vol. 100. Ithaca, New York: East Asia Program Cornell University, 1998: 1–39.

Yoshida, Tomoya. "Buraku mondai wa naze owaranai noka [Why Doesn't the Buraku Problem End?]." *Gendai shisō* 27 no. 2 (1999): 73–83.

Young, Iris Marion. *Justice and the Politics of Difference.* Princeton: Princeton University Press, 1990.

Žižek, Slavoj. "Against Human Rights." *New Left Review* 34 (July/August 2005): 130.

Electronic Sources

Alldritt, Leslie D. *The Burakumin: The Complicity of Japanese Buddhism in Oppression and an Opportunity for Liberation* (2000). Available at http://jbe.gold.ac.uk/7/alldritt001.html (accessed May 20, 2002).

Anand, S. "Caste and the World." *The Hindu.* Available at http://www.hindu.com/mag/2009/05/24/stories/2009052450180500.htm (accessed 1 July 2009).

Anand, Siriyavan. "Caste on the Couch: Do Brahminical Ideologies Permeate Indian Psychological Theory?" *Himal*, 24 April 2003. Available at http://www.countercurrents.org/dalit-anand24403.htm (accessed 16 May 2004).

Barmé, Geremie. "On New Sinology." Available at http://rspas.anu.edu.au/pah/chinaheritageproject/newsinology/ (accessed 31 July 2007).

Buraku kaihō dōmei zenkoku rengōkai. *Buraku sabetsu towa nanika* [What is Buraku Discrimination?]. Available at http://www.zenkokuren.org/whats/sabetu.htm (accessed 17 November 2004).

Buraku kaihō dōmei, "Sasayama Jiken Shiryōshitsu: Supplementary Report to the Fourth Periodic Report by the Government of Japan." Available at http://www.bll.gr.jp/sayama/s-sayam-counte.html (accessed 1 September 2008).

Buraku Liberation League. *What is Buraku Discrimination?* Available at http://www.bll.gr.jp/eng.html (accessed 17 November 2004).

Buraku Liberation and Human Rights Research Institute (BLHRRI). "What is Denunciation?" Available at http://www.blhrri.org/blhrri_e/blhrri/q&a.htm#What%20is%20Denunciation? (accessed 15 December 2004).

Buraku Liberation League, Tokyo. *'Renzoku / tairyō sabetsu hagaki jiken' yōgisha taihō* ['Mass Discriminatory Postcard Affair' Suspect Arrested]. Available at http://www.asahi-net.or.jp/~mg5s-hsgw/sabetu/hagaki/hagaki07.html (accessed 24 November 2004).

———. *'Renzoku / tairyō sabetsu hagaki jiken' no shinsō* [The Truth Concerning the'Mass Discriminatory Postcard Affair']. Available at http://www.asahi-net.or.jp/~mg5s-hsgw/sabetu/hagaki/h_sinsou.html (accessed 24 November 2004).

———. *Tonai no dōmei intaku ni tairyō no sabetsu tegami/hagaki ga* [Mass Discriminatory Letters and Postcards Sent to Innercity (Buraku Liberation) League Employee]. Available at http://www.asahi-net.or.jp/~mg5s-hsgw/sabetu/hagaki/hagaki1.html (accessed 24 November 2004).

———. *'Sabetsu hagaki jiken' yōgisha ga kiso* ['Discriminatory Postcard Incident' Suspect Indicted]. Available at http://www.asahi-net.or.jp/~mg5shsgw/sabetu/hagaki/hagaki08.html (accessed 24 November 2004).

"Burakumin - Current Numbers, Terminology, Historical origins, End of feudal era, Postwar situation, Burakumin rights movement." Available at http://encyclopedia.stateuniversity.com/pages/3395/Burakumin.html (accessed 15 July 2009).

Buraku mondai kenkyūjo. *Shakai hōjin buraku mondai kenkyūjo teikan* [The Charter of the Buraku mondai kenkyūjo Foundation]. Available at http://www.burakken.jp/cgi/file/1065076993__1027402929__teikan.html (accessed 20 November 2004).

Census of India: Scheduled Castes & Scheduled Tribes Population, Registrar General & Census Commissioner, India. Available at http://www.censusindia.gov.in/Census_Data_2001/India_at_Glance/scst.aspx; (accessed 29 September 2009).

Ermath, Elizabeth Deeds. "Postmodernism." In *Routledge Encyclopedia of Social Science* [online], edited by E. Craig. London: Routledge, 1998. Available at http://www.rep.routledge.com/article/N044SECT2 (accessed 23 August 2005).

Hansenbyō kaifuku kanja to furusato wo musubu. *Oita to hansenbyō no rekishi* [The History of Hansen's Disease in Oita Prefecture]. Available at http://www.geocities.jp/furusatohp/panerurten/oita/matogahama.html (accessed 6 June 2005).

Henomatsu jinken rekishikan. Available at http://www.city.sakai.osaka.jp/fureai/henomatsu/index.html (accessed 3 October 2007).

International Movement Against all forms of Discrimination and Racism (IMADR). "Descent-based discrimination." Available at http://imadr.org/descent/.(accessed 1 December 2007).

Jinken yōgokyoku [The Human Rights Protection Agency]. Available at http://www.moj.go.jp/JINKEN (accessed 17 November 2007).

Kitaguchi, Suehiro. "Aratana buraku chimei sōkan [New Buraku Residence Lists]," *Gendai kokusai jinken kō* [Thoughts on Contemporary International

Human Rights]. No. 66 (March 2006). Available at http://www.hurights.or.jp/newsletter/J_NL/066/01.html (accessed 22 February 2008).

Laidlaw, Ian. "Interview with T_, of the Buraku Liberation League and Human Rights Research Centre." Available at http://www.geocities.com/gaijindo4dan/BLHRRI.html (accessed 6 June 2005).

Matsushita, Tatsuhito, 'Taishōki no sabetsu chōsa shiryō ga mitsukaru [Documents Discovered Concerning a Taishō Period Discriminatory Survey].' Available at http://blhrri.org/topics/topics_0087.html (accessed 7 December 2006).

Osaka Prefectural Government. "Dōwa taisaku kankei shiryō [Sources Related to Dōwa Measures]." Available at http://www.pref.osaka.jp/osaka-pref/jinken/measure/kunidowa/d1_2.html (accessed 7 October 2008).

"Sakai City Peace and Human Rights Museum." Available at http://www.city.sakai.osaka.jp/city/info/_jinken/index.html (accessed 7 December 2007).

Saitama kenchō sōmubu jinken suishinka. *Dōwa mondai* [Dōwa Problem]. Available at http://www.pref.saitama.lg.jp/A01/BI00/contents/4.html (accessed 23 December 2004).

"Setsuritsu mokuteki to kihon rinen [Purpose for Establishment and Basic Philosophy]." Available at http://www.liberty.or.jp/cp_pf/index.html (accessed 11 September 2007).

"Settlement development through linking people. A Case of Kitagata Project in Japan," *Habitat International Coalition*. Available at http://www.hic-net.org/document.asp?PID=102 (accessed 16 January 2008).

Shakai hōjin buraku kaihō jinken kenkyūjo teikan [The Charter of the Buraku Liberation and Human Rights Research Institute Foundation]. Available at http://www.blhrri.org/blhrri/about/teikan.htm (accessed 27 June 2007).

Sōmusho, "Gyōsei kanri / sōgō chōri Hakusho (heisei 10 nen) [White Paper on Administrative Management and Comprehensive Regulation (1998)]." Available at http://www.soumu.go.jp/soumu/hokoku10.htm (accessed 11 September 2008).

Teraki, Nobuaki. "Buraku no rekishi wo indo no hisabetsu kāsuto to hikaku shinagara kangaeru [Thinking about Buraku History through a Comparison with India]." *Kenkyūjo tsūshin* 300 (August 2003). Available at http://blhrri.org/info/koza/koza_0068.htm (accessed 23 December 2006).

Terazono, Atsushi, "Ubawareta jinjiken to baibai sareta saiyōwaku (ge): 'dōwa' toiu yamai (4)" [Stolen Human Resource Rights and Brokered Employment Systems: The 'Disease' of Dōwa], *Mariido* (*Dōwa Gyōsei Obuzaabaa*) (July 2008) 156. Available at http://muhajirin.com/almarid/text/156.html (accessed 25 July 2009).

"The Centre for Human Rights Affairs." Available at http://www.jinken.or.jp/index-en.html (accessed 11 September 2007).

"Tokyo Meat Works." Available at http://www.tmmc.co.jp/saiyo.htm (accessed 1 June 2005).

Tsujimoto, Masanori. *Buraku sabetsu no kongen ni aru mono: kawa to niku no kegare (sono 2)* [At the Root of Buraku Discrimination: Pollution over Leather and Meat] [online]. Tokyo Jinken Keihatsu Kigyō Renrakukai, June 2005. Available at http://www.jinken-net.com/test/hiroba/hiroba0502.html (accessed 10 May 2007).

"United Nations Decade for Human Rights Education, Osaka Prefectural Government Plan of Action: Creating an Affluent Human Rights Culture—From Learning to Action." Available at http://www.pref.osaka.jp/jinken/measure/jinken/kouki10.htm (accessed 7 December 2007).

Wetherall, William. "Outcasts of History: Ferro-Concrete Monuments to Discrimination." Available at http://members.jcom.home.ne.jp/yosha/minorities/Murakoshi_1986_buraku_today_FEER.html#letters (accessed 7 December 2007).

Zaidan hōjin Osaka-shi jinken kyōkai [Osaka Municipal Human Rights Foundation]. Available at http://www.ochra.or.jp/event/2007_03/naniwa_070308.html (accessed 22 November 2007).

Zenkoku Chi'iki Jinken Undō Sōrengō, "What is Braku [sic] Problem?" Available at http://homepage3.nifty.com/zjr/english.html (accessed 30 November 2007).

Žižek, Slavoj. "Human Rights and its Discontents." 16 November 1999. Available at http://www.egs.edu/faculty/zizek/zizek-human-rights-and-its-discontents.html (accessed 30 November 2007).

Encyclopaedia / Magazine / Newspaper Articles

Akisada, Yoshikazu. "Dōwa [Dōwa]." In *Buraku mondai jinken jiten* [Buraku Problem and Human Rights Dictionary], edited by Buraku kaihō jinken kenkyūjo. Osaka: Kaihō Shuppansha, 2001: 721.

Fujita, Genji. "Saitama-ken [Saitama Prefecture]." In *Buraku mondai jinken jiten* [Buraku Problem and Human Rights Dictionary], edited by Buraku kaihō jinken kenkyūjo. Osaka: Kaihō Shuppansha, 2001: 366–67.

"Furīman senjutsu no shōri: joshi yon-hyaku hatsu v 97 sekai rikujō [Freeman's Victorious Strategy: A First in the Women's 400 Metres at the 1997 World Athletics Championship]." *Asahi Shinbun*, 6 August 1997, 19.

Hamashita, Akira et.al., eds, *Shakaigaku shōjiten* [Concise Dictionary of Sociology]. Tokyo: Yūhikaku, 2005.

Hasegawa, Yutaka, and Morimoto Hidehiko. "Kyōhaku: buraku kaihō dōmei no shokuin ni kyōhaku hagaki okuru mushoku no otoko taihō - keishichō asakusashō [Intimidation: An Unemployed Man is Arrested for the Intimidation of a Buraku Liberation League Employee – Asakusa Police]." *Mainichi Shinbun*, 20 October 2004.

Kawashima, Masao. "Eta [Eta]." In *Buraku mondai jinken jiten* [Buraku Problem and Human Rights Dictionary], edited by Buraku kaihō jinken kenkyūjo. Osaka: Kaihō Shuppansha, 2001: 94–96.

———. "Kiyome [Kiyome]." In *Buraku mondai jinken jiten*, edited by Buraku kaihō jinken kenkyūjo. Osaka: Kaihō Shuppansha, 2001: 249.

"Kenshō: Osaka-shi shokuin kōgu mondai" [Investigative Report: The Problem Surrounding the Preferential Treatment of Osaka Municipal Personnel], *Sankei shinbun*, 2 February 2005.

Kitagawa, Tadahiko. "Chūsei geinō [Medieval Entertainers]." In *Burakushi yōgo jiten* [Dictionary of Buraku Historical Terms], edited by Kobayashi Shigeru, *et al.* Tokyo: Kashiwa Shobō, 1985: 212–13.

Kobayashi, Takehiro. "Shakaigai no shakai eta hinin [A society outside society: eta / hinin]'." In *Buraku mondai jinken jiten* [Buraku Problem and Human Rights Dictionary], edited by Buraku kaihō jinken kenkyūjo. Osaka: Kaihō Shuppansha, 2001: 448.

Miura, Keichi. "Chūsei senmin [Medieval Outcasts]." In *Burakushi yōgo jiten* [Dictionary of Buraku Historical Terms], edited by Kobayashi Shigeru, et al. Tokyo: Kashiwa Shobō, 1985, 213–15.

Noguchi, Michihiko. "Sabetsu [Discrimination]." In *Buraku mondai jinken jiten* [Buraku Problem and Human Rights Dictionary], edited by Buraku kaihō jinken kenkyūjo. Osaka: Kaihō Shuppansha, 2001, 386–87.

"A Proud Champion." *The Canberra Times*, 8 August 1997.

Sethi, Sunil, "You can't wish away reservation." *Business Standard*, 22 April 2006.

Sterngold, James. "Ideas & Trends; Fear of Phrases." *The New York Times*, 18 December 1994.

Tamamuro, Fumio. "Shūmon ninbetsu aratame chō [Temple Population Registers]." In *Buraku mondai jinken jiten* [Buraku Problem and Human Rights Dictionary], edited by Buraku kaihō jinken iinkai. Osaka: Kaihō Shuppansha, 2001: 485.

Tatsuta, Hiroyuki. "Sanka [Mountain Nomads]." In *Yashi yobina jiten* [Dictionary of Names for Marginalized Groups], edited by Tatsuta Hiroyuki. Hiroshima: Menmehei Shuppan, 1998: 426.

Teraki, Nobuaki. "Buraku no rekishi: [Premodern Buraku History]." In *Buraku mondai jinken jiten* [Buraku Problem and Human Rights Dictionary], edited by Buraku kaihō jinken kenkyūjo. Osaka: Kaihō Shuppansha, 2001: 940–41.

———. "Sabetsu jōmoku kyohi tōsō [The Struggle to Protest Discriminatory Labels]." In *Buraku mondai jinken jiten*, edited by Buraku kaihō jinken kenkyūjo. Osaka: Kaihō Shuppansha, 2001: 391.

———. "Buraku no kigen [Buraku Origins]." In *Buraku mondai jinken jiten*, edited by Buraku kaihō jinken kenkyūjo. Osaka: Kaihō Shuppansha, 2001: 939.

Wakita, Osamu. "Mibunsei: kinsei [Status System: Early Modern Japan]." In *Buraku mondai jinken jiten* [Buraku Problem and Human Rights Dictionary], edited by Buraku kaihō jinken kenkyūjo. Osaka: Kaihō Shuppansha, 2001: 1016.

Warner, Adrian. "Athletics-Freeman becomes first aboriginal to win world title." *Reuter News*, 4 August 1997.

Yoshida, Akira. "Doreisei [The Slavery System]." In *Kokushi daijiten* [Japanese History Dictionary], edited by Kokushi daijiten henshū iinkai, vol. 10. Tokyo: Yoshikawa Kōbunkan, 1989.

Index

abnormality, 25, 71, 107;
see also normality
Ainu, 162, 174, 183
All Romance Incident, 156, 242n39
Ambedkar, B. R., 78–79, 247n2, 248n15; meeting with Suiheisha movement leader, 141
Anderson, Benedict, 234n52
anti-buraku; discrimination law, 162, structuralist narratives, 194–96
Arai Kōjirō, 53, 244n61
Asada Zennosuke (buraku activist), 63, 82, 144, 152–54, 156–59, 160–61, 167, 242n39, 263n19
Asakusa, 57–58, 61, 63, 86, 124, 127–28, 207, 250n38

Bakufu, 101
begging (occupational right), 42, 71, 85, 101, 110, 128, 250n38; see also *hinin*
bemin (outcast/e), 36
Benjamin, Walter, 195
binary, 28, 106, 109–10, 148, 208, 213, 224
birth (and status), 13, 29
Bolshevikism, 157
Botsman, Daniel, 220, 222, 228n5, 252n63, 267n17
brahmins, 221
Buddhism, 14, 222, 235n54
bunmei kaika (enlightenment), 44, 119, 255n93
Buraku Liberation Cultural Festivals, 165
Buraku Liberation Human Rights Research Institute, 63
Buraku Liberation League (BLL, *Buraku kaihō dōmei*), 6–7, 15, 17–19, 21, 28, 45–46, 57–58, 63, 93, 112–13, 116, 149–50, 152, 157–59, 161–73, 178, 184–87, 191, 193, 195, 229n17, 233n44, 235n56, 241n38, 242n38, 264n32
Buraku Mondai Kenkyūjo, *see* Research Institute for the Buraku Problem (RIBP)
Burakushi yōgo jiten (Dictionary of Buraku Historical Terms), 38
butchery, 39, 112–13, 125

Butler, Judith, 230n23, 268n24

cadastral registers/surveys, 40, 84, 239n18
candala, 30; *see also* sendara
capitalism/capitalist, 4, 22, 69, 71, 115, 125, 127, 160, 213, 215, 217; Japanese, 262n15
carcass(es), 42, 50, 76, 125, 220
Caron, Francois, 85, 249n36
Carr, David, 99–100, 252n67
caste (system), 3, 9–10, 29–32, 43, 81, 120, 219–24, 235n53 n56, 238n13, 242n41, 245n69, 270n4 n14
census(es), 7, 46, 125, 219, 229n18
Central Yūwa Project Council, 142
Centre for Human Rights Affairs, 173, 176, 265n52
China, 31, 36, 141
Chinese ideographs (referring to *eta* and *hinin*), 3, 47–48, 87, 146–47
Chiribukuro, 30–31
Christians, 14, 84–85
chūsei, *see* medieval period
citizens(hip), 36, 52, 69, 70–71, 110, 122, 127–28, 138, 182, 216; *see also* commoner-citizen
class, 27, 29, 40, 70, 80–81, 107, 134, 136, 140–41, 146, 148, 155–57, 160, 189, 215–216, 228n5
'comfort women', 184
commoners (status), 8, 25, 47–50, 52, 59, 77, 81, 83, 101, 104, 109, 118, 121, 229n18
commoner-citizens, 44, 46, 50–51, 69–70, 106–11, 118, 120–21, 130, 132–33, 199, 213, 241n33, 258n52; *see also* citizens
Confucian, 3, 29, 41, 235n54, 269n2
cordon sanitaire, 9, 25, 71, 76–79, 98, 100, 105, 106–10, 202, 213, 218, 247n2
Culture, Health and Welfare Assembly Hall Incident, 157–58

Dōaikai (Mutual Love Association), 142
dalits, and burakumin, 29–32, 77–79, 218–20, 222–24, 235n56, 245n69
Dan Naiki, 47, 52, 244n61; *see also* Danzaemon
Danzaemon (leader of *eta* and *hinin*), chapter 2 *passim*; 17, 43, 83–86, 100–04, 106, 108, 123, 126–27, 130, 248n24, 249n34–35, 253n79, 254n89, 267n22; Dan Naiki as, 47, 48; descendants of, 52, 244n61; history of, 204–06; map, 88; status promotion of, 47–48, 52, 89; Uramoto and, 60; 232n39, 241n31
democracy, 59–60, 80, 154, 170
denunciation campaigns, 45, 116, 144, 156, 172, 199, 241n38, 242n39
descent (and discrimination), 12, 223, 231n29, 235n56, 242n41
designated documents (*shitei bunsho*), 230n19, 244n58
discourses of difference, 22–26, 72–73, 110, 111–48 *passim*, 211–12, 214, 218, 223, 253n68
Dravidians, 219, 221
Dumont, Louis, 30
dōwa, 45, 53, 73, 92–95, 151–52, 163–64, 170–73, 176–77, 212, 242n40, 247n87; policy 158, 160; Special Measures, 45, 161, 166, 170

Emancipation Edict (*mibun kaihōrei*) (1871), 3, 26, 33, 35, 44, 46–53, 69, 77, 117–18, 120, 122–23,

125–27, 140, 147, 155, 213, 231n30, 241n33, 243n53, 244n59
Ekōin Temple, 60–62
endogamy, 55
enlightenment (*bunmei kaika*), 44, 119, 255n93
enlightenment activities (human rights), 28, 149, 173–79, 186–87
Enlightenment, the, 147–48
equality, 1–2, 15, 95, 98, 116, 142, 145–46, 159, 199, 220, 242n41
etori, 31, 39

fascism, 145, 157
'foreign' (origin of *eta*, *hinin*) 13, 31–32, 48, 70, 111, 132, 139, 258n65
Foucault, Michel, 107, 267n17
Fujin Sendara (film), 143, 217, 261n92
Fujitani Takashi, 119
Fujitani Toshio, 157–58, 160; *see also* Asada Zennosuke
fukashoku (untouchability), 37, 238n13
Fukuzawa, Yukichi, 121, 132, 263n29

Giyūdan, 140
gōmune, 101, 191, 206, 251n46, 266n5
Gountei Sadahide, 64–65
Groemer, Gerald, 8–10, 227n4, 241n31

Harada Tomohiko, 37, 251n52; on Japanese and Indian outcastes, 235n54
Harootunian, Harry, 68
Hatanaka Toshiyuki, 11, 66, 223, 244n66, 255n96, 268–69n26; on linking *eta*/*hinin* and burakumin, 53–54, 91
heimin, see commoner-citizens
heinin, *see* commoners/ commoner-citizens
Hibiya riots, 134
Hikaku kaikan (Leather Hall), 58
hinin, 4–5, 42; feature of, 108
hisabetsu/min, 8–10, 17, 25–28, 33, 36–37, 39, 53, 55–56, 63–64, 66, 73, 75, 88–94 *passim*, 190–92, 194–95, 211, 214, 220, 225; *see also* senmin, outcast/e(s)
Honda Yutaka, 46
Howell, David, 8
human garbage, 30
human rights culture (*jinken bunka*), 28, 149–52, 162–63, 166–67, 176–79, 181, 184–87
Human Rights Research Institute (BLHRRI), 63, 152, 163–64, 241–242n38; *see also* Buraku Liberation Human Rights Research Institute
Human Rights Week, 173–75
HURIGHTS, 169

Imado ('buraku area'), 35, 43, 52–53, 56–60, 63, 68, 86, 247n88
impurity, 36–37; *see also* kegare/pollution
India, *see* caste, dalit
Inoue Kiyoshi, chapter 3 *passim*; 80–82, 144, 153–54, 156–57, 159
intermarriage, 3, 77
International Movement Against All Forms of Discrimination and Racism (IMADR), 165
ippan (non-buraku), 6, 51, 77, 270n4

Japanese Communist Party (JCP), 159, 161, 264n32
jati(s), 29, 221; see also caste

Kaiho Seiryō, 70
Kaihō shinbun (newspaper), 18, 93, 232n39
Kameoka, 52, 123
Kang Sang-jung , 111, 113, 115
Kawamoto Yoshikazu, 78, 80
kawaramono, 31, 38–39, 71–72, 109, 239n21, 255n96; origin of, 236n62
kawata ('tanner'), 38–39, 73, 83–85, 104–05, 240n24, 245n70, 246n86, 249n35; governance of, 239n20, origin of, 239n18
kawaya, 83–84
kawazukuri, 83–84
kegare, 30, 36, 74, 76, 217, 219, 235n58; *see also* impurity/pollution
Kinegawa, 129–31
kiyome, 30–31, 38–39, 72, 236n60, 239n21
Kodama Kōta, 42
kojiki (beggars), 39, 84, 239n21, 250n38 n44; *see also* begging
Kurokawa Midori, 11, 72, 111, 113, 115, 122, 126, 131–32, 135–36, 190, 231n26, 244n66, 246n80
Kuruma Zenshichi (*hinin* leader), 85, 103, 127, 250n38
Kyoto, 16, 31, 124–25, 128, 135, 139, 152–54, 156–58, 168, 227n2
kyūdan, 45, 156, 241n38; *see also* denunciation
kyūmin (the destitute), 124, 127

Laclau, Ernesto, 96, 148
leather/work, 12, 42, 58–59, 67, 83–84, 108, 120, 125–26, 129–31, 141, 152, 162, 211, 220, 227n2, 239n18, 245n70, 246n86
Left(wing), 146, 155, 157, 187
leper/leprosy, 39, 85, 137, 238n17, 246n79
Liberal Democratic Party (LDP), 168–69
Liberty Osaka (*Libati Osaka*), 28, 63, 67, 149, 152, 162–63, 168, 178, 180–87, 265n55
lineage(s), 12, 14–15, 30–31, 33, 93, 229n18
Lower Wana Village, 13, 87–93, 98, 105, 231n32, 251n49

Maeda Katsumasa, 2, 14–19, 232n37
map(s) (and outcastes), 58, 64–66, 86–88, 176, 250n38 n43 n45
marriage(s), 1, 15, 36, 41, 43, 77; *see also* intermarriage
Marxism, 45, 146, 157, 215, 223, 263n21; kōzaha Marxism, 154–55, 215, 262n15
Mass Discriminatory Postcard Affair, 18, 191–95, 201, 208
Matogahama Incident, 137
Matsumoto Ji'ichirō, 140–41, 154, 263n19; meeting with Ambedkar, 154
McCormack, Noah, 6, 46, 120–21, 125, 133, 236n65, 268n26, 269n2
meat, 31, 48, 50, 112, 125, 191, 194, 219, 236n61
medieval period (and origins of outcast/e[s]), 3, 8–10, 29, 31, 37–39, 42–43, 72, 81, 94, 192, 206, 219, 221–22, 227–28n4, 236n60, n62, 237n11, 238n12 n17, 239n20 n21, 240n24
Meiji period/government, 6–7, 11, 14, 27, 44, 47, 49, 52, 69–71, 77, 110, 111–48 *passim*, 182, 191, 213, 215, 220, 222–23, 241n37, 242n42, 244n59, 245n67, 246n79, 262n15
Meiji Restoration, 13–14, 33,

43, 46, 57, 115, 123, 125, 140, 155, 228n7, 257n39
Minegishi Kentarō, 77, 83–85, 238n14, 240n23, 249n35
minzoku kokka (Japanese ethnic nation), 118
Miyazaki Manabu (buraku commentator), 16, 82, 115, 140, 203
modernity, 25, 52, 69, 73, 80, 82, 111, 114–15, 124, 136, 160, 214, 234n50, 255n4
Morris, Mark, 115, 231n28
Morris-Suzuki, Tessa, 271n26
Morse, Edward, 132

Nagasaki, 120
Nakano Itsuki, 49
Naniwa, 35, 56–57, 63–68, 124, 149–52, 161–62, 177–81, 185–86
Naniwa Human Rights Cultural Centre, 63–64, 67, 162, 177–80
National Association for the Advancement of Colored People (NAACP), 165
National Committee for Buraku Liberation (NCBL), 45, 152–58; *see also* Buraku Liberation League (BLL)
Neary, Ian, 6, 125, 143–44, 150, 167, 171, 214–16, 243n42, 263n21
new commoner-citizen; see shinheimin
'New Town' (*Shinchō*), 43, 52, 123–24, 128–30
normality (and buraku identity), 25, 35, 48, 79, 109, 187, 209; *see also* abnormality

occupation(s), (and identity) 3, 12–14, 33, 38, 40–43, 47–49, 56, 64, 80–81, 106, 115, 125–28, 132, 152, 194, 202, 220–22, 227n2
Okayama Prefecture, 6, 48, 50, 78, 135
Okinawa, 135, 138, 183
Omvedt, Gail, 219, 221–23
Ooms, Herman, 34, 98, 252n63
Osaka Prefecture, 2–3, 17, 63–67, 124, 126, 137, 150, 152, 161–62, 168–69, 178, 227n2; *see also* Liberty Osaka
Osaka Human Rights Museum, 63, 66, 149, 187; *see also* Liberty Osaka
Osatake Takeki, 143, 241n33
outcast/e(s), *passim* through the book; definition and usage, 8–10; Indian and Japanese, 29–32

Paekjong, 219–20
Pantawane, Gangadhar, 223
Pax Tokugawa, 3, 228n5
peasant(s), 29, 40–41, 81, 87, 90–91, 104–5, 227n3, 237n2, 253n69
performers, 38, 112, 131, 266n5
pollution, 30, 32, 37–38, 74, 129, 217, 219, 236n61, 247n2, and *eta*, 3, 11, 48, 87, ; in Indian context, 77, 219, 221; *see also* kegare, untouchability
positivism, 144, 271n25
postcard affair, *see* Mass Discriminatory Postcard Affair
postmodernism, 97
poverty, 16, 44, 85, 91, 107, 120, 124, 128, 131–34, 136, 143, 156–57, 216
Prefectures; Ehime, 50, 121; Hyōgo, 83, 104; Mie, 134–35; Nara, 135, 138–39, 163; Okayama, 6, 48, 50, 78, 135; Osaka, 2, 17; Saitama, 51,

93–94, 105, 201, 232n32; Shiga, 130; Tottori, 6, 65; Wakayama, 135
premodern (outcaste groups), 4–5, 7, 9, 12–13, 20, 23, 28–30, 33–34, 46, 53, 57, 63–68, 91, 94, 113, 117, 122, 129, 132, 143, 160, 183, 191–92, 197, 204–05, 211, 213, 216, 222, 228n7, 234n51, 244n66, 245n67, 255n3, 268n24
prewar, 4, 22, 66, 68, 116, 138, 141, 144, 148, 153–54, 215, 217, 229n8, 247n88
Pure Land Buddhism, 14, 139, 222, 235n54
purity, 30, 37–38, 76, 195, 219, 221; *see also* kiyome, pollution

race, 22, 54, 69, 71, 115, 120, 132, 136, 147, 182, 242n41
racial, 3, 60, 69–70, 136, 213, 235n53, 269n26; International/UN Convention on the Elimination of All Forms of Racial Discrimination (CERD), 166, 171
raisha (lepers), 39
religion/ religious, 12, 14, 29, 30, 28, 41, 71, 128, 190, 220–21, 235n54, 238n17, 270n14
Research Institute for the Buraku Problem (RIBP), 154, 158–59, 161; *see also* Buraku Mondai Kenkyūjo
Rice Riots (1918), 137, 241n37
ritsuryō system, 36, 237n3 n4
Russo–Japanese War (1904–05), 44, 134, 147

Said, Edward, 34
saimin (the poor), 124, 137
Saitama, 10, 51–52, 88–89, 92–94, 105, 201, 243–44n58
Sakai Naoki, 69, 234n50
samurai, 52, 109, 126, 230n21
sanitary cordon, *see* cordon sanitaire
Sendara, 30–31; see also candala
senmin, 3, 8–10, 25, 27–28, 33, 35–37, 39, 53–56, 71, 75, 88, 90–91, 93–94, 113, 137, 154, 190, 194–95, 211, 214, 225
Shinagawa, 102, 250n38
Shinchō, 43, 52, 123; see also 'New Town'
shinheimin (new commoner-citizen), 44, 69–70, 111, 116, 120, 132–33, 199, 211, 214, 229n18, 258n52
shogun/ate, *see* Tokugawa shogun/ate
shuku, 38, 238–39n17; *see also* kawaramono
shuzoku (special tribe), 121, 132
slum(s), 53, 70, 123–24, 127, 134, 137, 151
socialism, 135
special buraku (tokushu buraku), 4, 22, 44, 68, 70, 114, 134–37, 139–45, 156, 211, 214–15, 228n8, 230n21, 235n53, 247n88, 258n65, 259n75; establishment of associations, 134–35
Special Measures Law/ legislation, 45, 157, 160–61, 166–68, 170, 172–73, 260n77, 264n32
speciation, 27, 115, 117
status emancipation (*mibun hikiage*), 33, 47, 49, 51–52, 155
status emancipation edict (*mibun kaihō*), 3, 26, 33, 117–18, 122–23, 125–26, 140, 147, 155, 213, 231n30, 244n59
status system, 3, 8, 36, 41–42, 71, 82, 90, 117–18, 127, 240n24, and varna system, 29–30
structural/ist, aspects of buraku

identity, 4, 19, 24, 26, 74–75, 82, 98, 159–60, 189–90, 192, 194–96, 199, 203, 207–08, 212, 218
Suiheisha, 23, 44–45, 116, 139–44, 147, 152–53, 155, 163, 199, 232n34, 260n83; Declaration (1922) 1, 15, 73, 139–40, 232n34; denunciation or kyūdan, 45, 116, 144, 199, 241n38; Historical Museum, 163; movement, 44–45, 139–42, 144, 147, 157, 215, 217, 230n21; National Suiheisha Standing Committee, 143; Proclamation of 1922, 153
Suzuki family/household, 10–11, 13, 87–98, 105, 231n32, 251n49
Sword Hunt Edict (*katanagari-rei*), 3

taiko (drum), 60, 64–65, 67, 152, 180–81, 245n70; Taiko Drum Road, 151
Takahashi Sadaki, 230n21
Takahashi Yoshio, 132
Takakuwa Suehide, 155–56, 215
tanning, 3, 12, 39–40, 42–43, 59, 84, 125, 129–30, 152–53, 211, 227n2, 240n22; *see also* leatherwork
taxation/taxes, 40, 44, 49, 51, 81, 90, 134, 161, 266n5
Teikoku kōdōkai (Imperial Way Society), 136, 142
temple(s), Ekōin 60–62; Gokokuin, 127; Honganji, 135; Kōsaiji, 130; Shitennōji, 65; 139, 238n17, 240n27, 266n5, 270n14
Thorat, Sukhadeo, 77–78
tokken (special privileges), 31, 42, 47
Tokugawa, era/period/state/shogunate, 12–13, 25, 27, 29, 32, 40–43, 46–47, 49–50, 57, 59, 64–65, 70–71, 81–87 *passim*, 95, 98, 100–10, 126–29, 131, 138, 140, 143, 206, 213, 220, 225, 228n5, 229n18, 230n21, 239n20, 240n29, 250n38, 251n46, 267n17; culture, 91; and Danzaemon, 43, 47, 83, 100–03, 106, 108, 254n89; descendant of, 10; literature, 89–90, 99; status system in, 117–18
Tokugawa Iesato, 141
Tokugawa Tsunayoshi ('dog shogun'), 85, 250n39
tokushu buraku, 4, 11, 22–23, 44, 68, 72–73, 116, 134, 137, 139–40, 143, 211, 214, 228n8
Tokyo, 10, 17–19, 43, 44, 46, 52–53, 57–61, 63, 112, 119, 123–29, 134, 137, 190, 191, 192–93, 198, 201, 203–04, 206; university, 142
Tokyo Liberation Hall, 58
Tokyo Meat Market, 191, 194
Tomotsune Tsutomu, 116
Toyotomi Hideyoshi, 3, 42, 55
Tsukada Takashi, 40, 221–22, 240n24

United Nations, 149, 169–71, 173
United Nations Decade for Human Rights Education, 149
untouchability (*fukashoku*), 32, 37, 79, 222, 238n13, 270n14
untouchables, *see* dalits
Uramoto Yoshifumi, 2, 15, 17–22, 28, 57–63, 190–209, 232n39, 247n88, 266n3, 268n25

varna, 29

warrior(s), 25, 27, 29, 31, 40–42, 59, 64, 81, 84, 106–9, 141, 218, 227n3, 240n23
Watanabe (village), 47, 48, 64, 65
Watanabe Hiroshi, 238n12

Watanabe Toshio, 207, 247n1
Wetherall, William, 7, 229n17
World War II, 53, 145, 235n53

Yamato dōshikai (Yamato Brotherhood Society), 135
Yanagihara ('former outcaste' area), 125, 128–29, 132, 257n39
Yanagita Kunio, 71, 136, 239n17, 258–59n65 n68
Yayoi period, 36
Yokohama, 120, 125, 256n13
Yamanaka Yorimasa, 36
yoseba (enclosure), 103, 127
Yokoyama Gennosuke, 133
yūwa (integration) movement, 44, 135, 139, 142, 147, 241n37, 242n40

Zainichi Koreans, 12, 60, 156, 183, 193, 231n27
Zenkairen, 161, 166